Djoymi Baker is Lecturer in Cinema Studies at RMIT University, Australia, and wrote the first edition of *To Boldly Go* in her former position at the University of Melbourne. With a background in the television industry, she writes on myth in popular culture, film and television genres, the ethics of non-human representation, and children's screen cultures. Djoymi is the author of *The Encyclopedia of Epic Films* (Rowman & Littlefield 2014), with Constantine Santas, James M. Wilson, and Maria Colavito.

'In this ground-breaking exploration of the *Star Trek* universe, Djoymi Baker demonstrates the way mythologies emerge in and through a range of textual, commercial, and paratextual relationships. Beautifully written and full of innovative readings, *To Boldly Go* challenges us to see myth in new and exciting ways.'

– **Sean Redmond, Deakin University**

'A welcome addition to the scholarship on the *Star Trek* franchise. Baker's detailed analysis reveals the contemporary implications of myth as a combination of cultural descriptor and canny marketing strategy.'

– **Stan Beeler, University of Northern British Columbia**

TO BOLDLY GO

MARKETING THE MYTH OF *STAR TREK*

DJOYMI BAKER

BLOOMSBURY ACADEMIC
LONDON • NEW YORK • OXFORD • NEW DELHI • SYDNEY

BLOOMSBURY ACADEMIC
Bloomsbury Publishing Plc
50 Bedford Square, London, WC1B 3DP, UK
1385 Broadway, New York, NY 10018, USA
29 Earlsfort Terrace, Dublin 2, Ireland

BLOOMSBURY, BLOOMSBURY ACADEMIC and the Diana logo are trademarks of Bloomsbury Publishing Plc

First published in Great Britain 2018

Paperback edition published 2023

Copyright © Djoymi Baker 2018, 2023

Djoymi Baker has asserted her right under the Copyright, Designs and Patents Act, 1988, to be identified as Author of this work.

For legal purposes the Acknowledgements on p. vii constitute an extension of this copyright page.

Cover design: www.simonlevyassociates.co.uk
Cover image © Chris Goodney/Bloomberg via Getty Images

All rights reserved. No part of this publication may be reproduced or transmitted in any form or by any means, electronic or mechanical, including photocopying, recording, or any information storage or retrieval system, without prior permission in writing from the publishers.

Bloomsbury Publishing Plc does not have any control over, or responsibility for, any third-party websites referred to or in this book. All internet addresses given in this book were correct at the time of going to press. The author and publisher regret any inconvenience caused if addresses have changed or sites have ceased to exist, but can accept no responsibility for any such changes.

A catalogue record for this book is available from the British Library.

CIP Data Applied For

ISBN: HB: 978-1-7883-1008-6
PB: 978-1-3502-5236-3
ePDF: 978-1-8386-0974-0
eBook: 978-1-8386-0973-3

Typeset by Deanta Global Publishing Services, Chennai, India

To find out more about our authors and books visit www.bloomsbury.com and sign up for our newsletters.

Contents

List of Illustrations	vii
Acknowledgements	ix
Introduction	1
Beyond Roddenberry: *Star Trek* and the New Mythology	3
Persuasive Words and Outright Lies: A Brief History of Myth	7
Myth in the Age of *Star Trek*	14
1 Myth and Early US TV	23
Introduction	23
'Who Mourns for Adonais?'	25
Remediating Myth: The Cinematic Epic	29
Demographic Pitches and A New Search for Legitimacy	40
Science Fiction Myths	44
Superheroes and Camp: Remediating the Comic Book	49
Conclusion	54
2 The New Mythology	57
Introduction	57
Continuity and Discontinuity: New Myths and Old Process	58
Retelling Myth in *Star Trek*'s Future: Competing Discourses	63
History and *Star Trek*: 'Myth' in Quotations	76
Sci-Fi Sirens: Myth and 'Myth'	87
Conclusion	94

Contents

3	***Star Trek* Title Sequences and Cosmology as Myth**	95
	Introduction	95
	Cosmology, Myth and Science	97
	Cosmology and the Creative Arts	99
	The Original Series (1966–9)	105
	Star Trek: The Next Generation (1988–94)	113
	Star Trek: Deep Space Nine (1993–9)	117
	Star Trek: Voyager (1995–2001)	123
	Enterprise (2001–5)	125
	Conclusion	139
4	**Fans, Bards and Rituals**	141
	Introduction	141
	Myth and Ritual Theory	142
	Bardic Television	148
	Pilgrimage and *Star Trek: The Experience*	153
	Disneyland and Las Vegas: Three-Dimensional Texts	156
	Fan as Character/Hero and Identity Play	160
	Future's Past, Past Futures	166
	Playing with the Reality Experience	173
	Pilgrimage, Transformation and Control	176
	Beyond *The Experience*	179
	Fans as Internet Bards	181
	Conclusion	187
	Conclude ... Then Reboot	189
	Afterword	197
	Notes	201
	Bibliography	261
	Index	294

List of Illustrations

0.1 A young James T. Kirk leaps from a 1960s Corvette in *Star Trek* (Paramount Pictures 2009). 3

0.2 Leonard Nimoy and Zachary Quinto as Spock in *Star Trek* (Paramount Pictures 2009). 4

1.1 Walter Cronkite presents myth as news in *You Are There* (CBS 1953–7). 36

1.2 Apollo in *TOS* 'Who Mourns for Adonais?' (Paramount Television 1967). 38

1.3 *The Mighty Hercules* (Trans Lux 1963) encounters the Hydra. 39

1.4 *The Mighty Thor* (Famous Studios 1966) and its genre-blending iconography. 53

2.1 Data embodies technology and myth in *TNG* 'Masks' (Paramount Television 1994). 71

2.2 *DS9*'s Sisko meets Kirk in the 30th anniversary episode 'Trials and Tribble-ations' (Paramount Television 1996). 81

2.3 The Taresian aliens in *Voyager*'s 'Favorite Son' (Paramount Television 1997). 93

3.1 Captain Archer's childhood memories in *Enterprise* 'Broken Bow' (Paramount Television 2001). 132

3.2 Scott Bakula welcomes the USS *Enterprise* home (UPN 2001). 135

3.3 The new title sequence for *Enterprise* 'In a Mirror Darkly' (Paramount Television 2005), featuring the sword emblem. 138

4.1 The Millennium Gate in *Voyager* '11.59' (Paramount Television 1999). 169

List of Illustrations

4.2 Multiple alternate *Trek* worlds in *TNG* 'Parallels' (Paramount Television 1993).   171

5.1 Lens flare in the second *Star Trek: Discovery* teaser trailer (CBS 2017).   192

5.2 *Star Trek: Discovery*'s widescreen vista (CBS 2017).   192

Acknowledgements

I acknowledge the Traditional Owners of the land where I live and work, the Wurundjeri people of the Kulin Nations, and pay my respects to the Elders both past and present.

I would like to particularly thank my colleagues and mentors, Angela Ndalianis and Christopher Mackie. Special thanks also to Diana Sandars and Justin Shaw for reading early drafts, and to Barbara Creed, Jeanette Hoorn, Mark Nicholls, and Barbara Silliman for their support. I would like to express my appreciation for my new colleagues at RMIT University, where I wrote the Afterword, particularly Alexia Kannas, Lisa French, Adrian Danks, Smiljana Glisovic, and Daniel Binns.

Thank you to all the fellow *Star Trek* fans I have met along the way for their enthusiasm and support, particularly the crew at *Austrek*, the oldest *Star Trek* fan club in Australia.

I gratefully acknowledge the following bodies that provided financial assistance for much of the research for this project: the School of Culture and Communication at the University of Melbourne, the Alma Hansen Scholarship, the M. A. Bartlett Foundation, and the Faculty of Arts at the University of Melbourne.

I wish to thank the libraries at the University of Melbourne (particularly librarian Jane Brown); the UCLA Film and Television Library; MIT Humanities Library; the Library of Congress; the Margaret Herrick Library; and the Museum of Television and Radio, New York.

I would like to thank the following journals and publishing houses for permission to reprint revised versions of my previously published material:

Baker, Djoymi, ' "Every old trick is new again": myth in quotations and the Star Trek franchise', *Popular Culture Review* 12/1 (2001), pp. 67–77. From *Star Trek as Myth: Essays on Symbol and Archetype at the Final Frontier* © 2010 Edited by Matthew Wilhelm Kapell by permission of McFarland & Company, Inc., Box 611, Jefferson NC 28640. www.mcfarlandpub.com.

Acknowledgements

—— 'Contested spaces: the internet ate my TV, the TV company ate my internet site', *The Refractory: A Journal of Entertainment Media*, 1 (2002). Available at https://refractory-journal.com/contested-spaces-the-internet-ate-my-tv-the-tv-company-ate-my-internet-site-djoymi-baker/.

—— 'Are we there yet? Star Trek and the future history of space exploration', *Resistance is Futile*, exhibition catalogue (Southbank, VCA Margaret Lawrence Gallery, 2006). Reprinted in K. Daw and V. McInnes (eds), *Bureau* (Melbourne: VCA Margaret Lawrence Gallery, University of Melbourne, 2008).

—— '"The illusion of magnitude": Adapting the epic from film to television', *Senses of Cinema*, 41 (2006). Available at www.sensesofcinema.com/2006/film-history-conference-papers/adapting-epic-film-tv/.

This book is dedicated to Paul, Ava and Finn.

Introduction

This book charts how *Star Trek* has woven ancient storytelling traditions into its futuristic world, but has then promoted itself as the new mythology of our times. The flexible, often contradictory nature of myth forms the central premise of the book. Today, myth is often understood as a traditional story of cultural significance, but in practice myth is constantly in flux, a mixture of tradition and innovation. This is a process we find in both ancient myth and contemporary transmedia tales such as *Star Trek*, even as we must take into account how myth changes in a commercial entertainment context. Myth in the *Star Trek* franchise finds expression in numerous different forms, from mythic stories retold in its narratives, to the way it has been overtly marketed as a contemporary myth, and the fan experiences that bring myth into popular culture rituals. The myth of *Star Trek* can only be understood across its diverse textual, cultural and industrial practices with an equally multifaceted understanding of myth.

After the opening titles to the 11th *Star Trek* feature film – directed by J. J. Abrams in 2009 and called simply *Star Trek* – we see a sandy-haired youth racing a 1960s Corvette down a dirt road in Iowa to the strains of the Beastie Boys' 1994 song 'Sabotage'. As a futuristic airborne motorcycle gives chase, we know that this is not 1994. The boy jumps from the vehicle just in time to avoid joining it over the edge of a cliff. The audience is scarcely surprised when the recalcitrant youth identifies himself to the pursuing police officer as 'James Tiberius Kirk' – especially since most would have seen the sequence in one of the film's trailers in any case. What is Kirk doing listening to such an old track? It's so old that in Justin Lin's 2016 *Star Trek Beyond*, Doctor McCoy and Spock go so far as to agree the song is 'classical music'.

The 2009 feature film is another retelling of the origins of the *Star Trek* story following the cancelled *Enterprise* (2001–5), which itself had told a new beginning to the story. The opening sequence to the Abrams film brings together several generations of *Star Trek* and its viewers by means of a car from the same decade as *The Original Series* (*TOS*) and a generation-X song from the era of the *Star Trek* spin-off TV series *Star Trek: The Next Generation* (1987–94), *Star Trek: Deep Space Nine* (1993–9) and *Star Trek: Voyager* (1995–2001), from a band that has maintained its output and pop-cultural cachet. The 11th *Star Trek* film gives us a new Captain Kirk in the making – the original hero rebooted in an alternative *Star Trek* timeline for viewers new and old.

In our own timeline, the Beastie Boys dressed up as original-series characters Kirk, McCoy and Spock in their music video for the 2004 'Ch-Check It Out', and reference *Star Trek* in the lyrics for the 1998 track 'Intergalactic' and 2004's 'Brouhaha'. If this band apparently also exists in Kirk's timeline, then they have the curious distinction of being prophets of his destiny to become captain of the *Enterprise*. This is utter non-sense of course, and not in any way essential to understanding this scene. Except that this is how popular culture works, recycling and repackaging its history in such a way that it appears fresh and original, and yet evokes the past in a meaningful (or amusing) way. It is also the method used in mythic storytelling for millennia. The way that myth has been reimagined in *Star Trek* illustrates how myth in the twentieth and twenty-first centuries is not merely an unconscious replication of some ancient archetypal impulse, but rather has become a deliberate, conscious storytelling and promotional tool.

Introduction

Beyond Roddenberry: *Star Trek* and the New Mythology

The Beastie Boys' predilection for *Star Trek* was not the only apparent in-joke during this brief glimpse of Kirk's early delinquency. In *TOS* William Shatner as the first Captain Kirk had used the French pronunciation of 'sabotage'[1] in what many fans took to be a mispronunciation – and in turn fans assumed the use of the Beastie Boys' song in the *Star Trek* film was making fun of his 'error'. The bemused director J. J. Abrams responded by saying, 'I just dig the song.'[2] He similarly denied another fan speculation that the demise of the 1960s sports car was a metaphor for throwing off any restrictions from the original show – Kirk flinging himself from the Corvette to ensure not only his own survival but also that of the franchise (see Figure 0.1).[3] Despite Abrams' protestations, he nonetheless says 'the idea was to show the renegade, young Kirk and have a wildly anachronistic scene where you had an earthbound, almost back-looking scene combined with a forward-looking futuristic scene technologically.'[4]

Abrams' film uses a time-travel concept to create a new futuristic timeline for Kirk and his cohorts, known as the Kelvin Timeline as it is caused by the attack on the USS *Kelvin* by the time-travelling character Nero.[5] The

Figure 0.1 A young James T. Kirk leaps from a 1960s Corvette in *Star Trek* (Paramount Pictures 2009).

3

Figure 0.2 Leonard Nimoy and Zachary Quinto as Spock in *Star Trek* (Paramount Pictures 2009).

Kelvin Timeline reimagines the popular franchise[6] but links it to the past, particularly through Leonard Nimoy as Spock, who bridges the two timelines (see Figure 0.2). Although this complex mix of the new and the old may at first glance seem specific to the quirks of science fiction, it is also how ancient myth-making worked, retelling older stories by combining tradition and innovation to suit the changing needs of the audience and the culture.

This is a connection that the franchise itself has sought to promote. From *Star Trek: The Next Generation* (*TNG*) onwards, the television sequels have all been marketed by stressing the longevity of the *Star Trek* story and its connections with even older storytelling traditions of myth, legend and saga. Such connections would have come somewhat as a surprise in the 1960s: *TOS* first aired on US television in 1966 and was cancelled by NBC in 1969 due to the programme's low Nielsen ratings. By the sequels, *Star Trek* was overtly marketed as the futuristic myth of our times. The 2009 *Star Trek* feature film broke with this tradition by proclaiming in its trailers: 'This is not your father's *Star Trek*.' By implication, the trailer was asserting that this was, instead, a reimagined *Star Trek* for the current generation.

The original music video for the Beastie Boys' 'Sabotage' features the band in a parody of a 1970s cop show, complete with extra-large sideburns – a geeky but retro-cool parody. As much as the *Star Trek* trailers announced a break with the past, the 2009 feature film takes inspiration

Introduction

from the original 1960s series and fashions it into a retro-chic homage that simultaneously appeals to twenty-first-century filmgoers.

The debate about the Corvette scene might be taken as an example of how we can read too much into a film, and go beyond what the director intended. But media studies has long moved beyond assuming that meaning can be controlled in this way. *Star Trek* in particular cannot be contained to one vision of the future – not even that of creator Gene Roddenberry. It has seeped into popular culture across several generations and is inherently both 'back-looking' and 'forward-looking'. The fact that we come across *Star Trek* among myriad other, non-*Trek* sources affects the way that we respond to a film such as the 2009 *Star Trek*. Once we have seen the Beastie Boys in their *Star Trek* regalia, the image lurks in our minds as their song gives backing to Kirk's youthful escapades. It's an in-joke, whether or not Abrams intends it as such. There are other in-jokes in the film – both intended and unintended. Despite protestations in the trailers that 'This is not your father's *Star Trek*', the weight of this backstory and the place of *Star Trek* in popular culture are an intrinsic part of the film. Indeed, the recent television programme, *Star Trek: Discovery* (2017–), returns to the earlier campaign strategy by proclaiming in its second teaser trailer that the show is 'A new chapter in the *Star Trek* saga'.

In this book I argue that *Star Trek* is myth, twenty-first-century style: a complex set of stories passed on and updated from one generation to the next, in various media, that have become part of the broader cultural heritage. In turn they have been deliberately and consciously marketed as the new mythology. Ever since William Blake Tyrell's 1977 essay 'Star Trek as Myth and Television as Mythmaker', several decades of scholars have argued that *Star Trek* is the inheritor of an older mythic tradition.[7] Coming from a variety of backgrounds, authors have differed in precisely what they meant by this.

The commercial television, film and cross-media industry to which the expansive *Star Trek* franchise belongs has rarely been included as part of this mythological process. *Star Trek* increasingly situates itself as mythic not only in the texts themselves, but also in its paratexts such as title sequences, trailers, posters and other forms of advertising. As Jonathan Gray demonstrates, such paratexts help frame audience expectations and engagement,[8] and yet scholarship on *Star Trek* as a commercial franchise and *Star Trek* as myth-maker have tended to remain separate. Kapell's anthology *Star Trek as Myth* usefully charts much of the scholarship on *Star Trek* as myth, including foundational work by Tyrell, Peter J. Claus, C. Scott Littleton and John Shelton Lawrence, and yet marketing is mentioned only a few times in passing. This is also the case with significant earlier book-length examinations in the field, such as *Star Trek and Sacred Ground* and *Deep Space and Sacred Time: Star Trek in the American Mythos*.[9] There have nonetheless been some tentative steps towards bringing myth and its commercial context together. For example, in his introduction to *The Star Trek Universe: Franchising the Final Frontier*, Douglas Brode suggests a connection between the commercial expansion of the *Star Trek* franchise and its process of mythic retelling, but unfortunately this idea is not explored within the anthology itself.[10] In *Popular Media Cultures: Fans, Audiences and Paratexts*, Lincoln Geraghty advocates for scholarship that considers not only mythic popular culture texts themselves, but also the fan-produced and commercial paratexts that surround them, but again the specific connection between myth and commerce is not expanded upon.[11] Scholars have simply had a different focus. If myth-making connects authors, stories and cultural context, this book will suggest that *Star Trek*'s myth-making also includes and is shaped by commercial paratexts.

This commercial context also needs to include the television industry of the 1950s and 1960s that paved the way for *Star Trek*'s debut in 1966. The mythology of *Star Trek* has frequently been seen as reflecting not the future per se, but always and inevitably the culture and time in which it was created. Thus authors such as Rick Worland and Kapell have seen in *Star Trek* the continuation of America's frontier myth, which found new expression in the 1960s, both in the race to reach space and the conflict in Vietnam.[12] There has been extensive scholarship on the role of *Star Trek* in presenting a mythic version of US history.[13] *Star Trek*'s place within the history of the US television industry is examined in Roberta Pearson and Máire Messenger Davies' *Star Trek and American Television*; however, they see this as quite separate to mythic approaches.[14] Indeed, surprisingly little consideration has been given to the way *TOS*' use of myth reflects trends in the US television industry that spawned it.

Introduction

The fact that early television programmes up to and including *Star Trek* deliberately turned to myth for inspiration has deeper implications for the way we conceptualise myth. Writing in 1977, Tyrell suggests that the intentions of *Star Trek*'s writers and the true meaning of its episodes are often at odds, such that the mythic significance of the show is the result of an unconscious process.[15] This has been the dominant approach to myth in *Star Trek* ever since, with or without an overtly psychoanalytic methodology.[16] If myth serves and reflects cultural and psychological needs,[17] what does myth mean when its creation is no longer purely an unconscious process? Indeed, in our own era we can sit down with a copy of Vogler's 1998 *The Writer's Journey: Mythic Structure for Storytellers and Screenwriters*, a type of myth-by-numbers for screenwriters based on the work of Carl Jung and Joseph Campbell.[18] How do we arrive at an understanding of myth that makes room for Beastie Boys and heroic journeys, film trailers and ancient oral stories, *Star Trek* and Homer? The multilayered approach to myth that I develop in the book sees connections with the storytelling traditions from ancient Greece but also differences in the deliberate strategies around myth employed in our twentieth- and twenty-first-century media landscape.

Persuasive Words and Outright Lies: A Brief History of Myth

> 'All universal theories of myth are automatically wrong.'
> – G. S. Kirk.[19]

Star Trek borrows the cultural legitimacy and longevity often associated with myth to suggest and reinforce its own longevity within popular culture. However, defining myth is frustratingly problematic. Some theories seem to fit some myths extremely well, and yet not others. Ken Dowden suggests there cannot be a 'theory-free approach to myth', for every analysis of myth includes an implicit concept of myth itself. From the origins of the word 'myth' in Archaic Greece, the idea of myth has changed considerably.[20] At the same time, many of the debates surrounding the nature of myth continue over millennia. The mutable, contested status of myth is an important concept that runs through this book in various guises. This is particularly worth noting in the context of film and television studies, in which myth has tended to be associated with fixed, even universal, structures and meanings. By contrast, definitions and theories of myth have shifted considerably over time.[21] *Star Trek*'s futuristic version of myth becomes one in a long line of texts that rework what myth might mean in new contexts and time periods.

Myth has never been a static 'universal' concept. Myth comes from the Greek *muthos*; however, the Latin form *mythos* is most often used in English-language scholarship, and will be used throughout this book. The first surviving use of *mythos* appears in Homer's *Iliad* of *c*.700 BCE, where it may mean simply 'words', a 'speech', or perhaps 'oral storytelling' intended to be persuasive.[22] Thus, in the context of the *Iliad*, Richard P. Martin defines *mythos* as an 'authoritative speech-act'.[23] Hesiod (*c*.700 BCE) uses *mythos* in a similar way.[24] Despite a lack of consensus regarding this earliest extant use in the Archaic, pre-Classical period, what appears clear is an emphasis on the performative, spoken aspect: myth is not the story or account itself so much as the story in its telling.[25] This etymology of myth is quite different from traditional academic explanations of myth,[26] which tend to focus upon sacred stories that are orally composed and transmitted, set in ancient times and deal with subject matter that is supernatural, heroic or concerned with origins.[27] This book is particularly informed by the Archaic – but ever-shifting – understanding of myth as performative. It is important to consider the process by which *Star Trek* tells and retells its story in different texts, across different decades, generations and media forms, as well as the possibilities for fans to perform their own roles within the *Star Trek* story-world.

In the centuries following Homer, the ways in which Greek philosophers, playwrights and historians use *mythos* reveal some surprising changes in attitude towards the concept. By the sixth century BCE, the pre-Socratic philosophers criticised the stories described by Homer and Hesiod, but not the meaning of *mythos* itself. Their commentaries paved the way for critiques of *mythos* in the next century. Xenophanes of Colophon (570–460 BCE) notes that people invariably imagined gods in their own image, with their own foibles.[28] That said, he does not call the stories he rejects 'myths'.[29] Indeed, Xenophanes employs *mythos* only once, and favourably, saying, 'glad-hearted men must hymn the god with reverent words [*muthois*] and pure speech [*logois*]'.³⁰ However, Xenophanes' rationalisation of traditional stories was to have a broad-ranging impact, influencing, for example, Pindar (522–446 BCE), Euripides (480–406 BCE) and Plato (427–347 BCE).³¹ The notion that traditional stories might reflect human concerns also informed many nineteenth- and twentieth-century theories of myth, while the rationalisation of the fantastical elements in mythic tales continues into our own day. Thus, while the special effects of film and television have made much of mythical gods and monsters, other adaptations, such as Wolfgang Petersen's *Troy* of 2004, rationalise the stories even to the extent of removing the gods themselves. Indeed, as will become clear over the course of this book, traditional stories survive through adaptation, even if scholars do not always approve of the revisions that are made.

The Archaic period in Greece also brought the earliest allegorical reading of traditional stories.³² Theagenes of Rhêgium (*c.*525 BCE) argues that the gods of Homer metaphorically represent natural elements (for example, Apollo as fire, Artemis as the Moon), as well as essentialised human qualities (for example, Athena as intelligence).³³ This allegorical approach was later to become popular in the nineteenth century.

In the fifth century BCE, *mythos* undergoes a surprising and important shift: from being associated with truthfulness, to being associated with its direct opposite – deception.³⁴ In Ode Eight of the *Nemean Odes*, Pindar states (*c.*459 BCE): 'It seems that hateful Misrepresentation existed even long ago: a fellow traveller of flattering tales [*muthôn*],³⁵ deceitful-minded, a malignant disgrace.'³⁶ Traveller and historian Herodotus (born *c.*484 BCE) associates myth with ridiculous accounts, such that he disputes the idea that Heracles could kill a multitude of people single-handedly.³⁷ Thucydides (*c.*471–401 BCE), for his part, cautions in *The Peloponnesian War* that a distinction must be made between history and poetic myth.³⁸ This burgeoning distinction, as well as the correlation between myth and deception, survives today.

The idea that myths could be untruthful did not mean that they might not also be useful. In Plato's *Republic*, Socrates (*c.*469–399 BCE) states, 'we begin by telling children stories [*mythoi*]. These are, in general, fiction, though they contain some truth.'[39] Here, then, *mythoi* are a class of tale, closer to contemporary understandings of myth. The trick is to choose *mythoi* suitable for this educational purpose, while rejecting others.[40] Lincoln notes: 'What others had taken to be primordial revelations or undeniable truths now were treated as state propaganda.'[41] This ideological understanding of myth has survived in contemporary theory, particularly through the work of Roland Barthes.[42] Because myths could be useful, Plato was happy to create his own myths to serve a philosophical or moral purpose, for example 'The Myth of Er' and 'The Simile of the Cave' in *The Republic*.[43] Yet in Plato's *Timaeus* and *Critias*, Critias emphasises that the story of Atlantis is a true one, and 'not a made-up story', a seemingly ironic assertion.[44] The story itself is clearly fictional, albeit designed for a philosophical reading, a type of charter myth for the republic.[45] Similarly, *Star Trek* can be seen as assuring us of our continued importance in the cosmos even as Earth has been displaced from its centre, a myth for a post-Copernican, spacefaring era.

In the various periods of Greek culture, from Archaic through to Hellenistic, a process of demythologisation took place, although not necessarily in a strict linear progression. *Mythos* gradually moves from speech – often assertive and truthful in nature – to deceptive speech, irrational speech, and perhaps even a class of stories, which in turn became conceived in increasingly pragmatic and even dismissive terms. By the Hellenistic era (323–146 BCE), Euhemerus of Messene argues that the Homeric gods had originally been human, but had been deified over time.[46] Myth gradually comes to mean something quite different from Homer's notion of *mythos*. Kovacs even compares the gradual shift towards a more self-conscious understanding of myth in the Hellenistic era to the later sequels of the *Star Trek* franchise, and their 'attempts to expand earlier ideas and to reconcile perceived contradictions.'[47] Comparative works, particularly those such as this book, which seek to explore the use and reworking of myth in contemporary technologies such as television, must acknowledge the fluidity of the term 'myth'. The notion of 'traditional myth', so often invoked as a point of contrast with more recent adaptations, is itself slippery. Concepts of new and old myth, as a story, class of story, as a concept, or a mode of speech, must remain relative and unstable.

Introduction

Many of the Greek attitudes to myth would continue to have their effects felt down the centuries, with debates about myth focusing on many of the same issues. In the twentieth and twenty-first centuries, scholars have defined myth more broadly as a narrative that embodies communal ideas about the natural and social world.[48] Thus Walter Burkert argues that 'myth is a traditional tale with secondary, partial reference to something of collective importance.'[49] Conceptualised in this manner, myths can be seen to articulate universal themes and concerns of human life (such as birth and death), as well as reflecting and mediating specific cultural shifts.

The concept of a 'modern myth' has been anathema to many scholars working with more traditionally defined myths, and for whom distinctions between myth, legend and folklore are themselves much debated.[50] Drawing upon these traditional and popular understandings of the word, myth has become conceptualised in terms of an ever-broadening field of narrative and belief systems.[51] As R. W. Brockway notes:

> [S]ince the beginning of the nineteenth century, the definition of myth has been broadened to include sacred history [...] literary epics, and popular genre literature such as westerns, gothics, science fiction, fantasy tales, and romances. What is more, mythic implications are sometimes discerned in modern scientific theories, philosophical systems, theories of history and political ideologies.[52]

The broadened concept of myth has raised significant problems of identification and definition.

Cinema and television are technological products of an industrial culture. They differ markedly, therefore, from the oral transmission of myths of non-industrial cultures, at the very least by virtue of their technological status. Further, while the origins of many myths are difficult, if not impossible, to determine, film and television have identifiable production processes.[53] Despite these differences, theories of myth have been appropriated and adapted by film and television studies, particularly in the 1960s and 1970s, when the work of Claude Lévi-Strauss (1908–2009) was used to suggest that films by a particular director or within a particular genre might help to reconcile cultural oppositions.[54] Early *Star Trek* scholarship returned to these ideas to suggest that the franchise could be seen as a set of contemporary mythic stories that could symbolically resolve cultural contradictions.[55]

One of the reasons that mythic approaches to cinema fell out of favour was that screen scholars saw myth as essentially universal in nature, whereas genre was seen as more localised and therefore not myth.[56] In the late 1970s Schatz countered this approach by arguing 'a culturally specific narrative form *itself* can be mythic'.[57] However, Schatz also cautions that because myths are now told through new media, any study of film genres as myth must take into account considerations of film production, such as economics, the star system and film technology.[58] Bearing this caution in mind, this book argues that science fiction television programmes such as *Star Trek* function as popular culture myths; however, this mythic function is heavily conditioned by television industry trends and marketing.

Myth is now recognised as being both traditional and historically specific, but we must also be mindful of the multiplicity of myth. Jim Collins argues that complex contemporary societies reveal 'competition between different forms of "myth"'.[59] He contrasts this with the non-industrial tribal cultures explored by Lévi-Strauss. Collins suggests that:

> [Will] Wright is correct in arguing that myth as popular narrative is a form of legitimation, but he does not appreciate the processes or *self*-legitimation that form an essential part of the mythology they produce in response to other competing modes of representation.[60]

Contemporary cultures may produce different, even contradictory, forms of popular mythology, which attempt to assert their superiority over competing narratives in making meaning. In this context, different forms of popular narrative, generic or otherwise, can adopt different mythological roles within the same culture. The *Star Trek* franchise has adapted older story traditions in just such a process of '*self*-legitimation', attempting to forge a *Star Trek* popular mythology.

The idea that myth might be linked to legitimacy was also incorporated into the work of Roland Barthes (1915–80). In *Mythologies*, Barthes writes: 'What is myth today? I shall give at the outset a first, very simple answer, which is perfectly consistent with etymology: *myth is a type of speech*.'[61] What was important was the method rather than the content of this speech. 'Myth is not defined by the object of its message, but by the way in which it utters this message [...] Everything, then, can be a myth? Yes, I believe this.'[62]

Despite this broadness, myth in Barthes' system is neither universal nor eternal. Rather, it is the function of myth to *appear* universal. Barthes suggests that 'myth has the task of giving an historical intention a natural justification, and making contingency appear eternal.'[63] For example, that which is political is made to seem natural in myth, and for this reason Barthes argues that 'myth is depoliticized speech'.[64] The mythologist seeks to reveal that which lies within myth.[65] While Barthes never explored the etymology of myth beyond his brief statement quoted above, in his approach we can see a combination of Homer's use of myth as an 'authoritative speech-act', frequently spoken from a position of power,[66] with later Greek perspectives on the deceptive nature of myth.

In his 1971 essay 'Mythology Today', Barthes revisits *Mythologies*, stating, 'in our society the mythical still abounds, just as anonymous and slippery, fragmented and garrulous'.[67] Barthes argues that in the play of signs, there is no longer a direct relationship with ideology, for signs are 'infinitely citing one another'.[68] This requires a new form of interpretation whose task is 'no longer to simply *upend* (or *right*) the mythical message'.[69] The focus shifts to 'citation, reference, stereotype'.[70] Such citations could theoretically continue *ad infinitum*, and it is this journey that becomes the source of meaning.[71] Applying this idea to *Star Trek*, a journey through the franchise over time reveals twists and turns in its use of myth.

Signs refer to other signs, texts to other texts, sign systems to other sign systems. By referring to ancient mythology, the *Star Trek* franchise attempts to appropriate a mythological tint to its own story-world, as long-lasting and culturally significant. These movements help to create meaning within and around the text. Barthes argues that 'any text is an intertext; other texts are present in it, at varying levels, in more or less recognizable forms: the texts of the previous and surrounding culture. Any text is a new tissue of past citations.'[72]

Not only are different signs mixed together, but also different sign systems – different ways of speaking. Myth is an intertextual field of influence that is deliberately harnessed by *Star Trek* to borrow a sense of cultural legitimacy. However, this appropriation of myth exists within a broader set of quotes from multiple texts and multiple discourses.

The application of mythology to screen studies has, in some respects, been an attempt to deal with the presence of recurring structures while also wrestling with aspects of film and television that seem to distinguish them from ancient myth. In general, the move has been away from broader structuralist approaches,[73] towards more synthetic systems of analysis in which myth is one component. Recent studies of cinema and television as myth have turned away from broad models and have examined structures specific to a single myth rather than to all myths. Myth has also been understood as one communication system among a variety of possible systems that may be incorporated into specific contemporary texts, rather than applying to an entire medium.[74]

Myth has oscillated between a mode of speech and a classification of a story type, and the screen-myth alliance has attempted to deal with myth on both fronts. The shifting terrain of myth studies, especially as it has been applied to more recent media forms, indicates the difficulty in assigning precedence to any single model. Drawing on Collins' notion of the array,[75] myth can be seen as an array of texts and discourses that intersect one another. Collins' array can be extended to include both fictional texts and the wider discourses that inform those texts. A *mythological* array would include all texts and discourses around the concept of myth, including traditional stories, revamped versions of those myths, the definition and interpretation of myth, and storytelling rituals. Specifically, in the creation of a popular mythology, *Star Trek* intersects with its own accumulated textual past, older mythological stories that it adapts, and the cultural associations with the word 'myth' that it intentionally harnesses through marketing.

Myth in the Age of *Star Trek*

While the term myth has continually broadened in popular and academic use, it has also become the subject of a deliberate narrative strategy. The

Introduction

traditional myths of various cultures and time periods, but most frequently those of Classical Greece and Rome, have been mined by writers of television programmes. These programmes span ostensibly ancient settings, such as *Xena* (1995–2001); present-day settings, such as *Buffy: The Vampire Slayer* (1997–2003); and quasi-futuristic settings, such as *Battlestar Galactica* (2004–9) and the various *Star Trek* series, to name but a few. Whether or not television programmes function as myths, the conscious manipulation of mythic material at the very least produces shows that are *about* myth. These programmes enter into a long-standing dialogue about the nature of myth. Fans of *Star Trek* will not be surprised to discover the range of mythic references across the various shows, and even in this book there is insufficient room to do justice to them all.

Darcee McLaren notes that ' "*Star Trek* is a modern myth" is an often-heard phrase that resonates with, and is used by, scholars and fans alike [...] However, very little attention has been given to the referential meaning of the phrase.'[76] Matt Hills has taken up this suggestion, and asks: 'How might descriptions of "myth" [...] work not as blanket forms of cultural evaluation and valorisation, but rather as mobile discourses occupying different regimes of value for producers, audiences and critics, while seemingly binding these cultural groups together?'[77] This book explores a shifting concept of myth as it is articulated through industry television reviews, diegetic adaptations both overt and implicit, and marketing strategies. *Star Trek*'s live-action series of the 1980s, 1990s and 2000s (*TNG*, *DS9*, *Voyager* and *Enterprise*) have increasingly positioned *Star Trek* as a form of contemporary myth through an interplay between its own fictional world and the myths it has updated. The use of myth in *Star Trek* is explored not as an unconscious expression of universal tropes, but as an increasingly self-aware textual strategy. It is argued that competing mythic discourses are articulated and structured within and around the *Star Trek* franchise.

Whenever a writer begins to explore a fictional world or character that has kept reinventing itself (such as *Star Trek*, Superman, James Bond, *Doctor Who*[78] or *Star Wars*),[79] there is a practical problem created by the sheer scope of the different works. While this book examines the mythic elements of *Star Trek*, such an approach will necessarily highlight some aspects at the expense of others. As John Fiske notes, 'labels such as "realistic" or "mythic" are not just descriptors of textual characteristics but are active: they promote particular reading strategies which activate particular meanings in the text.'[80]

Henry Jenkins has shown that *Star Trek* has been interpreted in quite contradictory ways by fans and scholars alike.[81] Jenkins argues that *Star Trek* is constructed in such a way to facilitate this openness, leaving narrative gaps that can be filled in by viewers.[82] As Linda Johnston observes, 'fans are constantly filling in the gaps, speculating about the "actions" of nonexistent beings in a yet-to-be world [...] as if the Federation actually existed'.[83] Yet Tulloch and Jenkins note that even fans who produce completely different expansions upon this fictional world can see 'their position as totally consistent with the text's original and preferred meaning', so that a singular 'original' understanding of *Star Trek* becomes impossible.[84] This problem is compounded as the *Star Trek* story has expanded through films, spin-offs and a transmedia franchise, unfolding 'across multiple media platforms, with each new text making a distinctive and valuable contribution to the whole'.[85] As with many transmedia story-worlds, different offshoots of the tale 'introduce potential plots which cannot be fully told or extra details which hint at more than can be revealed', such that Jenkins suggests transmedia franchises continue to provide new vantage points and gaps for fans to speculate about and expand upon in multiple directions.[86] In the case of the *Star Trek* franchise, only the live-action television programmes and films are officially recognised as central 'canon', although even this status is debated.

Proctor argues that the canon issue has become complicated in recent years by *Star Trek* comic books such as *Star Trek: Countdown*, which was marketed as 'the official movie prequel' to the 2009 film and thereby muddies the waters.[87] Similarly, the cover of *Star Trek: Countdown to Darkness* proclaimed itself to be 'the official comic prequel to *Star Trek Into Darkness*'.[88] Some fans also argue for the inclusion of *The Animated Series* of 1973 in the canon, because Gene Roddenberry was closely involved with the series and it features the voices of *TOS* cast members (with the exception of Walter Koenig's Chekov). Roddenberry himself disowned the feature films *Star Trek V: The Final Frontier* (1989) and *Star Trek VI: The Undiscovered Country* (1991).[89] As Ndalianis argues in the case of comic book reboots, negating aspects of a story-world's past 'can't mean that they no longer exist because they still live in the memory and experiences of their readers.'[90] From the perspective of personal and cultural memory, *Star Trek* constitutes the entire array of transmedia stories, each of which situates itself within the fictional *Star Trek* world while simultaneously providing different narrative information (and modes of presentation).

While cross-media products can fill in temporal gaps prior to, between and after canon texts,[91] in many cases they introduce plot points that give their version of the story-world quite different timelines of significant events. For example, the *Star Trek: Telepathy War* comic brings together characters from *TNG*, *DS9*, the Marvel comic book characters of *Starfleet Academy* (1996–8), and the Talosian aliens last seen in *TOS*, in a wide-ranging war not acknowledged in the main, live-action canon.[92] As each new *Star Trek* text builds up more details that are exclusive to that version, they become splintered off from each other as similar yet different *Trek* worlds. This transmedia complexity has grown throughout its half-century existence.

Both Jenkins and Collins have suggested that we see the reader/viewer/user as a traveller, navigating his or her way through media products by a process of choice and appropriation.[93] Choosing one path over another produces one meaning within an array of possible meanings.[94] By focusing upon the role of myth in *Star Trek*, this book will produce one such meaning in the array of overlapping *Star Trek* texts and readings, within a broader array through which *Star Trek* connects with television history, other media, genre development, scientific discourses and myth theory. While mythic storytelling has always been intertextual in nature, it expands and connects in new ways in the contemporary transmedia environment.

Myth is at best a slippery word, affected in function through variations in communication methods. Such variations, rather than constituting a problem for myth analysis, are instead treated here as one of the means by which mythic meaning is generated and updated. Focus will be upon formal analysis of structuring systems (including serial form, title sequences, genre, intertextuality and mythic heroic models) and of representational devices (such as visual effects and iconography). As each chapter examines a different aspect of myth in and around *Star Trek*, tensions arise between these different modalities of myth. *Star Trek* quotes from old myths to align itself with high culture, but also begins to present itself as a futuristic inheritor of that mythic tradition. *Star Trek*'s use of the term 'myth' to refer both to older stories and to its own stories indicates the malleable nature of the concept within the *Star Trek* franchise. While myth may be a methodological filter that produces 'particular meanings',[95] acknowledging the varied history of myth and its slippery nature in turn produces different mythological readings. This flexible, shifting concept of myth is necessary when considering the complexities of contemporary transmedia culture. What myth means in *Star Trek* is quite varied across its stories, marketing and fan experiences. This requires a similarly multipronged methodology.

Chapter 1 looks at the way myth was updated in early television programmes of the 1950s and 1960s, leading up to *Star Trek*. The original *Star Trek* programme has itself been interpreted as mythic and as incorporating mythic patterns, but one episode explicitly takes ancient mythology and recasts it in a futuristic mould. In 'Who Mourns for Adonais?' (1967), Greek mythology is shown to have a basis in fact within the *Star Trek* storyworld, in that gods such as Apollo are really travelling aliens. Matt Hills argues that scholars tend to analyse 'Who Mourns for Adonais?' in purely diegetic terms, 'divorcing it from the detailed mechanisms and discourses of television production'.[96] Indeed, Pearson and Messenger Davies make this criticism of mythic approaches to *Star Trek* more generally.[97] In any consideration of the relationship between myth and *Star Trek*, 'Who Mourns for Adonais?' is impossible to ignore, because it so consciously reworks and rewrites Greek myth into *Star Trek*'s science fiction world. Bearing Hills' comments in mind, however, Chapter 1 asks how this episode might be informed by the trends in television preceding it. Examining television programmes from the 1940s, 1950s and 1960s leading up to 'Who Mourns for Adonais?', it is argued that television developed its own particular course in the adaptation of myth, favouring children's programmes and science fiction, and relying on multiple layers of textual and media referencing.

This referencing becomes increasingly complex over time. Although *Star Trek* struggled in the ratings, it inspired a dedicated fan following. This led to the 1973 animated series, and several live-action series from the late 1980s onwards, with 2017's *Star Trek: Discovery* being released on

Introduction

the heels of the 50th anniversary of the franchise the previous year, and the flagship for the new streaming service CBS All Access.[98] Like *TOS*, the spin-offs have each adapted older stories into their futuristic story-world. However, by the 1990s in particular, the *Star Trek* franchise deliberately marketed itself as legendary, epic and mythic in its various advertising campaigns. Due to its place within popular culture, the *Star Trek* franchise increasingly adapts mythological stories to suggest that *Star Trek* itself is also mythic in nature and status. Chapter 2 explores this process of retelling and quoting different forms of myth in the context of ongoing serial structures of storytelling.

The *Star Trek* franchise has become increasingly aware of its mythic resonances and references. Collins argues that some contemporary entertainment texts are so self-conscious in their multiple references that they no longer function as myth in any conventional sense.[99] Rather, they can only be understood as 'myth' in quotation marks, a form of self-reflexive citation.[100] This type of text appeals less to broad mythic or genre patterns, and more to a series of quotations within the text, of which the audience will have varying degrees of knowledge. Indeed, if contemporary texts operate as 'myth' only in quotations, then they should be more accurately conceptualised as 'myths'. It is impossible to investigate myth in contemporary serial texts such as *Star Trek*, for example, without acknowledging a coexistence of multiple mythic forms within the one text (let alone within the cross-media *Star Trek* array in which any one of its programmes is situated). Chapter 2 will argue that such quotational practices in the context of *Star Trek* undergo a process of mutual retelling in which more than one tradition is juxtaposed and transformed. The notion of mutual retelling has been harnessed by the *Star Trek* franchise to align *Star Trek* with high culture, including mythic texts.

The longevity of the *Star Trek* story means that it has become part of the way we think about space exploration. The *Star Trek* shows have attempted to draw and expand on known science to speculate on the future. Chapter 3 explores the way *Star Trek* continues a long tradition of using stories and images to communicate cosmology to the general public. Stories about the origin and nature of the cosmos can be found in both myth and science. During the scientific revolution of the sixteenth and seventeenth centuries, visual material and speculative stories were used by scientists and non-scientists alike to communicate in simplified terms the new cosmological theories of the time. Although separated by centuries, the original *Star Trek* also emerged during a scientific paradigm shift, in the context of the Cold War Space Race between the US and USSR. Just as scientific frontispieces summarised the cosmological ideas found within written treatises of the scientific revolution, the title sequences of the various *Star Trek* programmes concisely indicate the scientific and textual discourses regarding the nature of the cosmos that the programmes would then explore. The title sequences reflect and inform contemporary shifts in conceptions and concerns about outer space. If this cosmological discourse is arguably latent in *TOS* through to *Voyager*, *Enterprise* makes the connection overt in its title sequence by linking imagery from the sixteenth-century scientific revolution, the 1960s Space Race and *Star Trek*.

Chapter 4 analyses the award-winning themed attraction *Star Trek: The Experience* in Las Vegas, which transformed the *Star Trek* story-world into a three-dimensional, ritual pilgrimage space from 1998 to 2008. Segal argues that a dual approach that considers both myth and its related rituals has the benefit of putting stories into their broader context, looking at both 'narrative and action'.[101] Marketing for the themed attraction sought to centralise the *Star Trek* fan as its narrative hero, a strategy continued in the rides at *The Experience*. The franchise thereby incorporated fans into the heroic *Star Trek* mythos, but this could only be partially successful given the narrative constraints of the site. In the ancient multi-authored system, myths were told, retold and reinvented by storytellers and bards. In the contemporary era, this bardic function is contested between fans and the corporate copyright-holders that seek to frame permissible fan rituals.

The Experience site closed just prior to the Abrams 2009 feature film reboot, for no mythic 'tradition' is ever static, but rather must change with different eras and different generations to continue its story. Each *Star Trek* television episode may tell a cohesive story, but it also reworks myriad related generic conventions, mythic tropes and consciously quoted sources. In this sense, to tell a story is to always retell another story, if only by allusion. This notion of retelling becomes particularly overt in the Abrams and Lin feature films, which remind us that enduring franchises such as *Star*

Introduction

Trek do not ever really conclude, but can always be added to or started over along alternate lines that nonetheless always look back to a complex serial history. Similarly, ancient myths were never fixed, but rather combined tradition and innovation. Even Heracles' famous twelve labours were a later, Classical addition, and like James T. Kirk, his childhood exploits were 'prequel' material used to flesh out his backstory.[102] As he became Hercules for the Romans, his stories were revamped yet again for a new cultural context. So too, *Star Trek*'s continual process of retelling its story does not occur in a vacuum, but rather is affected by cultural shifts, television trends and commercial imperatives spanning half-a-century. As a result, myth in *Star Trek* is multiple: it is a textual strategy of legitimisation, a marketing ploy to maintain the franchise's commercial viability, and a popular culture phenomenon where stories are transformed into fan rituals, both official and unofficial. This is the complexity, multiplicity and richness of myth in the current era.

Through the television programmes and the supporting texts of advertising, games and interactive theme attractions, *Star Trek* is positioned as contemporary myth, consciously exploiting the term's associations with longevity, heroic tales and high culture. The official StarTrek.com website now even includes articles that argue *Star Trek* and its fandom are mythic.[103] Inherent in this project is the way in which *Star Trek* is constructed and marketed as myth. No one book can definitively answer why *Star Trek* has been so popular for so long. Its deliberate ties with older mythologies tap into an ancient mythic tradition that resonates across generations, while at the same time *Star Trek*'s complex mythic discourse can help to reveal our understanding of myth specifically in the twentieth and early twenty-first centuries. As any *Star Trek* fan knows, *Star Trek* is also special in and of itself. When the Beastie Boys' 'Sabotage' reappeared in the first trailer for *Star Trek Beyond*, it was set to a montage of action sequences, such that some fans tagged it *Star Trek Fast and Furious*, after director Lin's previous franchise.[104] Even writer/actor Simon Pegg lamented that the trailer did not contain more of the '*Star Trek* stuff' that would feature in the film.[105] This is the challenge of story traditions – ancient and contemporary – to be retold for new audiences over new generations, without losing their core: in this case, '*Star Trek* stuff'.

1

Myth and Early US TV

Introduction

The reinterpretation of myth within the original series of *Star Trek* reflected the way that television adapted myth in the 1940s, 1950s and 1960s. In 1967, *Star Trek* broadcast an episode entitled 'Who Mourns for Adonais [sic]?',[1] in which Captain Kirk and his crew discover the Greek god Apollo in space. Because it so overtly reworks Greek myth, 'Who Mourns for Adonais?' has frequently been discussed by academics in relation to *Star Trek*'s association with myth.[2] However, such studies have tended to ignore television production trends that might have helped shape the episode.[3] By the time 'Who Mourns for Adonais?' went to air in the USA, at least 32 other television programmes had already adapted mythological material for US television. Using 'Who Mourns for Adonais?' as an underlying framing episode, this chapter explores the use of myth on US television of the 1940–60s, and its reception in contemporary reviews.

Rather than merely reflecting concerns specific to the *Star Trek* storyworld, 'Who Mourns for Adonais?' followed television industry trends of the previous decades. Television adaptations of myth in the 1940–60s most often appeared in children's programmes and science fiction shows. Although some programmes set mythological stories in the ancient past, most, like *Star Trek*, transposed myth into quite varied settings. Myth was used in these shows to validate both the television medium itself and maligned television genres such as science fiction.

This chapter, therefore, examines television programmes from the pre-*Star Trek* period that retell mythological stories, or integrate mythic tropes within otherwise non-mythical diegeses. Most of these TV programmes have received little if any academic attention. While mythological subjects in cinema during the 1950s and 1960s have been the subject of studies in relation to the epic genre, little has been written about the connection between cinema epics and television adaptations of the same mythological material during this period.[4] This chapter argues that 'Who Mourns for Adonais?' reflects pre-existing television trends in the use of myth, but it also seeks to open up a new area of study that has heretofore been neglected: the adaptation of myth in the early decades of television.

That examinations of early television can still reveal such gaps is indicative of the methodological constraints of such studies. Incomplete holdings of early television and the disintegration of early kinescope stock mean that comprehensive examinations of a particular programme, time period or genre are often difficult, if not impossible. This chapter can only be a partial interrogation of early television's adaptation of myth for precisely these reasons, examining a series of trends established across numerous programmes and their reception by the industry. 'Early' here is bounded at one end by the availability of material from the late 1940s, and at the other by the mid- to late 1960s, when the original *Star Trek* series was aired.[5]

For the purposes of this chapter, myth is understood as a set of traditional stories, a model of myth that necessarily becomes more complex in the chapters that follow, as the spin-off series that followed *TOS* engage with different concepts of myth on multiple fronts. In the early years of television, myth was carried across media forms and genres in its transition to television. These genre links were often new, revealing television-specific alignments that affected the meaning of myth. The specific language used in reviews is of particular importance in establishing the terms of reference through which myth-based programmes were understood. As noted earlier, Jonathan Gray argues paratexts such as reviews help shape how audiences approach a text and 'the menu of intertexts' they are invited to think about.[6] The methodology of this chapter, therefore, combines textual analysis with analysis of contemporary reviews in publications such as *Variety* and *TV Guide*. The way traditional stories were negotiated in early television programmes, and the way reviews discursively constructed those programmes, reveal continuing and shifting ideas about myth.

'Who Mourns for Adonais?'

In the original *Star Trek* series episode 'Who Mourns for Adonais?' the Greek god Apollo is found living on an alien planet, and is revealed to be a member of a spacefaring alien race. The humans of the twenty-third-century *Star Trek* world are accustomed to dealing with alien beings, and refuse to become Apollo's new worshippers. *Enterprise* crew member Lieutenant Carolyn Palamas forms a romantic bond with Apollo, yet rejects his advances, at the behest of Captain Kirk. Apollo's subsequent rage drains the technological source of his power, enabling his defeat by the *Enterprise* crew. Apollo eventually accepts the change in human belief systems, and proclaims that his 'time has passed. There is no room for gods,' upon which he fades into a non-corporeal form.

Kirk and his crew reject Apollo partly because they can recognise him as simply another alien. By contrast, Kirk realises that the ancient Greeks, 'simple shepherds and tribesmen', must have mistaken Apollo's powerful alien race for gods. Despite this case of mistaken identity, Greek mythology is nonetheless given a basis in fact within the *Star Trek* story-world. The Greek gods are depicted as real beings who once visited Earth, immortal but not necessarily divine. Apollo compares Captain Kirk and his 'away team'[7] with the heroes of Greek epic: Agamemnon, Hector and Odysseus. This similarly suggests that these heroes of mythology actually lived.[8] The comparison further implies that the *Enterprise* crew have taken up the heroic role of these figures. Thus 'Who Mourns for Adonais?' retells its mythic subject matter to both renounce the past and yet embody its heroic nature in an imagined future. The distant future and the distant mythic past are therefore simultaneously marked by continuity and discontinuity. The fictional future may share heroic characteristics of myth suggested by Apollo, yet it is paradoxically also marked by a renunciation of mythic and religious belief structures.

'Who Mourns for Adonais?' has therefore been interpreted primarily in terms of the demise of myth or religion. Jeffrey Lamp argues that while *Star Trek* itself might be conceptualised as 'mythology', its use of myth in 'Who Mourns for Adonais?' functions in the context of other *Star Trek* episodes that reveal would-be deities as merely more advanced in either biology or technology.[9] Anne MacKenzie Pearson argues that the story suggests that, by the twenty-third century, humans will have overcome their need for gods and religion.[10] Similarly, while Robert Asa explores the episode in the context of Greek myth, his overall argument is that the episode reflects and informs the 1960s move towards secularism.[11] Thus what the episode really asks is 'who mourns for a dead God?'[12]

Asa notes that while the episode as a whole rejects the concept of gods and worship, Kirk does tell Apollo that 'we find the one [God] quite adequate.'[13] This contradiction makes sense primarily in non-diegetic terms, as a tension between creator Gene Roddenberry's atheist vision of the future and the realities of 1960s television. Thus Matt Hills has countered that it is possible that

> Kirk's one-liner is actually a sop to 'public opinion' as constructed by the network. When the greatest fear is one of offending an audience, and of losing audience share through the representation of unpalatable ideas (be these interracial relationships or a stridently God-less universe) then contradictions and cryptic allusions to an un-named but singular 'one' God are perhaps one route towards hegemonic recuperation. To take such comments as a basis for textual exegesis seems to miss the point slightly.[14]

Hills criticises scholars for analysing 'Who Mourns for Adonais?' only in diegetic terms, instead of taking its industrial context into account.[15] To an extent this can be a methodological trap of television scholarship, given that any episode has myriad other episodes to which it can be compared, even if episodes have different authors. This is particularly the case with *Star Trek*, partly by virtue of the perceived unity of vision achieved by Roddenberry, and partly due to the expanded *Star Trek* text from the 1970s right through to the early twenty-first century. Chapter 2 will examine *Star Trek*'s relationship with myth in the context of its ever-expanding diegesis; however, Hills' criticism highlights the need to examine the broader television context in which *TOS* emerged. This chapter therefore examines television industry trends that may have affected *Star Trek*'s use of myth.

The adaptation of myth in 'Who Mourns for Adonais?' – as with its religious commentary – indicates fissures that can just as easily be attributed to the production process as textual motivation. Asa, for example, tries to find diegetic explanations for the fact that Spock knows Apollo's identity, even though it is only subsequently revealed to the away party of which Spock is not part.[16] Although Asa acknowledges this as 'a plot oversight', he also argues that Spock would be smart enough to guess Apollo's identity from the clues that had been presented to him.[17] Wagner and Lundeen display a similar desire to integrate potential production mistakes into the diegesis. During the episode, Apollo courts away team member Lieutenant Carolyn Palamas. He tells her that his own mother was a human mortal, and that the lieutenant can similarly become mother to a new race of gods. However, Wagner and Lundeen note that Apollo's mother is usually identified as the goddess Leto or Latona, 'a daughter of the Titans'.[18] Wagner and Lundeen suggest this could be a 'typically male deception' to help seduce the lieutenant, but do not consider the possibility that the writers simply got Apollo's genealogy wrong.[19] Such work exposes the limitations of examining *Star Trek* only as a fictional story-world and not as a television programme aired in the 1960s under the constraints of the industry. Winkler notes that in 'Who Mourns', Palamas is an expert in ancient civilisations who *also* misidentifies Apollo's mother as mortal.[20] Winkler suggests this is a deliberate deviation from tradition intended to educate the audience about the fact that gods and mortals could be lovers, leading into the romantic subplot with Apollo and Palamas.[21] There is, in general, a tendency in scholarship to try to arrive at a seamless and non-contradictory *Star Trek* text, a tendency that does not always adequately acknowledge the realities of fallible television production. As George Kovacs argues in his examination of myth and antiquity in *TOS*,

> [C]onstraints of time and budget meant that episodes were often written and produced quickly. Writers were only loosely concerned with standards of continuity and consistency of detail – the obsessive examination of the series' fans had not yet manifested.[22]

Adaptations of myth necessarily add, remove and alter elements of a story tradition. The attempts by many scholars to justify these changes in the context of purely diegetic explanations suggest a denial of extratextual factors that might inform an adaptation.

Such explanations also negate the possibility that changes to a myth, both deliberate and unintentional, can be used not to expose the inaccuracy of an adaptation, but rather to help us understand the various forces at play in shaping those changes. Drawing on the work of Pierre Sorlin, Maria Wyke argues: 'Historians should try to understand not whether a particular cinematic account of history is true [...] but what the logic of that account may be.'[23] Wyke examines cinematic representations of ancient Rome, but her comments can also be applied to television adaptations of myth. Rather than focusing on how television programmes may digress from a mythic tradition, this chapter shifts the emphasis to asking why myths have been adapted by early television in a particular manner. In light of Hills' criticisms, this question can be interrogated not by comparing 'Who Mourns for Adonais?' with *Star Trek*'s other episodes, but rather by placing it in the context of the many other early television programmes that adapted myth in previous decades. The textual, commercial and moral imperatives that inform television's use of myth in the 1940s, 1950s and 1960s implicitly help to shape 'Who Mourns for Adonais?'

Here, then, the organising axis is thematic, comparing programmes from the early years of US broadcasting with a view to uncovering series or episodes that adapt mythological stories within the new medium. Some programmes set stories solely in a mythological 'past'; others use a fictional scientific device that allows some access to this realm (such as time travel); and finally, programmes adapt characters or narratives from pre-existing mythological tales into a new diegetic setting altogether. Early television uses all these methods in appropriating and reworking mythological material, pitching such programmes primarily at children, and merging the stories into popular children's genres, science fiction in particular. By the advent of programmes such as *Star Trek* and *The Time Tunnel* in 1966, mythological subjects on TV begin to change focus to an older demographic. *Star Trek* nonetheless continues trends that had been established in previous decades, combining myth with science fiction, heroic conflicts, and a camp aesthetic that was more specific to 1960s sensibilities.

Remediating Myth: The Cinematic Epic

In the process of remediating myth, early television responded to and against cinematic trends. 'Remediation' is a term coined by Jay David Bolter and Richard Grusin to describe those works in which one medium has appropriated from another medium, a process that may either high-light or attempt to hide the adoption. 'The very act of remediation, however, ensures that the older medium cannot be entirely effaced.'[24] Although Bolter and Grusin are primarily concerned with new media, they stress that remediation itself has a long history in a variety of different media.[25] In its use of mythological material, television remediated not only ancient epics and plays, but also the more recent adaptations of those materials in cinema and other media. Because they responded to cinematic trends, television adaptations of myth were often reviewed using similar terms of reference. This overlap exposes perceived similarities and differences between cinematic and television versions of myth. The terminology used in contemporary television reviews reveals an understanding of myth that had been filtered through cinema. The reviews nonetheless acknowledge the different features of the television medium and its ability to depict mythological stories.

Recognising the remediation of mythological subjects from cinema into television, TV reviews frequently adopted cinematic genre classifications. In cinema, mythological subject matter tended to be grouped under the wider genre term of the 'epic'. However, Rick Altman points out that all genre classifications change over time and according to who uses them.[26] By examining promotional material such as movie posters, for example, Altman traces producers' classification terms, which may or may not tally with scholars' subsequent genre groupings.[27] 'Regenrification' may take place when either producers or critics group films together under a new category, or reassign a classification to a particular film.[28] Altman's perspective makes genre a malleable, historically grounded process that reveals not the essence of the film or genre, but rather the nature of a genre discourse as it interacts with industry, scholarly or audience concerns at any point in time. While television reviews are thereby only one potential axis of genre identification, the continued use of the term 'epic' in reviews of television programmes based on myth reveals the way that the epic genre was remediated, and reconstructed, from cinema into television.

The epic has always been associated with a sense of scale and history. In the work of Aristotle, the epic is 'a lengthy recitation, usually sung or chanted, which treats the quasi-historical exploits of notable heroes from the culture's past'.[29] In the cinema, the term epic has been applied to films that are simply very large in scale and extreme in length. But in keeping with older epic traditions, film epics are usually heroic tales that merge different versions of the past – 'mythic, biblical, folkloric, and quasi- or "properly" historical'.[30] Vivian Sobchack links these melded categories through the notion of a historical consciousness, a sense of '*general historical eventfulness*', regardless of accuracy or origin.[31] George MacDonald Fraser therefore argues that the ancient world depicted by Hollywood can be located in 'the Egypto-Biblo-Classical era, since threads from all three were often intertwined in its productions'.[32] The epic genre in cinema, therefore, has a rather fluid geographic and temporal terrain. Because the epic attempts to convey an overall sense of time, it does not possess a fixed relationship with history or myth, but rather a melding of such categories. Despite this, as Steve Neale has pointed out, scholarly works on the epic tend to divide films according to the different historical (or mythical) eras portrayed in the films themselves, rather than the era in which they were made.[33] This is a form of regenrification, of scholars regrouping epic films into more specific categories.

Any subgroup of the epic can nonetheless be historicised by examining the way in which it functions or changes in key periods of a given industry. By focusing specifically on mythological subject matter, this chapter constitutes another such regenrification in the specific context of early US television. Instead of assuming that the term epic does indeed encompass all mythological subjects, we might ask: does the label 'epic' correspond to how mythological subjects on television were received? If the term 'epic' is not in fact used in some cases, what other terms of reference appear? What do these various terms contribute to our understanding of myth at particular points of time in the television industry? The specific language of reviews, therefore, becomes a prime means through which we can glean both the remediation and regenrification of myth in television, establishing a field of reference that may or may not correspond to the epic label usually applied to mythological subjects.

Epic films, and mythological stories within that genre classification, had peaked in the silent era in the years 1897–1918 and again in the mid-1950s to late 1960s.[34] Television adaptations of myth largely coincided with this second wave of myth-based films, which started to appear with greater frequency after Cecil B. DeMille's commercially successful *Samson and Delilah* in 1949 renewed the ancient-world epic in all its guises. The new cycle had been brought about at least in part as a response to the popularity of television and the subsequent drop at the cinema box office, although increases in leisure time and activities were also a factor.[35] Nonetheless, cinema could provide a budget, scale and spectacle that television could not. Consequently, 'historical' stories, whether factual, fictional or mythological, provided the scope for impressive locales and battle scenes played out on a larger screen. Indeed, widescreen technologies trialled at this time further emphasised a cinematic expanse that dwarfed the television screen.[36]

Sobchack argues that the epic lost its 'expansiveness' when it was transferred to television. Adopting the miniseries format, it was reduced to a small screen, with lower budgets, and temporal fragmentation caused by advertisements and the miniseries format itself.[37] Although unable to match the scale of cinematic epics, the miniseries of the late 1960s and the 1970s usually enjoyed a higher budget and longer episode duration than other television programmes. Earlier attempts to bring myth to US television included one-off specials and children's programmes in the 1950s and 1960s, which tried to harness the popularity of the epic within the limitations of television as a small-screen domestic medium. Relative to these early television shows, the miniseries was in fact an expansion of scale. Thus, when Franco Rossi's Italian miniseries production of *The Odyssey* (1968) was imported to US television, it was reviewed in terms similar to those for cinematic epics. *Variety* emphasised that it was 'the costliest venture in Italy to date', and the programme was commended for

> adapting one of the oldest literary masterpieces [...] 'The Odyssey' becomes a demonstration of how to preserve the dignity and epic tone of a classic while infusing the fabulous adventure with a realistic popularization of fact and legend [...] Special effects are considerable and slick, to preserve the mystery of divine necromancy.[38]

Here, then, the *Odyssey* is described using the terms 'epic', 'classic' and 'legend', while simultaneously being applauded for its spectacle.

This duality between the so-called 'dignity' of an old story and its visual appeal could be found in reviews of cinema renditions of myth as far back as the silent era. When Francesco Bertolini, Adolfo Padovan and Giuseppe de Liguoro's *Homer's Odyssey* (1911) was released in the US in 1912, it was praised as beginning 'a new epoch in the history of the motion picture as a factor in education', to both 'entertain and instruct the average moving picture audience'.[39] While stressing the 'classic' source of the story and 'the genius of Homer', the review nonetheless also praised the scenery and special effects as 'a delight to the eye'.[40] Industry magazine *The Moving Picture World* suggested that the film be promoted to professors, schools and churches as a way of overcoming their prejudice against the new cinematic medium.[41] But the journal also stressed that 'only the Greek scholars will want to see the Odyssey as such', while other potential customers will be drawn in by 'the adventures in the Cyclops' cave [...] the allurements of the sirens, the escape past the dragons'.[42] Therefore, both the reviews and promotion of *Homer's Odyssey* suggest an attempt to balance an appeal to the 'classic' and educational status of the original text with the promotion of spectacle. It is this same duality that finds expression in reviews when myth was adapted by television. De Liguoro's film release of 1912 and *The Odyssey* television miniseries of 1968 were received by critics in remarkably similar terms, revealing a degree of continuity in the association of myth with cultural status but also with modes of display.

The association of the epic with spectacle, and an excess of physical and temporal scale, explains why little work has been done on television's earlier attempts to adapt the epic. In turn, it also goes some way to explain why *Star Trek*'s early foray into mythology has not been seen in the context of television's broader treatment of ancient myth leading up to *TOS*. The relative silence about television's textual and visual treatment of epic subjects before the 1970s may be due to the choice of the term 'epic' to describe the genre. Due to the literal smallness of the screen, the complete lack of cinema's lush colour, the minimal number of programmes dealing with comparable subject matter, and the brevity of programme duration (particularly in contrast to the later miniseries format), early television seems to have little that is 'epic' about it.

Despite these differences in physical, economic and temporal scale, attempts to adapt mythological stories for television were nonetheless reviewed in terms surprisingly similar to those applied to cinema epics. Following Altman's observations about shifts in genre classifications over time, reviews of US television from the 1950s and 1960s make it clear that reviewers saw the connections between epic films and their television counterparts, even if subsequent scholars have been slow to do so. For example, in 1955, the adult drama anthology *Omnibus* (1952–61)

> turned the whole 90-minute works over to Homer's 'The Iliad' in an elaborate, DeMillean playout depicting the siege of Troy in the 10th year of the great war to return Helen to her Agamemmon [*sic*]. It was impressive as a spectacle supplying the illusion of magnitude and managing to convey a sense [of] the bitter personal conflict between the two camps.[43]

This *Variety* review merits a breakdown of terms. By calling the production 'DeMillean', the reviewer makes an explicit link with the cinematic tradition of films set in the ancient world, with Cecil B. DeMille directing films such as *The Ten Commandments* (1923), *King of Kings* (1927), *The Sign of the Cross* (1932), *Cleopatra* (1934) and *Samson and Delilah* (1949). The review commends the programme as 'impressive as a spectacle', yet this receives what must be considered a television-specific qualification: the spectacle is achieved only through 'the illusion of magnitude'. *Variety* continues to commend the 'large cast', again emphasising the scale of the production.[44] Rather than merely comparing the Homeric epic directly with its television adaptation, *Variety* understands this textual relationship via the mediation of cinema. While cinema in its cycle of silent epics had looked to earlier media as a way of borrowing cultural legitimacy, by the time of *Omnibus* cinema had become the reference point for television.

In other cases, reviews of mythological subjects on television focused primarily on the high arts, such as the original texts or theatre. However, this too was a strategy also used by cinema. Television programmes were praised for adapting ancient 'masterpieces', such as Homer's *Odyssey*,[45] or for combining 'masters of music and drama', such as the combination of Sophocles' *Oedipus Rex* with Igor Stravinksy's operatic version.[46] In 1960 a combined rendition of Sophocles' *Oedipus Rex* and *Oedipus at Colonus* was commended for including Elliot Norton as host, for 'Norton [...] also serves as lecturer in dramatic literature at Boston U., [and therefore] lent authorativeness and pro critique-narration to the program'.[47] These theatre reproductions, of which myth played only a minor role, mirrored a larger trend in television to equate television drama anthologies with theatre, a strategy emphasised by titles such as *Cameo Theatre* (1950–5), *Fireside Theatre* (1949–55)[48] and *The General Electric Theater* (1953–62). The wide-screen cinema epics, for their part, suggested a theatre connection through the use of heavy velvet curtains opening the feature (see, for example, Henry Koster's *The Robe* of 1953). Lynn Spigel notes how advertisements in the 1950s characterised television in terms of ' "family theater," the "video theater," the "chairside theater," the "living room theater," and so forth', which could be taken as reference both to the movie theatre as well as live theatre.[49] Spigel has shown that early television frequently used ' "theatrical" modes of representation, which produced the simulation of live theater'.[50] For the rendition of actual plays such as *Oedipus Rex*, this remediation of theatre was overt, emphasised by the specialist commentary that accompanied it.

The high-cultural status applied to 'masterpiece' works of myth, and plays based on myth, was qualified, however. In the 1966 one-hour special *Search for Ulysses*, a recreation of the possible journey taken in the *Odyssey* was criticised for having 'actor James Mason cut in occasionally, reading appropriate passages from Homer [...] his delivery inclined to be overly aesthetic and reverential and therefore out of key with the ruggedness of the adventure.'[51] Here the spectacle 'of exotic scenery and seascapes' outweighs a desire to engage with the Homeric epic itself.⁵² Indeed, Homer is praised 'not as a poet-fictionalist who authored adult fairy-tales, but rather as one of the earliest and most elegant journalists who made generous use of his poetic license'.⁵³ Myth, then, is historical journalism in disguise, a characterisation that lends itself to a mainstay of television broadcasting and is judged according to that standard. If the adult myth adaptations were generally praised for their spectacle combined with their reverential use of myth, *Search for Ulysses* was praised for its spectacle combined with its journalistic mode (Mason's delivery notwithstanding), and for tropes of realism rather than myth.

With its on-location filming, *Search for Ulysses* was a relatively expensive programme. In general, however, while mythological subjects received a relatively large budget in the cinema, television for the most part needed creative low-budget means to depict the material. For example, 'The Fall of Troy' (1953) episode of *You Are There* was filmed in black and white, used a restricted number of static sets, and a cast too small to depict the final conflict. However, the programme downplayed spectacle and created an entirely different focus: a mock news programme pitched at children, through which historical and mythological events could be explored. Walter Cronkite as anchor announced the story as news, crossing 'live' to events, which were covered by journalists' interviews and a voice-over narration (see Figure 1.1).⁵⁴ In this case then, the modes of journalism were invoked not to promote on-location spectacle, but rather to shift emphasis to geopolitical events and characters. In treating myth as news, *You Are There* favoured interpersonal, political exchange over spectacle, a focus more readily achievable on television. 'The Fall of Troy' thereby illustrates how mythological subjects were reinterpreted in television-specific ways, moving away from the cinema-informed adaptations attempted by more expensive television specials.

By mimicking journalistic tropes of news and documentary, the educational legitimacy of the programme could also be stressed. 'The Fall of Troy' did not need to be spectacular, because it was masquerading as serious news, not entertainment per se. *You Are There* shifted the terms of reference away from cinematic adaptations of myth, instead drawing inspiration from television programming. Myth was still being used for

Figure 1.1 Walter Cronkite presents myth as news in *You Are There* (CBS 1953–7).

its association with educational and cultural value, but it was depicted using television-specific codes of journalism that were more affordable to produce.

Television reviews followed cinema trends, associating Homeric works with cultural legitimacy, yet criticising mythological muscle-man stories. In 1965, Albert Brand's one-hour movie *Hercules* was broadcast as a pilot for a series, but the series itself never eventuated.[55] *Variety* printed a scathing review of the pilot, saying the 'busted sword-and-sandal pilot should have been kept in the vault altogether [...] As one among many soupbones in the genre, this one looked like it had been picked dry on the Cinecitta sound stages.'[56]

This review suggests a different field of reference from the Homeric adaptations. By comparing *Hercules* with the 'many soupbones in the genre', the *Variety* review sets up a direct comparison with the muscle-man 'sword-and-sandal' films in circulation, and Hercules films in particular, which had saturated the market in the late 1950s through to the 1960s following the success of Pietro Francisci's *Hercules* of 1958, released in the USA in 1959 at a phenomenal profit. Although the Hollywood epic cycle included films set in the ancient world, the Italian Hercules films were comparatively low-budget concerns. Despite their commercial success, the critics were mostly hostile to such films. The attempt to establish an ongoing *Hercules* television programme was evidently aimed at harnessing the popularity of these films with audiences, if not reviewers.

These depictions of a mytho-historic past were met with mixed responses; however, their arrival on television paralleled the cinema's own revival of muscle-man and mythological subjects. This correlation can be seen in the terms of reference of the television reviews. Like the *Hercules* films, the *Hercules* pilot was criticised as a poor sound-stage production, its spectacle value consisting primarily of its 'muscle beach refugee' star.[57] The review thereby highlights television's lack of budget and scale in its treatment of mythological subjects, but also sets up an alignment with the less critically favoured side of the epic revival in the muscle-man films.

While the failed *Hercules* had been intended as an ongoing series, most television adaptations of myth were intended purely as one-off specials or episodes. For example, *Captain Video and his Video Rangers* (1949–55), *Mr. I. Magination* (1949–52), *Space Patrol* (1950–5), *Tom Corbett, Space Cadet* (1950–5), *The Whistling Wizard* (1951–2), *You Are There* (1953–7), *Rocky Jones, Space Ranger* (1953), *Omnibus* (1952–61), *The Adventures of Danny Dee* (1954–5), *The Finder* (1954–5), *Flash Gordon* (1954–5) and *Beany and Cecil* (1963) all reworked mythological stories within individual episodes, although references to myth did not necessarily weave through the whole series. In parallel with the cinematic adaptation of myth, single episodes based on myth became more numerous on television into the 1960s.

Star Trek's 1967 rendition of Greek myth in 'Who Mourns for Adonais?' coincided with the tail-end of the epic cinema revival, and a general increase in the use of myth by television programmes, particularly as single-episode adventures within a series structure. *Star Trek*'s use of special effects, such as Apollo's giant hand holding the Starship *Enterprise* in space, tapped into the spectacle tradition of mythological subjects in film and television. However, like *Hercules* and *You Are There*, *Star Trek* struggled with a paucity of set funds. Instead, the episode suggested an outpost of the Greek gods through Greek columns and vaguely Greco-Roman (lamé) clothing – the latter of which displayed a large amount of flesh in the 'muscle beach' tradition (see Figure 1.2). Scantily clad extras were common on *Star Trek*; however, in 'Who Mourns for Adonais?', costuming implicitly

Figure 1.2 Apollo in *TOS* 'Who Mourns for Adonais?' (Paramount Television 1967).

referenced not ancient Greece itself, but rather cinema and television-mediated ancient Greece, transposed into the future.

Given the difficulties of budget, it is perhaps not surprising that the first US television programme to use myth as its ongoing premise was an animated children's show, *The Mighty Hercules* (1963). As an animation, *The Mighty Hercules* could simply draw mythological creatures such as the Hydra, rather than building models for expensive stop-motion animation (see Figure 1.3). The five-and-a-half-minute running time of *The Mighty Hercules* could not have been further from the cinematic epic, even the lower-budget Hercules films.

The series focused on Hercules' battles against various foes, some from Greek myth and some new inventions. This premise is emphasised in the opening theme song, which mentions his 'ancient glory' and origins in 'song and glory', but focuses overwhelmingly on his strength and goodness. This is much the same in the series itself, in that the mythological tradition provided the setting but the exposition relied upon a broader good/evil superhero pattern that did not restrict itself to Greek myth. Thus, Hercules

Myth and Early US TV

Figure 1.3 *The Mighty Hercules* (Trans Lux 1963) encounters the Hydra.

had a magic ring that was used as a type of laser beam, and most episodes were structured around a battle against an evil foe (such as the 'wizard' Daedalus in episode 128). This binary formula emphasised the alignment with popular superhero comic books of the time, which were to inspire a plethora of superhero animations in the 1960s. The 1973, *Star Trek: The Animated Series* can also be seen as following on from this trend.

Like the big-screen films that inspired it, *The Mighty Hercules* often displayed only a tenuous connection with mythology. Thus, 'although the series gave cursory treatment to some of the twelve tasks of Hercules, it ignored his other [...] legendary exploits in favor of a science-fiction approach.'[58] The series thereby simultaneously harnessed the continued success of children's science fiction programmes, a genre on the air continuously since *Captain Video and His Video Rangers* began the trend in 1949. The Hercules myths were subservient to the specific commercial and cultural needs of the time, aligning *The Mighty Hercules* with muscle-man Hercules films, superhero comic book characters and children's science fiction programmes. Myth-based programmes thereby drew on more than one genre or media tradition.

The Mighty Hercules was unusual to the extent that its diegesis was situated in the mythological 'past'. While adult specials placed mythological stories in a mytho-historical time frame, by far the greater number of programmes accessed mythological elements via a circuitous route, either visiting a mythological past through time travel, or adapting specific elements from a myth into a new setting. Thus *Mr. I. Magination* (1949–52) had taken children back in time, or to the world of literature or myth, through his special imaginative powers. One such journey recast a child in the role of Hercules.[59] *Mr. I. Magination* was so popular, it became the first television show to return to the air as a result of audience protests against its initial axing in 1951.[60] In *The Whistling Wizard* (1951–2) mythological characters were encountered in the 'Land of Beyond', a realm of myth, legend and fairytale accessible through an enchanted well.[61] Like *Mr. I. Magination*, myths and legends were usually updated and were geared towards teaching a lesson or conveying educational information, within an overall fantastic context. Both programmes emphasised imaginative engagement with the past.[62] Even the educational accuracy attempted by *You Are There* had an implied element of time travel. Although an intertitle proclaimed the year to be 1185 B.C. in 'The Fall of Troy' episode, Cronkite and his crew nonetheless had 1950s microphones and suits, suggesting that they could travel back in time. Thus, *Variety* noted that the show 'has dared to confront viewers with all the modern physical trappings of newsmen and their mikes and posted these vis-a-vis the great events of history'.[63]

By contrast, the greater trend in epic and muscle-man films was to begin and end purely in the ancient world, whether historical, mythological or a blend of the two. If the cinematic and televisual adaptations of myth were connected both through their subject matter and through the peak cycle of their activity, television for the most part had a younger audience in mind. This, as much as the technical and budgetary restrictions of the medium, had implications for the manner in which myths were reworked.

Demographic Pitches and A New Search for Legitimacy

From the 1940s to the 1980s, the overwhelming majority of television programmes adapting mythological material were children's shows. The first children's series to air in the US was *Small Fry Club*, which debuted on 11

March 1947.[64] In the early broadcast years, networks such as DuMont 'competed fiercely [...] for a young audience, one that would maintain an allegiance' to their particular network, hopefully surviving into adulthood.[65] Children's programming proliferated in this early era, with puppet shows, storytelling anthologies and science fiction particularly popular in the first five years. Westerns were soon to follow. Within these programmes, myths provided pre-existing stories, without copyright complications, that were largely known to parents and socially approved by virtue of their high-culture status.[66] Myths could be considered educational in their own right. While such programmes constituted a relatively small portion of television's output, the adaptation of myth in early TV has alignments with the use of mythological subjects in early cinema as a means of lending authority and acceptability to a new medium.

The educational status of programming material became increasingly important as social groups and commentators argued about the detrimental effect of television on children and a possible link to delinquency. These concerns resulted in an enquiry held by the House Interstate Commerce Subcommittee in 1952, and a Senate Juvenile Delinquency Subcommittee in 1954–5.[67] The 1952 enquiry found that television was bringing the family together, and keeping potentially wayward youngsters at home, but expressed concern that the content of programming needed to be suitable.[68] By 1954, connections were being made between violence on television and youth violence in real life.[69] Subsequent cycles in hearings, reports and speeches in the following decades saw violence temporarily toned down in children's programmes to varying degrees. Although myths can themselves be extremely violent, the judicious appropriation of myth within children's programming could nonetheless be seen as a means of legitimisation, a strategy used by other maligned media such as comic books. As Richard Reynolds notes, 'There has arguably been a tendency for comic creators to legitimize their offspring by stressing their resemblance to legendary heroes or gods: a strategy to give their disregarded medium a degree of moral and intellectual uplift.'[70] Rather than unconsciously replicating hero myths, comic books and television programmes alike consciously reworked mythological material while making those connections overt to curry cultural favour.

Myth was used in educational storytelling anthologies for children, such as *Mr. I. Magination*, which was praised for its

> reduction of classic literature and historical incident to juvenile levels [...] [creating] excellent fodder for all age brackets. It's still a series which [...] should pick up vast audiences by virtue of imprimateur [sic] of educators and parent groups. It's a rare blend of educational and entertainment values.[71]

Other educational anthologies to incorporate myth included *The Finder* (1954–5), which featured Odysseus and the Cyclops as clay models, and *The Adventures of Danny Dee* (1954–5), in which host Roy Doty would draw in chalk the mishaps of Danny and his sister Debbie.[72] Although the stories were new, at the end of the drawing adventure Doty would explain how they related to great works of literature, or mythological tales. Consequently, one episode drew simultaneously on 'Gulliver in Lilliput, the Colossus of Rhodes, and the feats of Ulysses and Hercules', stories that were explained to the audience once Danny and Debbie had finished their own adventures.[73] The programme thereby trained children to recognise references to myth and literature as they were adapted and recombined. Myth formed part of a larger agenda to ensure suitably educational programming for children.

Parents could often monitor the educational content of children's shows by virtue of their scheduling. While many children's programmes were scheduled for Saturday morning, others had an early evening slot, such as *Mr. I. Magination*, aired at 6.30pm, and *Captain Video*, which ran for six years in the prime-time position of 7.00–7.30pm.[74] As Lynn Spigel argues, 'adults seem to have watched the shows supposedly aimed at children. Since children's shows were often scheduled during the late afternoon and early evening hours, adults would have ample occasion to view these programs.'[75] As this became recognised in the industry, programmes began deliberately to address both their younger and older audience members. This can be seen in the television version of *You Are There*, initially broadcast by CBS in the 6.00–6.30pm time slot, but quickly moved to 6.30–7.00pm, where it remained, just shy of prime time.[76] The programme was designed for children, but its serious news format and its address to both an informed and uninformed audience made *You Are There* an early crossover show.

'The Fall of Troy' episode of *You Are There* demonstrates this dual-address logic. This episode supplies information for audience members who are unfamiliar with the myth of Troy, while providing in-jokes for those who know the general story. The mock journalists provide geopolitical background to the conflict: 'The Greeks are on the move, pushed from behind by waves of Barbarians sweeping down from the Danube Valley.' They also provide background to the Troy story: 'It was just about here that Achilles caught and killed Hector.' Information is thereby pitched to an audience with no knowledge of the myth. However, as the Greeks depart from the city of Troy and leave the wooden horse, the priest Laocoon and his sons do not believe the Greeks have really left, suggesting instead that they are 'in hiding'. When a guard retorts 'Where, in the horse?', his fellow guards laugh. The Greeks are indeed hiding in the horse, and this joke works only for audience members who already know the story. Similarly, the departing Agamemnon gives a 'live' interview and asserts his intention to leave Troy. If we know the myth, we also know that Agamemnon is lying, in effect using the reporter to plant false information. Thus, the programme speaks to both audience members who are familiar with the story and those to whom it is new. The programme also asserts its educational worth by citing Homer's *Iliad* as its authority (although the wooden horse is not in fact mentioned in this epic).

You Are There ended in October 1957, but its five-year success can be seen in the context of an emerging trend towards programmes with a crossover appeal to children and adults. Indeed, 1957 saw a reduction in purely children's programming in favour of 'kidult' crossover series.[77] However, the legitimising strategy of programmes such as *You Are There* does not explain the relative paucity of adult programming based upon mythology until the plethora of adult–child crossover programmes in the 1990s (most notably *Xena* in 1995–2001 and *Hercules* in 1995–99). In this respect, the correlation with epic cinema could be both cause and deterrent. While an increase in children's programmes based on myth corresponds with the enormous popularity of epic films and Hercules films in particular in the late 1950s and the 1960s, adult programming shows only a small increase. Television programmes could not compete with the literal scale of screen, cast and set used in cinema depictions of myth, a disparity perhaps acceptable to children but not to adults. Reviews of adult programmes demonstrate that a clear distinction was made between those that had been able to put the money into spectacle and those that had not. By contrast, many of the myth-based children's programmes from the 1960s were animated, which overcame the spectacle problem by drawing grand or imaginative sets that could not be built affordably for adult live-action series.

Science Fiction Myths

There was also an issue of generational taste situated around genre, given that many of the early children's programmes using myth were either science fiction or superhero programmes, or a mixture of both. During the 1960s in particular, 'the line between science-fiction and superhero shows [...] was often indistinct.'[78] Like the superhero comic book, on television the science fiction genre was associated purely with children, despite the fact that there were adult followers for both formats. As Jeffrey Sconce suggests, in the early years of television 'conventional industry wisdom considered science fiction to be a genre ill suited to television', where budgetary constraints limited the ability to bring its fantastical concepts to life.[79] By contrast, the industry believed that children would overlook a cheap visual aesthetic, a belief confirmed through the phenomenal success of *Captain Video*.[80] This very success helped to cement a television-specific alignment between the science fiction genre and children. As we shall see, the reception of *TOS* was directly impacted by this alignment and the perception that its viewers were much younger than they actually were.

Thus, in a review of *Space Patrol*, *Variety* suggested that 'this science-fiction stuff will be disdained by adults, but the kids should eat it up'.[81] There was some acknowledgement that adults might find themselves not minding their children's viewing. *Daily Variety* argues, 'Should an adult be trapped into seeing "Space Patrol," it will take him [sic] back to the early days of cinema when cliff-hangers were quite popular.'[82] The possibility of adult viewers was thereby considered in terms of nostalgia, albeit brought about by being 'trapped' by the viewing habits of younger family members.[83] Indeed, adults who did watch science fiction programmes aimed at children were themselves denigrated as infantile. In *The Honeymooners* episode 'TV or Not TV' (1955), Ed is shown as a *Captain Video* fan who loyally pledges to 'obey his mommy and daddy'.[84] Alice chides the men, saying: 'Stop acting like babies and try to grow up a little.' This depiction of science fiction television fans as infantile remained in subsequent decades, an issue that will be explored in more detail in Chapter 4. The mythological foes encountered by Captain Video and other science fiction heroes went unnoticed by reviewers, for whom the children's adventure formula retained disdainful prominence.

Even in the 1950s, the infantilisation of science fiction fans grated with older fans, pleased with the very few science fiction programmes aimed at an older audience. As future *Twilight Zone* (1959–64) creator Rod Serling noted in *TV Guide* in 1955,

> Although most science-fiction devotees are well past the elementary school level, TV has made little effort to appeal to this not inconsiderable audience, which scoffs at the likes of *Captain Video* and *Space Patrol*. The new *Science Fiction Theater* [...] remedies this oversight.[85]

Tales of Tomorrow (1951–3), *Science Fiction Theater* (1955–7), *The Twilight Zone* and *One Step Beyond* (1959–61) prefigured the rise of adult science fiction programmes in the 1960s, including *Star Trek*. Science fiction stories would also sometimes be featured in adult drama anthologies, such as *Conflict* (1956–7).[86] These programmes were, however, exceptions to the overall alignment of science fiction with children's television in the 1940s and 1950s.[87]

While the cycle of cinematic epics had grown increasingly removed from their mythic origins, most nonetheless persisted in their ancient settings.[88] In television, the balance was reversed, with the majority of programmes integrating mythological stories, characters or names into contemporary or futuristic settings. Distant future frequently replaced distant past. While the adult programmes were more likely to be set in a mytho-historic past, programmes such as *You Are There* and *The Time Tunnel* (1966–7) used implied or overt time travel to reach such a mytho-historic time and place.

In futuristic programmes, myth provided names for characters, ships, space stations, planets and storylines. For example, in *Captain Video and His Video Rangers*,[89] a 1953 storyline focused on the capture of the space liner *Telemachus* by the Space Pirate,[90] the liner's name derived from the son of Odysseus in Homer's *Odyssey*. In the 1954 story 'Odyssey into Peril', Captain Video encounters numerous phenomena that belong in the Classics tradition. Also in 1954 episodes, he visits a planet that resembles the society of ancient Rome, meets Circe, and his companion Tucker is turned to stone by the Medusa.[91] Both allies and villains in the series also drew on mythical inspiration, with Hermes of Jupiter and Neptune of an underwater kingdom making appearances.[92] Again it is tempting to read these appropriations of myth as an attempt to lend legitimacy to the programme, particularly as the National Association for Better Radio and Television had branded it one of the 'most objectionable' television programmes.[93] Indeed, in October of 1954, actor Al Hodge, who played Captain Video, appeared before the Senate Subcommittee on Juvenile Delinquency to defend the show.[94] By 1955, *Variety* noted that *Captain Video*'s return as a weekly clips programme overseen by Hodge usually included 'a film of a semi-educational or educational nature (it's good for the kids and impresses parents and critics).'[95]

A number of science fiction programmes turned to mythology for their naming strategies.[96] *Space Patrol* destroyed an old space station named Prometheus, and the Patrol also encountered alien Amazons in 'Amazons of Cydonia' (1954). In the *Rocky Jones, Space Ranger* episode 'Inferno in Space' (1954), Rocky's enemies visited the planet Herculon, a name derived from Hercules. In the television version of *Flash Gordon*, 'Death in the Negative' (1955) revealed a number of planets with the names of the Greek gods, including Apollo, Artemis, Athena, Hera and Ares.[97] The animated *Rod Rocket* (1963) featured hero Rod Rocket's adventures in his ship *The Little Argo*, a name taken from the vessel used by Jason and the Argonauts in the *Argonautica*. In *Tom Corbett, Space Cadet*, the episode entitled 'The Trojan Planets' based its name on the Trojan war of Homer's *Iliad*.[98] While villains in programmes such as *Captain Video* were named after Greek gods but were actually aliens, elsewhere creatures emerged that resembled those of mythology without being explicitly named. For example, in the

Space Ghost episode 'The Sorcerer' (1966), Space Ghost was attacked by a Cyclops creature conjured by a crazed sorcerer. Thus, science fiction looked to myth for its names and creatures, only to rework them in a new guise.

While anthology science fiction dramas that emerged in the 1950s and 1960s were pitched at adult viewers, spacefaring and adventure-based science fiction shows retained their youth association well into the 1960s. When *Star Trek* debuted in 1966, *Variety* argued that 'by a generous stretch of the imagination, it could lure a small coterie of the small-fry, though not happily time slotted in that direction', namely 8.30pm on Thursday evenings.[99] 'It's better suited to the Saturday morning kidvid bloc.'[100] Premiering in the same season as *Star Trek*, *The Time Tunnel* was similarly met with initial caution by reviewers, due to the science fiction adventure format and its association with younger audiences.[101] In 1967, another science fiction programme aiming for the 'kidult' market, *The Invaders*, was called by *TV Guide* 'a great show for the kids' but not 'for the rest of you'.[102] Only in *Star Trek*'s third season did *Variety* concede that ' "*Star Trek*" has drifted far demographically since its days as kid fare and has now made the transition complete with a move into the late hours', of 10pm.[103]

By reworking myth in the context of science fiction, *Star Trek* continued the genre-blending trend of earlier television programmes, while also attracting the demographic bias associated with science fiction, at least in its television guise. Contemporary network standards and the association between science fiction, *Star Trek* and a youthful demographic meant that *Star Trek*'s scripts were sometimes toned down in their references to sex and violence. In 'Who Mourns for Adonais?' Lieutenant Palamas is caught in a god-induced lightning storm, as an airborne Apollo approaches her. Her cries and subsequent unkempt appearance have been interpreted as rape imagery, a reading consistent with the fact that the original script indicated Palamas was pregnant at the end of the episode.[104] As Wagner and Lundeen note, the rape of human women by the Greek gods is 'consistent with Greek mythic tradition'.[105] However, the judicious pruning of the script reflects not Greek mythology nor *Star Trek*'s diegetic concerns, but rather the limitations of 1960s broadcasting standards, and an ongoing uncertainty about just who might be watching a space-themed programme.

Television's space heroes were seen in a different light once space travel shifted from mere fantasy into reality. In the 1950s, science fiction heroes such as Captain Video had merchandise that included 'helmets, toy rockets, games […] records' and a comic book.[106] *Tom Corbett, Space Cadet* had 'a syndicated comic strip, over a hundred toys and products, eight full-length hardback novels and countless comic books.'[107] By the 1960s, along-side science fiction merchandising, children could also buy toys based on the real test flights. Play activities not only included re-enacting science fictional adventures in space, but also the real space missions. Advertisements promised that children could ' "Ride" The New *Apollo* Moonship! Follow the thrilling Apollo test flights with an authentic Revell Apollo model. Yours for only 10¢.'[108] The preponderance of science fiction heroes on early television coincided with the emergence of the Cold War Space Race and the proliferation of space imagery in US popular culture. Television's space heroes attracted a new cultural currency once their activities were seen less as fantastic children's fare and more as imaginative extensions of real efforts to explore space.

Drucker and Cathcart argue that 'The hero myth […] is transformed in the telling and retelling, according to the time and place, and, most importantly, by the means of conveying *the story*.'[109] Thus, Strate suggests, 'It is through communication that we come to know our heroes, and consequently, different kinds of communication will result in different kinds of heroes.'[110] While Drucker, Cathcart and Strate cite the celebrity as the contemporary mass-media hero, this mediated and temporally specific model of the hero myth has applications to fictional mass-media heroes as well.

With space heroes being the fictional and then factual order of the day, making alignments with larger-than-life heroes of mythology served to underscore the space hero's own cultural status and bravery. When battling with villains named after Greek gods as well as foes taken directly from the *Odyssey*, Captain Video becomes a futuristic Odysseus by association. In undertaking his space adventures in his ship *The Little Argo*, Rod Rocket is a futuristic Jason with his own spacefaring Argonauts. In *Star Trek*'s 'Who Mourns for Adonais?', Apollo explicitly compares the *Enterprise* away team with the Greek and Trojan heroes Agamemnon, Hector and Odysseus. In doing so, the heroic alignments implicit in earlier myth/science fiction renditions are made overt. However, these latter-day mythological heroes had a different cultural resonance once their adventures in space were paralleled, albeit less fantastically, by the real space missions. Of all the gods to choose as representative of the Greek pantheon, Apollo resonates with the Apollo space missions of the time. NASA's Dr Abe Silverstein named the Moon missions after the Greek god in 1960, recalling that he thought the idea of 'Apollo riding his chariot across the Sun was appropriate to the grand scale of the proposed program'.[111] While maintaining NASA's alignment between the Greek gods and human space travel, 'Who Mourns for Adonais?' emphasises the 'grand scale' of human efforts in space, rather than those of the gods.

On a broader genre level, Elley has argued only the far future and the vastness of space can substitute for the mythic past.[112] He suggests that space is a physical and temporal realm in which the extraordinary and unexpected might still take place.[113] Like the realm of myth, in outer space strange creatures are at least possible. Mythic beasts in outer space need new mythic heroes to deal with them, albeit in a newly futuristic guise. While Apollo may compare Kirk and his crew with the heroes of old, it is by defeating a Greek god that Kirk elevates his own heroic status, even though he immediately expresses regret for doing so. Kirk admits to McCoy that Apollo and his fellow aliens 'gave us so much […] Would it have hurt us, I wonder, just to have gathered a few laurel leaves?'

Superheroes and Camp: Remediating the Comic Book

While Kirk originated as a television hero, the television heroes pitted against mythological monsters were frequently adapted from other media, including radio, cinema, cinema serials, comic strips, comic books and novels. The process of dual remediation can be found in *Captain Video and His Video Rangers*, *Space Patrol*, *Tom Corbett*, *Space Cadet*, *You Are There*, *Flash Gordon*, *Batman* (1966–8), *Aquaman* (1967–9), *Mighty Thor* (1966) and *Sub-Mariner* (1966), all of which rework their own pre-existing stories across different media while at the same time reworking myth within that story-world.

The adaptation of comic strips and comic books to television increased in frequency from the mid-1950s. For example, *Flash Gordon* had a weekly newspaper comic strip from 1934, a daily strip from 1940, a radio serial from 1935 to 1936, and cinema serials in 1936, 1938 and 1940.[114] In 1954, the *Flash Gordon* cinema serials were broadcast on television under new episode titles, followed by made-for-television episodes featuring Steve Holland as the new Flash. Not only did *Flash Gordon* adapt myth, using Greek mythology to name many of its planets, it simultaneously adapted its own hero and backstory across media. Both myth and the *Flash* franchise were remediated through the television programme.

While *Flash* had several incarnations before reaching television, the practice of adapting comic strips was becoming widespread. In 1954, the year that *Flash* debuted on television, *TV Guide* noted the high number of television series based on comic strips, arguing that 'television producers have been even more eager to serialize the strippers, figuring that TV series featuring the heroes and heroines of the more popular cartoon stories automatically would have tremendous audiences'.[115] By remediating comics into television, producers sought to engage an established audience. Comic book superheroes were also adapted, becoming more frequent on television in the 1960s, a decade that also witnessed the rebirth of Marvel Comics at the hands of Stan Lee and Jack Kirby.

Such shows were frequently met with derision. Indeed, 'comic-book' and 'comic-strip' became generic, disparaging terms for simplistic children's texts. In 1953, Fredric Wertham notes: 'We speak of [...] a comic-book-level show on television', one that is influenced by 'the lowest medium'.[116] By the 1960s, this type of comparison became common in television reviews. For example, *TV Guide* argued that *Star Trek* belonged to 'the comic-strip world of series television'.[117] Although *Star Trek* had a spin-off comic book from 1967, this is not what the *TV Guide* article was referring to. Rather, the television programme and the television series format were being compared with comic strips as an implicit negative value judgment. This judgement becomes clearer in a review of the 1968 debut of *Land of the Giants*. *Variety* notes 'the comic-strip plots shouldn't matter too much', given that the show as a whole is 'scaled strictly to the juvenile mentality'.[118] In other words, 'comic-strip' television equalled simple plots for children or older viewers with a similar 'mentality'.

This attitude was undoubtedly a debt to a long-standing controversy surrounding comic books and children,[119] particularly promoted by Wertham's *Seduction of the Innocent* of 1954. Wertham argues, 'Classic books, mutilated in comic-book form, have been adapted to the television screen.'[120] In other words, comic books and the television programmes based on them may rework older 'classic' texts, including novels and myths, but in a 'mutilated' form that thereby robs them of all worth. Although comic book heroes transferred to television were not to peak for nearly another decade, the heritage of the Wertham attack helps to explain why the mythological content of such programmes went largely unnoticed.

The relocation of superheroes to television included *The Mighty Thor*, the first successful comic book explicitly appropriating a pre-existing hero from mythology for its central character.[121] Thor was originally the Norse god of thunder.[122] Introduced to the Marvel catalogue in 1962, the superhero then became an animated children's programme in 1966. The initial comic book story introduced a mortal man, Dr Donald Blake, who could become Thor with the help of a magical walking stick.[123] Creator Stan Lee later changed the story to reveal Blake was the real god Thor in disguise all along.[124] The TV show took this latter premise, revealing its place in the redevelopment and continuity not only of the myth of Thor, but also of Marvel's Thor as well. In the comic book, Thor was conveniently relocated to New York, where the rest of the Marvel superheroes worked, and where he became one of the founding members of the superhero team *The Avengers*.[125] Myth was adapted to be culturally relevant, with a contemporary US setting, and commercially expedient, with a location that allowed the god to join with other Marvel creations.

When transferred to an animated television programme, *The Mighty Thor* appeared within *Marvel Superheroes* (1966), a syndicated series that featured a different superhero each day. *Thor* stylistically reflected its media origins through a relatively static animation style that tended to look like separate comic book panels or pages transferred to the television screen. This aesthetic was primarily economic in origin, however: one example of the 'limited animation' style that came to prominence in the 1950s.[126] Upon its airing, a *Variety* review linked the look of the programme with contemporary art movements and aesthetics:

> The resurgence of interest in comic books [...] plus the impact of Pop art and the camp syndrome have inevitably produced this comic book TV series [...] While the series' basic appeal is to the kids, it will no doubt pick up its share of post-high school hippies addicted to the old comics.[127]

The updated *mythos* of the Norse–Marvel Thor also harnessed the cross-generational comic book revival, pop art and camp aesthetic,[128] a strategy also employed by *Batman*, which debuted in the same year.[129] Both *Thor* and *Batman* emphasised their remediation from comics into television by using written text 'sound' effects. For example, when Thor engages in a fight in 'Enter Hercules' (1966), the clash is accented by the words 'Pow! Pow! Klang! Thop! Zap! Splat! Clunk! Blap! Pow!'

Star Trek's 1967 episode 'Who Mourns for Adonais?' can also be seen in the context of this camp aesthetic, with its brightly coloured lamé Greco-Roman costumes. The potential camp quality of the entire show was acknowledged in a 1967 letter to *TV Guide*. A *Star Trek* fan argues that to keep the show on air everyone should 'tell the sponsors the show is the newest kind of CAMP! Then tell the public that if they listen close the dialogue is really DIRTY! This should please everybody.'[130] Although intended as ironic, given that the fan also notes, 'it is the kiss of death to tell anyone a program is intellectually stimulating', the letter nonetheless suggests that *Star Trek* was seen as open to a camp reading when it was aired. This creates an alignment with contemporaneous programmes such as the *Marvel Superheroes* that were reviewed in terms of camp and pop art on aesthetic grounds. The mixing of myth with science fiction in *Star Trek* continued the blending of cultural forms that were perceived as high and low respectively. While this might be seen in terms of the legitimising strategies of earlier programmes, the high–low combination just as easily suggests the pop and camp aesthetic of other 1960s television programmes.

Shows such as *Star Trek* and *Thor* readily mixed the iconography of a mythological 'past' with a contemporary and futuristic *mise-en-scène*.[131] In *Thor*'s 'Enter Hercules' (1966), Odin calls on Zeus to help deal with

Myth and Early US TV

his errant son. Like Asgard, home of the Norse gods, Mount Olympus is located somewhat ambiguously in outer space, and from here Zeus sends Hercules to Earth. While using the characters and locations from mythology, the costumes and set decorations of Asgard are a mix of old and new, combining winged helmets with the body-hugging garb common to superheroes. And while Odin learns of Thor's rebellious activities through his 'immortal extra-sensory perception', he watches the battle between Thor and Hercules taking place in contemporary 1960s New York via a type of video display unit (see Figure 1.4). Similarly, while *Star Trek*'s Apollo retains a liking for Greek drapery and columns, his powers actually emanate from a technological device. The iconography of ancient Greece is juxtaposed with *Star Trek*'s futuristic technology and costuming. Like *The Mighty Hercules*, *The Mighty Thor* was able to tap into more than one tradition for its characters, plots and its *mise-en-scène*, making Thor a contemporary, science-fictional, mythological, pop-art, camp, comic book television superhero. *Star Trek* similarly combined its references to myth

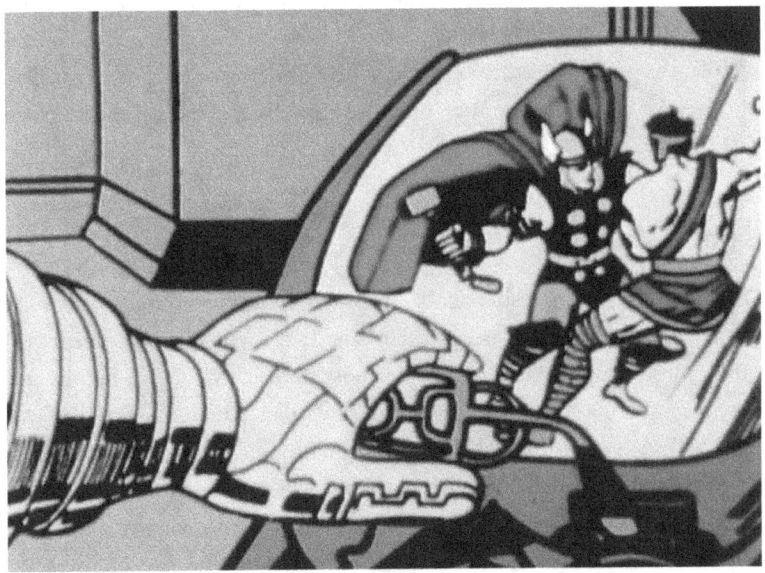

Figure 1.4 *The Mighty Thor* (Famous Studios 1966) and its genre-blending iconography.

within a science fiction programme with a camp aesthetic and a perceived 'comic-strip' simplicity. Programmes such as *The Mighty Thor* and *Star Trek* indicate the complexity of mutual and multiple retellings of different genres, story traditions and representational aesthetics. *Star Trek*'s mutual retelling of different textual traditions becomes more complex as it spawns its own ever-increasing sequels in subsequent decades, an issue that will be explored in Chapter 2.

Even myth-inspired animation heroes that did not have a prior comic book existence, such as *The Mighty Hercules* or *Birdman* (1967–8),[132] nonetheless borrowed from the superhero format. Aside from superheroes such as Thor, Aquaman and Sub-Mariner, who were all overtly based on myth, Reynolds argues that the superhero format itself draws heavily from a variety of mythological traditions.[133] Like mythological heroes, comic book superheroes possess noticeably and preternaturally superior abilities.[134] For example, at the developmental stage Superman was conceived as having the strength of Hercules, even though in the comic book and its subsequent cross-media spin-offs he has no connection with the Greek gods, and instead originates from an alien planet.[135] From this perspective, superheroes were drawing upon the same mythological template as popular culture versions of mythic heroes and gods, regardless of whether superhero comics or animations made overt references to myth.

Conclusion

On early television, mythological subjects were primarily found in children's programmes. As such, it is not surprising that myth was combined with other genres popular with children, most noticeably science fiction and superhero formats. At the same time, myth in adult programmes was reviewed in terms of superior cultural quality. Consequently, the use of myth in children's programmes could be seen as a legitimising strategy. The adaptation of myth into television also had alignments with industry trends and commercial concerns. An increase in the use of myth on television is found in the same decades that myth was popular in cinema as part of the epic film genre. Television programmes also harnessed the comic strip and comic book market, the superheroes of which were often based explicitly or implicitly on the heroes of myth. Many of the hero-based programmes incorporating myth had pre-existing and subsequent cross-media ties, as television used merchandising to hold children's interest and diversify its product. While myth provided pre-existing stories that could be reworked by television, the manner and frequency with which this was done corresponded to intersecting patterns of genre popularity and television industry positioning.

Star Trek's 1967 episode 'Who Mourns for Adonais?' must be placed within the context of these trends. Others have investigated 'Who Mourns for Adonais?' in the context of the *Star Trek* canon, or as a reflection of 1960s attitudes towards religion. These studies have failed to consider whether the episode's use of Greek myth speaks not to *Star Trek*-specific concerns, nor those of its creator Gene Roddenberry, but rather to industry trends in the use and depiction of mythological subjects. Placed in the context of earlier programmes that adapted myth, 'Who Mourns for Adonais?' can be seen not as an exemplar of the secularism of the 1960s, nor of Roddenberry's vision of the future, but rather as part of a continuum of trends in the use of myth that encompasses issues of high and low culture, genre blending, cinema competition, demographic appeals, camp aesthetic, cross-media adaptations and morality debates.

In its iconographic and narrative mix of science fiction and myth, 'Who Mourns for Adonais?' continues the trend established by programmes such as *Captain Video and His Video Rangers*, *Space Patrol*, *Rocky Jones*, *Flash Gordon*, *Rod Rocket* and *The Mighty Thor*. As with *Captain Video*, the characters of myth could be encountered in the future vistas of space. Like *The Mighty Thor*, the ancient gods had survived for millennia after their initial stories, and had both natural and technological abilities. Both *Star Trek* and *Thor* were reviewed in terms of their camp qualities that appealed to a young adult market, undermining the conventional association of science fiction and superheroes with children. Like *The Time Tunnel*, *Star Trek* appropriated myth within a programme deemed by *TV Guide* to be primarily 'adventure' and secondarily 'science-fiction',[136] while trying to attract an older demographic than this particular stream of science fiction had previously harnessed.

Television programmes that used mythological material overtly or implicitly stressed their own continuity with a mythological and heroic tradition, yet they did so primarily within a radically transformed diegesis. These differences and the manner in which they were articulated are important in positioning a historically specific reworking of myth. That said, the alignments both consciously and implicitly made between television characters and their mythic forebears raise the question of whether such reworkings themselves constitute a continuation of myth, an issue explored in the next chapter. On the one hand, the relation between myth and *Star Trek* that forms the central case study for this book is specific to its own franchise, and its particular place within the history of popular culture. On the other hand, the transposition of myth into a futuristic science fictional world is found in many of the earlier programmes examined here. So too, rituals of fandom associated with *Star Trek* and its cross-media manifestations find their origins in early programmes such as *Captain Video* and *Tom Corbett*. Both of these earlier texts had substantial merchandising and a highly developed fan base directly linked with that merchandising. While the remainder of this book explores the case study of *Star Trek* from 1966 to the present in terms of its use of myth, and the positioning of a *Star Trek* myth with associated fan rituals, the franchise does not occur in a vacuum. Rather, as this chapter demonstrates, *Star Trek*'s textual strategies mirror trends in early television history in the use of mythological material. On television, myth proves itself to be extremely malleable (as indeed it is in antiquity), frequently transposed in time and place, reworked in detail, but speaking simultaneously to its mythic origins and the specific cultural and industry needs of the time.

2

The New Mythology

Introduction

Early television programmes appropriate myth, but alter story traditions to such an extent that it is difficult to see these programmes as a form of contemporary myth in their own right. Television programmes create an intertextual, cultural and industrial dialogue on the nature and cultural status of myth as it is reworked across various programmes, within changing cultural needs and crises. However, this dynamic system of myth appropriation has synergies with Greek storytelling and *mythos*. As the cultural interpretation of *mythos* changed from the eighth to fifth centuries BCE, so too traditional stories within Greek culture were transformed over time.[1] Stories also referred to other stories, making the audience aware of the larger set of tales to which they belonged. Taking this active process as its lead, this chapter argues for an intertextual, dialogic approach to myth, using the *Star Trek* franchise as a case study, and drawing on the theories of Ken Dowden, Mikhail Bakhtin and Jim Collins. Since the 1980s, the *Star Trek* franchise has not only appropriated older myths, but has also increasingly presented the *Star Trek* story-world as a form of popular culture mythology. This strategy not only reflects the success of the *Star Trek* franchise as a cultural phenomenon, but also a very pragmatic commercial desire to maintain that success by emphasising *Star Trek*'s mythic importance.

Chapter 1 revealed a number of trends that filtered through the use of myth by early television programmes. In particular, early television programmes placed mythological stories and characters in contemporary and futuristic settings, visited the mythological 'past' by fantasy and pseudo-scientific means, and blended genres, themes and iconography. While some attempts were made in these early decades to depict mythological stories without these contemporary interventions, children's programmes that mixed story traditions freely outnumbered adult-oriented programmes that aspired to a sense of authenticity. These trends cannot be simplified into a singular use and understanding of myth. Just as traditional stories were reworked, so too texts and reviewers activated different cultural associations of myth. This chapter argues that *Star Trek* similarly activates different meanings of myth across its 50-year-old multi-authored transmedia franchise. Precisely because of its textual, commercial and cultural longevity, the *Star Trek* franchise begins to appropriate myth as a means of drawing parallels with its own status as a cross-generational storytelling tradition. As noted in Chapter 1, the retelling of two or more pre-existing story traditions was evident in numerous early television programmes that appropriated myth. In *Star Trek: Deep Space Nine* (*DS9*) and *Star Trek: Voyager*, this mutual retelling reaches a new level of self-conscious manipulation, in an attempt to reinforce the perceived 'mythic' status of *Star Trek* among reviewers, fans and scholars. *Enterprise* will be given a closer examination in Chapter 3, because it markets itself less in terms of ancient mythologies that will be explored here, but rather in terms of *Star Trek*'s own myth of progress, where *Star Trek* becomes the ultimate and inevitable consequence of human achievements.

Continuity and Discontinuity: New Myths and Old Process

As noted in the introduction to this book, the earliest surviving use of the word *mythos* placed importance on the process of telling the story.[2] Myth also draws upon a tradition of previous stories and versions of a story that are known to the audience. As Edmunds notes:

> Against the traditionality of myth and its meaningfulness as a collective expression of society [...] must be set the consideration that a traditional story can survive only if it can be retold, and it can be retold only if it can be applied to new circumstances [...] [O]n the occasion of any retelling, the present, individualist version is the authoritative one. Myth occurs, one could say, at the juncture of performance with tradition.[3]

Myth, therefore, has its own tradition that it draws upon and adds to through the process of retelling. Edmunds' model is process-driven, a perspective that has implications for myth in its contemporary guise and its continuation of retelling. The difficulty lies in locating the point at which the retelling of myths becomes merely the telling of stories about myths.

The history of retelling myth cannot be viewed as inconsistent with myth conceived of in more traditional terms. *Mythos* occurred within a culture that prized storytelling and poetry performed to music. This was not merely a static replication of learnt tales. In Homer's *Odyssey* (*c*.700 BCE), Telemachus notes that 'people, surely, always give more applause to that song which is the latest to circulate among the listeners', suggesting that innovations were not only common, but indeed welcomed.[4] Features of numerous Greek myths can be directly linked with historically specific trade connections, colonisation or political changes.[5] Bremmer argues:

> The respective audiences of these *mythoi* must surely have recognised the novelty of these tales at the time of their first performances, even though they soon became incorporated into the traditional corpus of myths. Mythology, then, was an open-ended system.[6]

Myth must therefore be conceived of in terms of both tradition and innovation, of speaking to the present through a mythic past. The public performance of oral poetry and myth would seem to lend itself to subtle reformulation in response to a specific audience's tastes.[7] The notion that myth is both systemic and malleable has also been applied to myth in its later literate forms.[8]

While a myth may be represented by many different versions over a length of time, not all versions necessarily survive in material forms such as writing or art.[9] It is in this respect that the initial orality of myth and the vagaries of text preservation have perhaps left us with both a distorted picture of myth and the desire to make up for that distortion. Within scholarship that has traced changes in myth over time, there has often been an underlying assumption that the ultimate aim was the reconstruction of a lost original.[10] But as Parker argues:

> There is perhaps no helpful discrimination to be drawn in terms of 'authenticity' between different variants of a myth or stages in its development, or between 'real myth' and 'literary myth' or the like [...] Perhaps we should consider the history of mythology not as a decline from myth into non-myth but as a succession of periods or styles, developing out of one another, as in art. That metaphor, however, does not remove but emphasises the need to distinguish between the products of different periods.[11]

From this perspective, to attempt to determine and fix the boundaries between myth and non-myth may be to misunderstand the way myth is transformed over time. Instead, this book shifts the focus to the process of change, whereby specific myths alter over time, while the *concept* of myth itself is also gradually transformed.[12] Each variant of a specific myth is situated within a progression of earlier variants, but can also be understood in terms of historically specific trends. Although Parker does not extend such an approach to contemporary media versions of myth, his ideas provide a model through which the retelling of myths in different times and through different media can still be addressed. Within this model, myth is reconceptualised by any given era, maintaining some elements of continuity yet transforming others.

Parker suggests a linear model of progression; however, there is also a sense in which a myth gains an overall cumulative identity, full of both continuities and contradictions. As such, Ken Dowden has argued:

> Greek Mythology is an 'intertext', because it is constituted by all the representations of myths ever experienced by its audience and because every new representation gains its sense

from how it is positioned in relation to this totality of previous representations.[13]

Dowden argues that such a 'model is applicable equally to oral and literary traditions'.[14] Although similar to Parker's model, in which new forms of myth are situated in relation to preceding ones, Dowden's conceptualisation of myth as intertext differs in its perception of a cumulative whole created out of this history of retellings. Each new version of a myth is not merely the next instalment to be plotted in linear succession, but rather gets its meaning from the entire backlog of retellings that coexist, particularly through the memory of the audience. For example, in Homer's *Odyssey*, Odysseus visits places and meets characters also featured in the story of Jason and his ship, the *Argo*, whose adventure, we are told, 'is in all men's minds'.[15] The *Odyssey* provides an opportunity to revisit and rework elements of another myth in the guise of a new story, but also relies upon the story of Jason also being in the audience's mind. Jason is mentioned so that the two stories can be understood alongside one another.

Dowden notes a number of references to other stories in both the *Iliad* and the *Odyssey*.[16] Although in general he takes the neoanalytic view that Homer is alluding to specific texts,[17] Dowden notes: 'There is no way of telling from these references whether Homer refers [...] to common stories or particular poems'.[18] In other words, an audience member's knowledge of a mythic allusion, such as the story of Jason, may itself be a composite. While myth may be conceived as traditional in its appeal to prior knowledge,[19] such prior knowledge may draw from numerous representations that need not be consistent. All of this jostling knowledge constitutes an intertextual understanding of Greek mythology.[20]

Intertextuality may consist not only of explicit textual references but also a field of influence. Oral-formulaic approaches to myth can also be understood as intertextual in this broader sense, through the use of metonymic codes.[21] Thus Foley, in his discussion of stylised and repeated phrases in Homeric poetry, argues that epithet formulas (such as 'swift-footed Achilles') are used as shorthand to stand in for 'the entire heroic portrayal, complete with its mythic history and contradictions, as known to the tradition and as signaled by this phrase'.[22] A brief formulaic code is able to conjure up a multitude of story traditions. These traditions are activated through poetic formulas understood by poet and audience alike. Foley sees such a code also operating on the level of other traditional elements such as thematics and story-pattern, which, along with phraseology, 'command fields of reference much larger than the single line, passage, or even text in which they occur. Traditional elements reach out of the immediate instance in which they appear to the [...] totality of the entire tradition.'[23]

Both Foley's metonymy and Dowden's intertextuality are grounded in the notion that the specific (phrase, theme or myth) can evoke and stand in for a larger mythic tradition.[24] Thus various elements of the past are subsumed into the new version of the myth. Past and present coexist to create if not a whole, then a dialogue between the various competing and complementary aspects of the tradition in the very process of being reworked. Foley's metonymic elements are also similar to Edmunds' theory of myth occurring 'at the juncture of performance with tradition', in that Foley sees epithet formulas as operating within an exchange 'between an always impinging tradition and the momentary and nominal fossilization of a text or version'.[25] Meaning occurs at the nexus between retelling and tradition.

The scholars quoted above have formulated their theories by examining traditional mythic form in ancient Greece, while also acknowledging that such traditions are changeable.[26] They nonetheless bring us somewhat closer to how we might conceptualise myth as it is appropriated and reworked beyond this (etymologically) original context: as drawing upon a tradition yet transforming it; as existing in a succession of different understandings of myth and different versions of specific myths, each of which has a historical context; as an intertext made up of the various versions of the myth; and as an economic means of suggesting a cultural tradition while simultaneously adding to that tradition. When myth is conceptualised as itself inherently changeable, as dependent upon an interplay between tradition and retelling, narratives created in a different time with different communication technologies become the next phase of transformation, the most recent instalment in the 'succession of periods or styles' of myth.[27]

Retelling Myth in *Star Trek*'s Future: Competing Discourses

As examined in Chapter 1, the appropriation of myth in *TOS* episode 'Who Mourns for Adonais?' in many respects reflects early television trends in the depiction of mythological subjects. However, this original series has since inspired sequels in which myth is depicted in varied, even conflicting ways. The sequels may refer to a mythological intertext, but they also have an increasing *Star Trek* textual tradition. In this context, references to myth become a means of suggesting parallels between two traditions, mythological and *Star Trek*, each adding to the other.

By appropriating myths, futuristic works such as the *Star Trek* franchise transform the traditional association between myth and the past. As noted in Chapter 1, explicit references to myth in film have tended to be classified within the broader category of the historical epic, a genre made up of 'an admixture of different kinds (and not merely periods) of past events: mythic, biblical, folkloric, and quasi- or "properly" historical'.[28] Thus myth in its cinematic and televisual manifestations has been subsumed into a larger discourse on the relationship between the (represented) past and the present. Pierre Sorlin, for example, has argued that the use of history in film creates a dialogue between the present and the past, but the past as it is constituted by the present.[29] Drawing on a culture's shared sense of history, a film can offer up 'a few details from this [history] for the audience to know that it is watching an historical film and to place it, at least approximately'.[30] The 'history' film both draws on and becomes part of a broader historical consciousness.[31] However, by relocating myth into a fictional future, futuristic science fiction television programmes, such as *Ulysses 31* (1981), *Red Dwarf* (1988-) and the various *Star Trek* series, rework this historical consciousness as a connection between past, present and future. In this futuristic context, 'a few details' may still be able to 'place' a myth, but not necessarily in a manner that corresponds to the imagined time depicted on the screen. Rather, like Foley's metonymic myth, a visual, verbal or narrative element is able to conjure up a cultural and mythic tradition that is nonetheless a transferable unit of composition.[32]

For example, in the *TOS* episode 'Who Mourns for Adonais?', centuries after leaving ancient Earth, the god/alien Apollo is dressed in gold Greco-Roman draped clothing, gold sandals and a gold laurel wreath, and is furnished in a temple supported by columns. Apollo's proclamation of his identity is both prefigured and upheld by an iconography that only broadly denotes the ancient world, albeit one relocated both spatially and temporally.[33] Specific elements of iconography are consonant with the figure of Apollo in Greek myth – such as his lyre, which was an instrument given to him by Hermes as recompense for stealing Apollo's cattle, recounted in the *Homeric Hymn to Hermes*. These iconographic features create not only the possibility of an intertextual referent, but also a culturally informed shorthand for creating an impression of antiquity. Like Foley's poetic phrases, iconography functions metonymically, standing in for a larger tradition through the cultural memory of the audience.

The mythic tradition provides a narrative model for the episode and points of connection with a broader intertext of myth (as conceived by Dowden). Thus, Asa has examined the way in which Apollo's rejection by Lieutenant Carolyn Palamas and a subsequent implied rape draw upon a mythic tradition in which Apollo suffers multiple rejections in love, and also inflicts much harm upon unwilling women.[34] Yet of all the gods mentioned in this episode, each of whom could be similarly situated within a broader mythic tradition, only Apollo is actually depicted. He therefore (literally) embodies not only his own tradition, but stands in for an absent pantheon, which is similarly characterised by dangerous changes in temperament. Apollo operates as a metonymic focal point, a momentarily fixed nexus between the retelling and the told in which the 'traditional' component of myth can operate as a broad cultural resonance or as a link to a specific set of intertexts.

In *TOS* a Greek god is lifted from mythology and relocated in time and space, as if the myths were real and the gods had lived into the future, their love of drapery unchanging over the millennia, only to be juxtaposed with twenty-third-century phasers.[35] Iconographic and textual juxtapositions activate different and sometimes competing discourses for the creation of meaning. Collins argues that when two different discourses are invoked by the same text, part of the meaning is informed by the relative weight given to the discourses – whether one is valorised over the other or, by contrast, if 'both of the conflicting discourses are given equal footing'.[36] Apollo finally accepts that his 'time has passed', and 'Who Mourns for Adonais?' thereby gives primacy to the scientific, predominantly secular discourse of *Star Trek* over the mythic and religious discourse that Apollo attempts to reassert. The episode evokes a mythological intertext, but also, on a more fundamental level, a different system of meaning from the technological world of *TOS*' heroes. That the Starfleet discourse is victorious is signalled by the crew's ability to expose Apollo's mythic power as technologically based, destroying his power source hidden within the temple. Apollo fails to convert the crew to his worldview, and instead the *Enterprise* crew literally and conceptually capture him in their own secular, technological discourse.

What characterises the allusion to myth across the *Star Trek* franchise is the shifting way in which it is set in harmony or conflict with other discourses, a fact that is evident in 'Who Mourns for Adonais?' Having defeated Apollo, Kirk almost immediately expresses reservations about his actions, recognising the importance of Greek myth and culture to the development of humanity. This ambivalence threads through the sequels, extending into newly created 'future' and alien myths.

Characters from *The Next Generation* do not meet figures from pre-existing myths. However, the series does draw on myth to create new alien myths. While an intertextual field of reference is activated by visual cues in *TOS* episode 'Who Mourns for Adonais?', a mythic tradition may also be activated by aural cues. In *TNG*'s 'When the Bough Breaks' (1988), for example, Riker notes that the area of space the *Enterprise* is travelling through is associated with

> Aldea, the wondrous mythical world. Like Atlantis of ancient Earth ... Advanced culture, centuries-old, self-contained, peaceful; incredible technical sophistication providing the daily needs of the citizens, so that they could dedicate themselves over to art and culture.

> TASHA: Where is it supposed to be?
> RIKER: That's the myth. Somehow, as the legend goes, the Aldeans were able to cloak their planet in darkness and go unseen by marauders.

In 'When the Bough Breaks' our first mythic cue is verbal. Atlantis is never mentioned again in this episode. Instead, the passing mention of a pre-existing Greek myth establishes a cultural prototype with which Aldea itself, and the myth of Aldea, can be compared. Just as Homer's *Odyssey* makes only the briefest mention of Jason and his similarities with Odysseus,[37] so too a fleeting mention of Atlantis can generate an entire mythological field of reference stretching from Plato to the present.

In this episode, the *Enterprise* discovers a spatial distortion, from which a planet – Aldea – suddenly appears. Captain Picard notes that he had 'heard stories about Aldea, but frankly, I never believed they could be true ... Amazing. To exist only in that dream-world of mythology and then suddenly to be here, right in front of us.' The Aldeans attempt to negotiate a trade for some of the *Enterprise*'s gifted children, but when Picard refuses, they take the children by force. Dr Crusher discovers that the Aldeans' infertility has been caused by radiation poisoning seeping through their damaged planetary shield. The children are restored to the *Enterprise* in return for medical and technological help to rectify the problem. The *Enterprise* helps the Aldeans 're-seed' their atmosphere, but they will have to remain uncloaked, visible to all. Picard concludes that 'the legend will die, but the people will live'. Although this episode depicts the production of new myths in the twenty-fourth century, the maintenance of the myth by the Aldeans is at the cost of their health and other forms of knowledge, such as the science required to maintain their advanced shielding. In this episode, myths must die in order that people can live. Scientific rationalism is posited as the necessary mode of thought to replace myth and ensure survival. As in 'Adonais', myth in this episode is revealed as having a basis in fact and a living presence in the future, but ultimately it belongs in the past.

Aldea is compared both with Atlantis and 'Nineminozetzi 7', the latter of which is not explained in the episode. These comparisons suggest a continuing tradition of lost worlds from the ancient past through to new examples in the distant future. Atlantis is the prototype lost world, while Nineminozetzi 7 and Aldea extend this tradition.[38] Aldea and Atlantis are both said to have an 'advanced culture'. Aldea is thereby aligned with the city of Atlantis, first described by Plato in his *Timaeus* and *Critias* in the fourth century BCE. However, in Plato's account Atlantis is destroyed by a geological disaster.³⁹ 'When the Bough Breaks' ultimately owes more to the nineteenth-century notion that Atlantis might actually have existed, and awaits discovery,⁴⁰ as indeed does Aldea. Aldea is forced to relinquish its mythic status and mystery, but its comparison with Atlantis draws upon a pre-existing mythic tradition. Aldea reinvents the Atlantis tradition in a new guise, suggesting a lineage of such reinvention that includes Nineminozetzi 7. Bremmer argues that myth is subjected to change in a manner evident to the audience, yet also incorporates itself into an evolving mythic tradition.⁴¹ Just as Aldea is situated in a diegetic mythic tradition it then transforms (the myth of the lost world of Aldea), so too this episode explicitly positions itself as part of an Atlantis tradition it references and reworks.

In both 'Who Mourns for Adonais?' and 'When the Bough Breaks', a mythological discourse is given voice, only to be declared outmoded. By contrast, in *TNG* episode 'Darmok' (1991), knowledge of myth is essential for establishing and continuing communication with alien species. In this episode, Picard and his crew are drawn to a planet by an alien race called the Children of Tama, with whom the Federation have unsuccessfully made contact. This lack of success is due to the fact that the supposedly 'universal' translators possessed by the Federation are unable to adequately translate the Tamarian language, instead only giving descriptions of people and places the crew cannot interpret. The words are translated, but the meaning and context is still unclear. The Tamarians, in turn, are confused. The Tamarians beam their own Captain Dathon with Picard onto the nearby planet's surface and cut off all means of rescue. Rather than an aggressive act, the Tamarians seek to explain their words by enacting one of their mythological stories through Dathon and Picard: the story of 'Darmok and Jalad at Tenagra', in which two strangers fight a beast together and leave as friends. For the Tamarians, to say 'Darmok and Jalad at Tenagra' is to suggest a friendship forged through common adversity. Picard, in turn, tells Dathon the Earth story of Gilgamesh and Enkidu, in which two combatants similarly become friends.⁴²

In their encounter with a beast, Captain Dathon is killed, but Picard has understood enough to make rudimentary communication with the Tamarians. Because further or more sophisticated communication would require knowledge of the Tamarians' entire 'mytho-historical' accounts,[43] their ability to communicate with one another has not greatly changed. At the end of the episode, Picard reads the Greek Homeric Hymns, with the reasoning that 'more familiarity with our own mythology might help us to relate to theirs'. This creates a somewhat contradictory model of myth and mythic communication. Specific people and places lie at the heart of the Tamarians' myths and language, yet Picard hopes to understand the underlying logic by drawing broad cross-cultural comparisons. As Data notes earlier in the episode, this is still 'analogous to understanding the grammar of a language but none of the vocabulary'. In this respect the depiction of Picard's understanding of myth appears to draw on structuralist approaches to myth. Lévi-Strauss' notion that myth functions like language[44] is made literal in 'Darmok', in which myth is language, or conversely, language is myth. This also replicates the emphasis on the spoken aspect of myth identified by Edmunds.[45] Myth in this instance cannot die because it is the Tamarians' living form of communication – and the Federation's only hope of future communication with them. Myth is both familiar and (literally) alien.

Translation alone is insufficient to the task of communication, because the Tamarians have a different way of using words. Dathon and Picard must enter into a dialogue on a more fundamental level of distinct systems of meaning.[46] Mikhail Bakhtin argues that 'dialogic' works encompass different voices and different ways of speaking. Dialogism is characterised by 'the battle between points of view, value judgments and emphases'.[47] Therefore, Bakhtin argues: 'Discourse lives, as it were, on the boundary between its own context and another, alien, context'.[48] The struggle between discourses denies the possibility of singular meaning, a 'monologic', unified speaking position. Bakhtin argues that, in the novel, different world views are often personified by characters through literal dialogue, a function that can also be applied to film and television.[49] Picard and Dathon can exchange words, different ways of speaking words, and different ways of understanding the world. However, 'each word tastes of the context and contexts in which it has lived its socially charged life.'[50] Picard lacks this contextual, social and historical knowledge. The words of Dathon cannot activate for him a metonymic charge, for they are translated but still meaningless. Such an

The New Mythology

interpretation deliberately plays with Bakhtin's sense of the 'alien', made literal in 'Darmok'. Each individual

> strives to get a reading on his [sic] own word, and on his own conceptual system that defines this word, within the alien conceptual system of the understanding receiver; he enters into dialogical relationships with certain aspects of this system. The speaker [...] constructs his own utterance on alien territory.[51]

Picard enters into this dialogic space, and he and Dathon are able to have a limited encounter on the boundary of each other's discourse. Indeed, Bakhtin argues that dialogism is often highlighted through characters who struggle or indeed fail to understand 'someone else's discourse'.[52]

By the end of the episode, Picard searches for a monologic, cross-cultural, universal language within mythology. Bakhtin conceptualises myth as inherently monologic, for it presents human ideology as a single, universal truth.[53] For Bakhtin, myths are exposed as human constructions only when a culture becomes aware of other cultures, of other ways of understanding the world.[54] Picard must acknowledge limitations in his ability to understand the Tamarians, yet he seeks the answers to this understanding within his own mythological heritage. This constitutes a degree of disavowal of Tamarian difference, but also an acknowledgement of discursive difference within human culture, between the mythological discourse of the past and the scientific rationalism of Picard's futuristic 'present'. The encounter with an alien discourse thereby has potential to shed light on human heteroglossia, the dialogue of various *human* discourses, rather than necessarily leading to an understanding of the alien other.[55]

In 'Masks' (1994), the monologism that Bakhtin sees in myth is taken to a more profoundly universal degree. In this episode, the *Enterprise* discovers the cultural archive of an ancient but technologically advanced alien race from the D'Arsay system. When the archive is made active by a sensor scan, matter on the *Enterprise* is gradually transformed into alien artefacts and architecture. As the archive takes over the ship and resists attempts to close it down, android Lieutenant Commander Data is taken over and begins speaking as various characters from the archive. Picard is able to draw upon his own interest in ancient cultures and his knowledge of mythic tropes to gain an understanding of the myth being enacted through Data, continually noting elements common to ceremonial, ritualistic cultures that are heavily founded 'on symbol and myth'. Picard is then able to successfully participate in the mythic ritual with the possessed Data, improvising by drawing on the 'similarities between this culture and others that I've studied'. Through this ritual Picard regains control of the ship, participating in the performance of myth.

The notion of myth represented in this episode is, therefore, universal in the broadest, most literal sense, suggesting recurring mythic structures are held in common throughout the known universe. Picard prevails because he is able to understand mythic modes of thought in a situation in which scientific rationalism has failed.[56] However, there is no strict dichotomy between myth and science. Although Riker characterises the alien artefacts as 'primitive', he is corrected by Picard, who acknowledges that the archive is itself technologically advanced, and seems to accept from this that myth and science need not be mutually exclusive. Myth is nonetheless assigned to the past even in its alien guise: the makers of the archive have long since disappeared. While myth is a relic of the past, it is also posited as a valuable form of knowledge, which can be understood from both a scholarly and intuitive perspective. This suggests that myth is not just the conscious object of study but exists simultaneously in the unconscious. Myth may be of the past, but this episode continually stresses the universal, the common and the shared aspects of myth. That Picard is able to be part of these shared mythic structures suggests an underlying continuity of myth, rather than its cessation.

Myth in 'Masks' is depicted as based on truly universal patterns and ways of thinking, and is, therefore, monologic. However, mythic discourse is encountered on the boundary of Starfleet's scientific and technological worldview. The archive represents the melding of myth with (alien) technology, the merging of two ways of understanding the world that Riker initially assumes to be separate. The alien voices of the archive are provided with an outlet via Data, an android who is both technological yet sentient (see Figure 2.1). As Wagner and Lundeen note, Data's possession by the archive enables him to experience not only the alien mythological records but also the recorded thoughts of thousands of individuals, real

The New Mythology

Figure 2.1 Data embodies technology and myth in *TNG* 'Masks' (Paramount Television 1994).

and mythic.[57] The encounter with the archive mythology is, therefore, dialogic. As Robert Stam notes:

> Bakhtin is not always consistent in his views on dialogism [...] At times he describes it as an inherent characteristic of language itself, but elsewhere he posits it as a liberatory praxis exclusive to the novel as a multivocal genre.[58]

Although myths may contain a singular worldview of a particular culture, mythological systems change over time, creating both complementary and conflicting stories within the same 'tradition'.[59] Mythological stories might contain internal contradictions and points of view. Lillian Eileen Doherty, for example, points out that 'the *Odyssey* often juxtaposes two accounts so as to suggest a competition between their narrators', while also depicting different opinions among audience members within the story.[60] As Bakhtin himself notes in another context, without an understanding of the 'dialogizing background' to an old work, we may turn 'a two-voiced image into one that is flat, single-voiced'.⁶¹ This methodological danger increases as the work grows older, because it becomes more likely that we will misunderstand the 'dialogizing background'. Even if we were to accept Bakhtin's characterisation of myth as inherently monologic, when mythic discourse is brought into other conceptual frameworks this is no longer the case. Instead we might consider dialogism as a sliding scale: that some 'utterances' (whether words, texts or images) are simply more or less dialogic than others.

Dialogic works bring together different systems of meaning, creating a boundary zone in which meanings are negotiated. Collins suggests that textual meaning is created partly from the relationship between different intertextual discourses: whether one discourse is given primacy over another, or if the two reach an equilibrium, even a hybrid.⁶² Individual episodes within the *Star Trek* franchise may prioritise the scientific rationalism of Starfleet over mythological discourse; however, this balance shifts between episodes and between series. As Bakhtin points out, dialogism cannot be reduced to 'mere conversations between persons', but rather includes different 'points of view' expressed in artistic works through various means, including visual and physical cues.⁶³ Furthermore, even when embodied in characters, discourses 'may be resolved as far as plot is concerned', but the discourses themselves may 'remain incomplete and unresolved'.⁶⁴ Different discourses may be present in individual works, but also intertextually between works. Television series, serials and sequels particularly lend themselves to a broader understanding of dialogic frames, as texts that are explicitly tied to one another, yet separated by formal divisions.⁶⁵ Therefore, the dialogic nature of *Star Trek* (and its attempts to control that dialogism) can be seen not merely in individual episodes nor individual series, but rather across the franchise as a whole.

Of *TOS*' sequels, *DS9* frequently explores myth in the form of (diegetic) Bajoran myths, blurring the distinction between myth and scientific fact. Two apparently different ways of understanding the world begin to merge, not merely as a passing concern in transient alien encounters within a single episode, but rather within the central serial narrative. *DS9*'s engagement with myth forms part of a larger narrative concern with religious belief and the Bajoran story arc.⁶⁶ Just as 'When the Bough Breaks' uses

The New Mythology

myth and legend interchangeably, so too in *DS9* the lines between myth, legend, prophecy and religion are continually blurred, as indeed is the line between the mythic and the (diegetically) real. In 'The Assignment' (1996), Miles O'Brien's botanist wife Keiko returns from studying plants in a series of Bajoran caves, only to announce that she is in fact an alien who has taken control of Keiko's body. Miles is forced to make modifications to the space station under threat of Keiko's death at the hands of the alien. A clue to the alien's identity occurs by chance when Commander Sisko's son Jake asks Keiko whether she encountered any Pah-wraiths in the fire caves, super-natural beings of Bajoran legend. But with little time and 6,427 computer entries on Pah-wraiths, Miles is unable to follow up the possibility that Keiko might be possessed by one of them. That is, until his assistant Rom notes that the modifications he is helping to make to the station will be able to kill a group of aliens who live in the wormhole, a nearby spatial phenomenon. As O'Brien notes: 'They're not just wormhole aliens, they're Prophets. Part of Bajoran mythology. Just like the Pah-wraiths of the fire caves.' According to Bajoran myth/legend (again used interchangeably in this episode), the Prophets and the Pah-wraiths once lived together in the wormhole, until the Pah-wraiths were declared false prophets, expelled and imprisoned in the fire caves. Because they are basically the same species (with a long-standing ideological disagreement), the weapon intended to kill the wormhole Prophets will also kill the Pah-wraiths. With this knowledge, Miles is able to readjust the space station modifications to kill the Pah-wraith occupying his wife, rather than the Prophets in the wormhole.

As in 'Darmok', the specific details of particular myths hold the key to understanding and survival. Even when he knows the name of the Pah-wraiths and suspects their involvement, Miles cannot understand the alien's motivations and aims without some further guide to the 6,427 mythical stories he has to choose from on the computer database. While the computer cannot help him, memory and the spoken word can. Jake tells him about the Pah-wraiths, having been told of them himself by Odo, the chief of security on the space station. And Rom tells Miles the story of the Prophets and Pah-wraiths, having heard it from Leto, a worker at the station's gambling bar. Myth in its most useful (indeed life-saving) guise is handed down from person to person by word of mouth. In this respect, myth in 'The Assignment' comes close to Homer's *mythos*, by stressing not so much the corpus of stories themselves but rather the process of telling and the spoken word.[67] However, it is only in remembering that the wormhole aliens are both Prophets from ancient myth *and* real aliens in the present that Miles finally understands what has been happening and how to prevail. Armed with his knowledge of myth, Miles uses his technological knowledge to kill the alien. Only by drawing on both his technological and mythological knowledge does he succeed. A 'collision between different points of view on the world' in Bakhtin's terms creates a discursive hybrid, which is more meaningful.[68] Throughout the episode, neither myth nor technology alone can make sense of the situation, suggesting the continued relevance of myth from the past and into the future.

The specific technology used to overcome the aliens also draws upon this temporal continuity of myth. The adjustments to the space station create a 'chroniton beam' that is harmless to humanoids, but 'its temporal disruption would kill a wormhole alien instantly'. This is technobabble, or simply 'TECH' as it is designated in scripts: dialogue that sounds pseudotechnological in order to support a plot device that is not really explained.[69] So while we are never sure what a 'chroniton beam' really is, nor how it works, its narrative function as a weapon against the Prophets and Pah-wraiths is made clear. The beam causes a temporal disruption harmful to the Prophets because they do not experience time in a linear fashion, but rather occupy all time simultaneously.[70] If *Star Trek* episodes dealing with myth frequently link it with the relationship between past and future, the centrality of the Prophets to Bajoran mythology and religion sets up a different temporal dynamic in which past, present and future are seen as one.[71] While the Prophets exist in a realm beyond time, the humanoids who relate to and interact with this mythology live in a linear, temporally situated world. However, by the Season 7 episode 'Shadows and Symbols' (1998), it is revealed that Captain Sisko's mother was taken over by a Prophet, making Sisko '*half* divine, much like Hercules, son of Zeus and a human woman'.[72] By the last episode, 'What You Leave Behind' (1999), Sisko has joined the Prophets.[73] The timeless Prophets of Bajoran mythology, and the humans of *DS9*'s linear existence, have merged. Myth – its stories, characters and telling – is therefore paradoxically both of time and timeless.

The New Mythology

The issues of time and technology continually present themselves in the various *Star Trek* episodes that explicitly engage with the issue of myth. In 'When the Bough Breaks', myth must die and science replaces it, whereas in 'The Assignment' both myth and technological knowledge are needed together. In episodes such as 'Who Mourns for Adonais?' and 'When the Bough Breaks', myth must be consigned to the past, whereas in 'Darmok' and 'The Assignment' myth has a continued active existence in the future, especially through the spoken word. In all these episodes, myth is aligned with technology and with the future, because in each case myth exists within the futuristic, technologically advanced *Star Trek* world, whether as a living process or a powerful cultural heritage. 'Masks' and 'The Assignment' posit technology and myth as complementary modes of thought, an alignment that is implicit in all the myth episodes simply by virtue of their choice of narrative. Clute and Nicholls argue 'Mythology in sf [*sic*] reflects a familiar truth, that in undergoing social and technological change we do not escape the old altogether, but carry it […] within us.'[74] The construction of an imagined world is necessarily the reconstruction and reworking of a past one. Myth in *Star Trek* cannot exist purely in the past, because it is a cultural heritage for humans and aliens alike that continually makes its presence felt.

That myth is often both the threat and the solution in these episodes indicates an underlying ambivalence towards myth, an ambivalence also to be found in the fact that even those episodes that are critical of myth nonetheless uphold it as a valued form of storytelling by making it the subject of the episode. 'Who Mourns for Adonais?' proclaims the mythic realm to belong to the past, yet continues the tradition by adding another instalment to Greek mythology and that of Apollo in particular. Apollo disappears, along with the other gods, and this lends a sense of finality both to his myth and to myth itself. But in its choice of subject matter, the episode also suggests that myths are never really finished: someone can always add another chapter, even centuries later. Similarly, if the Prophets and Pahwraiths of 'The Assignment' exist both as aliens and as figures of Bajoran mythology, so too do Miles and his co-workers occupy both realms in their interaction with a real Pah-wraith and a new chapter in the Bajoran Pahwraith mythology – story 6,428 to add to the computer database. Although these various episodes have different constructions of what myth is, and varying value judgements on myth, read together as a *Star Trek* intertext they suggest a process by which myth, even when denounced, is kept alive for both the diegetic world and the extra-diegetic audience.

Star Trek refashions older, pre-existing myths, but also reconceptualises what myth might mean in a contemporary and futuristic context. As Parker suggests, the transformation of myth over time should not be considered 'the decline from myth into non-myth but as a succession of periods or styles'.[75] Continuity between different forms of myth as it changes over time does not negate the differences between various stages of its development. Rather, each stage of mythic reinvention must be situated historically.[76] The reworking of myth within the *Star Trek* franchise must, therefore, be seen in relation to its late twentieth- and early twenty-first-century context and its televisual medium.

History and *Star Trek*: 'Myth' in Quotations

Of the episodes discussed above, 'Masks' and 'The Assignment' mention no pre-existing human, Earth myths. They do, however, create alien diegetic stories and refer to them explicitly as myth. These are not, then, unconscious replications of myth. Myth in its origins (as much as we can extrapolate) cannot itself be seen as unknowing in its deliberate reformulation of story traditions. In the twentieth and twenty-first centuries, scriptwriters not only have an accumulated mythic tradition from which to draw, but also a multitude of other sources that include cinematic and television history. The *Star Trek* franchise has usually been called mythic by scholars and fans not because of its use and discussion of myth in its episodes, but rather because *Star Trek* has itself been reworked for 50 years and has gathered a large fan following in that time. In this sense, *Star Trek* has generated its own popular culture myths.

Umberto Eco has argued that cult popularity of films arises from the unconscious repetition of cinematic intertextual archetypes, which are not conceived as psychoanalytic, mythic or universal, but rather are 'derived from preceding textual tradition' that may be quite recent.[77] Thus, he explains the popularity of *Casablanca* (1942) as arising from its pastiche of 'the already said', an improvised plot in which 'everything they chose

The New Mythology

came from a repertoire that had stood the test of time [...] stock formulas' to which people respond.[78] Eco is able to claim this improvised, intuitive use because the script was still being developed during filming, with no one knowing how it would end.[79] But Eco is careful to distinguish this effect from films developed within a textually aware culture, because 'what the semiotician can find in them is exactly what the directors put there'.[80] Self-conscious and deliberate use of stock forms and earlier cinematic traditions is not at all interesting to Eco, particularly when compared with examples of 'instinctive' use.[81]

Jim Collins has argued, however, that Eco's perspective is nostalgic in its claim for a purer, lost form of cinema.[82] Collins instead suggests that 'retro' is appealing because 'popular culture has a *history*', and our 'cultural memory' maintains that history alongside new retellings.[83] Thus we not only accumulate a textual and popular culture history, but also develop a means of responding to this sense of history.[84] This process is particularly evident when a specific story or character is retold many times over, for each new text responds not only to a broad popular culture history, but also to its own specific textual and cultural past.

Tony Bennett and Janet Woollacott have argued that James Bond, a franchise character reworked over numerous decades, is a 'mobile signifier'.[85] Each new version of Bond adds to the original text and ultimately undermines its significance and identity as an original.[86] For enduring fictional worlds and characters, retelling the tale in a new story does not merely add to the sheer volume of texts, nor simply add to its growing importance in the history of popular culture. Rather, new additions in such a context function to alter our understanding of fictional creations as existing beyond the confines of any given version.

Collins has extended upon Bennett and Woollacott in his exploration of the Batman character. Collins argues that in recent retellings of Batman there is an elevated awareness of 'their own status as mobile signifiers' – that is, the texts display a heightened acknowledgement of their own textual relations and past.[87] Each 're-telling' necessitates some reworking of the previous retellings, for these 'have become as inseparable from the "text" as any generic convention or plot function'.[88] It is impossible to completely sever a new Batman text from previous Batman texts, because this textual and cultural history exists simultaneously, and does not simply disappear from cultural memory. But more than that, new Batman texts draw on the figure's accumulated history as part of their very composition, reworking it and highlighting its relational intertextuality.

Collins argues that in such a self-aware, 'hyperconscious' text, there can be no master narrative producing a myth, but rather only 'myth' presented in quotation marks, one in a multitude of quotations of which audience members will have varying degrees of knowledge.[89] Further, in contemporary societies there will be 'competition between different forms of "myth"'.[90] For example, Collins accepts Will Wright's argument that genres can function as myths, 'but only if we make one essential adjustment – that several different forms of myth represent the diverse consciousness of a heterogeneous culture'.[91] There is no longer, if indeed there ever was, one overarching mythological narrative that brings everything together, or gives the various stories a sense of unity. Contemporary texts, such as those in the Batman franchise, revel in this multiplicity, highlighting both their traditions and their inconsistencies.

Collins does not extensively explore his idea of 'myth' as presented in quotations, and in other contexts he uses the term myth in more conventional ways.[92] Storytelling traditions that might once have functioned as myths may be presented as 'myth' in contemporary texts, but as self-conscious citations within a larger expanse of citations, whose significance is ultimately relational and dependent upon audience knowledge.[93] 'Myth' thereby becomes merely one or more nodes in an interconnecting array of texts.

Dowden has argued that myth (as more traditionally defined) may be conceived as an intertext.[94] Audiences of Greek myth gained a cumulative memory of different, interconnected stories within the mythological system.[95] While new stories and variations must have been noticeable, they were subsumed into the corpus of stories.[96] In an oral system of composition and transmission, direct comparisons between different versions of the same story would have been more difficult than in a literate culture. Collins' notions of 'myth' also relies on cultural memory, but this memory can be renewed through textual artefacts that remain alongside new versions, facilitating direct comparison even over a considerable length of time. Collins' notion of 'myth' presented in quotation also has alignments with Foley's metonymy, in its ability to evoke a larger tradition while in the process of reworking it.[97] The field of reference created by Collins' 'myth' is specifically that of late twentieth- and early twenty-first-century texts that have created their own storytelling tradition,[98] and are able to quote back from that tradition alongside any number of other quotations from various sources.

TOS lacks an extensive field of self-reference by virtue of its newness. While 'Who Mourns for Adonais?' suggests that Captain Kirk and his crew are similar in nature to the heroes of Greek myth, this suggestion has no resonance beyond the diegesis itself. As a struggling series with low ratings,[99] *TOS* cannot claim at this stage to have forged a great place for itself in popular culture. It may quote pre-existing myths, but cannot quote from its own textual history in order to present itself as a form of 'myth' within popular culture.

TOS' appropriation of myth does, however, occur within the context of multilayered, cross-genre quotations. Greco-Roman myth and culture form part of a number of non-*Star Trek* sources that are reworked in *TOS*.[100] Thus 'Elaan of Troyius' (1968) takes its name from Helen of Troy, but little, if any, of its plot or scenario – indeed, this episode is loosely based upon Shakespeare's play *The Taming of the Shrew*.[101] Other sources that are brought into *TOS*' science fictional world include the horror genre,[102] a retelling of Jack the Ripper,[103] the gangster genre,[104] the Western genre,[105] Shakespeare,[106] and other science fiction texts, such as the silent film *Metropolis* (1926).[107] Further, *TOS* also engages with various periods of Earth history, both directly through time travel and through the analogy of alien cultures. The crew travel back in time to the 1930s[108] and the 1960s,[109] and discover alien cultures resembling those of Nazi Germany[110] and of Indigenous Americans before European invasion.[111] Gene Roddenberry may have conceived of *TOS* as '*Wagon Train* to the stars', but the multi-authored world of *Star Trek* clearly has a much broader field of reference.[112] The discovery of a living Apollo in *TOS* must, therefore, be viewed within the broader context not only of television history (as explored in Chapter 1), but also of multiple cross-genre appropriations within the series' various episodes, in which myth is by no means privileged as a site of meaning.[113] Multiple intertexts, and multiple voices, occupy the discursive boundary of the text.

As the *Star Trek* franchise has extended, so too has the range of material it quotes and reworks within its science fiction setting. While Greek myth is revisited in the *Voyager* series (in an episode examined in depth below), and later again in *Enterprise*,[114] new sources of appropriation in the *Star Trek* televison sequels have included the legends of King Arthur[115] and Robin Hood,[116] the medieval epic *Beowulf*,[117] the Irish hero Brian Boru,[118] the Bible,[119] *Moby Dick*,[120] *The Three Musketeers*[121] and Arthur Conan Doyle's Sherlock Holmes character,[122] to name but a few. Ilsa Bick argues that the *Star Trek* franchise continually alludes 'to canonical texts such as Dickens, Twain, Doyle, and [...] Shakespeare [...] to legitimate and elevate its narrative to immutable *mythos*'.[123] While essentially critical of its textual strategies, Bick acknowledges that *Star Trek* holds a prime place within the history of popular culture, and is able to draw upon that sense of history in order, paradoxically, to suggest its own timelessness – creating a 'cultural mythology' that aligns itself with the lasting quality of great works of literature and their esteemed *oeuvre*.[124] It is a type of 'neverending story', Bick argues, that keeps moving forward yet essentially only into its own past.[125] Bick shares Eco's misgivings about self-aware texts that draw on popular culture history. Bick's perspective is nonetheless useful in that she sees the construction of a popular culture form of mythology both in terms of the ability of a text to draw on its own popular culture tradition, and in terms of intertextual connections with more traditional texts.

Given that the *Star Trek* franchise is 50 years old and extends over many different media, in its more recent forms it is particularly well placed to draw upon its own history to produce and promote a (popular) 'myth' about itself. The *Star Trek* of the 1990s and beyond is aware of its textual past and place within popular culture, and occasionally displays this awareness in a heightened, deliberate manner. To coincide with the 30th anniversary of the series, for example, the *DS9* episode 'Trials and Tribble-ations' (1996) has the crew of Deep Space Nine taken back in time to an incident depicted in *TOS* episode 'The Trouble with Tribbles' (1967).[126] With the benefit of digital technology, characters from the new series are able to rub shoulders with Captain Kirk and Mr Spock of *TOS* (see Figure 2.2).

The New Mythology

Figure 2.2 *DS9*'s Sisko meets Kirk in the 30th anniversary episode 'Trials and Tribble-ations' (Paramount Television 1996).

One of the *DS9* characters, an alien called Dax who has lived over the span of many human lifetimes, articulates the nostalgic aspect of this journey when she says, 'I remember this time. I lived in this time and it's … it's hard to not want to be a part of it again.' Dax's sentiments echo those of many of the audience who, through rewatching *TOS* and its reworking in 'Trials and Tribble-ations', can 'remember' the *Star Trek* of the 1960s, but only through the mediation of a 1990s perspective. A retrospective understanding of *TOS* is filtered through the knowledge of its textual growth as a fictional realm, and the emergence of its cult status in the history of popular culture.[127] The textual and cultural history of *Star Trek* is maintained quite literally alongside a new retelling in this episode.

'Trials and Tribble-ations' was one of many promotional strategies around the 30th anniversary of the franchise. Prior to broadcasting, toy tribbles were distributed across US city public transport systems to promote the episode – and, of course, the franchise as a whole.[128] *Voyager*'s own anniversary episode, 'Flashback' (1996), retrospectively reveals that

Tuvok once served under Captain Sulu (George Takei), the episode's flashback sequences enabling a similar combination of generations. These endeavours may have been pitched as celebrating *Star Trek*'s 30th anniversary, but they were also aimed at bolstering ratings and potentially bringing some *TOS* fans back to the franchise. Cross-generational guest appearances reoccur across *Star Trek* – most recently in the 2009 *Star Trek* feature film, which has Spocks from the old and new timeline, played by an original and new actor respectively, coexisting alongside one another (Figure 0.2). Where 'Trials and Tribble-ations' differs is in the literal insertion of the new into the old pre-existing footage. Collins argues that in the hyperconscious text, 'distinctions between the telling and the told […] the diegetic action and the extra-diegetic intertextual references become not only difficult to make, but decidedly misleading […] Both now form part of the "action" generated by the text.'[129] While 'Trials and Tribble-ations' is by no means as fractured as the texts Collins examines, its telling of a new story is indivisible from its use of the previous story, 'The Trouble with Tribbles'. Here the 'action' of the text sets up connections with the *Star Trek* history, suturing *TOS* episode into *DS9*, through which it can be re-read, while simultaneously suggesting that *DS9* is bound into the tradition that Dax, and the audience, see in *TOS*. If, then, the literal quotation of *Star Trek*'s past can be seen in terms of 'myth', *DS9* attempts not only to recall its own mythic past but also to become part of it.

While Dax yearns for the time of *TOS*, the episode also makes fun of this textual past. Attention is drawn to the fact that the alien Klingons look totally different in the new series to how they looked in *TOS*. Seated in a space station bar, the Klingon Worf appears uncomfortable as his *DS9* crewmates Odo, Miles O'Brien and Dr Julian Bashir survey the other Klingons in the bar. Worf, with his ridged forehead partially covered by headgear, uncomfortably avoids the gaze of his crewmates; the Klingons around him are distinguishable from humans only by a distinctive uniform and a predilection for goatee beards.

JULIAN: Those are Klingons?
WORF: They *are* Klingons. And it is a long story.
O'BRIEN: What happened? Some kind of genetic engineering?

The New Mythology

JULIAN: A viral mutation?
WORF: We do not discuss it with outsiders.

The official *Star Trek* website even set up a page with eight 'theories' to explain the changes in the Klingons in diegetic, *Star Trek* terms.[130] In Season 4 of *Enterprise*, during which the prequel programme pitched itself more strongly at a knowledgeable *Star Trek* fan base, given that most other viewers had trailed off,[131] it is finally 'revealed' in 'Divergence' (2005) that attempts to create genetically enhanced Klingons results in a virus altering millions of Klingons and removing their cranial ridges. Despite this retrospective explanation, the seasoned *Star Trek* viewer knows exactly what caused this racial transformation so vexing to Worf. Better make-up techniques and higher budgets led to a production decision that broke continuity between *TOS* and its subsequent film and television manifestations. The knowledge of the textual and cultural tradition of *Star Trek* is thereby utilised to achieve different effects even within the same *DS9* episode. If 'Trials and Tribble-ations' attempts to quote itself as 'myth', its hyperconsciousness about this process does not allow the portrayal of a seamless continuity between series.

The changes between *TOS* and its sequels are such that when viewed as an entire fictional world, *Star Trek* does not merely revisit its past, but rewrites it. The original VHS release of 'Trials and Tribble-ations' includes a summary of the original 'Trouble with Tribbles' episode on its sleeve. However, the narrative of this 'past' has been overwritten by the events depicted in the *DS9* episode – events that take the twenty-fourth-century characters of *DS9* into their twenty-third-century past. This twenty-third-century 'past' is our future, except that it simultaneously represents our past in terms of an episode produced in the 1960s. Following the description of the original episode, the videotape sleeve tells us that 'Kirk was blissfully unaware, however, that a personal threat to him was being frantically averted by time-travelling Starfleet officers from a future century'. The events of the *DS9* episode are thereby depicted as having occurred all along, even though the episode itself makes clear that the presence of the *DS9* crew in the past was not originally part of 'history'. More than just aligning itself with its textual past, *DS9* here legitimises and promotes its own 'mythology' by overlaying its presence in this past: its own 'myth' and the 'myth' it quotes become one and the same. Once individual VHS editions were superseded by DVD season and series box sets, this information was no longer provided on the covers, but DVD special features included two documentaries on the making of the episode, including 'Trials and Tribble-ations: Uniting Two Legends' (2003), again emphasising the continuing heroic lineage between the two shows, even as the 'Trials and Tribble-ations' episode rewrites that very history.

'Trials and Tribble-ations', its paratextual video sleeve notes and documentary extras thereby promote the episode's position within the history of *Star Trek*, but also facilitate a particular path through the *Star Trek* array. The episode allows viewers simultaneous access to two separate timeframes and two separate series, signalling both breaks and continuities along the way. This process is extended beyond the narrative to production details, from the make-up used for Klingons to the more complex use of special effects. Although the new episode features painstakingly recreated models of the old *Enterprise* and space station using old-school techniques, digital technology originally developed for *Forrest Gump* (1994) is used to place *DS9* characters in *TOS* shots and to remaster the original footage to create greater clarity.[132] This draws attention to changes in visual technology between *TOS* and its subsequent sequels such as *DS9*. The achievements of contemporary, real-life digital technologies displayed in such an episode mirror the diegetic concern with displaying technological marvels of the future. The episode simultaneously flaunts a self-awareness of *Star Trek*'s evolution as a fictional text and as a television production dependent on existing technologies. The episode thereby presents the 'myth' of *Star Trek* in a manner possible only in the late twentieth century, linking its own development of a textual and popular culture tradition with developments in technology that both restore this past yet also provide an improved present.

'Trials and Tribble-ations' is more than merely a parody of the old *Star Trek* versus the new, as it combines self-reflexive highlighting of continuity changes[133] with an attempt to weave *DS9* into the very fabric of this textual past. Bick conceptualises *Star Trek* as a type of master narrative that creates a 'cultural mythology' through the 'temporal seamlessness of sequels'.[134]

The New Mythology

However, the discontinuous elements between the various *Star Trek* texts, combined with the quotation of outside texts, produces a far more complex textual array than she can account for in a model of a unified master narrative.

Textual discrepancies, and the specific way they are dealt with, become as much a source of meaning as textual alignments. Bakhtin argues, 'New images in literature are very often created through reaccentuating old images, by translating them from one accentual register to another (from the comic plane to the tragic, for instance, or the other way around).'[135] Collins, in turn, has suggested that as quotation has become a favoured narrative device from the late twentieth century onwards, register is more important to the narrative. Register hinges on 'the degree of ironic distance or empathic involvement that the viewer is expected to mobilize from scene to scene.'[136] This, in turn, can vary depending on the degree to which the text attempts to create the illusion of a real diegesis, or whether by contrast it self-reflexively highlights its place within entertainment history.[137] In an ongoing series or serial, however, register can vary from scene to scene, from episode to episode, or from series to series.

While 'Trials and Tribble-ations' cites *TOS* in order to both parody and valorise it, *DS9*'s 'Way of the Warrior' (1995) begins the process of turning *TNG* into a newly finished tradition that can be quoted in a mythic guise. In this episode, Worf mourns the passing of his time on board the *Enterprise* depicted in *TNG* (1987–94), both as an expression of nostalgia and as a means of articulating his new role. 'We were like warriors from the ancient sagas,' says Worf. 'There was nothing we could not do ... The *Enterprise* I knew is gone. Those were good years. But now it is time for me to move on.' In his nostalgia for a time that has only just finished, Worf has already begun to idealise *TNG* in terms of ancient saga[138] and heroic deeds. While the audience is fairly sure that Worf will indeed have an heroic future on *DS9*, his reflections occur in the midst of political upheavals in the diegesis and the personal doubts of his character.[139] Reference to *Star Trek*'s own past here serves both nostalgia and product differentiation, as Worf accepts his new role on the troubled space station, and actor Michael Dorn accepts his role on a different series. So too, these parallels draw on audience knowledge and facilitate the transition to a new set of *Star Trek* stories whereby its 'saga' can be continued.

The characterisation of *Star Trek* in terms of older storytelling traditions is also drawn upon in advertisements for the various *Star Trek* series, which ran at the beginning of the original release *Voyager* VHS tapes. One advertisement describes the passing of the tradition from *TOS* through the sequels, so that *DS9* is described as 'a place where legends are forged', and that 'the legend continues with *Star Trek: Voyager*'.[140] Official Paramount merchandise also situated *Voyager* in terms of the *mythos* of *Star Trek*.[141] While the next (prequel) series initially called itself simply *Enterprise* rather than *Star Trek: Enterprise*, and seemed on this basis at least to be cutting itself off from its past,[142] television advertisements stated 'This is how the *Star Trek* saga begins'[143] and 'Every legend has a beginning'. Similarly, when *Enterprise* was first released on DVD, the advertising tagline that was used for online sales sites such as Amazon.com proclaimed, 'Before Janeway ... and Picard ... before Spock ... and Kirk ... the *Star Trek* saga began.' Each sequel series positions itself through marketing in relation to a preceding *Star Trek* tradition, a tradition which in turn is explicitly compared with saga, legend and *mythos*. These texts and paratexts quote their own *Star Trek* history as 'myth', while trying to attach a mythic quality to new *Star Trek* texts. That they are also marketed in terms of saga and legend suggests a common appeal to ancient forms of storytelling, which *Star Trek*'s own tradition is overtly promoted as continuing. The recent television programme, *Star Trek: Discovery*, continues this trend, its second promotional teaser proclaiming it as 'A new chapter in the *Star Trek* saga'.

The sequel series of *Star Trek* are aware of their place within the history of popular culture, an awareness activated whenever *Star Trek* quotes itself, such as in 'Trials and Tribble-ations'. Each retelling of *Star Trek*, whether in a new series or an individual episode, situates itself in a much larger *Star Trek* text that is made up of, but ultimately not contained by, its textual manifestations. Within such a context, to retell a story appropriated from an outside source is to simultaneously and necessarily retell the *Star Trek* story in a new guise. When the *Star Trek* of the late twentieth and early twenty-first centuries quotes an external myth, it is automatically, at the very least, a twofold endeavour, because it is aware not only of its source material, but also of its own carefully maintained status as a form of popular mythology. *Star Trek* not only contextualises outside myths within *Star Trek*'s fictional realm, but also attempts to contextualise its own mythology through that quotation. The *Voyager* episode 'Favorite Son' (1997), which retells the encounter of Odysseus with the Sirens, is an example of this heightened form of mutual retelling.

Sci-Fi Sirens: Myth and 'Myth'

Like *TNG* and *DS9*, *Voyager* is set in the twenty-fourth century. It centres on the Starship *Voyager*, which is flung into distant space by an alien who subsequently dies. The crew of *Voyager*, led by Captain Kathryn Janeway, embark on a 70-year journey home to Earth, searching for any means of shortening their passage. The Season 3 episode 'Favorite Son' revises Odysseus' confrontation with the Sirens from Homer's *Odyssey* (c.700 BCE). The *Odyssey* recounts individual heroic encounters occurring within the overall structure of the return home by Odysseus, his crew and his ship. In adapting the Sirens episode, 'Favorite Son' situates *Voyager* in the context of Greek myth, as well as situating Greek myth in the context of *Star Trek*.

In 'Favorite Son', *Voyager* crew member Harry Kim begins to experience déjà vu, even though the ship is travelling through an area of space never before explored by humans. After undergoing a series of genetic transformations, Harry directs the ship to a planet on which he is warmly greeted. The inhabitants inform Harry that he is, in fact, not human, but rather an alien who has fulfilled his latent genetic urge to return home to take a mate. On a planet with a population of 90 per cent women, this revelation seems too good to be true for young, straight Harry. Unfortunately, the imbalance of the sexes on the planet Taresia has led its people to infect male aliens such as Harry with a gene-altering virus, changing the victims to make them suitable for procreation. The combination of the virus and an abundance of women provide the Taresians with enough willing husbands. The men, however, are killed during the mating process – as Harry finds out just in time, when he stumbles across the corpse of an unlucky husband.

In the tag of the episode, Harry sits in the mess hall telling fellow crew members Neelix and Paris about the parallels between Odysseus and the Sirens, and his experience with the Taresian women.

HARRY: But Odysseus had been warned that these women, the Sirens, sang a song so beautiful that any man who heard it would be lured to his death.

NEELIX: So how did he get the ship past them?

HARRY: He told his crew to cover their ears so they couldn't hear the Sirens' song. But he also had them tie him to the mast of the ship so he could listen himself without being led astray as they sailed past.

PARIS: Anyone would have been drawn in by these Taresians. I have never seen so many beautiful women in my life.

HARRY: It wasn't just the women [...] There was also something exciting about having a new identity. Being more than just young Ensign Kim.

Though remodelled to fit the concerns of a primarily science fiction programme, ancient Greek myth forms a basic framework for this episode's narrative. Harry briefly retells the original source, providing not only a short lesson on the original myth but also another means of quotation. A potential metonymic function here is delayed; it is only when Harry's encounter is over that we are explicitly given a mythic framework through which to understand it. The Sirens story is told twice: firstly through Harry's adventure, and secondly through Harry's storytelling.

The Sirens story has a third resonance in relation to *Voyager*'s series structure of the return home. While Homer's *Odyssey* tells of Odysseus' encounter with the Sirens in flashback,[144] the episodic nature of Odysseus' adventures within a quest to return home against great odds is a structure that *Voyager* follows as a series.[145] In an interview before 'Favorite Son' was in production, actor Kate Mulgrew, who plays Captain Janeway, noted the connection between *Voyager* and the *Odyssey* as both constituting 'mythic storytelling'.[146] Her comments form part of an official Paramount account of *Voyager*'s development, in which supervising producer Brannon Braga also states that '*Star Trek* is mythos'.[147] This

The New Mythology

suggests that 'Favorite Son' is quite conscious of the alignment it is setting up between *Voyager* and the *Odyssey*. Whether or not the viewer is aware of this alignment is another matter, given that 'Favorite Son' gives no more information about the *Odyssey* than Harry's brief retelling of the Sirens story at the end of the episode. The use of the *Odyssey* nonetheless situates *Voyager* within its mythic framework, inviting the viewer to relate the two tales to one another. Within the mythic intertext,[148] which here could lead us instead to Jason's encounter with the Sirens or myriad other Siren myths, we are directed specifically to Odysseus, thereby allowing us to understand the episode in terms of its use and manipulation of this myth.[149]

In the *Odyssey*, Odysseus is forewarned by Circe of the Sirens' deadly allure, and is therefore able to make preparations to protect himself and his men from the effects of their song.[150] In 'Favorite Son', Harry gradually gains knowledge of a different kind – a feeling of déjà vu and the gradual awareness of Taresian knowledge. This precognition is, in fact, part of the Taresians' method of ensnarement. Unlike Odysseus, whose characteristic use of intellect and craftiness allows him to pass by the Sirens unharmed,[151] Harry is the youngster of the *Voyager* team, often depicted as talented but a little naïve due to lack of experience. He is not the captain of his ship, nor the leader of his crew, like Odysseus. Indeed, if for Odysseus the lure of the Sirens lies in their ability to sing for him epic song in which his former heroic deeds will be praised,[152] Harry's temptation is to believe that he is more important than he has, as yet, become. As a junior officer, he longs to be special – an elevated status that the Taresians can offer. Although Harry becomes suspicious of the Taresians, it is the combined efforts of the *Voyager* crew by which he is rescued, not his own cunning.[153]

While 'Favorite Son' aligns the quest of Odysseus with that of Harry and the crew of *Voyager*, Harry's role in the narrative is adapted in order to be consistent with his character in the series, thereby drawing on the mythic tradition but also undermining its original dependence on Odysseus' leadership and cunning. While Harry may share with the rest of the crew the quest to return home, it is his personal quest for greater importance and respect that is highlighted. In the Season 4 episode 'Demon' (1998), Harry confidently asserts his opinion and expertise, and cites his heroic deeds in support of his new determination.

> I was young, inexperienced, and I acted like it. Nervous about giving my opinion, hesitant to make suggestions, so I usually just kept my mouth shut [...] But in the last four years a lot has happened. I've fought the Borg, been transformed into an alien [...] Hell, I've even come back from the dead.

Harry's encounter with the Taresians is part of a larger set of learning experiences that allow the development of his character over the length of many episodes. As noted earlier, changes in a myth are not themselves inconsistent with myth; indeed, they are needed to keep a myth alive. Just as the *Odyssey* places Odysseus' forthcoming encounters in the context of those previously experienced by Jason,[154] in 'Favorite Son' Harry's encounter is modelled on, and compared with, that of Odysseus, but changed in order to accommodate a different heroic figure.

In their promise to tell Odysseus epic poetry, which will flatter his ego as a hero, the Sirens embody the 'temptation of "forgetting the return" ' to his home and to the loved ones waiting there.[155] Harry's false memories, which gradually emerge, embody a similar temptation. To 'remember' the Taresians is to forget his place on board *Voyager* and his desire to return to Earth. As Odysseus continually chooses the glory of *nostos* (return home) over the possible delights to be had elsewhere,[156] so too the crew of *Voyager* consistently pass up opportunities to settle on hospitable alien planets. Although aliens often aid their journey home, alien planets themselves always pose the potential of a replacement Earth that will divert the crew from their quest. Foreign lands and alien planets thereby play a similar function within the overall structure of the quest to return home, suggesting that the mythic patterns deliberately used in this episode may resonate throughout the whole series.

The Sirens constitute Odysseus' first heroic encounter after his trip to Hades, and seem by implication to be close to the dead world 'of purely retrospective heroism'.[157] Their connection with death and stagnancy is emphasised by the still waters that surround them.[158] This stagnancy can be related not only to the Sirens' potential to halt the homeward journey, but also to Circe's warning that those who listen to the Sirens do not depart again.[159] Odysseus does not say whether there are indeed bones of the dead around the Sirens, as Circe claims, and the Sirens themselves claim that one can listen and then freely depart.[160] Unlike Odysseus in the *Odyssey*, in 'Favorite Son' Harry receives no warnings about the deadly intent of the Taresians,[161] and instead is lured by fake memories that make him believe he belongs with them. But while the presence of remains surrounding the Sirens is never corroborated in the *Odyssey*, the lethal nature of the Taresians in 'Favorite Son' is confirmed with the discovery of the corpse.

This threat is directly related to the Taresians' sexuality. The viewer of various *Star Trek* programmes will be aware that love interests from outside the central spaceship usually last only for one episode,[162] and are frequently treacherous or manipulative in nature. Despite the *Star Trek* edict of equality of races, this tendency seems little improved upon the *Odyssey*'s own distinction between Greek and non-Greek women.[163] Although the allure of Homer's Sirens lies in their promise of knowledge and epic poetry, the language they use is distinctly sexual, as is their location on a flowery meadow, which as Doherty notes is 'a setting connected elsewhere in archaic poetry with sexual encounters'.[164] The Taresians bypass such allusions, instead overtly offering the lure of no less than group sex. Their sexual drive is, however, channelled specifically for reproductive purposes. The Sirens of the *Odyssey* lack this feature, their subtle sexual connotations augmented in *Voyager*.[165]

Despite its twenty-fourth-century setting, then, 'Favorite Son' divests the Sirens of their role as holders of great knowledge, and instead depicts the Taresians in terms of the dangerous nature of female reproductive power. Significantly, while *Voyager* has a female captain, it is a male ensign through which the Sirens story is told, not Captain Kathryn Janeway. Although *Voyager*'s ensemble cast allows different characters to feature prominently in different episodes, Janeway is closer to Odysseus in rank and function as the leader of her ship and crew. 'Favorite Son' reworks the Sirens incident in order to adapt it to the *Star Trek* world and *Voyager* in particular; however, the choice of Harry and the addition of procreation as the source of the Taresian threat suggest a return to the type of gender stereotyping often present in *TOS*.[166]

'Favorite Son' aligns itself and *Voyager* as a whole with myth by retelling a famous mythic story, maintaining some elements and changing others. That the gender stereotyping of the episode is reminiscent of *TOS* leads us to consider this retelling in the context of the broader *Star Trek* array. The original release videotape sleeve for 'Favorite Son' explicitly links the episode with earlier episodes from *TOS* and *TNG*.[167] Under the heading 'Species Survival', the sleeve notes that in *TOS* episode 'Wink of an Eye' (1968), the crew encounter a species whose men have been rendered sterile. The queen of these aliens attempts to take all the men from the *Enterprise* in order to repopulate the planet, focusing her personal attentions on Captain Kirk. Although in terms of Greek myth this plot seems closer to the Lemnian women of the *Argonautica* than the Sirens of the *Odyssey*, the 'Favorite Son' VHS sleeve makes a different connection on our behalf, a paratextual invitation to read these two episodes in relation to one another.

The various alignments and discontinuities between Homer's description of Odysseus and the Sirens and *Voyager*'s version of the tale will be evident only if the viewer is in possession of specific knowledge. Similarly, the episode's alignment with earlier *Star Trek* series can only be appreciated if the viewer has either seen the other episodes in question or has read the video sleeve, which carries information that was not included on the later DVD box sets, and would also be absent when streaming.[168] Visually, the saturated reds and oranges of the Taresian costumes with their black neck trim are reminiscent of *TOS*' uniforms (see Figure 2.3). While in 'Who Mourns for Adonais?' Greek antiquity is suggested through the iconography of columns and gold Greco-Roman clothing, in 'Favorite Son' the iconography suggests not the *Odyssey* from which the plot is adapted, but rather *TOS*. The metonymic mythic function, as extended from Foley, here becomes multifaceted, visually denoting *TOS* tradition, verbally referencing the Sirens/Odysseus tradition and, through a shared narrative structure, combining the two. Both *Star Trek*'s own 'myth' and the myth of Odysseus are quoted and retold, blurring the boundary between myth and 'myth'.

Intertextuality consists of not only explicit textual and paratextual allusions, but also a broader field of reference that draws on cultural memory. The 'Favorite Son' video sleeve does *not* make a connection with *The Animated Series* episode 'The Lorelei Signal' (1973), which takes its name

The New Mythology

Figure 2.3 The Taresian aliens in *Voyager*'s 'Favorite Son' (Paramount Television 1997).

from the Germanic equivalent of the Sirens. In this episode, a group of alien women whose own men have all died ensnare the men of other species through beautiful visions, and then drain them of their life force. Not only does the Taurean system in which these women live closely resemble the planet Taresia from 'Favorite Son' in name, but the plot and Siren theme are also quite similar in both episodes. Yet this episode is not mentioned on the 'Favorite Son' VHS sleeve, nor in the DVD extras, thereby paratextually situating 'Favorite Son' within a specific *Star Trek* array that privileges the live-action series over other media forms. Actor Garrett Wang discusses the episode in the DVD extra '*Voyager* Time Capsule: Harry Kim' (2004) as the first instance of an Asian American male actor kissing an African American female actor on television. This recalls the first interracial kiss to appear in a scripted television programme in *TOS* episode 'Plato's Stepchildren' (1968), in this case between a white man (Kirk) and a black woman (Uhura). Although Wang does not specifically mention this connection, it is well-known *Star Trek* lore. While the 'Favorite Son' episode itself, and the video sleeve, suggest connections the viewer can make to other texts, this does not preclude other connections within or beyond the *Star Trek* array into other episodes and spin-offs, as each viewer mobilises their personal and shared popular culture memories. The current, official StarTrek.com guide to the episode makes no reference to any other episodes whatsoever, meaning that in this case any such connections rely entirely upon a viewer's memory. If both myth and 'myth' can be understood as intertexts, they are made up of all the different versions known to an audience,[169] which may be highlighted or ignored by the text or its official paratexts, but may nonetheless be activated by memory.

Irad Malkin argues that 'the *myth* of Odysseus' is made up not only of 'the epic narrative of the *Odyssey*, but also alternative versions and "sequels", pictorial images [...] and forms of cult'.[170] Although described in text, the myth of Odysseus is not contained in any single text. Even by the early Classical period, the Sirens in particular had been refashioned many times.[171] *Voyager*'s 'Favorite Son' episode is but one in a long line of retellings that retain some aspects of the tale, yet transform others. Equally, the Sirens and the *Odyssey* are used in order to retell *Star Trek*'s own form of popular culture 'mythology'. Both the Siren myth and *Star Trek*'s own 'myth' are retold in a continuous process of quotation.

Conclusion

Star Trek appropriates myth and transposes it into its futuristic, high-tech diegesis. Despite this shift in setting, the traditional mythic process of retelling is maintained. Popular culture texts also have their own textual and cultural traditions that can be drawn upon and reinvigorated. *Star Trek* is thereby able to present itself as a form of contemporary 'myth' both through its alignment with pre-existing myth, and through its self-quotation. In a television franchise that quotes its own past and consciously aligns itself with myth through quotation and advertising to bolster its cultural and economic position, the 'myth' of *Star Trek* is ultimately a set of relations between the varied notions of myth that are mobilised by writers, producers and audiences.

3

Star Trek Title Sequences and Cosmology as Myth

As long as there have been humans, we have searched for our place in the Cosmos [...] We find that we live on an insignificant planet of a humdrum star lost between two spiral arms in the outskirts of a galaxy which is a member of a sparse cluster of galaxies, tucked away in some forgotten corner of a universe in which there are far more galaxies than people [...] There are those who secretly deplore these great discoveries, who consider every step a demotion, who in their heart of hearts still pine for a universe whose center, focus and fulcrum is the Earth.[1]

Introduction

This chapter argues that the title sequences of the *Star Trek* television programmes situate us in space and provide not only a physical location, but also a way of mythologising the role of humanity and Earth within an expanded cosmos. *Star Trek* mediates scientific discourses about the cosmos through story and image, a role that in millennia past belonged to myth. Indeed, Karl S. Guthke argues that once science fiction goes beyond the limits of scientific knowledge in its depiction of the cosmos, it enters into the realm of myth. Guthke says, 'we cannot lightly dismiss the view that the mythology of science fiction has a grip on the minds of many people today comparable to that of myth in other societies in the past or at the present time'.[2] In the sixteenth century, Nicholas Copernicus suggested that we live in a Sun-centred cosmos, in which Earth was merely one of many planets. This prompted scientists to imagine that other worlds might also be inhabited. Centuries later, science fiction works such as the *Star Trek* franchise assume a multitude of inhabited worlds, affirming the implications of the Copernican world view.[3] At the same time, in the title sequences to programmes such as *TNG* and *Enterprise*, Earth is restored as the centre of our human cosmos, reasserting our lost primacy. The *Star Trek* franchise thereby attempts to mediate our scientific knowledge of a heliocentric system (and the possibility this opens up for multiple inhabited worlds) and our human sensory experience of an Earth-based existence. In this way, *Star Trek* forms a mythology that goes beyond science in order to comprehend our place within the post-Copernican cosmos.

Star Trek's advertising and official products increasingly and consciously market the franchise's longevity in terms of legend, myth and epic. In turn, each television series' title sequence implicitly constructs a cosmological perspective that draws on both mythological and scientific discourses on the nature, arrangement and origins of the cosmos, and the place of humanity within that cosmos. In particular, *Enterprise*'s title sequence harnesses the latent cosmological discourses of the earlier series in a deliberate attempt to meld *Star Trek* with the cosmological breakthroughs of the (real historic) past. In the previous chapter, *Voyager* was used to highlight *Star Trek*'s multiple engagement with the myths of antiquity and those *Star Trek* has forged for itself in popular culture. In this chapter, *Enterprise* will be given extended consideration because it so explicitly engages with the history of cosmological imagery in its furthering of the *Star Trek* mythos through its title sequences. As each *Star Trek* television series frames its episodes within title and credit sequences, it not only marks the boundaries of the text, but also positions us physically and ideologically within the cosmos.

Space-themed programmes, such as the various *Star Trek* series, take on the function once served by cosmological myths. Beginning in the scientific revolution of the sixteenth and seventeenth centuries, speculative science fiction became the inheritor of cosmological myth-making, blending astronomical science with speculation about alien species and the wider cosmos. Because *Star Trek*'s fictional cosmos is part science and part myth, it is important to set the franchise within the broader history of cosmology that it implicitly, and in many cases explicitly, draws upon.

Cosmology, Myth and Science

In a variety of ancient cultures, cosmogony (theories about the origins of the universe) and cosmology (theories about the ordering and nature of the universe) were explained through myth.[4] In oral storytelling, myths combined cosmogony and cosmology with heroic and divine narratives. This combination of a divine story and cosmological theory can still be found today in many practised religions. However, scientific teaching constitutes a primary means through which most of us reach a basic understanding of a wider universe we will never access firsthand. Storytelling still performs a cosmological function. The oral origins of storytelling are now reworked in literature, film and television. Even when fictional, stories can mediate our understanding of science, rendering it more accessible through narrative. In particular, science fiction frequently takes us off our own planet and into a real or imagined cosmos that draws imaginatively on science. *Star Trek* shares with older cosmological traditions a mythological underpinning, as well as continuing a relationship between science and the creative arts that has its own long tradition within scientific discourse.

Within the broader, if much debated, classification of myth, academics have further marked out types of myth with common narrative elements. Of all the different possible types of myth (for example, hero myths, myths of an underworld and afterlife), this chapter examines myths dealing with the origins and ordering of the universe. Such myths have been classified under a number of headings, such as cosmogony, cosmology and theogony. While theogony refers to the origin (literally begetting) of the gods and their genealogy, such tales often also involve the creation of the universe.

For example, in the Greek tradition, the Muses in Hesiod's *Theogony* (c.700 BCE) tell us:

> In truth at first Chaos came to be, but next wide-bosomed Earth [...] From Chaos came forth Erebus and black Night; but of Night were born Aether and Day, whom she conceived and bore from union in love with Erebus. And Earth first bore starry Heaven, equal to herself, to cover her on every side.[5]

Once the universe's physical foundations and the gods' genealogical trail have been set in motion, Hesiod's *Theogony* is ultimately concerned with the rule of Zeus over the other gods and the cosmos itself. Honko notes that cosmogonies and theogonies may be used to affirm social and political realities as natural and ordained.[6] Like other forms of myth, they can communicate communal ideas about both the natural and social world.[7] Myths can also be used as tools for connecting the cosmos to the smaller human sphere of activity. For example, an Assyrian incantation from 1000 BCE called 'The Worm and the Toothache' begins with the creation of the universe and ends with a cure for toothache.[8] The grandest and the smallest elements of existence are thereby bound together in the cosmos through an overarching origin story.[9]

In ancient oral cultures cosmology belonged to myth, in a blurring of storytelling, scientific theory, theology and history. Today, cosmology belongs primarily to science and theology. As Arlow argues: 'Each age and culture has proposed its own answers to the question of how the cosmos began [...] In our age, apprehension of the physical world is formulated in terms of science.'[10] While the exploratory tools differ, science must still convert its data into narratives, tiered for the expert and the layperson. Scientific cosmology in some instances does not stray very far from earlier mythological accounts. Arlow notes, 'Just as in the cosmologies of modern science, in many mythologies the origin of the universe begins with an epic clash or struggle that brings the primordial chaos to an end.'[11] The Greek cosmogony cited above begins with Chaos, out of which matter emerges. Scientific theories of the Big Bang similarly begin with chaotic explosion that brings the universe into being.[12] While the explanation of these events differs, neither myth nor science has answered the question of what pre-empted the first cataclysmic event at the dawn of the universe.[13] Arlow argues that:

> In the last analysis, after all that has been learned, must the final judgment of cosmology depend upon faith in the same way as more primitive people placed their faith in the cosmogonic theories of their mythology? If there was indeed a unique moment marking the beginning of time, neither science nor mythology possesses a definitive answer concerning the nature of the first cause [...] In a special sense, a scientific cosmology is the mythology of the astronomer [...] a set of speculations that cannot be proven by observation or experiment, used to explain what cannot be experienced.[14]

As the complexity of science takes it beyond the detailed understanding of the layperson, the scientist becomes a myth-maker, providing stories to explain the universe that are accepted as a matter of belief.[15]

By prompting us to consider the vastness and mystery of the universe, astronomy and cosmology force us to look for meaning beyond science, and in doing so, to be open to new ideas and new discoveries that challenge our belief structure.[16] Stoeger argues that 'cosmology and astronomy play this role more forcefully and less ambiguously than many of the other sciences do. This is because their subject matter takes us beyond ourselves in space and time.'[17] We require imagination, as much as scientific thought, in order to contemplate cosmology. In this way, for Stoeger, science can be both empirical and mythological, providing new origin stories that tally with our scientific culture but have a mythological function in facilitating our relationship with the universe in a meaningful way.[18]

Cosmology and the Creative Arts

While origin stories in science are transmitted through scientific articles in academic books and journals, and in less detailed form in the popular press, science also has a long tradition of mediating new ideas in more creative forms, such as fiction and art. This tradition has been continued in newer technological forms of storytelling and visual representation, such as television and film. Garoian and Mathews argue that creativity has always had a place in scientific thought, in making conceptual leaps in experimental science or imagining new theories that are only then tested experimentally: 'For example, Einstein gave verbal/visual expression to the basics of general relativity (in the famous elevator 'thought experiment' [...]) well before the necessary mathematical structure for *precise* expression was in place.'[19] For Garoian and Mathews the role of creativity in science is hardly surprising, given that they see both science and the arts as 'products of human curiosity and creativity and the human need for expression.'[20] Both science and the arts are part of the need to understand the world and communicate a particular understanding of that world.

While creativity can precede and enable subsequent science, it also has a role in its dissemination, communicating cosmological ideas to the non-scientist in story form. Storytelling as a means of communicating ideas about the natural world has a long history. For example, it has been suggested that 'Greek myths might have been deliberate devices for organizing and transmitting information about the natural world to non-scientifically oriented people.'[21] As noted in the Introduction, Theagenes of Rhêgium (*c.*525 BCE) proposed a similar idea as far back as Archaic Greece, by suggesting the gods represented natural elements.[22] Nonetheless, stories overtly based upon scientific theory were rare in antiquity.[23]

It is, perhaps ironically, with the scientific revolution in the sixteenth and seventeenth centuries that we find scientists themselves deliberately using speculative fiction to explain new scientific findings and ideas. Nicholas Copernicus' *De Revolutionibus Orbium Coelestium Revolutionibus* of 1543 suggested that the Sun did not move, and that it lay near the centre of the universe.[24] Basing his publication on intellectual reasoning rather than new empirical work, the Copernican 'revolution' from a geocentric (Earth-centred) to a heliocentric (Sun-centred) understanding of the cosmos was, in fact, 'a *long-term* event – some one hundred fifty years in the making.'[25] The work of Copernicus nonetheless prompted other scientists to consider the implications of a heliocentric universe in which Earth is one of many planets that revolve around the Sun, drawing on speculative fantasy as much as science.

For example, in Johannes Kepler's *Somnium* (*The Dream*), written in 1609 and published in 1634, space travellers journey to the Moon, where they watch the Earth above.[26] The Moon inhabitants call their world Levania, and Kepler writes that 'Levania seems to its inhabitants to be stationary, while the stars go around it, just as the earth seems to us to be stationary.'[27] In an explanatory footnote, Kepler argues that perception, therefore, cannot be used as proof of a stationary Earth.[28] Following Galileo's discoveries of Moon craters with the use of his improved telescope in 1609–10, Kepler added an Appendix to *Somnium*, in which these craters are explained as the towns of Moon inhabitants.[29] Kepler's narrative thereby affirmed recent science in story form, but also went beyond established and observed scientific fact into speculation. It is, then, an early science fiction work.

Science fiction as a genre was new at this time and not distinguished from science proper. In Kepler's book, the hero's mother contacts spirits and calls forth a 'deamon' who is able to tell them about the Moon.[30] Due to the lack of distinction between science and science fiction at the time, Kepler's mother was charged with witchcraft on the basis of his book.[31] Indeed, superstition, magic, occultism, alchemy and astrology all remained prevalent in Kepler's time.[32] Kepler himself cast horoscopes for court.[33] That a number of sixteenth- and seventeenth-century works merged science with science fiction, and cosmological theory with story,[34] was in keeping with the fluidity between scientific rationalism and older beliefs at the time.

Speculation about the nature of heavenly bodies extended to speculation about worlds yet to be discovered. Giordano Bruno was the first person to explicitly state that there may be other worlds around other suns;[35] however, in their time, some people had thought this was implied in the work of Copernicus and Kepler.[36] In his 1698 work *The Celestial Worlds Discov'd* (also known as *Cosmotheoros*), Christiaan Huygens imagined that there might be societies on other planets that mirrored our own.[37] The possibility of new worlds in the cosmos coincided with the new and strange lands being discovered on Earth during the sixteenth and seventeenth centuries. As Cohen notes, in art, geographical exploration and the exploration of new scientific ideas were linked through seafaring imagery, in particular the 'explorer's ship'.[38] For example, the title page to Francis Bacon's 1620 treatise *Instauratio magna* or *Great Instauration* depicts a ship sailing beyond the Pillars of Hercules that were said to have marked the edge of the known world in antiquity. By implication, Bacon was suggesting his work went beyond the previous limits of human exploration and knowledge.[39]

Images of the newly discovered worlds and their inhabitants drew as much, and sometimes more, on imagination and fantasy traditions as they did on observation. A 1599 depiction of a tribe of Indigenous Americans drew on a belief that there were men and women without heads, with faces in their chests.[40] This fantasy had been present in speculative travel books from the medieval period.[41] Maps similarly depicted fantasy and mythological creatures inhabiting the edges of the known world.[42] In the context of existing information, misinformation and speculation about different creatures that might be living on Earth itself, Kepler's crater-making Moon-men and other speculative tales about space seemed all the more credible.

While both accurate and highly imaginative images transmitted ideas about the new worlds to be found on Earth, so too cosmological ideas were expressed through visual imagery. As William B. Ashworth Jr. has noted, seventeenth-century writers often used illustrations in the place of long, explanatory introductions.[43] The illustrations used allusions and allegories that would have been familiar to readers at the time, even if their meaning can at first appear obscure today.[44] The use of imagery also tied into a broader understanding of the universe in symbolic terms. Ashworth explains that 'until the mid-1600s, the universe itself was seen as a vast hieroglyph, filled with concealed significance. One studied the natural world by sorting through the signs, symbols, and correspondences that were built into the cosmic structure.'[45] This worldview 'overlapped' with 'the more mechanical view of nature that followed', such that there was a period in which 'astronomy and allegory combined to produce a rich visual vocabulary'.[46] Central to this visual exposition of scientific ideas was the emblem, which combined an image with a motto in order to communicate an idea, including the new cosmological ideas.[47]

Rather than merely asserting one cosmological model, some frontispieces attested to their truthfulness through direct comparison with rival models. For example, the frontispiece to Riccioli's *New Algamest* of 1651 shows the Copernican model of the universe being weighed against the Tychonic model, in which the Sun and Moon orbit around Earth, while the rest of the planets orbit the Sun.[48] In the *New Algamest*, Riccioli outlines his own variation on the Tychonic model, and as such the frontispiece image shows the Tychonic model as being weightier than the light (and therefore less worthy) Copernican model.[49] Rival scientific approaches were fought through artistic representation and not merely through written argument or story.

Representations of the new science also found their way into art in a non-science context. In 1612, Ludovico Cigoli frescoed the Moon with shadowed craters in the chapel of Pope Paul V in Santa Maria Maggiore, Rome. This was against artistic convention but in keeping with Galileo's images of the Moon, published two years earlier.[50] Scientific cosmological discourses were filtered through art, both within and beyond scientific works themselves. Art was a means of mediating new scientific thought, serving as a creative means of understanding the cosmos and our place within it.

In the seventeenth century, the distinction between science and science fiction simply did not exist, or was at the very least in the process of being articulated.[51] Similarly, argument through image and argument through word were closely connected. Today, fictional narratives, images, film and television (which combine the two) draw on scientific knowledge and new scientific ideas. Science fiction became the inheritor of the blending of astronomical science with speculation about alien species and cultures initiated in the sixteenth and seventeenth centuries. Although not often explicitly intended as an educational tool, science fiction continues to be a means through which science can be transformed into image and story, and in so doing, communicate scientific concepts.[52] Just as the scientific cosmological discourses of the sixteenth and seventeenth centuries found expression in non-scientific artwork, today fictional works reimagine contemporary science for a lay audience.

There is a considerable variation in the degree of speculation within science fiction texts, but the role of the popular media in conveying scientific information arguably increases as research science becomes too complex for the layperson to understand. Apple and Apple note the importance of popular media within the scientific discourse, particularly if science cannot be accessed directly by a non-specialist:

> Popular-cultural forms, including films and television, play a crucial role in teaching a large population about what science was, is, and should be. These media may not portray the histories of science and scientists in ways that make historians comfortable – they popularize, distort, stereotype, and simplify. But it is clear that many people learn just as much about the history of science from, say, films as they do from their formal education.[53]

While Apple and Apple are primarily concerned with the history of science and its representation, their comments are also more broadly applicable. Film and television take on new areas of science and present them in narrative form, finding ways to turn them into speculative gadgetry or plot twists. As Constance Penley argues:

> Popular science involves the efforts of scientists, science writers, and scientific institutions to attract interest and support for advancing science and technology. Popular science includes the many science fiction television shows (and fewer films) that offer a personalized, utopian reflection on men and women in space. Popular science is fictional work that carries on this reflection.[54]

Science fiction programmes need not always be a 'utopian reflection' of the development of science and the journey of humanity into space. However, science fiction can be regarded as loosely belonging to a broader scientific discourse in the popular domain. Science fiction personalises and simplifies scientific concepts, while sometimes broadening the consideration of their impact upon humanity by extending those consequences to an as-yet-unrealised degree or application. In the intersection of known science and imagined narrative, science fiction takes on the functional role of cosmological myth, explaining the cosmos and our place within it through story and image.

Aside from speculative narratives involving possible alien species, technology and future history, science fiction in film and television has also

Star Trek Title Sequences and Cosmology as Myth

visually represented the solar system and broader universe as its backdrop. This is particularly the case with programmes focused on space travel. As David Pringle argues, 'Given the interstellar-tending-to-intergalactic settings of most space opera, it seems natural that the form should often embody cosmic or even cosmological themes.'[55] Even when not pivotal to the plot, science fiction can nonetheless communicate underlying assumptions about the cosmos.

The Original Series (1966-9)

The longevity of the *Star Trek* franchise means that it has become a recognised component within a popular culture discourse of science and space, even for those who have never seen the programme. A search on NASA's homepage will bring up numerous entries for *Star Trek* and its relationship with NASA's own real endeavours, a recent indication of Constance Penley's argument that NASA/*Trek* has become a combined discourse on space travel.[56] By linking itself with *Star Trek*, NASA promotes the *Star Trek* mythology of a more successful future of space exploration, for which NASA becomes the necessary precursor. The NASA/*Trek* connection has continued although its nature has changed over the decades between *TOS* and *Enterprise*. The *Star Trek* franchise reveals changing fictional and factual discourses on the nature of space and our human place within it.

In a 1988 interview, the creator of *Star Trek*, Gene Roddenberry, recalled:

> I was very afraid when I started *Star Trek* that scientists would say 'Oh God, you're so inaccurate, and you're so wrong,' and I almost hated to deal with them at first. Until I discovered that they're not like that. They're intelligent, and because they're intelligent, they understand the problems of show business. And they understand that I had to appeal to a mass audience as well as a specialised audience.[57]

Like the Copernican 'revolution' of the sixteenth and seventeenth centuries, the late 1950s and the 1960s mark another profound change in the way people looked at the cosmos. New discoveries were made through space exploration and not just through the telescope. Science fiction formats such as *Star Trek* could draw on the burgeoning space programme and imagine its future potential through fiction, blurring real concerns with fantasy.

Science and science fiction discourses are never entirely separate. Curator Mary Henderson of the Smithsonian's National Air and Space Museum defended the inclusion of a *Star Trek* exhibition in 1992 because 'there is no other fantasy more pervasive in the conceptualization of space flight than Star Trek'.[58] Futuristic fiction provides a forum in which the potential implications of space travel for humanity can be explored. In his foreword to *The Physics of Star Trek*, physicist Stephen Hawking writes, 'Science fiction like *Star Trek* is not only good fun but it also serves a serious purpose, that of expanding the human imagination.'[59] Indeed, in the 1993 *TNG* episode 'Descent', Hawking made a guest appearance in a poker game with Albert Einstein, Isaac Newton and Lieutenant Commander Data on the holodeck[60] of the *Enterprise*. Hawking's guest appearance blurred the lines between contemporary science, past science, contemporary fiction about the future and the potential of that future itself. Unlike Kepler's readers, the *Star Trek* viewer realises that science fiction uses imaginary elements that separate it from science itself. However, this does not negate the cultural role that science fiction plays in mediating new scientific discoveries for a lay audience, simplifying their underlying scientific premises, yet complicating the potential implications for humanity and our place in the cosmos. As Consolmagno noted in 1996, 'with more than 10 million households tuned in every week' to *Star Trek* programmes, 'probably more people today learn about modern astronomy from this show than from any other single source'.[61]

As noted in Chapter 1, in the late 1940s and early 1950s, science fiction in its television form had been closely associated with children's fantasy adventure programmes. However, what had seemed merely fantastic speculation for children was drawing closer to fact as the decade progressed, with the launch of Sputnik by the USSR on 4 October 1957. By contrast, the US Vanguard I was nicknamed 'Flopnik', 'Kaputnik' and 'Stayputnik' after it exploded on the launch pad on 6 December 1957.[62] Despite the formation of NASA in 1958, Russian successes continued to pre-empt US efforts. As

Star Trek Title Sequences and Cosmology as Myth

Edward W. Ploman points out, 'the Russians had managed both Sputnik 2 and the space dog Lajka [...] before the Americans had launched their first satellite, Explorer 1' on 31 January 1958.[63] On 12 April 1961, Russian Yuri Gagarin became the first human in space. On 5 May 1961, Alan Shepard became the first US astronaut in space, but the US space programme itself was still lagging behind. However, President John F. Kennedy's hopes for an invigorated (and more heavily funded) US space effort cast imagined space missions in a new, more realistic light.

In his speech before a Joint Session of Congress on 25 May 1961, Kennedy declared:

> Now it is time to take longer strides – time for a great new American enterprise – time for this nation to take a clearly leading role in space achievement, which in many ways may hold the key to our future on earth [...] Recognizing the head start obtained by the Soviets [...] we nevertheless are required to make new efforts on our own. [...] But this is not merely a race. Space is open to us now [...] First, I believe that this nation should commit itself to achieving the goal, before this decade is out, of landing a man on the moon and returning him safely to the earth [...] no one can predict with certainty what the ultimate meaning will be of mastery of space.[64]

Kennedy expanded on the meaning of this new Space Race in an address at Rice University, Texas, on 12 September 1962, where he used seafaring imagery that harked back to the earlier era of exploration and scientific advancement:

> We set sail on this new sea because there is new knowledge to be gained, and new rights to be won, and they must be won and used for the progress of all people [...] I do say that space can be explored and mastered without feeding the fires of war, without repeating the mistakes that man made in extending his writ around this globe of ours.[65]

TOS affirmed Kennedy's vision through a multinational, multiracial crew, which suggested that in the age of space exploration humans could indeed overcome their differences. Even television critic Cleveland Amory, who dismissed the show as kids' fare, noted of the *Enterprise* crew, that 'altogether, they're so darn well-integrated internationally that it seems a pity to waste them on outer space. We need them right here on Earth.'[66] In the 1967 time-travel episode 'Tomorrow is Yesterday', Captain Kirk confirmed that the first manned Moon shot would take place in the late 1960s, in keeping with Kennedy's proclamation.[67] The original air date for the episode, 26 January 1967, was just one day before a fire in a NASA module claimed the lives of three Apollo astronauts.[68] *Star Trek* affirmed the future success of a then-struggling space programme, encapsulating the possibilities of science.

The potential of television science fiction to contribute to the discourse of the Space Race had not been taken particularly seriously due to the genre's association with children, at least on the small screen, as discussed in Chapter 1. When *Star Trek* debuted in September 1966, it was classified as 'Adventure' by *TV Guide*, and given a prime-time adult slot of 8.30pm on a Thursday evening.[69] In the descriptive blurb, it was also called 'science fiction' and was said to be on a 'space patrol', a reference to the earlier children's television programme of the same name. Early TV science fiction had been split between space adventures for children and anthologies (of which only a few episodes were spacefaring) for adults.[70] In this context *Star Trek* was an anomaly, as an evening space adventure programme for both adults and older children. The wider tendency towards bifurcation of the genre on television can be seen in an early review of *Star Trek*. Cleveland Amory suggested that adult viewers follow Captain Kirk's advice to a crew member in 'Shore Leave' (1966): 'Face front. Don't talk. Don't think. Don't breathe. For the kids, though, let 'em breathe. Let 'em even hallucinate. They'll love it.'[71] For Amory, *Star Trek* remained the domain of children, partly, it would seem, because most episodes 'involve shoot-'em-ups of one sort or other', aligning the programme with earlier space adventures for the younger set.[72]

As fictional space travel was increasingly paralleled by real attempts at space travel, other commentators in the contemporary media began to see cultural alignments between the two. Rather than being dismissed as merely speculative fantasy for children, space-based science fiction television programmes in the 1960s were linked in the popular press with

Star Trek Title Sequences and Cosmology as Myth

the real Space Race, albeit often disparagingly. Science fiction writer Isaac Asimov writes of the 1966 season of science fiction programmes (including *Star Trek*):

> We are faced with a television achievement this season that must surely make the bosom of every space-conscious American glow with pride and make him [sic] thankful to the great men of the TV world who are contributing so much to the educational enrichment of our children and to the Space Race we are conducting against the Chaps On The Other Side. Our science-fiction programs are, I am glad to report, accurate except for occasional slips like not knowing what a galaxy is, or a star, or a planet, or possible speeds, or actual distances, or the nature of space and time. Everything else, like, for instance, the fact that men and women have two arms and two legs apiece, they've got perfect.[73]

However, *Star Trek* soon became popular with many scientists involved with the real Space Race. At a meeting of the National Space Club in March 1966, Leonard Nimoy (Mr Spock) was told, 'Cape Kennedy practically shuts down when *Star Trek* is on'.[74] The designs for the *Enterprise* were arrived at in consultation with NASA's Jet Propulsion Laboratory.[75] As creator Gene Roddenberry noted in 1967, 'We seem to appeal to everybody, from the kids through the science-fiction buffs to the top scientists in the country'.[76] Despite his initial criticisms, Asimov himself came to love *Star Trek*, 'because it is well-done, because it is exciting, because it says things (subtly and neatly) that are difficult to say in "straight" drama, and because science fiction, properly presented, is the type of literature most appropriate to our generation'.[77] The adventures of *Star Trek*'s Starship *Enterprise* could harness the excitement surrounding Kennedy's vision for 'a great new American enterprise' in space.[78]

This synergy is evident in the programme's titles. Kennedy's desire to travel to 'the furthest outpost on the new frontier of science and space'[79] was reflected in *Star Trek*'s voice-over, in which Captain Kirk (William Shatner) proclaims: 'Space, the final frontier. These are the voyages of the Starship *Enterprise*. Its five-year mission to explore strange new worlds, to seek out new life and new civilizations, to boldly go where no man has gone before.' Roland Barthes argues that words serve to fix the interpretation of images, offering a legitimised way of reading them.[80] Similarly, voice-overs can be seen as delivering information about the diegetic images and narrative realm, but also a particular point of view,[81] even if the meaning provided is not as securely 'anchored' as Barthes suggests. The title imagery of *TOS* situates us in unidentified space, moving slowly forward among the stars. In doing so, the programme was drawing upon pre-existing tropes in the title sequences to earlier science fiction programmes that had also featured unidentified space in their opening titles, from the television version of *Flash Gordon* (1954–5), to *Lost in Space* (1965–8), which had debuted the year before *TOS*. The Starship *Enterprise* appears, and then travels past a large red planet, which is not named in the titles. Through its colour, this new alien world is visually associated with our planetary neighbour Mars, although in the programme the *Enterprise* visits many red planets. Kirk/Shatner's voice-over suggests that we are placed near one of the 'strange new worlds', going where no human has ventured either in the 1960s or in the *Star Trek* future. The *mise-en-scène* and voice-over of the title sequence thereby set the physical scene for the story. But they also establish a connection between the viewer and that setting, and a particular perspective, much as the frontispieces of seventeenth-century books situated the reader before they undertook the written scientific treatise itself.

Film title-maker Saul Bass argued that titles are designed 'to set mood and to prime the underlying core of the film [...as] a way of conditioning the audience, so that when the film actually began, viewers would already have an emotional resonance with it'.[82] The title sequence is another form of paratext, in this case a specific boundary zone designed to lead us into the text, intellectually and emotionally.[83] However, because of the series and serial structure common to television, the titles are repeated from episode to episode, creating a ritualised boundary.[84] This opening sequence also serves to advertise what the television show can offer the viewer, particularly a viewer not yet committed to the programme. Cathy Schwichtenberg argues that 'the opening sequence functions as a kind of rhetorical "hook" or interest-statement which provides the viewer with a context and a promise of what the show's narrative will fulfil',[85] either in the individual episode or across the entire series. The title sequence thereby initiates a set of expectations about the show, designed to keep our viewing interest. Thus, John Ellis has argued that 'the title sequence is in effect a commercial for the programme itself'.[86] In *TOS* we are positioned in space near a 'strange new world' with the promise that there will be more to come in the series. By mirroring the language of Kennedy's speeches on space travel, *TOS*' voice-over promises to see the president's ambitions for the new frontier realised. The myth of space prevails over the contemporary reality of space.

In an audiovisual medium such as television, repeated titles are often identified as much through distinctive music as any visual components. Indeed, John Ellis and Rick Altman argue that, for broadcast television, sound has precedence over image, because it can call us back from our domestic activities and draw our attention to what is happening on the screen.[87] More specifically, Janet K. Halfyard calls the television theme tune 'a call to attention'.[88] Sound cues such as music, lyrics, voice-overs, dialogue and sound effects in the opening sequences can, therefore, be as important as what is shown, if not more so. Music can also establish a sense of time, place and emotion.[89]

TOS' title tune, written by Alexander Courage, begins 'with a four note, *mysterioso* theme played by chimes over tremulous strings'.[90] This is followed by the brass '*Enterprise* Fanfare', before leading into the main title theme itself, characterised by bongo drums and a soprano melody, replaced in Season 3 by a synthesised voice.[91] Each component musically suggests quite different themes: beginning with intrigue; then the stridently official, even military, associations of a brass fanfare; and the otherworldly jazz/pop of what Jeff Bond calls the 'siren song'.[92] Composer Courage recalls that *Star Trek*'s creator, Gene Roddenberry, had instructed him to avoid 'goddamned funny-sounding space science fiction music' and instead wanted 'adventure music'.[93] Courage personally 'wanted to have a kind of exotic feel to it'.[94] Therefore, the main tune is based on a Scottish folk song, with 'a fast-moving accompaniment to get the adventure and the speed'.[95] The journey to 'strange new worlds' that Kirk's voice-over promised is suggested through the 'questing and heroic' sounds of the brass fanfare.[96] Neil Lerner interprets the subsequent main theme, with its beguine tempo and Latin American percussion, as Captain Kirk's personal theme, a type of 'bachelor pad music'.[97] Jessica L. Getman in turn notes that Gene Roddenberry's unused lyrics to the tune feature a female narrator and suggest a heterosexual love theme.[98] Given the mysterious sound of the soprano melody, we can also read it as the alien other: the 'new life and new civilizations' of which Kirk speaks.

Human proficiency in these new areas of space is suggested through the Starship *Enterprise* as an advanced piece of technology. The title theme tune increases in volume as the voice-over ends, and written credits appear between fly-bys of the *Enterprise* through starry space. In a somewhat disorienting move, the *Enterprise* leaves the screen at the lower right foreground, only to re-emerge in far space and head left.[99] The extraordinary ability of the *Enterprise* to loop around in space between written credits emphasises the camera's role as our reference point, where there are no other stable objects in view. The speed of the ship highlights its technological abilities, and its mastery – and indeed that of the predominantly human crew running it – over the expanding frontier.

Star Trek affirms the post-Copernican consideration of multiple inhabited planets, yet does so within a new era of changing perceptions of space and the place of humanity within it. The Space Race opened up for the first time the real possibility of actually reaching some of those 'strange new worlds', beginning with the journey to our nearest neighbour, the Moon. The seemingly effortless technological mastery of the *Enterprise* over space, exemplified by the opening titles, suggests that contemporary human endeavours would indeed be successful. Kennedy's 'time for a great new American enterprise' is transposed from the 1960s to the twenty-third century, embodied in the Starship *Enterprise*. Spacefaring television programmes of the late 1950s through to the 1960s attracted a cultural resonance that they had previously lacked. Indeed, programmes such as *TOS* fulfilled in fictional form the real-life attempts to enter space, contributing to the conceptual shift in our human relationship with the cosmos around us.[100] As a cosmological myth of the 1960s, *TOS* communicated science in narrative form, but also went beyond contemporary achievements in order to speculate on a grander future in which the human role in the expanded cosmos was assured.

Star Trek: The Next Generation (1988–94)

NASA fulfilled the vision of both Kennedy and *Star Trek* by getting humans to the Moon on 20 July 1969, 47 days after the last episode of *TOS* went to air.[101] The real Space Race had itself been a television event that had served the television industry's need for cultural legitimacy.[102] However, interest in the television broadcasts and the space programme itself soon waned. In an editorial on 22 August 1969, *Life* magazine proclaimed: 'The first requirement for a sensible post-Apollo 11 program is that President Nixon decline to sign the sort of blank check for an all-out manned Mars landing that vocal space agency partisans are urging him on.'[103] In 1967, NASA boasted a staff high of 35,000, but by the late 1970s this had dropped to 14,000.[104] *The Animated Series* in 1973 thereby came about during the rise of *Star Trek* fandom and the decline of NASA. Norm Prescott and Ray Ellis penned a new theme tune under pseudonyms, which musically closely mirrored Courage's work,[105] but visually the title sequence directly copied *TOS*.

By the time a new live-action spin-off series of *Star Trek* was broadcast in 1988, NASA's *Challenger* disaster on 28 January 1986 was still relatively recent.[106] Indeed, the feature film *Star Trek IV: The Voyage Home* (1986)[107] had been dedicated to the memory of the *Challenger* crew. Given that the 1967 module fire had occurred during the original *Star Trek* series, the ambiguous symbolism of NASA had not entirely changed between the production of the two series. What had changed was that both NASA and the public were aware that the space programme of the 1980s was on a shoestring budget by comparison, regardless of technological advances. Notably, the space shuttle, unlike the Mercury, Gemini and Apollo spacecraft, did not have an escape system due to budgetary constraints.[108] As Penley notes with deliberate and bitter punning, 'NASA's attempt to make the space program popular with young people all across America literally blew up in its face.'[109]

If NASA was the site of ambivalent feelings, *Star Trek* by comparison had become a popular-culture phenomenon, the very reason for a spin-off series. As noted in earlier chapters, designations of *Trek* as legendary, classic and mythic had become common in popular, commercial and academic discourse. As a sequel, *TNG*'s titles refer back to those of *TOS*, while highlighting ideological and technological shifts.[110]

From *TOS* to *TNG*, there had been significant cultural shifts that impacted on the latter's title sequence. In 1988, the use of 'man' to denote all of humanity was no longer acceptable, even though the *Star Trek* feature films were still using this version into the 1980s.[111] As Clyde Wilcox notes, 'The new *Star Trek* reflects a changed conception of women's roles. While the original series mission was to "boldly go where no *man* has gone before," the new *Star Trek* is gender neutral: it seeks to go "where no *one* has gone before".'[112] Whether or not the promise of gender neutrality was delivered in the series itself has been the subject of much debate.[113] In its function as series advertisement, the titles' voice-over by Captain Picard (Patrick Stewart) nonetheless creates an anticipation of a revised *Star Trek* cosmos affected by shifts in both the late twentieth century and the fictional twenty-fourth century.

The titles also reference *TOS* through their music, a mixture of the brass fanfare taken from *TOS*' soundtrack and the theme tune taken from Jerry Goldsmith's score for the first feature film.[114] The Goldsmith tune is a vigorous march, which musically has military overtones.[115] The ethereal soprano of *TOS* is not included, suggesting a less mysterious cosmos, but one that is nonetheless explored with confidence. Walter Irwin notes that even in *TOS*, it was not long before 'Starfleet Command reached farther and farther out into space, until it seemed that in many episodes, Captain Kirk and his crew went home every night for dinner'.[116] Unknown space had increasingly become known place.[117] That the otherworldly associations of *TOS*' song is replaced with the strident tones of the Goldsmith march suggests this shift.[118] Thus aural elements such as the voice-over and theme tune cue earlier instalments of the franchise,[119] but also rework them. It is a specific *Star Trek* cosmos that we enter.

TNG had different opening sequences over its seven years, with the visuals changing in Season 3 and several text changes occurring throughout.[120] The original opening (shown without a teaser in the 1988 pilot episode, 'Encounter at Farpoint') begins with the image of one-third of Earth in space, pulling out to reveal the entire planet and the Sun behind it. *TNG* thereby centralises Earth in space. This echoes much earlier science fiction programmes, such as *Tom Corbett*, the titles of which include a shot of Earth in space from the point of view of a rocket ship, an image that upon the show's debut in 1950 had not in fact been seen in real life. The special effects may have vastly improved by the time of *TNG*, but the localising strategy remained the same. Thus Jindra notes that in beginning with Earth, the title sequence for *TNG* 'orients the viewer to envision the events as taking place in his [sic] own universe'.[121] Indeed, in 'The Best of Both Worlds, Part 1' (1990), the Federation 'sector' containing Earth is identified for the first time as Sector 001, again suggesting the primacy of both Earth and humanity.[122] This seems to return us to a pre-Copernican geocentrism. However, during the title sequence, the camera continues to pull out, and the Sun, rather than Earth, marks the furthest point of reference. By opening with Earth but moving out to reveal a solar reference point, the opening shot combines a geocentric and heliocentric depiction of the solar system. *TNG* implicitly attempts to mediate two seemingly contradictory worldviews – the heliocentric model we intellectually know to be true, and the geocentric model that our senses (and egocentrism) tell us is true. *TNG* tries to reconcile these models by subsuming them into the mythological *Star Trek* cosmos.[123]

While Kirk's voice-over in the titles of *TOS* suggested alignments with Kennedy's speeches and the real space technology of the 1960s, *TNG*'s title sequence highlights advances in *entertainment* technology of the late 1980s. Continuing the camera movement outwards, the titles reveal the Moon and then Jupiter and Saturn. After Saturn, the frame looks out into star-filled space as Picard proclaims it to be 'the final frontier'. As the voice-over continues, the new Starship *Enterprise* comes into shot, warping into the distance once Picard finishes his preamble. However, the warp visuals, followed by an echo flash of light in the distance, are achieved with new special effects technology. This highlights not only the achievements of the next generation of Starfleet ships within the *Star Trek* diegesis, but also the next generation of contemporary effects technology used in production. Indeed, the new 'rubber-band effect' had been developed specifically for the programme by Industrial Light and Magic (ILM) along with *TNG* staffer Rob Legato.[124] Brooks Landon, Albert J. La Valley, Stephen Neale and Garrett Stewart have argued that science fiction films are as much (and perhaps more) about the contemporary cinematic and special effects technology with which they are produced as about depicting future technologies.[125] This conflation is evident in *TNG*, where advances are signalled through CGI as much as through fictional new *Star Trek* diegetic technologies. The sense of time having passed between *TOS* and *TNG* is suggested by the *Next Generation* title, its improved *Enterprise* spaceship and its representational special effects. This blurring of fictional and factual technologies in the title sequence cues the viewer to expect a universe accessed via spaceships that are more advanced than their original series counterparts, rendered with special effects technology that is similarly more advanced. The diegetic and production realities reinforce one another, both enabling access to outer space through technological improvement.

TNG's title sequence mirrors *TOS* by suggesting a mastery over both technology and space.[126] Between the introduction of *TNG*'s main characters and actors in written text, the *Enterprise* again flies from deep space into the foreground, only to re-emerge in space to repeat the action in a different direction, screen left or screen right. At the end of the titles, the *Enterprise* slowly emerges below us and warps into the distance (complete with flash echo), leaving the viewer in empty space once more. Although we begin in close proximity to Earth, the viewer ends in space. The *Enterprise* disappears further out into space and out of sight, setting the spatial scene for episodes that could take place anywhere.

In Season 3, however, the titles were revamped, 'featuring an incoming route from outside the Milky Way rather than a departure angle from the solar system'.[127] While initially situating us in unknown space, then, these new titles in fact depict a homeward trajectory, a choice at odds with the *Enterprise*'s mission to head outwards into space in search of new places and peoples. Unknown space becomes somewhere you return from, in search of more familiar locations; a seemingly regressive move. While this was not, in fact, the *Enterprise*'s own trajectory, it would become the logic behind the fourth live-action *Star Trek* series, *Voyager*. The series made after *TNG* each suggest an ambiguous relationship with space exploration, challenging the scientific cosmological perspective in *DS9*, while giving a new primacy to Earth in *Voyager* and *Enterprise*.

Star Trek: Deep Space Nine (1993–9)

> This is where the adventure is. This is where heroes are made.
> Right here, in the wilderness.
> – Doctor Bashir, 'Emissary' (1993).

While *TNG*'s pilot launches straight into its title sequence, *DS9*'s first episode, 'Emissary', provides background to the new series by way of written text and a teaser before the title sequence itself. For programmes with a serial element, the opening sequence may recapitulate ('recap') previous events or 'ongoing storylines'.[128] For sequels such as *DS9*, the recap is used to refer back to events from the timeline of an older series, *TNG*, while leading immediately into a teaser for the new programme.[129] Teasers provide a segment of the episode to come; however, the title sequence or an advertisement break usually separate them from the body of the episode.[130] While titles succinctly introduce the general premise of the show, teasers provide information about the specific episode, setting up a narrative problem or moment of suspense designed to 'tease' the viewer and keep them sufficiently interested to stay tuned. Although recurring titles function as an advertisement for the programme as a whole, teasers function to advertise a particular episode, setting up an episode-specific set of expectations. Teasers and recaps are, therefore, additional paratextual materials that frame audience engagement with an episode. From the first decade of the medium, science fiction television programmes used teasers and recaps with varying degrees of complexity, such as the voice-over recaps of *Captain Video and His Video Rangers*, or the brief teasers of *The Outer Limits* (1963–5). In the case of a pilot episode, a teaser also functions as an advertisement for the entire series.

In white text over a black background, the *DS9* pilot recap states:

> ON STARDATE 43997, CAPTAIN JEAN LUC PICARD OF THE FEDERATION STARSHIP ENTERPRISE WAS KIDNAPPED FOR SIX DAYS BY AN INVADING FORCE KNOWN AS THE BORG. SURGICALLY ALTERED, HE WAS FORCED TO LEAD AN ASSAULT ON STARFLEET AT WOLF 359.

Larry Nemecek notes that Wolf 359 is a real star, 'the third closest system to Sol, after Alpha Centauri and Barnard's Star – just 7.6 light-years from our solar system.'[131] However, the teaser that follows begins in our future and in *Star Trek*'s past, contemporaneous with the *TNG* episode 'The Best of Both Worlds, Part II' (1990). Commander Benjamin Sisko's wife Jennifer is killed in the encounter with the Borg, and three years later Sisko is posted to the Deep Space Nine space station with his young son Jake. The title sequence then ensues. Although providing a new viewer with enough information to make sense of the series and characters, the teaser for the first episode, 'Emissary', is more overtly serial in form than *TNG*. While *TNG*'s titles refer back to *TOS* by replicating the basic format, voice-over and elements of the soundtrack, the characters and the twenty-fourth-century setting were, at that stage, completely new. 'Emissary' takes the audience back into *TNG* history, a move that would have more meaning to a *TNG* viewer. Like *TNG*, *DS9* references its own *Star Trek* backstory, giving further narrative weight to the *Star Trek* cosmos and history, rather than reflecting contemporary space missions as *TOS* had implicitly done. It is the *Star Trek* 'myth' of successful space travel that is given primacy over the real history of space exploration.

Because its events take place primarily on the space station and in its immediate environs, the titles for *DS9* are noticeably more static than those of the previous *Star Trek* series. Momentarily following the trajectory of an icy comet, the camera reveals the station in distant space as the series title appears. A shuttle leaving the station crosses in front of the camera and enables a cut to a medium close-up of the station, which is then shown from various angles while the cast credits appear. Production Designer Herman Zimmerman recalls his instructions for the station:

> It was to be recognizable from a long way off. If, from the corner of your eye, you saw the station very small on a video screen across the living room, you were to know instantly that it was Star Trek: Deep Space 9 [sic] that was about to happen. Deep Space 9's shape had to be like no other.[132]

The iconic value of a ship and planets are, therefore, replaced by the space station. Not even Bajor, the planet and people that would occupy many *DS9* scripts, is featured in the opening sequence. The station, rather, seems isolated in space. In its location in the 'deep space' of the Alpha Quadrant of the Milky Way, the station lacks the planetary reference points to our own solar system used in *TNG*. However, by remaining focused on the same space station, what begins as unknown space becomes, for the frequent viewer, a very well-known place.

During the pilot episode 'Emissary', a wormhole is discovered near the station, a type of tunnel of curved space connecting two points in space-time. In *DS9*, the wormhole connects two distant parts of the Milky Way galaxy. Mathematicians applying Einstein's theory of relativity have predicted the existence of wormholes; however, this has not been proven through astronomical observation.[133] Speculative astronomy, although tentatively proven through equation, is affirmed as fact through *DS9*. The wormhole features in the titles from the next episode, 'Past Prologue' (1992), reminding the viewer of wonders in space that contemporary science anticipates but cannot definitively prove. The wormhole and its presence in the titles thereby mythologises theoretical science through narrative.

Because the wormhole allows access to another region of space, Kathy E. Ferguson argues that the station in turn 'functions as both a border and a threshold, both marking the differences among contrasting spaces and inviting the traveller to journey from one space to another'.[134] Although it is, therefore, a type of 'frontier town',[135] the station also embodies the colonial conflict that has been associated with the expansion of frontiers on Earth. As a leftover from the Cardassian occupation of Bajor, the station reflects a bloody occupation, war crimes and an underground Bajoran resistance movement. Within the diegesis, the station itself is built by Bajoran slave labour. The underbelly of heroic space exploration is revealed as exploitation, of people and resources. Humans also become implicated in this colonialism. In 'Emissary', Bajoran Major Kira points out that although the Federation of planets (to which Earth belongs) claims only to want to help Bajor, the Cardassians made exactly the same claim before forcefully occupying the planet for 60 years. The human Doctor Bashir reveals his own colonial desires to practice 'frontier medicine' in 'the farthest reaches of the galaxy [...] the wilderness'. Major Kira retorts that for the friendly 'natives' such as herself, that wilderness is home.[136] The Bajoran region is only a frontier, only in 'deep space', from the perspective of an Earth-centric culture. What constitutes the frontier is entirely relative to a geocentric cosmos.

The space station may represent the future potential of a free Bajor, and its alignment with other species and organisations, but it also represents an oppressed past and potentially compromised present. The literal darkness of the station, and *DS9*'s title sequence as a whole, contrast noticeably with the luminous quality of *TNG*'s planets and highly lit *Enterprise*. *DS9*'s title aesthetic thereby cues the audience to expectations about the programme itself. The 'darker and grittier environment' of the station[137] reflects the popular perception that the show was 'edgier' and 'darker' than its predecessors, although there is some dispute over whether this connotation was entirely intended.[138]

The more sombre physical and political atmosphere of *DS9* is emphasised by a more ponderous, slow-paced theme tune. Dennis McCarthy's theme features a horn melody, which suggests an epic quality, but at the slower pace it is more contemplative. During *TOS*, the possibility of real space exploration and rapid technological development were still new concepts that required a shift in perspective, a different way of understanding our place in the cosmos facilitated by science fiction. By *TNG*, the dreams of space travel had been both realised and frustrated. *TNG* harks back to *Star Trek*'s *mythos*, attempting to recapture and continue the franchise's popular culture role in imagining space on our behalf. By the time *DS9* was developed, the successful revival of the franchise was assured, but contemporaneous science fiction television programmes, such as *The X-Files* (1993–2002, 2016) and *Babylon 5* (1993, 1994–8), suggested official organisations and scientific rationality could no longer be trusted absolutely.[139] Due to these cultural and textual developments, and a change in production team, *DS9* shifts its focus away from space exploration to the religious implications of a post-Copernican, many-worlds cosmos. By focusing on the different belief systems of alien cultures, *DS9* prompts its human inhabitants to question the scientific rationalism that, for the most part, underpins the earlier series.[140] The 'haunted' sounds of the *DS9* theme tune[141] suggest that, as heroic as the space station's inhabitants may be, some mysteries remain.

The shift in focus to a fundamentally more spiritual, less certain cosmos is also cued by the wormhole. To the Bajorans, the wormhole is the Celestial Temple of the Prophets. As Barrett and Barrett argue,

Star Trek Title Sequences and Cosmology as Myth

[I]t is worth stressing that the predominant force affecting the wormhole – a crucial portal between the Alpha and Gamma Quadrants – is not astronomical but religious. The wormhole is controlled by its resident 'prophets' rather than by processes which science can hope to analyse.[142]

The wormhole functions not merely as an astronomical means of accessing new space, but also as a visual reminder and embodiment of the Bajoran mythology and religion, the importance (narratively and spatially) of which marks an ideological shift in the scientific rationalist, secular discourse prevalent in the *Star Trek* franchise up to this point.[143] The wormhole provides access to a new region of space, but also a new spiritual way of understanding the cosmos. Although the new viewer would not appreciate this connection, for the repeat viewer the continued presence of the wormhole in the title sequence acts as a reminder of this shift in focus. Space itself is part of a Bajoran, mythological cosmos.

The wormhole/Celestial Temple is also important right from the first episode in the construction of Commander Sisko as the Emissary of the Prophets. In 'Emissary', the Bajoran religious leader Kai Opaka tells Sisko that he will find the temple, because 'it is quite simply, Commander, the journey you have always been destined to make'. The chosen mediator between the Bajoran people and their wormhole Prophets turns out to be a human. Consolmagno argues:

> The ultimate myth of science fiction that is tagged onto our astronomy turns out to be that, even with all those alien races, human beings are the central characters in the story of the universe. It is as if the Copernican Revolution never happened.[144]

Within the many worlds of the *Star Trek* cosmos, humans nonetheless retain the highest command roles in each series, and in the case of Sisko, are given a great heroic and divine destiny. Although Sisko continually resists his status as Emissary,[145] by the final season the writers decided to make Sisko half-Prophet, and therefore semi-divine in terms of Bajoran myth and religion.[146] In the last episode of the entire series, 'What You Leave Behind' (1999), Sisko joins the Prophets in the wormhole. The wormhole functions as a symbol of Sisko's destiny, suggested in the pilot episode but only fulfilled in the final episode, a meaning that would be retrospectively grafted onto the opening titles when rewatching the programme.

Despite the mythological, religious connotations of the wormhole, it is nonetheless the product of contemporary special effects technology. While Barrett and Barrett can argue that on a diegetic level the wormhole cannot be fully explained by science,[147] for the viewer the wormhole is simultaneously a feat of real-life technology. The wormhole is a religious wonder, a scientific wonder of speculative cosmology, and also a technological wonder of special effects. This does not necessarily make the wormhole any more explicable to the layperson, but it does make the wormhole part of a contemporary science fiction discourse in which the wonders of CGI are as important as the depiction of fictional technology.[148] Rather than functioning purely as a religious icon, the wormhole mediates religious and scientific paradigms in the liminal zone between the diegesis and the real world, reflecting the diegetic concerns with Bajoran spiritualism and Starfleet's scientific rationalism.

After the *Defiant* ship was introduced to *DS9* in 'The Search, Part 1' (1994), it became part of a revamped title sequence from Season 4, starting with 'The Way of the Warrior' (1995). Michael Dorn's name was added to the credits and Siddig El Fadil changed to a stage name of Alexander Siddig. The new titles included 'a new arrangement of Dennis McCarthy's [...] score',[149] with a fuller musical backing, as well as new background visual details, with colour variations in the view of space beyond the space station. *DS9* Season 4 was visually and aurally busier than previous seasons, and while the titles retained their relatively static focus on the space station itself, with the *Defiant* in dock the programme suggested at least the potential for travel beyond the station. An increasingly serial structure meant that expansion was now primarily episodic and temporal,[150] with increased reliance on story arcs and a greater necessity for recaps ('Last time on *Star Trek: Deep Space Nine* ...'). Narrative extension across multiple episodes replaced spatial expansion into unknown space, the backbone of *TOS* and *TNG*. It is particularly the heroic, mythic life journey of Captain Sisko across the entire series, rather than literal space travel, that defines the *DS9* cosmos. The Prophets at the heart of this Bajoran mythology are beyond time, and their knowledge goes beyond mere physical scientific descriptions that would reduce a Celestial Temple to a mere wormhole.

Star Trek: Voyager (1995–2001)

By the time *Voyager* emerged, many of its special effects were 'created using off-the-shelf consumer computers and software'.[151] In accelerated obsolescence, what was wondrous technology in *DS9* had become domestically available by the time of *Voyager*. Like *DS9*, the pilot of *Voyager*, 'Caretaker' (1995), begins with a written introduction, this time scrolling up over a space background. This style of opening was famously used in *Star Wars* (1977), which in turn had borrowed the technique used in the early *Flash Gordon* cinema serials, such as *Flash Gordon Conquers the Universe* (1940), but not the *Flash Gordon* television series. The colonial theme overtly introduced in *DS9* provides the context for the new *Voyager* story. The introductory text states:

> UNHAPPY WITH A NEW TREATY, FEDERATION COLONISTS ALONG THE CARDASSIAN BORDER HAVE BANDED TOGETHER.
> CALLING THEMSELVES 'THE MAQUIS', THEY CONTINUE TO FIGHT THE CARDASSIANS.
> SOME CONSIDER THEM HEROES, BUT TO THE GOVERNMENTS OF THE FEDERATION AND CARDASSIA, THEY ARE OUTLAWS.

As with the *DS9* introduction, a *Star Trek* viewer would know this background, with the Maquis first introduced by name in the *DS9* double episode 'The Maquis' (1994).[152] The double episode had been written specifically to provide background for the upcoming *Voyager* programme.[153] Writer Jeri Taylor notes, 'in order to avoid having burdensome backstory and exposition in *Voyager*'s plot, we decided we could plant the idea of the Maquis in the shows that were already on air'.[154] The Cardassians had been introduced in the Season 4 *TNG* episode 'The Wounded' (1991). The negative consequences of the Federation–Cardassian treaty and the possibility of terrorist cells had also been explored in *TNG*'s Season 5 episode 'Ensign

Ro' (1991). However, two subsequent *TNG* episodes, Season 7's 'Journey's End' (1994) and 'Preemptive Strike' (1994), were made specifically with *Voyager* in mind.[155] In particular, the colony of Indigenous Americans[156] on Dorvan V shown in 'Journey's End' was intended 'to establish [...] the implied home of *Voyager*'s [...] American Indian character Chakotay'.[157] What gives *Voyager* narrative resonance is the other *Star Trek* series that provide its background story. By contrast, *TOS* was a utopian slant on the struggles of the Space Race being undertaken during its production, affirming the ability of humans to conquer this new frontier of space, and indeed, to conquer differences among humans while doing so. It had no textual, *Star Trek*-specific history at that point in time. *Voyager*'s connections with both *TNG* and *DS9* construct its field of reference within the *Star Trek* cosmos and textual tradition, rather than in a relationship with real space exploration of the 1990s. *Star Trek*'s popular culture 'mythology' takes precedence over contemporary space missions.

While *DS9*'s wormhole to the Gamma Quadrant opened up a new expanse of unexplored space, *Voyager*'s relocation in the Delta Quadrant, a distant part of the Milky Way, meant that alien vistas and species were completely unknown to the characters and the audience. However, through their pilot teasers, *DS9* and *Voyager* emphasise not so much spatial exploration as the temporal, serial expansion of the *Star Trek* franchise. Parallel universes, new quadrants and the holodeck all become means of overcoming familiarity. Despite this, *Voyager*'s premise of being lost in the Delta Quadrant more than a lifetime's journey away from home meant that the crew (and the audience with them) were not heading 'out there' but rather focused on 'getting back'.[158] Unlike all the previous *Star Trek* series, then, *Voyager* focused on getting home, and specifically getting home to Earth, in Sector 001, the centre of the human universe. That Earth is not literally the centre of the universe is rendered immaterial to its cultural centrality. The crew's nostalgia for their distant home by extension becomes nostalgia for Earth's primacy, for its lost centrality in a post-Copernican, many-worlds cosmos.

Voyager's title music suggests that the journey home is nonetheless heroic, with composer Jerry Goldsmith aiming for a 'very broad and noble' sound.[159] Similarly, the sheet music for the theme suggests that it should be played 'with grandeur'.¹⁶⁰ The epic tone evoked by the theme music would be reinforced by episodes in which *Voyager*'s characters re-enact the heroic epics of *Beowulf* and the *Odyssey*.¹⁶¹ *Voyager* asserts a nostalgic desire for the earlier years of *Star Trek* in which space was still an unexplored frontier, and a more profound nostalgia for a pre-Copernican worldview in which Earth was the centre of the cosmos. The word nostalgia is itself based on the Greek *nostos* (return home) and *algos* (pain), literally appropriate in the case of *Voyager*.

The homeward trajectory of *Voyager* is not, however, implied by the series' title sequence, which features the *Voyager* ship moving past a sun/ star, through a gaseous formation, past a ringed planet, by an Earth-like planet with a solitary moon, and into a nebula. The titles therefore visually situate us heliocentrically, moving outwards from a star, past planets that are presented in the wrong order to be our own solar system, but which iconographically refer us back to our known planetary neighbours. The unfamiliar is nonetheless rendered visually familiar; even in a distant quadrant, there is a pseudo-Earth and solar system to give us comfort.¹⁶²

Enterprise (2001–5)

Enterprise maintains the cycle between *Star Trek*'s unfamiliar and familiar space vistas by bringing us back home again – this time, to the real Earth. However, *Enterprise*'s titles consist of a montage of overlapping images, more complex than the previous programmes. This approach broadly mirrors the title sequence of lead actor Scott Bakula's previous science fiction programme *Quantum Leap* (1989–93), which features a historical montage of his character's leaps through time. The *Enterprise* title sequence begins in space, with only around one-third of the planet Earth in shot as the title appears (changing to the longer title of *Star Trek: Enterprise* in Season 3). This image fades into old drawings of the globe, maps and models of the solar system. An early sea vessel segues into HMS *Enterprize* [*sic*], inspired by several Royal Navy rigged sailing ships of this name, the first of which was a French Corvette captured by the British in 1705;¹⁶³ and the sea blurs into a runway. A number of aircraft and space vessels are shown, progressing from Earth's real past into *Star Trek*'s fictional future.

The titles of *TOS* implicitly referenced the 1960s Space Race that it reflected, but also informed, in popular culture discourse. While the titles of subsequent *Star Trek* series have tended to reference *Star Trek*'s own textual past rather than real space exploration, *Enterprise* returns to the NASA/*Trek* relationship, weaving 'real' scientific history with *Star Trek*'s history. The space shuttle *Enterprise* forms a nexus of these two timelines, as NASA's first shuttle of 1977 was named after the *Star Trek* spaceship, following a letter-writing campaign by fans.[164] The cast of *TOS* attended the shuttle's unveiling ceremony and Paramount advertised the occasion, stating 'It's nice to know that sometimes science fiction becomes science fact. Starship *Enterprise* will be joining the space shuttle *Enterprise* in its space travels very soon', referring to the first slated feature film.[165] By featuring the space shuttle *Enterprise*, the titles for *Enterprise* emphasise the role of the *Star Trek* franchise within the history of popular culture, but also its impact on the history of space exploration. Further, *Star Trek*'s narrative past is literally incorporated through images of the first human warp drive, footage of which is taken directly from the feature film *Star Trek: First Contact* (1996). The final step in this progression is the first *Enterprise* ship in the *Star Trek* timeline (but the last in terms of broadcast history at the time), which flies into distant space away from Earth. It is only as the titles and music come to a close that we finally leave the home planet.

Enterprise is set in the twenty-second century – in our future but *Star Trek*'s past. The series goes 'back' to an earlier time in *Star Trek*'s future, when space travel was new and exciting. When *Enterprise* was originally broadcast, NASA was also keen to promote itself as entering into a revitalised era of space exploration, buoyed by President George W. Bush's 'new vision' to undertake human missions to the Moon and Mars. A number of publicity stunts involving NASA and *Star Trek* in the *Enterprise* years stressed the connection between the two in the light of Bush's mission statement of 14 January 2004.[166] On 23 February 2004, *Voyager* and Paramount presented NASA with the *Voyager* Award to recognise their current and future missions. Accepting the award, astronaut and shuttle veteran Dr Janice Voss said: 'The line I take from President Bush's speech is – This is not a race but a journey. And that's what all the *Star Trek* series are about.'[167]

Star Trek Title Sequences and Cosmology as Myth

In May 2005, NASA astronauts Mike Fincke and Terry Virts appeared as extras in the finale of *Enterprise*, citing science fiction and *Star Trek* as the inspiration for their careers. Reporting the guest appearance, NASA author Amiko Nevills argued that, 'Today, the space frontier is expanding, and like the setting of 'Star Trek: Enterprise,' the nation's Vision for Space Exploration is at the brink of the early pioneering days of deep space exploration.'[168]

While the original *Star Trek* series suggested a harmonious, integrated outcome to the Space Race, *Enterprise* and NASA looked to one another to suggest that both our own time and *Enterprise*'s twenty-second-century future marked new heroic eras of exploration that could equal the excitement of the 1960s. Sharon Sharp notes that the *Enterprise* crew wear 'NASA blue jumpsuits with arm patches reminiscent of those from the space shuttle program. In this way, the series' spin is "the future is now", as it uses *mise-en-scène* to create a nostalgia for the future.'[169] The shared NASA/*Trek* vision and optimism of the era is stressed in the opening titles of *Enterprise* and their united timelines, even if subsequent funding cuts have, at least for now, thwarted such aspirations.

Combined with images from the history of Earth and space exploration, and images from an imagined *Star Trek* future history, are sketches from the scientific revolution depicting the new heliocentric system. The opening titles of *Enterprise*, therefore, trace a physical journey within and beyond Earth, but also the narrative of scientific and cosmological knowledge with which this chapter began. While acknowledging a post-Copernican, heliocentric system, *Enterprise* nonetheless visually harks back to a pre-Copernican geocentrism, championing our journey away from Earth yet retaining its primacy. If science fiction programmes such as *Star Trek* reimagine science through story, and thereby take on a function once assigned to myth, *Enterprise* praises technological progress but upholds an older, Earth-centred cosmos. This tendency had begun with the homeward journey of *Voyager*, but had not been expressed so literally in its opening titles. Just as *TNG*, *DS9* and *Voyager* appropriate traditional myths and create new myths in order to suggest an alignment with *Star Trek*'s own story tradition, *Enterprise* asserts *Star Trek*'s continuity of a spacefaring myth of progress, in which humans and the Earth hold prime importance.

The progression from HMS *Enterprize* to its later namesake the Starship *Enterprise* emphasises this journey of discovery. Ships have a long history as symbols of exploration, but in the sixteenth and seventeenth centuries they also became symbols of scientific knowledge, of the human capacity to travel beyond the known.[170] The exploration of Earth and the exploration of new scientific ideas, including new theories about the cosmos, were linked through the imagery of the ship. In the title sequence of *Enterprise*, exploration of Earth is linked with the exploration of space, the end point of the journey. Except, of course, that visually we stay with Earth. The theme song lyrics imply travelling far into space, but visually we remain with Earth until the lyrics have ended and the music draws to a close.

The sequence of images in the titles as a whole suggest that the destination of the *Enterprise* theme song 'Where My Heart Will Take Me' is anywhere away from home – across land, sea, air and ultimately space. The song's destination might also refer to the future, given the progression of images from the real and fictional past into the *Star Trek* future. While the visuals of the *Enterprise* titles emphasise a journey taken by generations of humans across centuries, the theme song's lyrics use the imagery of a journey from the personal perspective of an unnamed individual, the 'me' of the song's title. Simon Frith argues that theme songs from films released as singles can function as 'an extremely effective film trailer',[171] but within the film itself 'the song becomes a kind of *commentary* on the film: the singers represent us, the audience, and our response to the film, but also become our teachers, making sure we got the film's emotional message'.[172] Frith is writing specifically about theme songs played at the end of a film, channelling the emotional loose ends of the experience. Like his trailer analogy, however, title theme songs do not sum up what we have already seen, but rather help cue our expectations about a forthcoming programme, even though the 'voices and words' of a theme song may not 'have anything to do with the characters or dialogue in the film'.[173]

Originally titled 'Faith of the Heart', for *Enterprise* the song was renamed in the first person as 'Where My Heart Will Take Me'.[174] What meaning can the 'me' of the title have in the context of *Enterprise*? The only people depicted in the opening titles are historical figures involved in air and space travel, such as Alan Shepard, the first American in space. The first human in space, Yuri Gagarin, is not granted the same slow motion close-up. As Lincoln Geraghty notes, the *Enterprise* titles present a specifically 'American mythic history'.[175] While the *Star Trek* future is made an inherent part of this history, no characters from the *Enterprise* series are shown (unlike the *Quantum Leap* titles), just the starship itself.

The first-person singular 'I' or 'me' of a song would seem most obviously to belong to the singer of the song. In the case of 'Where My Heart Will Take Me', this would mean singer Russell Watson. But this answer is not as simple as it may seem, for songs can themselves be fictional narratives sung by the performer who functions as a fictional persona. What seems like a personal address from the performer 'may turn out to be, like the voice-over in film noir, a fictional invention, a character'.[176] Andrew Goodwin argues, 'When a pop singer tells a first-person narrative in song, he or she is simultaneously both the character in the song and the storyteller. Often the two positions become confused for audiences.'[177] However, Goodwin argues that for a performer who has become known, the storyteller/performer 'usually overwhelms characterization within the story'.[178] While some *Enterprise* viewers may be familiar with popular English tenor Watson, others may well have greater familiarity with the *Star Trek* storyworld.[179] The context and medium in which a song is used affects how we might interpret its first-person lyrics.

For as Roman Jakobson notes, personal pronouns (I/me, you, they, and so on) shift in meaning depending on their context and are consequently known as 'shifters' in linguistics.[180] In other words (and with a certain degree of circularity): '*I* means the person uttering *I* [...] Thus *I* means the addresser (and *you*, the addressee) of the message to which it belongs.'[181] However, Jakobson acknowledges that relations between addresser and addressee are complicated by communications technology. He notes, 'such technical media as telephone and radio', for which we cannot see the source of the sound we receive, must surely have 'consequences both for the perception and for the production of transmitted verbal messages'.[182]

While Jakobson does not explore these consequences himself, Schwichtenberg has analysed the function of the second person 'you' in her analysis of the theme song lyrics to *The Love Boat* (1977–86). Although in linguistics 'shifters are defined by the fact that they never apply to more than one thing at a time,[183] Schwichtenberg argues that this depends on the medium. She suggests that 'as a medium of mass-mediation, television [...] can] simultaneously' address individuals and the masses, 'that is, "you" as specific, and "you" as general, as collective.'[184]

Similarly, 'I' might not be spoken in a face-to-face conversation, but could be transmitted by technology without the receiver being able to see who is uttering the word. In this mediated form, 'I' may still mean 'the person uttering *I*', but particularly when it is addressed to a simultaneously singular and collective addressee, the lack of context (such as the image of the person uttering 'I') creates ambiguity. This ambiguity obviously does not occur if the voice itself is recognisable, which may be the case for some audience members familiar with Russell Watson. Without footage of Watson in the titles themselves, the song title and lyrics nonetheless become open to other interpretations.[185]

To interpret just who is the ambiguous first-person subject of the song, we can look at the narrative of the song itself, but also at the narrative of *Enterprise* which it fronts. In the teaser for the pilot episode 'Broken Bow' (2001), preceding the first title sequence, we see the future Captain Jonathan Archer as a young boy with his father, Henry Archer. Jonathan paints a model spacecraft and complains about the delays in the building of his father's real ship. Jonathan says, 'Billy Cook said we'd be flying at warp 5 by now if the Vulcans hadn't kept things from us.' Henry replies, 'Well, they have their reasons. God knows what they are.' Read in this context, the theme song 'Where My Heart Will Take Me' might refer either to Captain Archer or his father, their hopes for more advanced human spaceships, and ultimately their 'Faith of the Heart' that such hopes will eventually be fulfilled.

The association of the song with Captain Archer (Scott Bakula) is suggested through the franchise's history, given that both *TOS* and *TNG* feature voice-overs by the captains. Indeed, as he paints his spaceship model, the young Archer exclaims 'where no man has gone before', repeating the words of Captain Kirk's voice-over in a moment of self-reflexivity. Later in the pilot, these words are revealed to be part of a speech given by Zefram Cochrane,[186] the human inventor of the warp engine, at the dedication of the Warp 5 Complex: 'We'll be able to explore those strange new worlds, and seek out new life and new civilizations. This engine will let us go boldly where no man [sic] has gone before.' Although set in our future, *Enterprise* is profoundly backwards-looking in terms of both *Star Trek*'s fictional timeline and the 1960s to which *TOS* belonged. The titles for *Enterprise*, and its pilot episode, reveal nostalgia for real and imagined eras of scientific and technological advancement (not to mention a return to a specifically male outlook in the wording).[187] *TOS* fictionalised the possibilities of the Space Race, but in turn influenced the cultural reception of these changes. The rapid developments in space technology of the 1950s and 1960s were not continued to the same degree in subsequent decades, so this cultural resonance is more difficult to harness for a sequel *Star Trek* series. *Enterprise* goes back to an earlier time in *Star Trek*'s future history in order to recapture a sense of newness to space travel, to a period in which humans are just about to travel further into space with the aid of new technology. Mythological narrative takes precedence over fact.

Although the titles for *Enterprise* suggest the heroic exploits of humans as they develop new technologies of exploration, the pilot episode reveals a sense of stagnation. The fact that the realisation of human space ambitions has been a challenging one that has taken generations is suggested not only through the title images, but also through the teaser flashbacks to Archer's childhood, bathed in a golden, idealised light. The aspirations of Archer and his father are forestalled by the Vulcans, whose contact with Earth is signified through the warp vessel from *First Contact* featured in the *Enterprise* title sequence. The theme song asserts that 'they' will no longer hinder the song's protagonist, but the context of the pilot episode suggests that 'they' might be specifically identified as the Vulcans.[188] The pilot reinforces such an interpretation by showing a confrontational adult Jonathan Archer complaining about the Vulcans, saying 'We've been deferring to their judgment for a hundred years [...] How much longer?' Guthke suggests that the post-Copernican possibility of many inhabited worlds in the cosmos brings with it the 'fear that we might become the exploited colonial subjects of an extraterrestrial master race that does not share' our values.[189] In *TOS* and *TNG*, the mission is to seek out 'new life and new civilizations', yet this also has darker colonial implications. Indeed, Andreadis questions whether we should even seek out alien life on other planets, 'given the dismal record of human colonization on Earth'.[190] The frontier colonialism implied in the earlier series is made explicit in *DS9*, but in *Enterprise* the Earth has, in effect, become a colony of the Vulcans, beholden to their superior knowledge. The Vulcans may claim to have human interests in mind, but from the perspective of Archer, 'they' are simply controlling humans and keeping them back.

By the end of the pilot episode, Archer has modified his opinion of the Vulcans, saying to the Vulcan T'Pol: 'Ever since I can remember I've seen Vulcans as an obstacle, always keeping us from standing on our own two feet [...] If I'm going to pull this off, there are a few things I need to leave behind. Things like preconceptions and holding grudges.' This shift in mindset is necessary if Archer and his crew are to one day reach the 'darn well-integrated' *Star Trek* future that was praised back in the 1960s.[191] The *Enterprise* pilot episode ends where it begins, in the golden-hued past, as the two Archers fly their toy spacecraft (see Figure 3.1). Archer's speech to T'Pol suggests he sees the mission of the *Enterprise* in very personal terms ('If *I'm* going to pull this off '). Although the audience is free to take an interest in any or all of the characters, Archer is privileged not only by his rank but also by the use of his subjective flashbacks, which open and end

Figure 3.1 Captain Archer's childhood memories in *Enterprise* 'Broken Bow' (Paramount Television 2001).

the pilot episode. This framing, and the conventions of *TOS* and *TNG* in privileging the voice-over of the captain during the opening titles, suggests the first-person I/me of *Enterprise*'s song is Archer.

In *Enterprise* Archer does, however, have his own theme tune, available on the *Enterprise* soundtrack. Indeed, one fan laments, 'I wish [Dennis] McCarthy's Archer theme could have been used in a sweeping orchestral arrangement to underscore the opening credits', rather than the existing song.[192] This preference for the epic grandeur of the previous *Star Trek* themes over the pop music of *Enterprise* is as much informed by heated fan debates over the suitability of the song as it is by the link to Archer. Reading the song's subject as Archer is also undercut by the disparity between the singing voices of Russell Watson and actor Scott Bakula, which may be noticeable to some viewers familiar with Bakula's music recordings.

The original song, entitled 'Faith of the Heart', was performed by Rod Stewart and featured in the end credits for *Patch Adams* (1998).[193] Just as Scott Bakula's singing career and role on the science fiction programme *Quantum Leap* open the possibility of an intertextual reading of his performance as Captain Archer, viewers who recognise the *Patch Adams* origin might be inflected in their reading of the *Enterprise* song. Jane Garcia notes that the song was 'written for the cloying film *Patch Adams* by Diane Warren, queen of the sickly power ballad'.[194] This assessment has as much to do with music genre associations as it has with the triumph-over-adversity narrative of *Patch Adams*. Similarly, Charles Murray and Mike Marqusee call the theme an 'excruciating sub-Bryan Adams power ballad',[195] while Lerner suggests the lyrics and music style evoke a Christian song, at odds with the *Star Trek* franchise.[196]

Simon Frith has argued, 'What's "good" [... about pop music] usually is described by its straight musical elements [...], but what matters is a tone of voice'.[197] Frith goes on to say that 'it is the sound of the voice, not the words sung, which suggests what a singer *really* means'.[198] Not only do lyrics occur in a musical context,[199] but songs also encompass 'emphases, sighs, hesitations, changes of tone'.[200] Music can draw on the historically determined connotations of musical meaning.[201] Putting aside for one moment the narrative of the *Enterprise* song, it is both the earnestness with which the song is performed and its stylistic connections with ballad arrangements from the 1980s that, emotionally and musically, suggest not a looking forward but a looking back.[202] This nostalgia is emphasised through the title images, and *Enterprise*'s setting in *Star Trek*'s past, in a time before *TOS*. *Enterprise* attempts to establish an origin story for an origin story, providing a background to *TOS* that began the *Star Trek* franchise, a retrospective move that is mirrored in the anachronistic style of its theme song.[203] In Season 3, a new upbeat arrangement was introduced, bringing a less sentimental feel to the music, if not the lyrics.

The style of the performance and the inflections of the voice also affect how we read the address of a song. Frith argues:

> Pop effects are usually explained in terms of identity – the key words in most pop songs are 'I' and 'You' [...] the best records (the ones that give most pleasure) are the ones that allow an ambiguity of response, letting us be both subject and object of the singers' needs (regardless of our or their gender). And what's crucial to this, of course, is the grain of the voice.[204]

Fans and reviewers alike are sharply divided on whether the *Enterprise* song and Russell Watson's voice are uplifting or saccharine. Frith's suggestion that there is greater ambiguity than is strictly suggested by the linguistics of lyrics, however, is surely played out not only through the qualities of voice, but also in the inter-relation between the song and its narrative and visual context that might make it difficult to fix any particular personal pronoun in a song.

The ambiguity inherent in the *Enterprise* titles extends to the elements around it. Titles often form part of a larger opening sequence, with a teaser of the episode to come in the case of *Enterprise*. Broadcasters may use additional promotional material for the programme leading up to the teaser. On 14 November 2001, Scott Bakula preceded the US teaser for 'Civilization' (2001) with a special message. Dressed in Captain Archer's Starfleet uniform, Bakula/Archer announced on UPN: 'We salute the brave men and women serving this country. From the Starship *Enterprise* to the aircraft carrier *Enterprise*, welcome home.' A graphic proclaimed 'Welcome Home USS *Enterprise*'. The *Enterprise* carrier was returning from service in Afghanistan, hostilities that had been undertaken in the wake of the

Star Trek Title Sequences and Cosmology as Myth

September 11 terrorist attacks on New York and Washington, DC, in 2001.[205] Bakula/Archer's paratextual announcement blurs *Star Trek* with the US Navy, attempting to legitimise contemporary US government politics and ideology through an alignment with the *mythos* of *Star Trek*. It is, then, a return to myth in its most ancient Homeric form, as discussed at the very beginning of this book: a persuasive speech from a person of authority – at least within the world of *Star Trek*.[206] Bakula's address, as both himself and as the captain, creates an intentional slippage between the real and imagined *Enterprise* vessels, and between their two missions. This blurring was underscored by the fact that for the 2001 welcome home message, 'Bakula wore a baseball cap reading "USS *Enterprise* CVN 65", representing the actual USS *Enterprise*, as opposed to the NX-01 he captains on the small screen'[207] (see Figure 3.2). The programme's newly invented adversary, the Suliban, was intended to echo the Afghani Taliban, an alignment that gained particular (and unexpected) resonance after September 11.[208] The *Enterprise* production subsequently maintained ties with its US Navy counterpart. In 2002 and again in 2003, winners of the aircraft

Figure 3.2 Scott Bakula welcomes the USS *Enterprise* home (UPN 2001).

carrier *Enterprise*'s 'Sailor of the Year' award were given walk-on roles on *Enterprise*.[209]

The military connections of *Enterprise* were not new to *Star Trek*. The original *Star Trek* spaceship had been named after a US Navy aircraft carrier of the same name.[210] In 1967, Gene Roddenberry explained, 'I've always had a soft spot in my heart for the Big E, since she broke the back of the Japanese Navy at Midway.'[211] This inspiration is cited in *Enterprise* through a picture of the *Enterprise* aircraft carrier featured on the wall of Captain Archer's quarters. The progression from sea to air and space from the opening titles is echoed in Archer's gallery of pictures, which move from a rendition of one of the HMS *Enterprize* tall ships to the USS *Enterprise* air carrier, the space shuttle *Enterprise*, and finally to the programme's own USS *Enterprise* spaceship.[212] Bakula/Archer's address implicitly attempts to add the latest USS *Enterprise* aircraft carrier to this collection, aligning a contemporary conflict with older historical conflicts (both military and scientific) and with *Star Trek*'s futuristic, heroic narrative. The different connotations of each vessel are subsumed into *Star Trek*'s mythology, which promises that all technological advances and all military conflicts will ultimately lead to a better *Star Trek* future. Indeed, the succession of images suggests that these earlier *Enterprise* vessels and their endeavours are the necessary precursors to that future, emphasising the timeline established in the opening title sequence.

Bakula's direct address as Bakula/Archer, *Enterprise* CVN 65/NX-01, at the beginning of 'Civilization' breaks the diegesis and realist conventions of *Enterprise*,[213] while harnessing the inherent liminal ambiguity of opening sequences as they lead us into the text. Opening sequences mark the beginning of a programme, yet in doing so they often incorporate elements from both the diegetic and non-diegetic realms. The written text that appears in the *Enterprise* titles includes the name of the programme but also the names of the real actors who take on fictional characterisations within that programme. The politics of Bakula's address may mark it out as noticeable; however, the slippage between diegetic and non-diegetic is a convention of opening sequences. Jane Feuer has gone so far as to claim, 'The very concept "diegesis" is unthinkable on television [...] disregard for the diegetic is a *conventional* television practice, not an exceptional one.'[214]

Star Trek Title Sequences and Cosmology as Myth

Titles highlight the programme as a programme, while at the same time leading us into, and identifying, its fictional realm. Bakula/Archer's speech reminds us that *Enterprise* is not, in fact, a sealed diegesis, but rather a nexus point in an array of fictional and popular culture texts and knowledge around the *Star Trek* franchise. In a collapse of fiction/fact, Archer/ Bakula, *Enterprise* NX-01/CVN 65, Space/Afghanistan, Suliban/Taliban, Starfleet/ Navy, Bakula's address highlights the already-present ambiguity of these boundary zones, inflected with military and political connections both intended and unintended.

Murray and Marqusee even suggested, 'If Shatner's Kirk evoked John F. Kennedy, Bakula's Archer, his facial expressions limited to a scowl and a smirk, brings to mind an elongated George W. Bush.'[215] In retrospect, commentators have reassessed Kennedy's rhetoric of 'the New Frontier and found in its words and deeds the blueprint for the Vietnam debacle.'[216] *TOS* alludes to Kennedy's 'new frontier' in its opening titles, while connecting this final frontier with political and military frontiers metaphorically in episodes such as 'A Private Little War' (1967).[217] *Enterprise* suggests a continuity and interchangeability with NASA but also the US Navy, both in the opening titles and in Archer/Bakula's address (before any specific episode content). While *TOS* plays out these contemporary parallels through fiction, *Enterprise* makes the connection explicit through the direct comments of Bakula/Archer.

In the Season 4 *Enterprise* episode 'Home' (2004), Captain Archer is troubled by the military consequences of his mission, but this is still bounded by the regular, upbeat titles and credits, which seem to announce that all is well in the journey towards a better *Star Trek* future. A new credit sequence that screened for only two episodes, 'In a Mirror Darkly, Part I' (2005) and 'In a Mirror Darkly, Part II' (2005), foregrounds the potential of this military connection to create an entirely different worldview. The mirror *Star Trek* universe was first seen in *TOS* episode 'Mirror, Mirror' (1967). In the mirror universe, the United Federation of Planets has become the Terran Empire, whose aggressive Earth-and-sword symbol features in *Enterprise*'s revamped titles (see Figure 3.3). For the mirror *Enterprise* opening, the customary ballad was replaced with a militaristic horn tune, and the *Star Trek: Enterprise* titles change from white to black to

Figure 3.3 The new title sequence for *Enterprise* 'In a Mirror Darkly' (Paramount Television 2005), featuring the sword emblem.

emphasise the shift in tone. In the new sequence, images of HMS *Enterprize* lead into footage of sea battles, and the subsequent montage of exploration is replaced by human military achievements on Earth and in space as part of an alternate timeline. Steffen Hantke suggests the ease with which this switch is achieved 'hints at a complicity between *Star Trek* and the spirit of American military aggression'.[218] Although *Enterprise*'s mirror title sequence acknowledges the role of violent conflict in human expansion, it is neatly contained in a separate mirror world rather than being acknowledged as a factor in the regular *Enterprise* and the main *Star Trek* timeline to which it belongs. Despite this, *Star Trek* writer/actor Simon Pegg has wondered whether the alternate timeline of the Abrams films may eventually reveal itself to be this mirror world,[219] his character Scotty complaining in *Star Trek Into Darkness* (2013) that 'this is clearly a military operation. Is that what we are now? 'Cause I thought we were explorers'.

In *Enterprise*, the journey from Earth into the cosmos is situated within both military and scientific discourses. If the titles of *DS9* suggested that space exploration could result in military oppression (exemplified by the Cardassian station) and spiritual salvation (embodied by the wormhole/Celestial Temple), Bakula/Archer's paratextual address to the crew of the aircraft carrier *Enterprise* at the beginning of the *Enterprise* programme instead suggests that military force in foreign lands can itself be a form of salvation, upholding the political doctrine of the time. Each new military conflict and scientific discovery is subsumed into the *Star Trek* mythology of the future,[220] in which political and military difficulties have been overcome and implicitly justified. Pearson and Messenger Davies argue that the new title sequence for the 'Mirror Darkly' episodes of *Enterprise* 'celebrates science and technology in the service of war and conquest, ironically constructing an alternate possible world that is the antithesis of *Star Trek*'s humanist philosophy'.[221] By contrast, what has been suggested here is that a military theme already runs through the *Star Trek* franchise and its paratextual framings, a fact that the 'Mirror Darkly' opening tries to anxiously deny with its assertion that conquest belongs to an alternate *Star Trek* world.

Conclusion

Since Copernicus argued that the Earth travels around the Sun rather than the other way around,[222] cosmology has no longer tallied with our everyday, lived experience. We still refer to the Sun rising and setting, not only because at one stage in human history we thought the Sun was moving around us, but because from our perspective here on Earth, that is still visually what appears to happen. Although we are not at the centre of the universe, Earth is the centre of our own existence and of our human perception of the cosmos. Our attempts to make sense of the universe in which we live will always be relational to our home on Earth and to our human bodily and cultural experience. As such, it is not surprising that many science fiction films and television programmes still visually centralise Earth. The *Star Trek* franchise has attempted to draw and expand on known science in order to speculate on future inventions; however, its title sequences reveal an ongoing tension between heliocentric knowledge and geocentric experience.

All of the *Star Trek* series implicitly fashion a cosmological perspective that is part science, part myth. By situating us in particular areas of space, from particular vantage points and trajectories, and with different musical and voice-over cues, each title sequence suggests a specific cosmological view. The *Star Trek* programmes position us in space not only physically but also ideologically. Therefore, while the *Star Trek* franchise is not itself science, it is nonetheless part of a scientific and cosmological discourse, where its special effects, science-inspired technobabble and sheer longevity have granted it a prime position in the popular culture mediation of space. The variations between the opening titles of the various series suggest that *Star Trek* has not created a master narrative cosmology. However, its assertion of the simultaneous importance of our solar system origins and the continued availability of new spatial (as well as temporal, narrative and series) frontiers suggests a cosmos that is an expansive yet knowable, vast yet local, space and place. Although the various *Star Trek* series promise to explore strange new worlds, those worlds are ultimately mappable and intelligible. Most of them are also Class-M planets – in other words, like Earth. Tyrell argues that the *Star Trek* cosmos is ordered by comprehensible causation, and that this 'causality functions as a myth; it is a story that *Star Trek* tells to affirm that there is nothing new or strange anywhere around us'.[223] Science fiction programmes such as the *Star Trek* franchise mediate contemporary scientific and cosmological knowledge, rendering it accessible to the non-scientist through narrative and image. However, the 'real' cosmos is subsumed into the *Star Trek* cosmos, a mythic realm in which the strange promises to be rendered familiar and safe, and where, ultimately, there's no place like home.

4

Fans, Bards and Rituals

Introduction

If title sequences provide a ritualised boundary zone through which we enter the television programme, this chapter argues that rituals of television viewing have extended to interactive rituals of storytelling and pilgrimage as the world of *Star Trek* has expanded into physical environments – taking as case study the award-winning *Star Trek: The Experience*,[1] which operated in Las Vegas from 1998 to 2008, during the tail end of what has become known as the 'Disney in the Desert' years. This period also coincided with the break-up of Viacom, the parent conglomerate that owned the *Star Trek* brand from 1994 to 2006, and which had become something of a symbol of corporate oppression of fans seeking to play out their own *Star Trek* narratives outside the (numerous) official transmedia products. *The Experience* closed just one year before the franchise was rebooted by J. J. Abrams' 2009 film *Star Trek*. Given the expected revival of interest in the story-world, particularly among new, young viewers, the timing of the closure may seem odd. *The Experience*, though, was devoted to the original *Star Trek* timeline, which the new film was about to overhaul. Mythic 'traditions' are always, in fact, in constant flux, particularly across generations, and *Star Trek* is no different in this respect. While ancient mythic traditions would expand across epic poetry, art and theatre, our contemporary mythologies find themselves played out in a transmedia expanse. Earlier chapters have noted that *Star Trek* has been deliberately marketed in its paratexts as legendary, mythic and epic, with its own set of heroes. But it is the fan who has been recast as the hero through the marketing and ride narratives for *The Experience*.

As there are limits to fan interactivity with official products such as *The Experience*, fans have continually asserted their right to enact their own *Star Trek* narratives. Rituals of viewing have extended to new rituals of storytelling by the fans themselves, as they take on the role of latter-day bards. This multi-authored mythic storytelling may have ancient precedence, but it frequently contravenes contemporary copyright laws. In a series of mergers and acquisitions, the Viacom conglomerate bought Paramount Communications (and with it *Star Trek*) in 1994, and merged with CBS in 1999. After their dissolution in 2006, the *Star Trek* brand as a whole went to what was now called CBS Corporation, while licensed film rights stayed with Paramount under a new Viacom company.[2] Particularly in the late 1990s, when the original Viacom was most actively attempting to crack down on fan use of copyrighted material, fans cast themselves as heroes of resistance against both Paramount and Viacom, articulating their stories of this struggle in very *Star Trek*-specific ways. While official Viacom products during this era attempted to make the fan a central character and hero through interactive products such as *Star Trek: The Experience* in Las Vegas, this chapter explores these attempts in the context of a contested *Star Trek* fan culture, and its official and unofficial rituals.

Myth and Ritual Theory

Although television fandom is not itself religious in nature, theories of secular, entertainment rituals have drawn heavily upon theories of myth and ritual from classics and anthropology, albeit in highly modified forms. In the late nineteenth and early twentieth centuries, the 'myth and ritual' or Cambridge school of theory argued that myth was the spoken equivalent or component of an enacted ritual. Myth was the words; ritual was the act.[3] From this perspective, 'there can be no myth without ritual, although time

Fans, Bards and Rituals

may have obliterated the act and left the narrative free to survive as myth or its debased subspecies (saga, legend, folktale, etc).'[4] The most notable figure in the movement was Sir James Frazer (1854–1941), whose imposing collection *The Golden Bough*, written from 1890 to 1915, tied a number of myths and rituals to one cross-cultural ritual.[5] This methodology suggested a universalism that was increasingly difficult to sustain as new research came to light. The myth–ritual theory was so popular that it was applied extremely broadly and with undue certainty. Rituals were 'discovered' at the base of numerous historical and literary accounts.[6] Despite this, contemporary theorists have maintained strands of the theory in contending that '*some* myths are tied by their *motifs* to local rituals, especially initiation rituals'.[7] This approach had been tentatively suggested in early myth theory, but the more literal connection had been prevalent.[8]

In a Greek example, Lucia Nixon has noted similarities between *The Homeric Hymn to Demeter* (c. seventh century BCE) and rituals performed in honour of the goddess of the harvest, Demeter.[9] In *The Homeric Hymn to Demeter*, Hades, the god of the underworld, abducts Persephone, daughter of Demeter. Demeter is overcome by grief and refuses to join the other gods in their activities. In her distress, Demeter takes the seeds that have been sown in the earth and hides them, causing a famine. Zeus finally intervenes, allowing Persephone to be fetched from the underworld. However, Hades tricks Persephone into eating pomegranate seeds in the underworld, which forces her to return to him for one third of every year. At the end of the *Hymn*, Demeter allows the seeds in the earth to sprout, and gives instructions about the rituals that must be performed within the sanctuary at Eleusis constructed in her honour.[10] Although the details of those rituals are not specified, the Mysteries are thought to have been similar to the *Hymn* in their focus on the process of death and rebirth, both agricultural and spiritual.[11] More specifically, Nixon points out that the plants mentioned in the *Hymn*, namely pennyroyal and pomegranate, were known by the Greeks to be anti-fertility treatments, the effects of which have been attested to by contemporary science.[12] At the Thesmophoria, female cult participants were forbidden from eating pomegranate seeds, and made offerings to Demeter of pine branches, another plant used for gynaecological purposes.[13] In Greek thought, women only housed the growing baby, while men alone provided the creative material.[14] However, in the *Hymn*, Demeter is able to control agricultural fertility by not allowing the seeds to grow.[15] The plants specified in *The Homeric Hymn to Demeter*, and used in rituals in honour of Demeter, suggest that the myth and ritual alike were used to confer knowledge of fertility-controlling herb lore to their female participants.[16] Myth and ritual, story and action, seem to relate directly to one another, even if there cannot be any certainty as to which came first.

Not all myths have such clearly related ritual sites, and conversely, not all ritual sites have clearly related myths. Thus, the Rome school of classical theory[17] suggested that myth may be linked to ritual where sufficient ethnological evidence exists, but is also related to the intertext of Greek mythology.[18] The Rome school was also mindful of the need to view 'religion in an historical context'.[19] In these respects, the Rome school, although perhaps not presenting as unified a theory as its title suggests, nonetheless broadened the context of the myth–ritual perspective.

Ritual has traditionally been most closely associated with religion and religious cult, where the term can cover a broad range of activities. However, in the context of myth–ritual theory, ritual has also been applied to apparently secular areas of ancient Greek life, as well as non-Greek secular literature.[20] Literary myth–ritual theory postulates that literature originates in myth, which in turn is tied to ritual; indeed, 'myth becomes literature when it is severed from ritual'.[21] The notion of ritual has also been extended to secular and contemporary examples, without necessarily appealing to myth.[22]

Although an interrelationship between myth and ritual is still considered controversial by many scholars, Segal suggests that one of its strengths lies in its willingness to tackle 'the relationship [...] between narrative and action. The theory also suggests parallels between myth and other cultural phenomena like science and literature that might otherwise get missed'.[23] Along similar lines, anthropologists such as Victor Turner have drawn comparisons between tribal ritual and the activities of secular, industrial cultures, most notably the '*leisure* genres of arts and entertainment'.[24] Because of this broad alignment, scholars of popular culture have continued to look to Turner when approaching the role of ritual in contemporary culture, including within television studies.[25]

In this broader, secular context, cinema theory attempted to come to terms with a possible myth–ritual connection, most notably in the context of genre theory approaches to myth of the 1960s and 1970s. Jim Kitses, for example, argued that the Western genre had a ritualistic aspect 'of displaced myth'.[26] While John Cawelti argued that cinema genres were not myths, he acknowledged the role of the Western as a 'cultural ritual'.[27] By the late 1970s, Thomas Schatz had incorporated broader scholarship on myth, noting that even secular ritual could perform a mythic function.[28] But just as cinema studies has tended to conflate myth with structuralism, so too genre theory's association with ritual has perhaps hindered our understanding of broader rituals in entertainment.

The ritual aspects of media fandom have most often been filtered through theories of cult and religion. What constitutes a cult text has, however, become quite broad. J. P. Telotte ultimately defines cult film not through the films themselves but through the activities surrounding them. Telotte argues:

> Memorizing dialogue, practising gestures, wearing costumes, and attending repeatedly are required. In effect, a body of ritual, of the sort that marks both the religious and theatrical experiences, attends the cult film experience and, in the process, gives it, almost in spite of itself, a clearly social dimension [...] every cult constitutes a community, a group that 'worships' similarly and regularly, and finds strength in that shared experience.[29]

The nature of the rituals surrounding a cult text obviously varies, according to the text, medium and fan.

Star Trek fandom occupies an in-between status as both a global mainstream conglomerate franchise and an often socially marginalised subculture. As Chris Gregory notes:

> If contemporary *Star Trek* 'fandom' with its network of conventions and fan clubs, [sic] constitutes a 'cult' it must be stressed that it is not – as the term perhaps implies – a small, self-contained group of 'fanatics' but a global 'community'. There are many parallels between rituals of religion and those connected with modern mass media forms. While the stars of popular

music, TV and film are 'worshipped' as modern 'icons', 'cult' TV series give their fans a sense of 'belonging' to an exclusive group which is one way in which they define their identity.[30]

As Henry Jenkins notes in his important monograph on media fandom, the characterisation of fandom as religious owes a debt to the origins of the word 'fan', the Latin *fanaticus*, meaning 'a temple servant, a devotee'.[31] However, the term soon became associated with any excessive and mistaken belief.[32] Comparisons between fandom and cult, religion and ritual often run the risk of being too literal, without adequate qualification. This can leave the reader free to make (sometimes incorrect) associations on their own, particularly about how fans themselves might conceptualise their activities.[33] While Gregory argues that the cult programme serves as the foundation for 'ritualised drama' enacted by fans, he goes on to say, 'It must be emphasised, however, that the vast majority of *Star Trek* fans participate in such activities with a self-deprecatingly ironic approach and few would claim to be serious "religious" devotees.'[34] Despite this, James A. Herrick has gone so far as to suggest that the substitute mythologies offered by science fiction are a potentially dangerous diversion from legitimate (and in his case, specifically Christian) religious teachings.[35]

Is the fandom that surrounds science fiction worlds such as *Star Trek* mere play or something more serious? And is this a distinction worth making? Michael Jindra has suggested that *Star Trek* fandom is 'a religious-type movement' with 'an origin myth, a set of beliefs, an organization' and, of course, members.[36] Part of the basis for his assertion are the mythic qualities of the *Star Trek* texts, with their utopian futurism; however, Jindra does not explain exactly how he is employing the term 'myth'.[37] Jindra notes: 'In calling the activities of ST [*Star Trek*] fandom "mythological," I do not intend to eliminate the "playful" or entertainment aspects of ST and claim it is only serious.'[38] Similarly, he states 'ST fandom does not have the thoroughgoing seriousness of established religions, but it is also not mere entertainment.'[39] Elsewhere he asserts that *Star Trek* fandom can involve 'utterly serious pretending [...] ST fandom, I believe, is an example of play and ritual coming back together, back to their "natural" condition of coexistence and ambiguity'.[40] The ambiguity Jindra identifies points to behaviour that might be both serious and playful at the same time. As mainstream yet marginal, serious and playful, a real engagement with the fictional, *Star Trek* fandom has a liminal ('in-between') status that will be explored in this chapter in a number of guises, through the filter of the myth–ritual connection.[41]

In the context of media cult and fandom studies, the story is created first and the rituals second. The order of this relationship in myth–ritual theory has varied depending on the theorist – myth first, then ritual; ritual first, then myth; or simultaneous development.[42] The relationship has also varied depending on the cultural context, leading Clyde Kluckholn to assert, 'the facts do not permit any universal generalizations as to ritual being the "cause" of myth or vice versa'.[43] Due to the frequent necessity of projecting back into pre-history, however, many theorists considered the potential relationship too difficult to reconstruct, if indeed there was a correlation to find. As a result, 'most theorists of myth continue to focus on myth alone, and most theorists of ritual continue to focus on ritual alone'.[44] In a contemporary context, the potential relationship between story and action is not clouded by distant time. While we should be cautious in the assertion of correlations between ancient or oral cultures and present multimedia culture, as Walter Burkert argues, 'there has yet to be a community without ritual.'[45] Rather, it is the nature of those rituals that is different in the context of media conglomerates that seek to create popular, profitable texts, and deliberately produce from them activities and sites that can generate further profit. This corporate structure does not *prima facie* preclude the possibility that such commercial rituals might be meaningful for their participants, nor has it prevented fans from creating their own (sometimes illegal) activities around the text.

Just as there exists a constant play between different notions of myth in our culture, so too ritual holds competing and complementary meanings, whereby it is understood both in terms of the ceremonial and in terms of the habitual. In some respects this distinction has been borne precisely of our perceived split between sacred events and secular, mundane ones. Television viewing, as an activity integrated into our daily routines, not only acts as a communication medium for the shifting notions of myth outlined in the preceding chapters, but also functions as ritualised act in itself.[46] This ritualistic aspect is emphasised by the predominance of series and serial forms in broadcast television in particular, which aim to attract repeat viewing at the same time each week or each day. Thus, John Fiske and John Hartley argue that 'television functions as a social ritual'.[47] While ritual may imply an activity beyond the story, the conditions of storytelling can themselves be the subject of ritual behaviour.

The nature of the viewing ritual has changed over time as television technology became part of the everyday. Hartley and Tom O'Regan note that when the first television sets arrived in homes, they created a social focus, as neighbours without sets would come over to watch television.[48]

> As ownership or rental became more widespread, and as the novelty wore off, television viewing began to lose its quasicinematic, social aspect, and to take on its more recently characteristic patterns – it became a private, family activity, with just one family per set.[49]

The television, in becoming more widespread, paradoxically also became more insular in its use. At the same time, the notion of 'one family per set' became a powerful cultural idea, an unrealistic image of how families used televisions. Indeed, elsewhere Hartley acknowledges that this concept created a 'tribalized' construction of the family.[50]

Once the technology became a familiar and presumed part of the home, it was subsumed into domesticity. John Ellis argues, 'Broadcast TV is […] intimate and everyday, a part of home life rather than any kind of special event.'[51] Emphasising this everyday status, early television theory suggested that television viewing was characterised by the distracted glance.[52] However, cult television fandom undermines this model. Fandom suggests a greater investment in the TV text, and therefore a more attentive viewing practice. With the advent of streaming services, it has become clear that this attentive and intense viewing of television programmes previously associated only with fandom is now mainstream.[53]

Bardic Television

The television has become an important storytelling medium in contemporary culture, even as its edges become blurred in an era of streaming. Fiske and Hartley go so far as to argue that television can be conceptualised as a type of oral storyteller in our homes analogous to the ancient bard.[54] As with this ancient bard, television works with and communicates myth, although Fiske and Hartley tend to blur myth with ideology, partly due to their use of Barthes.[55] Fiske and Hartley argue that 'the traditional bard rendered the central concerns of his [sic] day into verse', affirming the culture's self-image and acting as a *'mediator of language'*, as television does in contemporary culture.[56] They suggest that the resulting story was seen as belonging to the culture as a whole rather than the individual bard, and was constructed to respond to the needs of that culture and audience rather than 'to the internal demands of the "text"'.[57] Fiske and Hartley compare this to the 'multi-originated' television message.[58] They argue that both the bard and television provide a 'common center' for the culture; in the case of television, providing unity for 'our highly fragmented society'.[59] Fiske and Hartley are primarily interested in describing the functionality of television as opposed to the specifics of its reception. However, their gloss on the contemporary audience problematically assumes that the audience in a post-industrial culture is capable of being 'centred' in a manner similar to the much smaller, non-industrial tribal group or clan that traditional bards addressed.

Fiske and Hartley state that 'the bardic voice is *oral*, not literate'.[60] Like the oral storyteller, television communicates through speech. They later acknowledge a visual and literary aspect to television, but argue that an oral *logic* dominates.[61] The bard tries to find common ground between audience and subject matter, and where this is not possible a shift in culture will occur to accommodate the inadequacy.[62] Bardic television is, then, a 'dynamic' process, but Fiske and Hartley do not account for the fact that, unlike oral storytelling, television is separated from its audience in time and space.

Finally, Fiske and Hartley's bardic television selects and combines myths, and is able to communicate the resultant mythologies regardless of the degree of audience consciousness, because myths 'operate at the level of latent as opposed to manifest content'.[63] The audience is nonetheless capable of being 'multi-conscious' – of understanding various meanings 'simultaneously and without confusion'.[64]

While the preceding chapters argued that television can tell and retell myth in a variety of guises, Fiske and Hartley's concept of bardic television takes this correlation further by suggesting that television's mode of storytelling has not greatly changed from the ancient forms of storytelling through which myth was transmitted. They suggest that myth is an inherent part of this communication system – but that it must be analysed in order to reveal ideology. Thus, as Barthes suggests, the job of the mythologist is to reveal the assumptions that lie within the myth.[65] If the television medium as a whole has the ability to create popular culture myths, specific programmes such as the *Star Trek* franchise extend this function to further mythicise their fictional universe. Different layers of myth, and even different forms of myth, are built upon one another, from an implicit media-based function to a deliberate marketing and narrative strategy.

Fiske and Hartley interpret a newsreader, sports commentator and drama protagonist as bardic in their transformation of reality into myth; these televisual bards communicate their value judgement of the events around them, but their interpretations are presented as merely factual.[66] Here there appears to be a certain slippage between 'television as our own culture's *bard*' and figures featured on television as bards;[67] that is, between medium as bard and medium as communication device for individual bards. This is partly due to the fact that the figure of the bard remains obscure at best within the model. Fiske and Hartley use 'the classically conceived bard' as their basis, but do not offer the means by which this conception is reached.[68] Historically, the bard was governed by complex social and legal rules that can help us extend this bardic metaphor as a comparative model for contemporary storytelling. Etymologically, the word 'bard' is Celtic in origin (Irish *beird*, Welsh *bardd* and *beirdd*).[69] Over time the title of bard has been applied to poets of various cultures and time periods, from those of ancient Greece to William Shakespeare.[70] This points to the terminological slippage possible, particularly in the interplay between the written script and the spoken, enacted performance. It is unclear whether Fiske and Hartley's 'classical' bard references Greek and Roman antiquity, or if this is meant to suggest more broadly oral cultures in which the bard held a prime cultural position. Further, in its etymologically original setting, bard is but one word for a poet among a number of different classes of poet. There were also different types of bard in the Celtic tradition, including both wandering and resident bards, professionals and amateurs.[71] For example, in the Welsh tradition, one might have a *bardd teulu*, or 'household poet'.[72]

Proinsias Mac Cana notes that there were conventions – 'one might almost speak of ritual' – surrounding bardic storytelling in the Irish medieval context, which probably had their origins in older Celtic traditions.[73] Storytelling could be restricted to certain individuals, times and locations, and specific classes of story were used for special occasions.[74] Storytellers were paid for their efforts, and yet they performed in the homes of both the rich and the poor.[75] Some classes of storytellers would undergo years of training, learning story traditions and catalogues of allusions to be used in poetic compositions.[76] However, as a social practice, 'storytelling [itself] was [...] a normal and unremarkable part of life'.[77] Oral storytelling in the Celtic bardic tradition was both an integral part of life and a commercial exchange, as television is today. Both draw on formula in order to retell old stories and create new ones. Although they use the bard merely as an analogy, Fiske and Hartley underplay the significance of formula both to the bard and to television.

By contrast, Janet H. Murray has applied cross-cultural theories of storytelling and the bard in her correlation between oral bards and computer storytelling.[78] In particular, she cites the work of Milman Parry and Alfred Lord, whose groundbreaking shift to an oral, rather than literate, approach to the Greek epic poet Homer provided the basis of the oral-formulaic approach.[79] Unlike Fiske and Hartley, Murray stresses the bard's use of formula and pattern, from which the story is constructed. While the specific details of the story may be changed with each telling and are therefore quite fluid, the patterns themselves are preserved.[80] Murray cites the example of Vladimir Propp's work on the Russian oral folk tale, in which he was able to find a specific set of recurring story elements (morphemes) that occurred in a set order and yet were open to extremely varied combinations.[81] While dependent on repetition, the units of oral composition and the way in which they are used could be quite complex.[82] Although some of Propp's story elements are found in the computer stories and games explored by Murray (such as 'The hero defeats the villain'), Murray's argument is not that computer storytelling replicates morphemes from the Russian folk tale. Rather, morphemes and a morphological system can be found within other storytelling systems and groups of tales. The creation of a set of morphemes can become the basis of new story generation, such as within a computerised environment.[83] Murray's vision is for all users to become bards, constructing stories with the morphemes laid out by a programming bard. Here the orality of the storytelling is not literal, but rather constitutes a logic of story production based on oral story production. Murray is also interested in the way that the internet facilitates fandom; and by conceiving of us all as latent bards, this approach to storytelling can be expanded to include the way that fans – including those of *Star Trek* – can draw and expand upon the templates set out by pre-existing story-worlds.

Murray's model is applied to a medium that incorporates a direct interactivity on the level of narrative production, which is mostly unavailable to the television viewer, apart from voting off contestants or, less often, voting for story outcomes. The model nonetheless provides a more balanced approach than Fiske and Hartley to bardic storytelling in its interplay between formula and innovation. It also takes account of bardic storytelling as multi-authored. Individual bards draw upon earlier and coexistent stories and storytelling traditions of a culture, and in the case of the computer narratives discussed by Murray, play off other bards as well. Fans enter into this multi-authored array of shared cultural tales, engaging with different media offshoots of a story but adding their own adventures as well.

Partly due to her reliance on Propp and partly because she is interested in the computer generation of new stories, Murray does stress the maintenance of formula over the maintenance of surface details. In fact, specific stories (rather than just their underlying patterns) are maintained in the traditional bardic system of storytelling.[84] However, Murray does acknowledge that a storyteller (or computer program) that does not understand the importance of 'specific material' to enliven a formula will produce a story that is bland to incoherent.[85] She argues that 'the pleasure of storytelling lies not in the raw formulas but in the particularizing details. No one would curl up at night with a tale made out of a recitation of Propp's abstract morphemes.'[86]

Although Murray is primarily concerned with existing and emergent interactive technologies, she does note connections between potential forms of 'cyberdrama' and the demands of 'serving for several seasons as head writer of a multithreaded television drama',[87] particularly in terms of coordination of plotlines and the balance between formula and innovation. Most television series are multi-authored, even if they are headed up by a show-runner. While *TOS* was overseen by creator Gene Roddenberry, for example, individual episodes had different writers and directors. Within this multi-authored domain, a number of story traditions were drawn upon. The *Star Trek* franchise has increasingly adapted pre-existing myths into its futuristic diegesis, drawing on both broad mythic formulas and specific mythic stories. In turn, its advertising has attempted to strengthen its cultural status as a form of popular myth. We can characterise this multi-authored appropriation as a contemporary bardic function, using both innovation and older formulas in the process of adapting myth into a futuristic setting.[88] The *Star Trek* narrative has also been developed into three-dimensional spaces such as *Star Trek: The Experience* in Las Vegas, relying upon audience knowledge of specific *Star Trek* stories, and on a more general level, the conventions of the *Star Trek* story-world. By retelling the *Star Trek* 'myth' in new contexts, new rituals of engagement with the *Star Trek* story are facilitated. This creates spaces within which fans can generate ritual-based stories, memories and mementos of an experience. In turn, *Star Trek* fandom extends the multiple authorship inherent in a bardic system of storytelling, expanding upon pre-existing texts through new fan-generated stories.

Pilgrimage and *Star Trek: The Experience*

While *Star Trek* fans may have dedicated, ritualised viewing habits that take their viewing beyond the casual glance conventionally associated with television,[89] fan conventions have provided physical meeting points for fans to share their fandom at a special place and time. Rituals of the everyday (viewing) have been extended into the shared fan rituals of the convention. The *Star Trek* franchise has also been extended into a range of official interactive products. *Star Trek: The Experience* was one such interactive experiment: a themed environment, two rides and a convention site at the Las Vegas Hilton in Las Vegas, Nevada, USA, which operated from 1998 to 2008. The themed site was initially owned by Viacom through its Paramount Parks division, and after the 2006 split became part of CBS Corp., which in turn sold off the interest to theme park operator Cedar Fair Entertainment Company in the same year, before the attraction's closure in 2008 and the franchise's subsequent rebooting with J. J. Abrams' 2009 feature film *Star Trek*.

Star Trek: The Experience reproduced aspects of the *Star Trek* world in three dimensions, and included a restaurant, a museum and two simulation rides. Like Disneyland before it, *Star Trek: The Experience* was but one offshoot of a large, cross-media corporation, using a successful franchise to expand its concerns. It provided fans with the opportunity to enact their own embodied *Star Trek* narrative, while gearing that interactive experience towards predetermined trajectories. Upon entering the attraction, fans would be positioned as heroes charged with protecting the *Star Trek* timeline, a mythology of the future. The attraction thereby relied upon 'the relationship [...] between narrative and action' that Segal identifies at the juncture of myth and ritual, even in its secular guise.[90]

In the context of a story that spans several decades and has a dedicated fan following, *Star Trek: The Experience* operated as a pilgrimage site, transforming *Star Trek* from a fictional text into real locale. *Star Trek: The Experience* became the destination for fan journeys imbued with fan significance, offering a play between identities and realities in its mix of multiple fictive, physical and temporal realms. Jennifer E. Porter has suggested that fan journeys to *Star Trek* conventions can be conceptualised in terms of pilgrimage.[91] Drawing on the work of anthropologist Victor Turner, Porter explains that pilgrimage is 'a ritual journey in which participants are temporarily freed from the social constraints of everyday statuses, roles and expectations'.[92] By comparison, Alan Morinis defines pilgrimage as 'a journey undertaken by a person in quest of a place or state that he or she believes to embody a valued ideal'.[93] Thus pilgrimage can be an affirming experience, but can also provide a liminal zone in which social boundaries and identities can be blurred.[94] Pilgrimage allows the *spatial* expression of liminality and a communal fellowship ('communitas') between participants during a special journey.[95]

In non-industrial religious cultures, a number of different forms of ritual could provide communal affirmation and liminal transgression. During the rite of passage, a liminal period and communitas would 'mark changes in an individual's or a group's social status and/or cultural or psychological state in many societies past and present'.[96] The rite of passage can transform or restore social bonds.[97] Carnival has also been explored as a form of liminal, ritual behaviour in which social boundaries can be subverted, providing an outlet that 'both challenge[s] and support[s] the established order'.[98] Rites of passage, pilgrimage and carnival are all ritual encounters with ambivalent states that provide the opportunity for communal fellowship, and in some cases also transformation. While Turner identifies three different forms of communitas, pilgrimage is characterised by what he terms 'normative communitas', in which the communal experience has become organised into a system as a result of necessity and 'social control', particularly when dealing with large numbers.[99] Thus, the pilgrimage provides a structured format that nonetheless contains within it an attempt to recall a more spontaneous, liminal communitas of an earlier era.

Turner argues that industrial cultures do not have truly liminal experiences but rather what he terms 'liminoid', a secular version of liminality found in performance arts.[100] In a recreational context, social norms are played with, blurred and reversed. Turner also argues that pilgrimage may perform a liminoid function within secular industrial society, even though it too is an optional pursuit under the rubric of leisure.[101] Thus Erik Cohen argues that 'even as traditional pilgrimage becomes "mere" tourism, tourism [...] becomes for some the new pilgrimage'.[102] Within this liminoid experience, Turner suggests that there still remains at least the possibility of deeper liminal transformation.[103] Porter argues that the fan journey to *Star Trek* conventions can be characterised in this manner, leading to a state of 'communal fellowship' and a liminoid blurring of social roles.[104] She says, 'Although *Star Trek* convention attendance is not religious pilgrimage, it may well be an "inheritor" of pilgrimage in the contemporary, secular context.'[105]

Similarly, *Star Trek: The Experience* in Las Vegas functioned as a pilgrimage site for fans from around the world.[106] *The Experience* was both a themed site and the location of physical and virtual conventions. Alan

Morinis notes that not all pilgrimages necessarily involve 'communitas', and can indeed be highly individual.[107] Further, while pilgrimage may share features of the rite of passage, it may also be 'reinforcing, like a rite of intensification'.[108] In a commercial context such as *The Experience*, participants may be addressed as individuals in narrative and commercial terms, further complicating a pilgrimage model. Just as Turner argues that contemporary industrial cultures may include liminoid and liminal cultural forms and practices, we must not assume that resemblance to traditional pilgrimage necessarily results in communal fellowship. The experiences on offer at the attraction paralleled older pilgrimage models without being religious in nature, while drawing on the lessons of Disney's theme parks in their transformation of text into place, and of story into ritual.

Disneyland and Las Vegas: Three-Dimensional Texts

In the media conglomerate age, transmedia spin-offs and merchandising have become standard means of maximising profits around a popular product, story or character. Harnessing synergy between subsidiary companies, a big success in one medium soon appears in other forms, hoping to capture and cultivate the fan market, and using new media to enable increasingly performative experiences of the text. While the shift from narrative text to interactive experience of that text by no means began with Walt Disney's theme parks, the degree of synergy his company facilitated was unprecedented, providing a template for the conglomerates that followed. *Star Trek*'s expansion into a themed environment reflects the new conglomerate structure that was exemplified by Disney.

In an inspired marketing move, Disney named both his planned amusement park and his 1954 television series *Disneyland*. The television programme functioned as a long advertisement for Disney feature films and the park, which opened in July 1955. The TV show also offered a narrative template through which tourists could understand the park, as initially the programme used the same themed sections as the park.[109] Thomas Hine describes the park as 'a movie that could be walked into'.[110] Indeed, many of the rides within the park, such as Peter Pan's Flight, reiterate parts of Disney film narratives.[111]

The cinematic quality of the park was mediated by the television experience that grouped the films into themes, and linked those themes explicitly with the park. In the first episode of the television show, Disney informed the audience that 'Disneyland the place and *Disneyland* the show are all the same', emphasising this crossover synergy.[112] Indeed, K. A. Marling has argued that wandering through Disneyland

> is discontinuous and episodic, like watching television [...] each ride a four- or five-minute segment, slotted in among snacks, trips to the rest room, and 'commercials' in the form of souvenir emporia. And it is always possible to change the channel.[113]

Marling's metaphorical television set would seem to be a strange one, however, with only Disney programmes to choose from.[114] This is, after all, Disney's land, and not merely television-land, cinema-land or story-land.

In the early conceptual stages, Disney conceived of the park space as one of 'total merchandising'.[115] Christopher Anderson argues:

> In effect, Walt identified the program with the park in order to create an inhabitable text, one that would never be complete for a television-viewing family until they had [...] made a pilgrimage to the park itself. A trip to Disneyland – using the conceptual map provided by the program – offered the family viewer a chance to perform in the Disneyland narrative.[116]

Innovative in the mid-1950s, Disney's cross-media merchandising and interactive, three-dimensional reworking of cinema and television texts provided a successful example for other entertainment conglomerates to emulate.

Star Trek's textual and commercial expansion reflects the shift in the entertainment industry to a conglomerate structure, which began in the late 1950s.[117] By the 1990s, Disney-style synergy was a common expansion tactic. For example, T. L. Stanley notes that 'in the Disney mold', parent conglomerate Viacom has used its Paramount Parks division to increase the 'hands-on interface between consumers and popular products like *Star Trek*, Spelling and MTV properties and Hanna-Barbera "toons"'.[118] In the case of *Star Trek*, a themed attraction was developed at the Las Vegas

Hilton through the Paramount Parks division, using the design work of Landmark Entertainment Group.[119] Indeed, the shift towards themed family entertainment in Las Vegas during the 1990s[120] prompted some journalists to rename it 'Disney in the Desert'.[121] While these new complexes were themselves multimedia extravaganzas, the cross-media synergy exemplified by Disneyland as a park–television crossover can be seen most strongly in *Star Trek: The Experience* at the Las Vegas Hilton. Disney's park was being constructed as his television programme was in its first year. By contrast, *Star Trek: The Experience* capitalised on a pre-existing set of programmes, the first of which aired over 30 years prior to the site's development. However, like the Disneyland theme park, *The Experience* operated as performed narrative, an inhabitable *Star Trek* environment that made its story-world real while also providing new *Star Trek* stories on its rides, a transmedia expansion of the story-world. As Jenkins notes, transmedia storytelling extends the tale further with new instalments, but also seeks to enhance 'audience engagement' with that story-world as a 'unified and coordinated entertainment experience'.[122] Both Disneyland and *Star Trek: The Experience* create pilgrimage destinations for their fans, enabling fans to enter the text made manifest,[123] and arenas of secular, ritualistic play.

Opened on 3 January 1998 after a number of delays, the attraction was originally made up of '37 themed spaces',[124] grouped roughly together in terms of a *DS9* promenade including a merchandise store, a recreation of Quark's Bar from *DS9*, a museum of the *Star Trek* future, and the various spaces that made up the *Next Generation* ride, subsequently titled 'Klingon Encounter'. On the ride, guests would step into a small entrance room which then suffered an 'unexpected' blackout, after which they found themselves in the transporter room on *TNG*'s *Enterprise*. Guests were then taken to the bridge of the *Enterprise*, where characters Lieutenant Commander Geordi La Forge and Commander Will Riker explained that alien Klingons had abducted the guests from their own time. The renegade Klingons believed one of the guests to be the ancestor of Captain Jean-Luc Picard (from *TNG*), so by removing them from the proper timeline, Picard's birth could be prevented. Visitors were then taken through the Grand Corridor, arriving at a bay containing shuttle craft. Inside the shuttles, they would be taken on a simulated ride, trying to avoid fire from Klingons in order to make it back home and correct the timelines. The shuttles arrived over the Las Vegas skyline, and guests departed into a 'maintenance' area, to be led by a 'janitor' back to the themed environs. In 2004, a 'Borg Invasion 4D' ride was added, in which guests were rescued from the Borg by Admiral Kathryn Janeway of *Voyager*. On this ride, it was suspected that a guest may have a special genetic immunity to Borg technology.[125] The themed attraction finally closed its doors in September 2008. Props from the attraction were auctioned off in April 2010.[126]

Although prominently advertised in its signage, the attraction was nestled in a corner of the Las Vegas Hilton, a hotel located well off the main Strip, and at the time of its opening, a not inconsiderable walk in the heat of the Nevada sun. The attraction was, therefore, a dual effort to profitably expand the *Star Trek* franchise while at the same time bringing customers to the out-of-the-way Hilton.[127] In July 2004 access to the Hilton was improved with the Las Vegas Monorail extension.

While *Star Trek: The Experience* itself did not have gambling facilities, it sat adjacent to a space-themed 'SpaceQuest' slot machine room with vaguely *Star Trek* aesthetics and a pseudo-warp core at its centre, emphasising the desired spillage from one themed space into the other. Movement was thereby encouraged within the Hilton complex, from *Star Trek* theme environment, to space theme casino, to non-themed casino, and vice versa.[128] *Star Trek: The Experience* may have created an inhabitable television text, but again our options for changing channels were limited to Paramount and Hilton prescriptions. The transformation of story into space and the range of rituals possible within that space were strictly defined.

In the context of the wider Las Vegas environs, however, this metaphorical channel-hopping is more varied. Russell Belk argues that the town 'leaves us with the impression that we have just stepped into a three-dimensional television set with a wild agenda of disparate programming [...] a feeling familiar from theme parks, television, and shopping malls'.[129] This is hardly surprising, given that Las Vegas draws explicitly on all these modes, and on others as well – including movies, legends and quasi-history.[130] If these various sources jostling together are not unified under the same corporate banner in the manner of Disneyland, they still share a unified if competitive goal of profit making. Indeed, Mark Gottdiener notes that because the venues share the same primary product – gambling – 'thematic' differences become the focus of differentiation.¹³¹

While the themed environment and rides offered Viacom and Hilton the joint opportunity for further profit, *Star Trek: The Experience* offered fans the opportunity to inhabit, for a price, a re-creation of the fictional *Star Trek* world they knew and loved. Thus advertising for the attraction asserted that '*Star Trek: The Experience* is the only place in the universe where you can play, shop and dine in the 24th century',¹³² and that it is 'the only place on Earth where the world of *Star Trek* exists in three dimensions [...] visitors are immersed in a futuristic world'.¹³³ Commentators such as John Belton have argued that Disneyland consists of 'two-dimensional motion picture stories and space [...] reconstructed in three-dimensional space'.¹³⁴ *Star Trek: The Experience* not only followed this trajectory but also used it as a marketing tool, stressing that the site was the 'only place' where *Star Trek* exists as an inhabitable locale. The pilgrimage to *Star Trek: The Experience* extended viewing rituals into a ritual journey, for which the programmes provided 'the conceptual map' in the manner of Disneyland.¹³⁵ Within the growing conglomerate structure, *Star Trek* has been a useful pre-sold commodity, with its large fan following as a ready market for seemingly endless re-articulations that could be differentiated by media, and yet each be given the Paramount/Viacom seal of approval as an 'official' *Star Trek* text. *Star Trek*'s transmedia expansions have increased with each decade, entering into an era in which cross-media marketing has become the norm rather than the exception for successful media products.

Fan as Character/Hero and Identity Play

While the advertising for *The Experience* stressed the realisation (and exclusivity) of the *Star Trek* world in three dimensions, the role of the visitor and fan within that space was also carefully constructed. Similarly, more traditional forms of pilgrimage offer a zone of liminal play, but in quite standardised forms.¹³⁶ There are rules for breaking the rules within ritual liminality, shared conventions among participants in order to make pilgrimage groups manageable.¹³⁷ *Star Trek: The Experience* had commercial and legal rules of conduct, but also constructed a particular ritual role for us to occupy within the *Star Trek* story-world. The print advertising material for *The Experience* promised that we would not merely go on ride, but rather we would 'go on a mission'.[138] Brochures implored us to 'Join the crew and boldly go!', mirroring the opening words of the original and *TNG* series. These paratextual promotional materials emphasise our participation in the *Star Trek* narrative alongside our physical participation. A female alien Trill Starfleet officer looks directly at the reader, extending her hand to us in an invitation. This gives the appearance that we can take her hand and step into the *Star Trek* world with her. The idea that we are central to a *Star Trek* crew's mission and story is confirmed once we are on the 'Klingon Encounter' ride. We are told that one person in our group is crucial to bringing about the *Star Trek* future, as the ancestor of Captain Jean-Luc Picard.[139] However, the captain himself implores us not to tell anyone about what happens in the ride, for to do so might 'disrupt the future once again'. Picard tells the participants that 'each of you holds that future in your hands – guard it well'.

Similarly, on the 'Borg Invasion 4D' ride, the guest might hold the key to defeating the Borg through a special genetic immunity to this alien species and their mode of attack – assimilation. In this ride, a newly developed Steadicam 3D technique allowed 'the director to achieve shots from the "point of view" of the guest, placing the viewer in a "you are there" environment'.[140] Web advertisements for the ride proclaimed: 'Now, it is your time to be a true part in a *Star Trek* adventure.'[141] Again, it is the immersion of the fan guest in the *Star Trek* world and their positioning as central to that world that is emphasised.

These roles provide the ride equivalent of the fan fiction 'Mary Sue' story. This is a subgenre of fan fiction in which a young and talented new character saves the day. It arose specifically from *Star Trek* fan fiction, but has since been applied more broadly. The Mary Sue (or Marty Stu) character is usually interpreted as an idealised version of the author, a wish fulfilment of fans to insert themselves into the story-world and become important to its survival.[142] The narrative function of the Mary Sue goes beyond the mere walk-on roles offered to fans, either as a perk for crowd-sourcing (as was the case for the $10,000 Kickstarter contributor to Rob Thomas's 2014 *Veronica Mars* feature film),[143] or as a competition or joint promotional charity initiative – as was the case for *Star Trek Beyond*.[144] The appeal of being on the set among the cast and becoming part of a canon text is undeniable, but walk-on roles do not cast fans as heroes essential to the plot, and are not available to many fans in any case. The first 'Klingon Encounter' ride at *The Experience* gave many more fans the experience of being on a replica set in the midst of a *Star Trek* story. It transformed the fictional *Star Trek* future into a real future of which we are made guardians, as well as guardians of the ride's secrets. This gives us a role to play within the *Star Trek* narrative – as fan, consumer and (possible) ancestor. Like 'Mary Sue', we become central characters responsible for the survival of *Star Trek*. In effect, we are the heroes who save the day, merely through our existence (and, presumably, our procreation to create a future Picard and future *Star Trek* fans). However, unlike Mary Sue, Viacom controls our character construction and therefore how we save the day. We are subsumed into the *mythos* of *Star Trek* as it has developed and been marketed over the decades, but our narrative, ritual role is pre-written, and our actual actions on the 'Klingon Encounter' ride are minimal. The narrative declares us essential, but we only have to perform another version of a walk-on. While pilgrimages, and indeed rituals, have traditionally been quite regulated in nature, *Star Trek: The Experience* takes this regulation to a newly corporate level.

The Experience is not the first official product designed to personalise the *Star Trek* world and enable the story to be enacted, the myth to become ritual.[145] Via an avatar, the various *Star Trek* computer games similarly attempt to make us central heroes of a *Star Trek* narrative, even if our role within that story-world is articulated through gameplay and not story per se. As Markku Eskelinen notes, the relationship between preexisting story and subsequent game has been a point of focus for product placement and advertising, in an attempt to cash in on cross-media ties.[146] The mode of address of this marketing is itself of interest, for the way in which it attempts to position the player within the game but also within the story-world, whether or not this positioning is in fact successful. The role of paratextual advertising in constructing a desired form of fandom is often overlooked, given that it is not part of the official *Star Trek* story-world. The positioning of the game-player as a *Star Trek* hero in marketing is particularly evident in games in which we are given command, such as Activision's 2001 *Star Trek: Bridge Commander*. Activision's print advertisements, circulated at fan conventions, entreat us to 'Report for action' and 'Discover the responsibility of command'. Telling us 'You have the Con', Activision thereby attempts to personalise the game and mission, just as *Star Trek: The Experience* addresses participants on the ride as 'you'.

As noted in Chapter 3, Roman Jakobson identifies the linguistic 'you' as a shifter, requiring a context and a situation in order to define to whom the 'you' refers.[147] However, the medium used for this address is also important.[148] Thus, Cathy Schwichtenberg argues that even when using speech, television's use of 'you' is different. She argues, 'In the private space of the home the "you" seems personal, individual, but is [...] impersonal and removed in its general, collective articulation [...] due to television's technological ability to address a mass audience.'[149] The 'you' in Activision's advertisement potentially refers to all possible players, but becomes a defined 'you' only when read by a specific person. *Star Trek: The Experience*, by contrast, addresses a simultaneously singular and collective 'you', one that every participant in the group can interpret as personal. We can all, therefore, become 'the' *Star Trek* hero.

Participants would enter the 'Klingon Encounter' ride as fellow pilgrims seeking to inhabit a contemporary mythology transformed into a ritual space. But the mode of address attempted to single out participants, transforming the individual from visitor to Las Vegas to abductee, to ancestor of a great *Star Trek* hero. Turner argues that, like pilgrimage, the rite of passage is marked by a period of ritualised ambiguity. However, after a rite of passage, an individual or group adopts a new social status or cultural state.[150] Turner suggests that contemporary entertainment forms can mimic this process, potentially (but not necessarily) leading to genuine transformation of participants.[151] The 'transformation' conferred by *The Experience* upon its participants occurred within an entertainment space and did not continue into the real world in any socially recognised way. Indeed, participants were directly told not to disclose their new identity to outsiders. Although we are initiates only on the entertainment level of mimicry, the fan becomes central to the heroic *Experience* narrative and, through it, to the *Star Trek* realm as a whole. Indeed, this modelling of ritual initiation at the *Experience* upon the broader *Star Trek* story is consistent with the myth–ritual alignment. The 'secret' new *Star Trek* identity may have had significance beyond the transitory experience to fans who came to the site specifically to enter into the text-made-real. Thus, Turner argues that initiation into secular clubs and secret societies in contemporary culture can still be truly liminal from the perspective of the participants, for whom the transition continues to hold significance after the ritual event.[152]

By positioning the visitor as a central player in *Star Trek*'s unfolding future history, *The Experience* normalised the adoption of a fictional role by its participants. Visitors were invited to interact with *The Experience* as if they were something other than their ordinary selves. Porter notes that for conventions fans travel to a location outside their normal life, where the social stigma often attached to being a fan is removed. If they so choose, fans can masquerade as other people or even as other species.[153] Games, role-playing and mask-wearing are part of what Turner terms 'public liminality', incorporating play (ludic) elements into ritual.[154] By allowing a special space and time in which ordinary social and natural boundaries become ambiguous, 'ritual is both earnest and playful', itself a liminal blurring of categories.[155] Porter links playful elements, particularly role-playing and mask-wearing, with the adoption of *Trek* personas at fan conventions, which can be facilitated through costuming.[156] The adoption of new personas and the interchangeability (and performance) of roles, race and status could also be found at *Star Trek: The Experience*. While Roberts noted gender stereotyping of performers in the promenade and in the 'Klingon Encounter' ride at *The Experience*,[157] those staying for a whole day at the attraction, or returning to it, would find that the actors took turns in their roles. Actors with a passive, non-talking role on one ride took on active speaking parts in the next. Because at the time of my visit in 2001 one 'Klingon Encounter' ride ticket could be used for unlimited trips through the day, many fans did indeed experience the same script with different players, emphasising the performative nature of the various roles, and also, therefore, rank and the connection between rank and gender.[158] Although working within the narrative rules of the *Star Trek* story-world, the multiple versions of the ride provided a liminal space in which the relationship between rank and gender were in a constant state of flux. Although this achieved no lasting change, Turner notes that performative, public liminality still allows a ritual space for transitory liberation from ordinary rules.[159] Just as Porter has noted the performative nature of fans at conventions,[160] *The Experience* offered a space in which the adoption of different roles was highlighted.

On the promenade, race similarly adopted the features of performance and masquerade, created through literal masks merged with human actors through advanced prosthetics make-up. The costuming and performance enabled through the fan convention were heightened at *The Experience*, becoming an entire environment and cast playing out the *Star Trek* narrative realm. While the 'Klingon Encounter' ride conformed to a set script, in the promenade even set pieces required a high degree of improvisation in the unpredictable encounters with the fans. The conventions of the *Star Trek* story-world were maintained, but the actual narrative that was enacted had to rely on a degree of innovation, transferring a bardic logic into a three-dimensional themed environment. The more you engaged with the actors/aliens, the more complex the encounter, so that Klingons even attempted to converse with fans in the Klingon language – which some dedicated fans know, thanks to Klingon language books, audio lessons and even a Klingon Language Institute.[161] Because various costumes were available for sale in the promenade, and because many fans have their own home-made versions, fans also had the option of attending in full costume (and therefore full fictional persona) themselves, although on my visit this was less prevalent than at conventions. The performative nature of the site nonetheless occurs at the juncture between paid actors and the visitors who interact with them. We are invited to enter into a manifestation of the *Star Trek* story-world, to perform the role of a visitor to the Deep Space Nine space station. The ritual space, bounded by *Star Trek* rules but open to liminal play, makes us characters within the continuing popular mythology of *Star Trek*.

Conceptualising the journey to *Star Trek: The Experience* as secular pilgrimage and participation in its themed environment as liminoid play, the site offered multiple potential roles for the fan to play within the *Star Trek* text. While the script of *The Experience* and its related advertising attempts to position the fan as central hero within the *Trek* universe, this pre-written narrative is tempered by the fluidity of play that was at least potentially on offer. Such play does not so much abandon social rules as replace them with rules about the *Trek* universe. However, Turner himself notes:

> science fiction [...] provides many examples of just such a juggling of the factors of culture in new and often bizarre combinations and settings as was postulated earlier as a feature of liminality in initiations and mystery religions. Here we are dealing with [...] a mythology of the future.[162]

Following Turner, we can conceptualise futuristic science fiction as potentially taking the functional place of myth, as a fictional model for the social and physical reconfigurations associated with the liminal. Science fiction texts, as well as the role-playing enactment of those texts, open up at least the potential for a science fiction liminal experience that is paradoxically both fictional and real (itself a suitable liminal blurring of categories).

Future's Past, Past Futures

Morinis notes that 'the pilgrimage center is a locus for human gathering', but our understanding of such a site is mediated by 'the social field in legend, story, song, poem, film, and so on'.[163] In anthropology, most studies focus on the rituals performed at a pilgrimage site, with little work done on the relationship with stories about that site.[164] *The Experience* relied upon the *Star Trek* franchise on which it was based to provide the narrative template for its themed spaces, drawing upon the model established by the Disneyland television programme and theme park. Although acknowledging the fictional nature of its texts, *Star Trek: The Experience* also continually stressed the 'realness' of its fictional future, as a model for society we can strive for, but also as a future that has 'already' taken place. The reality of this future history (to which the fan participant personally belongs, courtesy of the 'Klingon Encounter' ride) was made concrete through the museum of *Star Trek* artefacts. Props and costumes were exhibited along-side a 'Prime' (pre-Abrams) future timeline display leading into the ride. This is archaeology of the future, the future that fans will be urged by Picard to protect.

Scott Bukatman has argued that many of Disneyland's images of the future (for example, within Tomorrowland) are so old and quaint as to be 'retro-futures', futures that never came to be realised but that we nonetheless feel nostalgic about.[165] *Star Trek* also has its retro-futures, in terms of its original programme of the 1960s. However, in the context of the museum of the future, *TOS* becomes one point in an ever-expanding *Star Trek* continuum, rather than an outmoded dead end – an oddity of how we imagined the future might be. The timeline, the succession of series and films, the physical artefacts that are both fictional and real, and the real physical experience of a fictional *Star Trek* within the rides, all serve to uphold the reality of *Star Trek* as historical future: a mythological Neverland that is both situated in time and yet is also timeless and eternal. The closure of the site in 2008 avoided the necessity to completely overhaul or at least radically complicate its museum timeline in the light of Abrams' 2009 feature film *Star Trek*, which presents an alternative trajectory for *TOS* characters (and by implication the rest of the *Star Trek* timeline as well). The new Kelvin Timeline extending from the Abrams feature reimagines an old future. The past of *Star Trek*'s future is open to constant retelling, in which both the original and new timelines are different forms of retro-futures. By conveniently using a time-travel premise to achieve the change, both timelines can remain 'real'.

As the *Star Trek* timeline has developed and warped, generations of viewers have entered that timeline at different points, and even non-viewers are aware of many *Star Trek* story elements as a broader cultural phenomenon. Judith Rubin notes, '*Star Trek* never really existed as a physical environment before in any form more solid than a television or movie set. At the same time, it is a place most of us have come to know.'[166] It is this cultural familiarity with the *Star Trek* universe that the attraction was geared to harness, among fans and casual visitors alike. Landmark's CEO Gary Goddard noted, '*Star Trek* is known to three generations, and is internationally popular.'[167] Indeed, *The Experience* was originally slated for a 1996 opening, to coincide with and promote the 30th anniversary of the *Star Trek* franchise,[168] thereby emphasising its place within the real history of popular culture – its familiarity with the public over three decades, as well as its long diegetic history. *The Experience* capitalised on the longevity of the franchise across generations and countries, and therefore could be seen as a seemingly perfect family attraction. As argued in Chapter 3, it is precisely through this longevity that *Star Trek* has both developed, and deliberately marketed, its status as contemporary myth. *Star Trek*'s intertextual, mythological array includes both its fictional storylines and its place within real entertainment history.

However, *Star Trek*'s 50-year history within popular culture, and its fictional history of the future, are not logically compatible. Fan writer Jeff Mason has argued that *Star Trek* has to be a future from an alternate timeline in which the television show never took place.[169] As Mason notes:

> If *Star Trek* is allowed to exist on the time line that will eventually produce the Federation, the very existence of the show and subculture in the twentieth century will paradoxically negate the universe of the *Enterprise* that we are familiar with in the twenty-third, as modelling an interplanetary government and defence force on a three-hundred-year-old video show would be considered ridiculous.[170]

Mason notes that this duality of timelines is evident in the feature film *Star Trek IV: The Voyage Home* (1986), in that no one recognises the crew from *TOS* when they travel back to 1987.[171] Indeed, the franchise post-*TOS* has constantly struggled with how best to deal with our history and its relationship with *Star Trek* history.

In the *Voyager* episode '11.59' (1999), the *Voyager* future flashbacks to the new millennium, but the years 2000/2001 are revealed to be quite different from our own real timeline. In *Voyager*'s version of 'history', a well-publicised, self-sufficient living environment called the Millennium Gate is being trialled, which will later become a model for Mars habitats in the *Star Trek* future history (see Figure 4.1).[172] The episode does not overtly explain why this *Trek* version of the millennium should be different to our own, but what is left is the implicit idea that the *Trek* timeline (past and future) is a separate, alternate world to our own, and not a plausible future that our timeline might lead towards.

By contrast, the Temporal Cold War depicted in *Enterprise* continually presents the possibility that a future conflict reaching across time would disrupt the *Star Trek* future that we know from the other programmes and movies, as well as our own real history.[173] As Proctor notes, *Enterprise*

Figure 4.1 The Millennium Gate in *Voyager* '11.59' (Paramount Television 1999).

'took severe liberties with hyperdiegetic continuity by rewriting elements of established textual history', such as introducing the Borg in Season 1 of *Enterprise*, despite what is supposed to be Starfleet's first encounter with this foe occurring in *TNG*, 150 years later.[174] The Temporal Cold War provides an overreaching diegetic reason for such contradictions, even when not explicitly invoked: a case of retrospective continuity ('retcon') justified by a science fictional device, even if many long-term fans could not stomach the changes.[175]

J. J. Abrams' 2009 feature film *Star Trek* performs an even more radical overhaul of the *Star Trek* timeline by giving *TOS* characters (and therefore also all those that follow on from them) an entirely new timeline altogether, while continually stressing points of similarity and rupture with the old timeline. In this respect, then, it is not a complete reboot that negates the existence of the first timeline, and yet it does start the story again, becoming what Teiwes has characterised as an instance of retcon, or what Proctor has termed a 'self-reflexive reboot'.[176] That the 2009 film provides a new

Star Trek timeline through a time-travel conceit keeps it squarely within its science fiction diegesis. There are entirely pragmatic and commercial reasons for wanting to restart the *Star Trek* timeline, as the complex history had become unwieldy for writers and new viewers alike.[177] What is pertinent here is the fact that the specific means by which this new beginning is achieved – in what Uhura explicitly calls 'an alternate reality' – is in keeping with a story-world *already* full of temporal rearrangements that change the past and the future, sometimes temporarily and sometimes permanently. As *Voyager*'s Captain Janeway exclaims:

> Ever since my first day on the job as a Starfleet captain, I swore I'd never let myself get caught in one of these godforsaken paradoxes. The future is the past, the past is the future. It all gives me a headache.[178]

In the (non-canon) 2016 computer game *Star Trek: Timelines*, a temporal anomaly even allows all the different canon *Star Trek* timelines to come together as the central gameplay attraction.

As well as temporal loops, paradoxes and offshoots, *Star Trek* also includes parallel, mirror universes, the most famous of which started with *TOS* episode 'Mirror, Mirror' (1967), and continued through the other series, as noted in the previous chapter. In *TNG*'s 'Parallels' (1993), an anomaly results in Worf travelling between different versions of the *Star Trek* universe, a manifestation of the 'many worlds' theory of quantum mechanics that suggests there is a separate alternate timeline and reality for each different possible decision that we make.[179] Although Worf is restored to his original reality, Wesley scans more than 10 million of them, suggesting a potentially infinite array of possible *Star Trek* worlds (see Figure 4.2). Proctor has suggested that this means *Star Trek* becomes 'not a singular universe, but a nexus of many worlds which interconnect and interlock within a vast story-system of parallel quantum realities'.[180] As Hark argues of the Temporal Cold War plot of *Enterprise*, the logic of the 'Parallels' approach threatens to destabilise 'everything known about the Trek mythology', by leaving it 'in perpetual flux'.[181] From this perspective even fan fiction becomes a manifestation of the different possible *Star Trek* realities discovered in 'Parallels', but what this comparison makes clear is

Figure 4.2 Multiple alternate *Trek* worlds in *TNG* 'Parallels' (Paramount Television 1993).

that some alternate realities are given 'canon' status while others are not. Abrams clarifies that from his 2009 feature film onwards, 'everything that people knew of *Star Trek* splits off into now another timeline', but that the original timeline still exists.[182] Exactly how this complex *Star Trek* 'history' might relate to our own timeline becomes difficult to determine in the light of its recognised, official alternate timelines.

This difficulty had, in any case, arisen once we entered into the 'future' forecast by *TOS*, which speculated about (what was then) the near future of the 1990s. In the official *Star Trek Chronology: The History of the Future*, the events recalled in *TOS* episode 'Space Seed' (1967) describe genetically engineered Khan Noonien Singh as having 'dictatorial control over one quarter of the planet Earth' in 1992.[183] Like *Star Trek: The Experience*, this involves a double play on the part of the authors (and readers), simultaneously presenting *Star Trek* as real future history while providing tongue-in-cheek editorials that acknowledge its fictional status, an alternate fictional reality that nonetheless reflects, responds to and interacts with our own.

The *Experience* extended upon a story-world that already contains narrative elements of liminal slippage between the real and the fictional, transferring this slippage into a three-dimensional space in which liminal play is encouraged. The *Experience* relied upon visitor knowledge of the *Star Trek* story-world, facilitating the enactment of the liminality it already contained.

In *Star Trek* advertisements, it is implied that the *Star Trek* world is not the history of the future so much as a futuristic legend or epic. In 1998, an advertisement placed at the beginning of *Voyager* home videos describes the passing of the tradition from *TOS* through the sequels, so that *DS9* is described as 'a place where legends are forged', and that 'the legend continues with *Star Trek: Voyager*'. Similarly, in 1999 an advertisement for the videos depicts highlights from various *Star Trek* texts set to Wagner's 'Flight of the Valkyries' from *The Ring of the Nibelung*, an operatic version of a Germanic epic. The advertisement thereby aligned *Star Trek* with both literary and musical epics, suggesting that *Star Trek*'s own story is similarly an epic for our own times. Television advertisements for *Enterprise* announced, 'The *Star Trek* saga begins with *Enterprise*.' As noted in Chapter 3, the sequels also reworked a number of high-culture texts that explicitly or implicitly compare *Star Trek* with the realms of myth, legend, saga and epic.[184] Thus narratives, paratextual marketing and transmedia offshoots from *Star Trek* have presented its futuristic tale as both a real possible future, and as a fantastic myth. This facilitates the performative space of *The Experience*, where the viewer could enact the *Star Trek* myth on the cusp of their real-life experience and a fictional narrative realm.

For many, arguing the logic of *Star Trek* as a real possible future would seem absurd.[185] Yet it is this possibility that *Star Trek: The Experience* tried to assert. Rene Echevarria, one of the show's creators, has said, 'We want to get people into the notion that *Star Trek* is real, and by odd coincidence, there is a TV show about it.'[186] The narrative of *Star Trek: Experience* posits *Star Trek* as not only our real potential future, but also our future in a very personal sense. As Robin Roberts notes, the 'Klingon Encounter' ride 'provides the illusion that you are central to the survival of Starfleet (which of course, as one of its consumers, you are)'.[187] It is the survival of the *Star Trek* story, its place within popular culture, and the economic franchise of which the fans are custodians. The blurring of boundaries is central to the liminal ritual experience, here transferred to liminoid entertainment in which we are nonetheless positioned as important ritual participants.[188] Although a form of secular play, *Star Trek: The Experience* continually stresses our importance in making *Star Trek* real, the transformation not only of participants into heroes, but also fiction into reality.

Playing with the Reality Experience

The fan convention provides a space in which ordinary rules are replaced by *Star Trek* rules, and in which the distinction between the real and the fictional enters into a state of play. In Roger Nygard's documentary *Trekkies* (1997), a number of actors from the various series recall encounters with fans who seemed not to recognise the distinction between fiction and reality. For example, John de Lancie, who plays Q in *TNG*, *DS9* and *Voyager*, remembered being approached by a fan in New York, who asked him, 'Are you Q?' De Lancie said, 'Yeah.' The man then asked whether or not he could bring people back from the dead. De Lancie replied, 'Only people I like.' At a 1999 fan convention in Melbourne, Australia, De Lancie said that he could understand the convention scene because it is the equivalent of going backstage after a play to tell an actor that you enjoyed their performance. But in retelling the New York story, he said that at the time he'd thought, 'Oh my God, a Trekker. Now I'm really in trouble.'[189] Despite this anecdote, some audience members at the convention kept asking him questions as if he were Q, eliciting the reminder 'No, I'm not Q, I'm the actor' from De Lancie. When a fan asked why he always keeps wearing the Starfleet uniform instead of making his own Q costume, De Lancie paused and replied, 'I *do* make all my own costumes ... what were you saying about reality?' This type of question, which seemed to assume that De Lancie was really the alien Q, was accompanied by embarrassed groans from the audience, indicating that not everyone shared or enjoyed their fact/fiction confusion/play.

Star Trek: The Experience actively required this slippage between fact and fiction from its participants in both the promenade spaces and the 'Klingon Encounter' ride, asking us to interact with the themed environment as if it were really the twenty-fourth century. And to a certain extent, it *was* real. You could eat real food at a real bar and interact with real people, even if they were dressed up as fictional aliens. Further, the food itself was a real approximation of fictional dishes – Romulan ale and Klingon Raktajino, for example. Consumption here was literal, participating in the (imagined) twenty-fourth-century culture of food, whereby the food and the activities surrounding its consumption became part of the transmedia expansion of the story-world, a sensory experience to 'deepen [...] audience engagement' in Jenkins' terms.[190]

At the same time, the attraction played on distinctions of real/not real and present/future for self-reflexive humour. The spaceships that invade our time and space were reported in a mock news report at the end of the ride as UFOs, but dismissed by officials as weather balloons. Fictional and factual television formats were blurred, while also tapping into UFO conspiracy theories. The participants are in on the joke, not only because they know the 'truth' behind the UFOs as revealed in the ride, but also because they recognise the double play being enacted. Here the confusion between reality and fiction is a source of humour rather than derision. Ride participants were returned from the future to a 'present-day' depiction of Las Vegas, which very quickly became an image of the past by virtue of the rapid changes to the Las Vegas skyline in the 1990s, when the attraction was operating. Departing from the ride and emerging in the promenade, guests were back in the present, but a present themed as the future they had just returned from. The two were therefore counterpoised as the real future they were taken to in the ride, and the fictional future in the promenade. *The Experience* site created layers of ritual spaces to enter and exit, with different levels of liminal play between the real and the fictional.

Even in the promenade, actors dressed in full *Star Trek* costume and prosthetics attempted to interact with guests as if they were indeed on a twenty-fourth-century space station, while simultaneously playing on the constructed nature of this exchange as a source of humour. While I was at the attraction, I was growled at by a Klingon who suspected I was up to no good, entreated by a Ferengi to contribute to his dubious orphanage fund (yet to make a profit due to his own management fees), and another Ferengi who wished me to ship an unnamed cargo back to Earth. The rules of the *Star Trek* fictional template still govern this performative interaction. As consumer/participants, we need to understand these diegetic rules to further enact the text. In order to move from the popular culture 'myth' of *Star Trek* into a ritual enactment of that myth, we need to understand the conventions of the *Star Trek* story-world.

These diegetic conventions were also enacted through commercial products available at the site. As Morinis notes, 'Pilgrims, regardless of the religious tradition, tend to carry souvenirs away with them.'[191] *The Experience* products act as valued relics, proof of pilgrimage that have been sold at inflated prices outside the USA.[192] Drawing on the slippage of real/not real as play, consumption itself was rendered another act of performance at *The Experience*. In the fictional *Star Trek* world, Ferengi are known for their money-hungry ways and for a complex set of rules of acquisition geared towards profit.[193] Thus it is entirely within the rules of the *Star Trek* world that I was berated by a Ferengi for not buying enough *Star Trek* merchandise at the store. Within *The Experience*'s rules of acquisition, consumption acts as a legitimate performance of *Star Trek*, increasing the fictional profits of a fictional Ferengi, played by a real actor increasing real profits for a real conglomerate, Viacom. This, surely, qualifies as Disney's 'total merchandising', where sales, narrative and play coalesce.[194] The consumer relics function as mementos of the pilgrimage to a special *Star Trek* site, but also of a particular performative encounter within this space.

The interactive experience in a shopping environment can be seen as part of the capitalist underpinning of the attraction, geared towards sales. However, the purchasing of products can equally be seen as part of the interactive, theatrical experience in which the fan, if brave and knowledgeable enough, could steer the encounter with the actors/aliens and thereby fashion their own *Star Trek* narrative (but not their own purchase price). Drawing on the narrative rules of the *Star Trek* story-world, the fan could create a bardic innovation on those conventions and create a new *Star Trek* narrative within the themed locale. Fan scholarship addresses the simultaneously creative and commercial aspects of fandom by suggesting that we need to challenge binaries between 'good' fan producers and 'bad' fan consumers, or between 'authentic experience' and commodification.[195] These distinctions become difficult to sustain given the degree to which *The*

Experience blurred material consumption with creative fan participation. Liminoid play in this context promotes consumption, but it can also facilitate a deeper liminal transformation: in this case, fans could get married at the site. Marriage is a rite of passage, a ritual that marks the transition from one social state into another.[196] Thus, a real-life legal ritual could be played out through *Star Trek* rituals. Although requiring a commercial transaction with Viacom for the use of the themed space, the marriage ritual is transformative, and recognised beyond the liminal play of the pilgrimage itself. While marriages at Las Vegas are not necessarily long-lasting, this blurring between 'real', legally recognised rituals, and rituals based on a fictional story-world, exemplifies the slippage between authentic and commodified fan experience. It is, therefore, difficult to suggest at exactly what point mimicry of the ritual pilgrimage experience becomes a 'genuine', meaningful liminal experience.

Pilgrimage, Transformation and Control

The consumption at sites such as *The Experience* has been perceived by some critics as undercutting the more positive aspects of liminal or liminoid playfulness they also offer.[197] Russell Belk has argued that Las Vegas as a whole creates a geographical and social zone in which liminal blurring is not only acceptable but in fact encouraged. He argues, 'Las Vegas resorts jointly participate in a theatrical farce meant to infantalize [*sic*] their adult patrons by creating a fantastic liminal time and place.'[198] In this way, Belk sees Las Vegas as drawing on older ritual traditions such as the rite of passage or the carnival, both of which centre around the inversion of everyday rules.[199] One can dress up, indulge in excesses of consumption and play, and ignore ordinary hours of rest or work.[200] For Belk, this is the true aim of the fantasy-themed Las Vegas, not to appeal to children as 'Disney in the Desert', but to create playful, infantilised adults who in turn make perfect, playful gamblers.[201] For Belk, the potential for performative, liminoid pleasure has been cynically subsumed into the commercial imperative.

Belk's argument takes on an additional dimension when applied to *Star Trek: The Experience*, as fans – and *Star Trek* fans in particular – have often been portrayed within popular culture as infantile.[202] It is true that

Fans, Bards and Rituals

in Turner's formation, non-industrial liminality within the rite of passage often involves symbols of infancy.[203] But in liminal blurring, no one state is ever absolute:

> [T]he most characteristic midliminal symbolism is that of paradox, or being *both* this *and* that. Novices are portrayed and act as androgynous, or as both living *and* dead, at once ghosts and babes, both cultural and natural creatures, human *and* animal.[204]

These categories must be broken down so that the individual can be remade into a new identity, and to foster new social ties with fellow initiates.[205] The infantile is but one of many symbols of liminality, paradoxically existing with its exact opposite of death, as well as a number of other possible and contradictory states. In the context of the liminoid, a blurring of categories may take place without necessarily leading to a new identity recognised by society, but it may nonetheless create strong social bonds among participants.[206] For the individual at the slot machine who is not engaged with their fellow gamblers, this creation of 'communitas' would seem a stretch. But in the environs of *Star Trek: The Experience*, the shared play of fandom at least opened a space for this possibility, the creation of social bonds rather than merely the breakdown of the individual to an infantile level as suggested by Belk. These social bonds rely on knowledge of the *Star Trek* story-world, the underlying popular culture myth that serves as the model for the ritual (and commercial) activities.

A number of theorists have also applied Turner's theory of pilgrimage, as a form of liminal ritual, to the various Disney theme parks. As sites removed from the everyday, Disney's parks provide aspects of blurred categories (such as between animal and human), and a sense of new community, but also an extensive array of products.[207] However, Bryman has questioned the degree to which play within Disney can ever really be a spontaneous abandonment of rules, given that 'the visitor/pilgrim is to a very significant extent controlled by the structure of the theme park experience and by the ever-present security staff'.[208] This perspective ignores the fact that even traditional forms of pilgrimage offer highly institutionalised liminal experiences within a larger structural system.[209] A dislike of these structures is more prevalent in contemporary tourism than in pilgrimage, where they in fact help to create meaning.[210] *Star Trek: The Experience* selected particular aspects from the *Star Trek* world, and was not, therefore, a free-form *Trek* realm for fans. The *Star Trek* structures that gave the attraction meaning simultaneously had the potential to close off other avenues of meaning-production within the *Star Trek* story-world.

At the same time, as the attraction was nestled into a relatively small corner of the Hilton, its ability to control the physical experience of the Las Vegas visitor was more limited than that of Disneyland. As Paramount Parks' Anthony Esparza said, 'It's food, it's retail and an attraction, but it's not a theme park.'[211] Las Vegas as a whole lacks the controlled vistas of Disneyland, jostling a number of differently themed facilities together, with no particular overarching plan or thematic sympathy.[212] Thus, Alan Hess argues:

> [W]here Disneyland firmly controls its imagery, Las Vegas' laissez-faire planning allows the unexpected to occur [...] It is a city with theme elements, not a theme park which is a city. Las Vegas is not, in fact, a Disneyland for adults.[213]

While dedicated fans may have travelled to Las Vegas specifically for *The Experience*, in the broader city context this mini-themed environment becomes one of many experiences on offer.

In his critique of Disney pilgrimage, Bryman also argues that 'unlike the conventional pilgrim, he or she does not return home with a new sense of reality'.[214] Bryman's account of a single, non-transformative Disney experience is too suspiciously totalising to sustain. Morinis argues that central to pilgrimage is 'an intensified version of some ideal that the pilgrim values but cannot achieve at home'.[215] Porter connects this to the 'communitas' experienced at *Star Trek* conventions,[216] a fellowship that might not be so easily achieved in Disney pilgrimage, as individuals and families visit Disneyland without necessarily being encouraged to meet one another. However, it is precisely the aim of Disneyland to intensify an experience of the Disney text that cannot be achieved through the television programme or films alone.

In the case of *Star Trek: The Experience*, the attraction offered a deliberate play between reality and fiction, inviting participants to join in such blurring as a site of humour but also with a degree of seriousness that posits the *Star Trek* universe as real, both in the present and the (already written) future. Porter suggests that at conventions most fans 'find themselves suspended in a liminal frame between seriousness and play',[217] a blurring of boundaries not only found at *Star Trek: The Experience*, but in fact deliberately fostered. The interaction with actors privileges fan knowledge as the source of both information and in-jokes, which help with role-playing on the promenade. Fan knowledge is real knowledge here, providing perhaps not transformation but at the very least affirmation. Following Morinis, *The Experience* provides 'an intensified version' of the *Star Trek* story-world 'that the pilgrim values but cannot achieve at home'.[218]

Beyond *The Experience*

Star Trek: The Experience was used as a geographic and online site for official fan conventions, merging these two pilgrimage destinations in the one location.[219] The conflation of the attraction with conventions came at a time when Viacom was trying to to keep *Star Trek* fandom as centralised as possible, cracking down on fans' copyright infringements and offering its own physical and virtual forums for fan community in their place.[220] If the liminal escape from *usual* boundaries characterises pilgrimage, *Star Trek: The Experience* could only be partly successful, for the rules of Viacom still existed there. It was, then, a space of negotiation between free-form play and predetermined (financial and narrative) action. The commercial nature of pilgrimage activities and sites cannot fully detract from the pleasures of play between reality and fiction that they offer, just as the interactive theatrical elements cannot extinguish the commercial nature of such sites.

In an effort to please as broad a spectrum of fans as possible, Viacom asked fans to contribute their suggestions for a second *Star Trek* attraction in Las Vegas.[221] Subsequently, the 'Borg Invasion 4D' ride/experience was added to the attraction, opening on 18 March 2004.[222] For many of the themed casino complexes, however, the 'Disney in the Desert' experiment was not particularly profitable.[223] From the mid-1990s many casinos began to return to either a mass-market approach or to old-fashioned strip clubs.[224] As one visitor noted, 'You can't be Sin City and a family attraction at the same time.'[225] Disney executives were heartened by this development. Disney designer Peter Rummell argued that Disney 'will endure, long after the Las Vegases have come and gone'.[226] Although a themed environment, *The Experience* targeted fans across the demographic range.[227] *The Experience* nonetheless struggled to meet expected customer numbers, but was revived somewhat by the addition of 'Borg Invasion 4D'.[228] Despite this, rumours of the attraction's closure frequently circulated online,[229] and *Star Trek: The Experience* finally closed its doors on 1 September 2008. In true fan fashion, a petition to reopen the attraction in some form was immediately started.[230]

Rather than relying solely on pilgrimage to its Las Vegas reliquary, Viacom sent *Star Trek* on the road with *Star Trek: The Adventure* in London in 2002.[231] In its operating years of 1998 to 2008, the Las Vegas site may have positioned itself as *the* experience of *Star Trek* made real,[232] without which our experience of *Star Trek* would be incomplete. But *Star Trek: The Adventure* dispelled this suggestion of a singular experience. If you couldn't come to *The Experience*, *The Adventure* might come to you, as a travelling themed fairground. After the closure of *The Experience*, CBS, the new entity in charge of the *Star Trek* franchise, produced *Star Trek: The Exploration* in Spain in 2010, and *Star Trek: The Exhibition* in the US in 2010, an attraction of *Star Trek* artefacts updated with items from the reboot films for its appearance at county and state fairs in 2013.[233] More recently, to celebrate and promote the 50th anniversary of the *Star Trek* franchise, *The Starfleet Academy Experience* featured for four months at the Intrepid Sea, Air & Space Museum in New York City, before a national tour, with attendees receiving training as Starfleet cadets.[234]

Meanwhile, spare a thought for the original future birthplace of Captain James T. Kirk, claimed by the town of Riverside, Iowa, where in the early 2000s one could purchase, for the undoubtedly reasonable price of $3, a relic-to-be: vials of dirt from Kirk's future birth site in the original timeline.[235] Drawing on the slippage between the real and the fictional, the *Star Trek* future and our real future, the dirt functions as a relic of an event yet to happen. Riverside even holds a festival to celebrate its 'future historical event'.[236] If you really want to guard the future of *Star Trek* by becoming one of its ancestors, apparently you have to move to Riverside. While the community might have been understandably a little peeved that Kirk is born in space in the rebooted timeline of the 2009 *Star Trek* feature film, this was more than compensated for by the fact that the film acknowledges Riverside as his home. What began as fan tourism has become canon.

The liminal slippages between present and imagined future, and between the real and fictional, were literally built into *Star Trek: The Experience*, providing a space for liminoid (or potentially even liminal) play for its visitors. Whether we see the attraction as an interactive fan pilgrimage or as the cynical venture of a controlling conglomerate must also remain in murky in-between-ness, a negotiated space between fan and conglomerate. Although not conceived in concert with the development of the TV series it depicts, *Star Trek: The Experience* nonetheless drew on the Disney synergy of programme and programme-made-space. Despite the franchise's longevity and revival in the Abrams feature films, with its closure *The Experience* has in effect become another 'retro-future', even as the continuing, transmedia *Star Trek* narrative tries to absorb its retro-futures in the creation of its own sense of historical weight.

Fans as Internet Bards

While *Star Trek: The Experience* transformed the *Star Trek* story-world into a pilgrimage space in which specific Viacom-determined rituals could be enacted, fandom has also created its own unofficial *Star Trek* stories and rituals. Some of these have been subsumed into the official *Star Trek* mythos – Riverside being a case in point – while others have been cause for conflict. Used by fans both as a story realm and as a language of metaphor, *Star Trek* has proven to be extremely malleable, including its web manifestations. As Janet Murray and Henry Jenkins argue, 'like larger fan culture, online *Trek* worlds extend the possibilities of the narrative without being bound by canonical events',[237] free to continue the *Star Trek* story endlessly in multiple directions. As noted in earlier chapters, Jim Collins has argued that for long-lasting fictional worlds, each 're-telling' necessitates some reworking of the previous retellings, for these 'have become as inseparable from the "text" as any generic convention or plot function'.[238] This process also has alignment with mythic intertexts, as new versions are created within a story tradition. Unlike oral storytelling traditions, the bardic reinvention of contemporary texts occurs alongside tangible records of earlier versions, in books, on videotapes, DVDs, CDs, streaming and so on. Within the popular culture array of texts, we are able to follow a character, fictional world or actor through a series of interconnected texts that extend the story realm, in both official and unofficial forms. Just as *Star Trek: The Experience* retold the *Star Trek* story-world in a three-dimensional form, fandom adds to the *Star Trek* text, creating another performative space.

Television rituals do not merely extend into physical spaces such as *The Experience*. Rather, they include virtual spaces in which fans appropriate a bardic function, refashioning the *Star Trek* story-world and their relationship with that world. *The Experience* provided a corporately defined, physical space in which fans could, to a degree, play out their *Star Trek* fantasies. Online, the virtual replaces the physical pilgrimage, and indeed internet fan conventions have harnessed the already social aspects of online fandom.[239] Unofficial fan internet sites operate outside official corporate guidelines, and therefore open up a potentially more free-form social 'space' for expansion of the *Star Trek* story-world.

Because 'the Internet encourages interpretation and editorializing' by the public, Havick argues that it offers sufficiently different communication properties to existing media, and television in particular.[240] Critics such as James A. Knapp have approached 'discussion groups and bulletin boards of the Internet' in terms of creating a space for public debate, albeit one that blurs this distinction between the public and private, both spatially and discursively.[241] Drawing on Jurgen Habermas' notion of public space as one that facilitates 'public debate by private individuals', Knapp argues that the internet provides a 'public sphere' for multiple voices, even if different perspectives are often curtailed from interacting with one another by virtue of segregated, topic-specific sites.[242] By contrast, Richard Wise argues that while Habermas' ideal serves as a useful and powerful model to aspire to, the notion that it has been achieved on and through the internet is highly ideological, masking the inequality of access to the technology, as well as its military origins and subsequent commodification.[243] For Wise, it has been important ideologically that the internet be seen as a democratic public space, particularly in relation to 'virtual communities' made up of minority groups, because this serves to offset and detract from an 'increasing domination by monopolistic capitalist media conglomerates'.[244] Since the early 1990s, academic fan theory has tended to move away from models of the ideologically and commercially passive fan in favour of more active models.[245] Although this has counteracted simplistic ideas of the fan-as-dupe, it is equally important to see the fan as a discursive and contested figure, and one under considerable pressure from media conglomerates. While *The Experience* encouraged fans to think of themselves as participatory heroes, as we have seen, the interactive possibilities were limited and relatively predetermined by the corporate and narrative rules of the site. Rather than a physical pilgrimage to *The Experience*, virtual pilgrimages online to fan sites, and indeed the creation of such sites, provide fans with an alternative opportunity to take on the role of *Star Trek* hero, transforming their everyday identities and entering into another example of liminal blurring of reality/play/fiction.

Official products cannot hope to respond to all the different types of pleasures that fans have in relating to the *Star Trek* world, including the ability to do so on their own terms – a feature difficult if not impossible to program into a product, no matter how interactive. Writing in 1999, Jenkins argues that interactive products and technologies have 'the potential of controlling and regulating fan pleasures at a time when Viacom has increasingly sought to centralize and constrain grassroots fan activities'.[246] Indeed, late in 1996, *Star Trek* fan sites began to close down under the threat of legal action by Viacom for the use of copyright material.[247] Having received mail from concerned fans, Paramount issued an open letter to fans outlining their policy, which was aimed at stopping website operators from gaining any financial advantage from the sites, and the removal of copyright material.[248] The letter also took the opportunity to advertise the new official site, although Viacom denied that its crackdown was related to this launch.[249] There was considerable fan debate over the move, due in part to substantial confusion over how far copyright might be seen to extend into fan activities.[250] Although Viacom was concerned with copyright protection and profits generated by illegal use of copyright material, for the fans themselves the unofficial sites are a means of exercising their own control over the story-world, drawing on the conventions of *Star Trek* in order to express fan opinions and even create new fan stories. By contrast, *The Experience* enabled a creative enactment of the *Star Trek* story-world, but within a physical, corporate space that selected only specific elements of that world. Entering into virtual space, engagement with the *Star Trek* story-world on fan internet sites becomes more overtly bardic when corporate rules are violated. Stories enter a communal, multi-authored zone that extends to fans, creating new possibilities for the relationship between story and action – myth and ritual – in this virtual space. Copyright becomes redundant to fans in the process of retelling, where the 'original' story is only the springboard for further stories. It is precisely by violating these legal rules that new liminal zones of ritual play are opened up.

Viacom's attempts to curtail web-based fan activities were quickly subsumed by fans into the larger *Star Trek* text.[251] Websites such 'Viacom as Borg' proclaimed, 'Like the Borg Viacom is trying to assimilate the internet, but this time resistance is not futile.'[252] Like the cyborgs of the series, who take over humanoid life-forms and divest them of all individuality, Viacom was seen as denying fans their autonomy and attempting to remove it by force – albeit legal force in this instance. In successive *Star Trek* series, resistance against the Borg has been anything but futile. First introduced as a formidable enemy in Season 2 of *TNG* in 'Q Who' (1989), by Season 5 the potential for individuated, even sympathetic Borg was posited.[253] By Season 6, a faction-group of individuated Borg was introduced in 'Descent, Parts I and II' (1993). The introduction of an ex- or semi-Borg female as a lead member of the cast in *Voyager* further humanised and individualised the Borg, and in the double episode 'Unamatrix Zero' (2000), at the end of Season 6 and the start of Season 7, the programme revealed that even for Borg still part of the collective, individuality is possible within a communal dream-world. The assertion of individual identity has been the key means of undermining the Borg collective within the *Star Trek* story-world.

The correlation of Viacom with the Borg on fan protest sites integrated fan resistance into the *Star Trek* story-world, using a model not only of ruthless assimilation but also of the continued fight for individual expression in the face of such assimilation. Scholars have expressed caution in the use of terms such as 'resistance' to characterise media fandom, with Davies suggesting that the term has become 'over-romanticised' when in fact fandom is part of the capitalist system.[254] While I agree that we can easily overstate the limited power available to fans, here I am specifically interested in the terms that fans themselves use to construct a narrative around resistance that deliberately and knowingly plays on the blurring of fact and fiction to create another *Star Trek* story. Fan fiction, fan editorialising and fan protest become part of the same process of retelling *Star Trek*, in which the heroic struggles from the television diegesis are replicated in fans' constructions of their own stories and activities.[255] While *The Experience* cast the fan guest as a hero within the *Star Trek* story-world, as ancestor to Captain Picard, fan internet sites such as 'Viacom as Borg' situated the fan as a resistance hero against this type of corporately controlled *Star Trek* product run by the Viacom/Borg. To many it would be tempting to read this as yet another example of fans' loss of distinction between the real and the fictional; however, the language is clearly metaphorical: nowhere is it suggested that the fans literally mistake corporate representatives for aliens. Rather, the metaphorical language of *Star Trek* is used as the base of both fictional and factual storytelling, to speak to real concerns through the language of fiction, and enabling performative connections to both realms. The story conventions of *Star Trek* are used as a template for innovative storytelling, extending the bardic function into the boundary zone between the real and the fictional. With franchise story-worlds such as *Star Trek*, the process of retelling begins in a corporate framework, where the multi-authorship common to mythic systems is subsumed within conglomerate ownership. Fandom marks a return to mythic, bardic retelling in an illegal form, with the creation of non-corporate ritual spaces in which ordinary legal and narrative rules are flouted. In this liminal inversion, communal fellowship may be created through shared fan activities and narratives of resistance.

In a 1996 internet editorial for *Wired Magazine Online* at the height of the fan site crackdown, Jason Ellis advised fans, 'If you want to help save Trek on the web [...] you must act [...] stop using copyrighted materials on your Web site. If there's nothing there that is illegal, Viacom can't shut you down.'[256] The media and textual dynamics of the debate highlight the way in which fans have developed a virtual, public discursive forum, which extends the private viewing practice, yet ultimately blurs distinctions between the non-diegetic and diegetic, public and private, bard and audience. While liminal slippage could be found in the textual and corporate strategies of *Star Trek: The Experience*, the resistance websites of the era asserted an anti-corporate stance, creating quite a different mythic fanhero than that offered by *The Experience*. The sites also created a forum where the textual rules were indicated (but not necessarily contained) by *Star Trek* texts but not set by Viacom, even if they lingered under the threat of legal intervention. While Viacom offered official *Star Trek* virtual ritual spaces, such as the 'Vir-Con' online conventions run from the Las Vegas attraction, the resistance sites invited shared fan rituals, but as individual authorship claims over their virtual spaces.

When the *Star Trek* franchise went to the new CBS Corp. formed out of the old Viacom in 2006, the official website remained online but was stagnant for some time without any updates. Once it was revamped, the CBS approach to fans, their material and their websites had undergone a noticeable shift in approach and tone. Although fans were still warned not to reproduce any *Star Trek* material from the official website (including images of characters and ships), StarTrek.com would now directly link to some of the most popular of those non-profit fan websites. It will hardly come as a surprise to note that those fan sites all feature *Star Trek* images of characters, ships and so on, but with an acknowledgement that *Star Trek* is the trademark of CBS. Not only would this not have been tolerated in the (original) Viacom years, but linking directly to them from the official site would have been unthinkable in the light of the ongoing legal threats. The new CBS seemed to have learnt the lessons from the tense Viacom years in recognising that *Star Trek*'s most ardent fans were also necessarily its best customers, and that it was counterproductive to get them offside. Indeed, Kozinets has gone as far as to suggest that the lack of more comprehensive copyright crackdowns on *Star Trek* fandom, even in the 1990s, suggests an 'uncharacteristically charitable corporate parental acceptance' in order to maintain 'the culture of consumption' around the franchise.[257]

The shift in policy and practice is emblematic of the turn from Web 1.0, which emphasised content delivery, to Web 2.0, which instead encourages user-generated content. Indeed, Jenkins suggests that it is fandom that has led to the Web 2.0 model, whereby previously marginal fan practices have become mainstream over time.[258] Green and Jenkins are careful to clarify that the current era does not mean copyright is no longer an issue, but rather that recent decades have seen the goalposts shift somewhat to accommodate, to a degree, some online activities that have become commonplace.[259] That fan-generated content may now be actively encouraged does not mean that copyright-holders no longer seek to control online fandom. Web 2.0 may promote fan content, but fans often have to waive rights to their material. As Green and Jenkins argue, the term Web 2.0 should ultimately not be used to describe all online participatory culture in the current era, but rather to describe a specific business model designed to harness free labour.[260] Within this model, some forms of fandom and storylines are encouraged, while others may be actively discouraged. Being linked to an official site may come with substantial strings attached.[261] The rules of engagement are still in flux: sometimes collaborative, sometimes prohibitive.[262]

There have, then, been recurrent waves of fan panic that new crackdowns on their websites could occur at any moment, particularly after the popular *Star Trek New Voyages: Phase II* fan series was blocked by CBS in 2012 from using an unused script from *TOS*.[263] Although CBS was within its rights as the legal owner of the script, another unused *Trek* script by David Gerrold (who penned the highly popular 1967 *TOS* episode 'The Trouble with Tribbles') had been used for a *Phase II* production without difficulty. *Phase II* Senior Executive Producer James Cawley, who plays Captain Kirk in the production, insists that he continues to have a good relationship with CBS, who provide him with detailed feedback on what is and isn't allowed. But these copyright boundary zones remain confusingly grey for many fans running their own websites,[264] and this uncertainty has led to angry fears of a return to the bad old Viacom days. As Gerrold warned, ' "Star Trek" fans … are not a sleeping dragon that you want to poke.'[265]

Conclusion

Television is itself a ritualistic medium. Scheduling and fan attachment to texts create habitual patterns of viewing. For many programmes, including

Star Trek, television is a platform for other related texts, media, consumption and fan activities. Fandom is not religion. Rather, fan pilgrimage is a secular version of older sacred journeys, creating new forms of meaning that combine fandom and commercial tourism. Like traditional pilgrimage, secular pilgrimage can offer a realm in which social norms are inverted, even if its ultimate aim is entertainment and profit rather than transformation. However, the liminoid play on offer may nonetheless open up a space for meaning beyond mere amusement and profit. Understanding the desire of fans to be part of the *Star Trek* mythos, Viacom cast fans as heroes in its interactive Las Vegas attraction and computer games. Fans have also written themselves into roles as heroes resisting corporate control of fandom. With the change of ownership in 2006, and as part of the broader transition to the logic of Web 2.0, CBS sought to smooth this distinction by positioning itself as a supporter of fans and their websites, even as it continues to proclaim its legal rights. Coming from a myth-ritual theory perspective, Mircea Eliade argues that the hero of myth physically undertakes what the neophyte symbolically undertakes in ritual.[266] In the case of *Star Trek*, the fan undertaking both physical and virtual fan rituals becomes a liminal, intertextual figure at the juncture of fictional and factual discourses surrounding *Star Trek*.

Conclude ... Then Reboot

It's a cold winter night. It's raining. It's Thursday and I'll be teaching tomorrow. All in all, it's probably a good night to be staying in, warm and dry, with a nice cup of tea (Earl Grey, hot). But instead I'm on my way to The Astor, a beautiful art deco single-screen establishment specialising in double features, second runs and cult films. Despite being midweek and miserable weather, there's a queue that stretches from the ticket box all the way across the sizeable lobby to the entrance doors and then around some. The theatre itself is packed. Completely. People hover at the stairs as they scan for the few remaining seats, but everyone is chatting happily, with each other and strangers. They're a mixed bunch, from early tweens through to the elderly, different ethnicities, different fashion tastes. There are families, couples, groups of friends, people on their own. No apparent common denominator. In other words, a typical *Star Trek* audience. The film is *Star Trek Into Darkness* (2013), the 12th *Star Trek* feature film, the second in the rebooted Kelvin Timeline, and an homage to the second *Star Trek* feature film in the original timeline, *Star Trek II: The Wrath of Khan* (1982) – a reimagining of 'Khaaaaaaan!' that sought (if not always successfully) to reward the audience for its knowledge of the *Star Trek* backstory across its many incarnations.

To Boldly Go

In the closing sequences of the final episode of *Enterprise*, 'These Are the Voyages ...' (2005), Captain Kirk's famous opening monologue is recited by Picard, Kirk and Archer, emphasising its place within the epic expansion of the *Star Trek* world across television decades and futuristic centuries. Although this is all now a retro-future, the earlier timeline continues to exist – through reruns, DVDs, online, and in the memory of the audience – alongside the new timeline. The franchise's actors also carry the mythic status of their former characters with them as they move on to other projects, their *Star Trek* pedigree becoming an integral way in which many of their roles are written, let alone received.[1] Similarly, while it is not necessary to know *Star Trek* to comprehend or enjoy the plot of *Star Trek Into Darkness* (thereby broadening the potential market for the reboot films), the backstory of the old timeline across its various cross-media incarnations – particularly, in this case, *The Wrath of Khan* – means that memory and recognition, tradition and innovation lie at the heart of its appeal for many fans.[2]

While it was the highest grossing of any *Star Trek* feature film worldwide,[3] *Into Darkness* was nonetheless voted the worst *Star Trek* film of all time at the annual fan convention at Las Vegas in 2013.[4] Their favourite film? *The Wrath of Khan*. This is the challenge of long-lasting story-worlds – to revise their stories for new generations and new cultural circumstances, without alienating the existing fan base. As H. A. Shapiro notes, in ancient Greece, if a myth could no longer be reimagined, it simply died.[5] In the case of *Into Darkness*, many fans took particular exception to the 'whitewashing' of Khan through the casting of Caucasian Benedict Cumberbatch, a move ironically enough intended to avoid potential offence caused by 'demonising' a non-white terrorist character.[6] The inclusion of Sulu's same-sex partnership in *Star Trek Beyond* also raised arguments of fidelity with the past versus the need to reinvent the franchise for a new era.[7]

Star Trek is constantly coming up with these reimaginings, new beginnings and further adventures that nonetheless draw upon its past, such that any 'end' feels entirely provisional. The poster for *Star Trek: The Motion Picture* (1979), which saw the return of *TOS* crew, proclaimed, 'The human adventure is just beginning'. With the transition of the feature films from the crew of *TOS* to that of *TNG*, the trailer for *Star Trek: Generations* (1994)

Conclude ... Then Reboot

emphasised that 'in space there is no beginning and no end' and promised a film in which 'the past and the future connect'. While the tagline for *Star Trek: Nemesis* (2002) was somewhat of a lament, proclaiming that 'a generation's final journey begins', Abrams' near-reboot starts the process all over again, stating 'the future begins' on its poster. This new beginning was also reflected in the title of the first Abrams film, as simply *Star Trek* (and not *Star Trek 11* nor *Star Trek: Insert Subheading Here*). By comparison, the title of Justin Lin's 2016 film *Star Trek Beyond* emphasises the continued expansion of the franchise in time and space. Visually, though, one of the main *Beyond* posters harks back to a poster for the very first feature film, *The Motion Picture*. Both feature an alien female at the centre in a shaft of white light, with Captain Kirk looking upwards to the left in a red shaft, while on the right Spock is in a blue shaft. The base of both posters features the Starship *Enterprise* and the movie title. While writer and actor Simon Pegg shared fans' frustrations that the film was marketed primarily as an action film rather than focusing on features unique to *Star Trek*,[8] the poster nonetheless deliberately reaches out to the memory of fans, and asserts the film's connection to *Trek*'s accumulated backstory and original timeline.

As the new television programme *Star Trek: Discovery* is nearly upon us, many discussion pieces have predictably debated what type of *Trek* it will be – original style or reboot style?[9] At the time of writing, teaser trailers provide some early indications. As a paratext that promotes a new show and attempts to shape audience expectations,[10] the second trailer reveals yet another new beginning, a prequel set 'ten years before Kirk'. It also indicates a continuity break, with the Klingons retconned with yet another makeover. In other respects, though, it aesthetically links back to its textual past – both old and recent – featuring the distinctive lens flare that director J. J. Abrams brought to the franchise in the 2009 feature film (see Figure 5.1). While it may not be Vasquez Rocks, the grand rocky vista in the trailer nonetheless visually recalls 'Kirk's Rock' from *TOS*, while simultaneously showing off the higher budget and widescreen format of the new programme (see Figure 5.2). By calling *Discovery* a 'new chapter in the *Star Trek* saga', the trailer continues the promotional strategy of the series that followed after *TOS*, which similarly sought to deliberately link the franchise with myth, legend and saga.

Figure 5.1 Lens flare in the second *Star Trek: Discovery* teaser trailer (CBS 2017).

Figure 5.2 *Star Trek: Discovery*'s widescreen vista (CBS 2017).

It is the textual, commercial and cultural survival of *Star Trek* for 50 years that has particularly enabled fans and scholars, Viacom, Paramount and CBS to associate the franchise with a new form of popular culture mythology. In the context of contemporary media texts, mythological resonance is not merely an unconscious replication of universal tropes. In a commercial context, myth operates as a corpus of traditional stories and storytelling processes that can be deliberately harnessed as a narrative and marketing strategy. This commercial status does not necessarily mean that *Star Trek*'s

Conclude ... Then Reboot

mythological function is purely economic. While Viacom and CBS have provided commercial pilgrimage sites and themed attractions based on the franchise, this does not preclude a meaningful ritual engagement with such sites. This book has argued that myth is still a useful metaphor in the study of twentieth- and twenty-first-century media forms, as long as it is acknowledged that the notion of myth is changeable, multilayered, and is based on the process of telling and retelling in new contexts.

Since its inception in the 1960s, *Star Trek* has provided a key means through which rapid scientific changes could be mediated within a narrative sphere, extrapolating beyond known science in order to mythologise a future in which the cosmos is knowable and conquerable. While stories about the origins and meaning of the cosmos were once the province of myth, science fiction has taken over this function, particularly in the era of space exploration. *Star Trek*'s mythologising of space extends from the depiction of outer space within its various series to themed physical spaces and virtual fan spaces. In each new context, the *Star Trek* story-world is retold and extended. Like myth, long-lasting transmedia stories use both formula and innovation to maintain a storytelling tradition and yet refashion it to suit changing cultural and media needs. *Star Trek*'s narrative and marketing manipulation of heroic myth and cult fandom has been under-pinned by the franchise's unusual survival over several decades.

That words such as myth, legend, saga and epic are used by television programmes, advertising, reviews and fans means that such terms continue to have cultural significance, even if their meaning becomes reworked in these newer media contexts. Twentieth- and twenty-first-century adaptations of myth, and deliberate attempts to create and market new 'myths', are commercial, technological products. In this respect, they cannot be seen as continuous with older storytelling traditions and the Homeric works where the term myth originates. Yet Homer uses the term myth to mean not a set of story themes or formulas, but a form of persuasive speech. This understanding of myth has changed continually over the millennia, attracting new cultural connotations in its wake that do not entirely disappear. Rather, notions of myth as a form of storytelling, as a type of subject matter, as deceptive and political speech, as a narrative expression of ritual, and as a way of dealing with human concerns through narrative, all continue to have resonance in the contemporary era. This makes myth an inherently complex term, one that activates numerous different associations. We cannot stop such a process, and it is simply not possible to assert, once and for all, a singular understanding of myth. Rather, contemporary, multi-authored texts such as the *Star Trek* franchise reflect the different modalities of myth, while simultaneously attempting to harness heroic associations of the term for their own purposes.

The brief foray of cinema studies into myth theory in the 1960s and 1970s left a scholarly tendency in this field to associate myth with structuralism and the universal. However, as this book has demonstrated, to conceptualise myth as being inherently ahistorical and universal is fundamentally to misunderstand both the history of the term 'myth', and the way that older, oral storytelling traditions could use both formula and innovation in a constant process of retelling. If we are to understand the continuing reinterpretation of older story traditions, we must be mindful that even tradition is a malleable concept. As noted earlier in this book, Robert Parker argues:

> Perhaps we should consider the history of mythology not as a decline from myth into non-myth but as a succession of periods or styles, developing out of one another, as in art. That metaphor, however, does not remove but emphasises the need to distinguish between the products of different periods.[11]

This book has isolated one particular shift in the understanding of myth in a particular period, through a franchise that has survived and developed over half-a-century. In the early decades of television, numerous programmes deliberately adapted myth into new genre-bending contexts. *TOS* followed this trend. However, the franchise's unusual longevity meant that it became particularly well placed to assert its *own* epic, mythic status. The way that the alignment between *Star Trek* and myth is played out through television episodes, video, print and online advertisements, themed physical spaces and online fan environments, indicates that *Star Trek*'s use of myth collides with media forms and practices specific to the late twentieth and early twenty-first centuries.

Future work examining the mythic status of contemporary entertainment forms, and their adaptation of older mythological stories, must

Conclude ... Then Reboot

therefore bear in mind both the malleability of the term myth and the specific technological, commercial and cultural conditions of that adaptation. Exploring media texts through myth 'promote[s] particular reading strategies which activate particular meanings in the text'.[12] So, too, different models of myth bring with them different assumptions and produce different readings.

On 3 January 2013, Canadian astronaut Chris Hadfield was delighted to receive a query from actor William Shatner (Captain Kirk in *TOS*) to ask whether he was tweeting from space. Hadfield responded, 'Yes, Standard Orbit, Captain. And we're detecting signs of life on the surface.' George Takei (Sulu) and Leonard Nimoy (Spock) joined in the conversation, before Buzz Aldrin commented, 'Neil and I would have tweeted from the Moon if we could have but I would prefer to tweet from Mars. Maybe by 2040.'[13] If (or when) we get there, it seems more than likely that at least one astronaut will find a way to give some of the credit to *Star Trek*.

Afterword

To Boldly Go: Marketing the Myth of Star Trek was written just as the first teaser trailers for *Star Trek: Discovery* were being circulated, declaring it a 'new chapter in the *Star Trek* saga'. It also marked the beginning of an unprecedented era of expansion for the franchise, after the post-Viacom legal restrictions on CBS expired.[1] In this new proliferation, *Star Trek* has continued to use the language of myth in promotional materials, as well as building mythology into its stories. As Sarah Iles Johnston notes, Greek myth was a constantly evolving system of storytelling, in that across media forms such as theatre, oral epic and vase paintings, 'interesting prequels, sequels, midquels, and paraquels could emerge, keeping the stories and their characters vigorously alive'.[2] We should be mindful of not overplaying the newness of contemporary media complexity, while also noting the historical specificity in how mythic narratives are played out in entertainment industries in often very deliberate ways.

CBS is positioning *Star Trek* as its tentpole franchise in a competitive streaming marketplace, conditions specific to the twenty-first century. While *TOS* and *TAS* were broadcast on NBC, for their part *TNG* and *DS9* were syndicated, and the pilot for *Voyager* launched the United Paramount Network (UPN). *Discovery* in turn premiered on CBS but thereafter was available only through the streaming service CBS All Access, a contentious move among fans.³ CBS All Access then released the anthology *Star Trek: Short Treks* (2018–), the series *Star Trek: Picard* (2020–) and the animated parody *Star Trek: Lower Decks* (2020–). In 2021, the streaming service rebranded itself as Paramount+ and announced production had started on *Star Trek: Strange New Worlds* (2022–) and the CG-animated *Star Trek: Prodigy* (2021–), aimed at a younger audience. Writing has commenced on a planned *Section 31* spinoff, starring Michelle Yeoh continuing her role from *Discovery* as Emperor Philippa Georgiou. Whispers are also circulating about 'a Khan Noonien Singh limited series'.⁴ Reflecting on this rapid growth, *Star Trek* writer-producer Akiva Goldsman hopefully asserts, 'you can never have enough *Star Trek* shows'.⁵

The distinction between 'prequels, sequels, midquels, and paraquels' has started to get complicated in the suite of current and upcoming *Star Trek* programmes. *Discovery* was initially situated in the Prime *Star Trek* timeline after *Enterprise* but before *TOS*, yet at the end of Season 2, the USS *Discovery* jumps into the thirty-second century. *Lower Decks* is placed in the Prime timeline, one year after *Nemesis*, but before *Picard*, which is set twenty years after the feature film. *Star Trek: Strange New Worlds*, headed up by Captain Christopher Pike (Anson Mount), sits between *Discovery* Season 2 and *TOS*. Meanwhile, producer Alex Kurtzman has suggested viewers 'are going to be very surprised about the world that [*Section 31*] occupies'.⁶

Indeed, Kurtzman proclaims *Section 31* is intended to have 'a new mythology to it'.⁷ The use of myth here may be cursory but the language is not incidental. The association between *Star Trek* and myth remains a conscious reference point for cast and crew, circulating in a range of promotional and publicity materials. *Discovery* showrunner Aaron Harberts declares, the *Star Trek* 'mythology will just continue to grow'.⁸ In the *Star Trek* texts themselves, writers continue to draw on established myths and build new 'ancient' mythologies among its various species. Of the latter kind, the Romulan myth of the Seb-Cheneb, the Destroyer, is central to the first season of *Star Trek: Picard*. Indeed, writer and Season 1 showrunner Michael Gabon subsequently posted a blog entry purportedly written by mythologist professor Ramdha of K'mu University, Romulus, to give greater context to the Romulan collection of myths around the creation

Afterword

and destruction of the world that inform *Picard*'s first season arc.[9] Of the former type, the stand-alone *Star Trek: Short Treks* episode 'Calypso' (2018) is inspired by the mythic figure of the same name from Homer's *Odyssey*, marking a return to Greek myth initiated by *TOS*.[10]

Star Trek has nonetheless sought to diversify its mythic references in the current era to align with its new casts, continuing a trajectory that began back in the 1990s with *Voyager* and *DS9*.[11] Eva Miller argues that even in *TNG*, *Star Trek* posits a future in which there will be greater cultural, canonical equivalency between Western and non-Western myth than there is today, citing the fact that Captain Picard knows both his Gilgamesh and Homer (albeit rather broadly) in 'Darmok' (1991).[12] In *Discovery*'s 'Brother' (2019), Michael Burnham (Sonequa Martin-Green) briefly tells the |Xam myth from southern Africa in which a young girl throws ash into the sky to create the Milky Way.[13] A more detailed retelling of the myth in *Short Treks*' animation 'The Girl Who Made the Stars' (2019) transforms what was once a coming-of-age tale centred on menstruation into one of alien first contact.[14] Writer Brandon Schultz wanted to provide a *Star Trek* version of an 'oral tradition' being passed on through the generations, as a young Burnham is told the bedtime story by her biological father.[15] The idea of myth resonating through the generations echoes the way post-*TOS Trek* cites ancient myths in its texts and then asserts its own status as an intergenerational myth in its promotional materials.

Although the continued complexity of these more recent intersections is beyond my scope here, exciting new work on the *Trek*/myth nexus has been conducted by Eva Miller, Kwasu David Tembo[16] and Leora Hadas,[17] and I look forward to more such work in the future.

As M. Keith Booker notes, in promotional *Star Trek* materials, 'the mythic significance' of the franchise is often couched in 'simplistic' terms.[18] In *To Boldly Go*, I suggest it is important for us to grapple with the multifaceted and often contradictory use of myth that circulates in our popular culture, from the glib to the reflective. It is only then that we can understand the multiple myths of *Star Trek*.

Djoymi Baker
RMIT University, Australia

Notes

Introduction

1. My thanks to Caroline-Isabelle Caron for confirming this issue of pronunciation.
2. Larry Carroll, 'J. J. Abrams Responds to "Star Trek" Fans' Theories', *MTV* (2009). Available at www.mtv.com/news/1611878/jj-abrams-responds-to-star-trek-fans-theories/ (accessed 22 September 2016).
3. Ibid.
4. Ibid.
5. Carl Wilson and Garrath T. Wilson, 'Future Technology in the "Star Trek" Reboots: Complex Future(s)', *Pop Matters*, 13 October 2016. Available at www.popmatters.com/feature/future-technology-in-the-star-trek-reboots-complex-futures/ (accessed 17 December 2016).
6. On the Paramount studio lot, the business of *Star Trek* as a whole is referred to collectively as 'the franchise'. Stephen Edward Poe, *A Vision of the Future: Star Trek Voyager* (New York: Pocket Books, 1998), p. 57.
7. William Blake Tyrell, '*Star Trek* as myth and television as mythmaker', *Journal of Popular Culture* 10/4 (1977), pp. 711–19. Reprinted in M. W. Kapell (ed.), *Star Trek as Myth: Essays on Symbol and Archetype at the Final Frontier* (Jefferson, NC: McFarland, 2010). See also William Blake Tyrell, 'Greek myth and *Star Trek*', *The Classical Bulletin*, 53, January (1977), pp. 36–9.
8. Jonathan Gray, *Show Sold Separately: Promos, Spoilers, and Other Media Paratexts* (New York: New York University Press, 2010). See also Cornelia Klecker, 'The other kind of film frames: a research report on paratexts in film', *Word & Image* 31 (2015), pp. 402–13.
9. Jennifer E. Porter and Darcee L. McLaren (eds), *Star Trek and Sacred Ground* (Albany, NY: State University of New York Press, 1999). Jon Wagner and Jan Lundeen, *Deep Space and Sacred Time: Star Trek in the American Mythos* (Westport, CT: Praeger, 1998).
10. Douglas Brode, 'Introduction' in D. Brode and S. T. Brode (eds), *The Star Trek Universe: Franchising the Final Frontier* (Lanham, MD: Rowman & Littlefield, 2015), pp. xxii–xxiii.

11. Lincoln Geraghty, 'Introduction: fans and paratexts', in L. Geraghty (ed.), *Popular Media Cultures: Fans, Audiences and Paratexts* (New York: Palgrave Macmillan, 2015), p. 1.
12. Matthew Kapell, *Exploring the Next Frontier: Vietnam, NASA, Star Trek and Utopia in 1960s and 70s American Myth and History* (New York: Routledge, 2016). Rick Worland, 'From the new frontier to the final frontier: Star Trek from Kennedy to Gorbachev', *Film & History*, 24/1–2 (1994), pp. 22–3. See also: Walter Irwin, 'Boots and starships', in W. Irwin and G. B. Love (eds), *The Best of the Best of Trek II* (New York: ROC, 1992). Mark Siegel, 'Science fiction and fantasy TV', in B. G. Rose (ed.), *TV Genres* (Westport, CT: Greenwood Press, 1985), p. 94. Karin Blair, 'The garden in the machine: the why of *Star Trek*', *Journal of Popular Culture*, 13/2, Fall (1979), pp. 310–20. Tyrell, '*Star Trek* as myth and television as mythmaker'.
13. See also Lincoln Geraghty, *Living with Star Trek: American Culture and the Star Trek Universe* (London: I.B.Tauris, 2007).
14. Roberta Pearson and Máire Messenger Davies, *Star Trek and American Television* (Berkeley, CA: University of California Press, 2014), p. 10.
15. Tyrell, '*Star Trek* as myth and television as mythmaker', pp. 20, 25.
16. For overtly psychoanalytic approaches to *Star Trek*, see, for example: Jane E. Ellington and Joseph W. Critelli, 'Analysis of a modern myth: the *Star Trek* series', *Extrapolation* 24/3 (1983), pp. 241–50. Louis A. Woods and Gary L. Harmon, 'Jung and *Star Trek*: The *Coincidentia Oppositorium* and images of the shadow', *Journal of Popular Culture*, 28/2 (1994), pp. 169–84. Steve Myers, 'Psychological vs. visionary sources of myth in film', *International Journal of Jungian Studies*, 4/2 (2012), pp. 150–61.
17. For psychoanalytic approaches to myth, see: Stephen L. Harris and Gloria Platzner, *Classical Mythology: Images and Insights*, 3rd edn (Mountain View, CA: Mayfield Publishing, 2001), p. 41. Justin Glenn, 'Psychoanalytic writings on Classical mythology and religion: 1909–1960', *The Classical World*, December/January (1976/77), p. 226. Richard S. Caldwell, *The Origins of the Gods: A Psychoanalytic Study of Greek Theogonic Myth* (New York and Oxford: Oxford University Press, 1989), p. 6. Sigmund Freud, *The Standard Edition of the Complete Psychological Works of Sigmund Freud*, trans. James Strachey (London: Hogarth, 1955). Laurence Coupe, *Myth* (London and New York: Routledge, 1997), p. 127. Carl G. Jung, *Flying Saucers: A Modern Myth of Things Seen in the Skies*, trans. R. F. C. Hull (Princeton, NJ: Princeton University Press, 1978), p. 42. Carl G. Jung, *Jung: Selected Writings*, A. Storr (ed.) (Bungay, Suffolk: Fontana, 1983), pp. 84–5. James F. Iaccino, *Jungian Reflections Within the Cinema: A Psychological Analysis of Sci-Fi and Fantasy Archetypes* (Westport, CT: Praeger, 1998), pp. xii, 15–34.

18. Christopher Vogler, *The Writer's Journey: Mythic Structure for Storytellers and Screenwriters* (Studio City, CA: M. Wiese, 1998).
19. Quoted in Ken Dowden, *The Uses of Greek Mythology* (London and New York: Routledge, 1992), p. 22.
20. Ibid., p. 23.
21. See, for example: G. S. Kirk, *The Nature of Greek Myths* (Harmondsworth, Middlesex: Penguin, 1974). Alan Dundes (ed.), *Sacred Narrative: Readings in the Theory of Myth* (Berkeley, CA: University of California Press, 1984). Coupe, *Myth*. Bruce Lincoln, *Theorizing Myth: Narrative, Ideology, Scholarship* (Chicago, IL, and London: University of Chicago Press, 1999).
22. See, for example: Richard Lattimore (trans.), *The Iliad of Homer* (London: University of Chicago Press, 1951), p. 29, 6.381–2, 9.431, 9.443. Jan Bremmer (ed.), *Interpretations of Greek Mythology* (London: Croom Helm, 1987), p. 4. Dowden, *The Uses of Greek Mythology*, pp. 4–5. Lowell Edmunds, 'Myth in Homer', in I. Morris and B. Powell (eds), *A New Companion to Homer* (Leiden and New York: Brill, 1997), p. 416.
23. Richard P. Martin, *The Language of Heroes: Speech and Performance in the Iliad* (Ithaca, NY, and London: Cornell University Press, 1989), p. xiv. For a critique, see J. Griffin, 'Speech in the *Iliad*', *The Classical Review*, New Series XLI/ I (1991), pp. 1–5.
24. See also Lincoln, *Theorizing Myth*, p. 17.
25. Edmunds, 'Myth in Homer', pp. 415–18, 420. Martin, *The Language of Heroes*, p. 12.
26. As Bruce Lincoln notes, nowhere in the *Iliad* does *mythos* 'mean "false story," "symbolic story," "sacred story," or anything of the sort'. Lincoln, *Theorizing Myth*, p. 18.
27. See, for example: Alan Dundes, *Sacred Narrative*, p. 1. Lauri Honko, 'The problem of defining myth', in A. Dundes (ed.), *Sacred Narrative: Readings in the Theory of Myth* (Berkeley, CA: University of California Press, 1984), pp. 50–1. J. W. Rogerson, 'Slippery words: myth', in A. Dundes (ed.), *Sacred Narrative: Readings in the Theory of Myth*, p. 64.
28. Xenophanes of Colophon, *Fragments*, trans. J. H. Lesher (Toronto: University of Toronto Press, 1992), fragment 11, 12, 16.
29. Lincoln, *Theorizing Myth*, p. 29.
30. Xenophanes of Colophon, *Fragments*, Fragment 1, pp. 47–8.
31. Kathleen Freeman, *Ancilla to the Pre-Socratic Philosophers* (Oxford: Basil Blackwell, 1948), p. 94. Harris and Platzner, *Classical Mythology*, p. 36.
32. Freeman, *Ancilla to the Pre-Socratic Philosophers*, p. 15. Kathleen Freeman, *The Pre-Socratic Philosophers* (Oxford: Basil Blackwell, 1953), p. 41. Harris and Platzner, *Classical Mythology*, p. 35.

33. Theagenes' own work has not survived. Freeman, *The Pre-Socratic Philosophers*, pp. 15, 41. Harris and Platzner, *Classical Mythology*, p. 35.
34. Lincoln, *Theorizing Myth*, p. 226.
35. Masculine genitive plural of *muthos*.
36. Pindar, *Odes*, trans. Diane Svarlien, revised by T. K. Hubbard (1990). Available at www.perseus.tufts.edu/cgi-bin/ptext?doc=Perseus%3Atext%3A1999.01.0162 (accessed 8 December 2004), 8.33, see also 1.25–29.
37. Herodotus, *The Histories*, trans. A. D. Godley (Cambridge, MA: Harvard University Press, 1920), 2.45.1–2.45.3. Marcel Detienne, *The Creation of Mythology*, trans. Margaret Cook (Chicago, IL: University of Chicago Press, 1986), pp. 49–50.
38. Thucydides, *The Peloponnesian War*, trans. Richard Crawley, J. M. Dent (London and New York: E. P. Dutton, 2008), 1.21.1.
39. Plato, *The Republic*, trans. Desmond Lee, 2nd edn (London: Penguin Books, 2003), ll 377a, see also ll 382d.
40. Plato, *The Republic*, ll 377c–d.
41. Lincoln, *Theorizing Myth*, p. 42.
42. Roland Barthes, *Mythologies*, trans. Annette Lavers (London: Vintage, 1957, 1993), p. 143.
43. Desmond Lee in Plato, *The Republic*, p. 361. Plato, *The Republic*, ll 382d. See also Christopher Gill, 'Plato on falsehood – not fiction', in C. Gill and T. P. Wiseman (eds), *Lies and Fiction in the Ancient World* (Exeter, Devon: University of Exeter Press, 1993), pp. 43–4, 56. M. R. Wright, 'Myth, science and reason in the *Timaeus*', *Reason and Necessity: Essays on Plato's* Timaeus (London: Duckworth, 2000), p. 7. For a loose application of Plato to *Star Trek*, see: Linda Johnston, 'The classic *Star Trek*', in W. Irwin and G. B. Love (eds), *The Best of the Best of Trek II* (New York: ROC, 1992). Plato's Atlantis is also referenced in *TNG* episode 'When the Bough Breaks' (1988), and to a lesser extent Plato's story of the cave is employed in various holodeck adventures, such as *TNG*'s 'The Big Goodbye' (1988).
44. Gill, 'Plato on falsehood – not fiction', p. 63. Kathryn A. Morgan, 'Designer history: Plato's Atlantis story and fourth-century ideology', *Journal of Hellenic Studies* 118 (1998), pp. 102–103.
45. Gill, 'Plato on falsehood – not fiction', p. 63. Plato, 'Extract from *Timaeus*', and '*Critias*', in M. Richardson (ed.), *The Halstead Treasury of Ancient Science Fiction* (Rushcutters Bay, NSW: Halstead Classics, 2001). Morgan 'Designer history', pp. 101–102, 112.
46. Coupe, *Myth*, p. 104. Harris and Platzner, *Classical Mythology*, p. 36. Harry Thurston Peck, 'Euhemerus', *Harpers Dictionary of Classical Antiquities* (New York: Harper and Brothers, 1898). Pieter Van der Horst, 'M. Winiarczk, *Euhemeros von Messene. Leben, Werk und Nachwirkung*', *Bryn Mawr Classical*

Review (2002). Available at http://bmcr.brynmawr.edu/2002/2002-07-21.html (accessed 10 September 2016).
47. George Kovacs, 'Moral and mortal in Star Trek: The Original Series', in B. M. Rogers and B. E. Stevens, *Classical Traditions in Science Fiction* (New York: Oxford University Press, 2015), p. 203.
48. Gregory Nagy, *Greek Mythology and Poetics* (Ithaca, NY and London: Cornell University Press, 1990), p. 8.
49. Walter Burkert, *Structure and History in Greek Mythology and Ritual* (Berkeley, CA: University of California Press, 1979), p. 23.
50. See, for example: William Bascom, 'The forms of folklore: prose narratives', *Journal of American Folklore* 78 (1965), pp. 3–20. Reprinted in A. Dundes (ed.), *Sacred Narrative: Readings in the Theory of Myth* (Berkeley, CA: University of California Press, 1984). Kirk, *The Nature of Greek Myths*, pp. 23–7. G. S. Kirk, 'On defining myths', *Phronesis: A Journal for Ancient Philosophy*, 1 (1973), pp. 61–9. Reprinted in A. Dundes (ed.), *Sacred Narrative: Readings in the Theory of Myth* (Berkeley, CA: University of California Press, 1984). See also Jon Wagner and Jan Lundeen, *Deep Space and Sacred Time: Star Trek in the American Mythos* (Westport, CT: Praeger, 1998), pp. 6–7.
51. Barthes, *Mythologies*. Robert W. Brockway, *Myth: From the Ice Age to Mickey Mouse* (Albany, NY: State University of New York Press, 1993), p. 2. Kirk, *The Nature of Greek Myths*, p. 25, emphasis in original.
52. Brockway, *Myth: From the Ice Age to Mickey Mouse*, p. 2.
53. Brian Henderson, 'Critique of cine-structuralism, part 1', *Film Quarterly*, 26/ 5 Autumn (1973), pp. 25–34. Sheila Johnston, 'Film narrative and the structuralist controversy', in P. Cook (ed.), *The Cinema Book* (London: BFI, 1985), p. 233.
54. Claude Lévi-Strauss, 'The structural study of myth', in R. and F. De George (eds), *The Structuralists from Marx to Levi-Strauss* (New York: Doubleday, Anchor, 1972), p. 181. Charles W. Eckert, 'The English cine-structuralists', *Film Comment* 9/3 (1973), pp. 46–51. Geoffrey Nowell Smith, 'I was a Star*Struck Structuralist', *Screen*, 14/3, Autumn (1973), pp. 92–9. Peter Wollen, *Signs and Meaning in the Cinema* (London: Thames and Hudson & BFI, 1969), p. 191.
55. Donna Reid-Jeffery, 'Star Trek: the last frontier in modern American myth', *Folklore and Mythology Studies*, 6, Spring (1982), pp. 34–41. Peter J. Claus, 'A structuralist appreciation of "Star Trek"', in J. B. Cole (ed.), *Anthropology for the Eighties* (New York: The Free Press, 1982).
56. Andrew Tudor, 'Genre: theory and mispractice in film criticism', *Screen*, 11/6, November–December (1970), p. 42. John G. Cawelti, *The Six-Gun Mystique* (Bowling Green, OH: Bowling Green University Press, 1971), p. 30.

57. Thomas Schatz, 'The structural influence: new directions in film genre study', in B. K. Grant (ed.), *Film Genre Reader* (Austin, TX: University of Texas Press, 1986), p. 100, n. 8, emphasis in original.
58. Ibid., p. 98.
59. Jim Collins, *Uncommon Cultures: Popular Culture and Post-Modernism* (New York: Routledge, 1989), pp. 97–8.
60. Ibid., p. 99, emphasis in original.
61. Barthes, *Mythologies*, p. 109, emphasis in original.
62. Ibid.
63. Ibid., p. 142.
64. Ibid., p. 143.
65. Ibid., p. 157.
66. Martin, *The Language of Heroes*, p. xiv. For a semiotic approach to Greek myth, see: Charles Segal, 'Greek myth as a semiotic and structural system and the problem of tragedy', *Interpreting Greek Tragedy: Myth, Poetry, Text* (Ithaca, NY: Cornell University Press, 1986).
67. Roland Barthes, *Image Music Text*, trans. Stephen Heath (London: Fontana Press, 1977), p. 166.
68. Ibid., pp. 167–8.
69. Ibid., p. 169, emphasis in original.
70. Ibid., p. 168. Eric Gould, *Mythical Intentions in Modern Literature* (Princeton, NJ: Princeton University Press, 1981), p. 26.
71. Barthes, *Image Music Text*, p. 166. In the context of Greek myth, see John Peradotto, *Man in the Middle Voice: Name and Narration in the* Odyssey (Princeton, NJ: Princeton University Press, 1990).
72. Roland Barthes, 'Theory of the text', in R. Young (ed.), *Unifying the Text: A Post-Structuralist Reader* (London and New York: Routledge, 1981), p. 39.
73. Such as Eckert, 'The English cine-structuralists', p. 49.
74. James W. Chesebro, 'Communication, values, and popular television series – a four year assessment', in H. Newcomb (ed.), *Television: The Critical View* (New York: Oxford University Press, 1987).
75. Jim Collins, *Architectures of Excess: Cultural Life in the Information Age* (New York: Routledge, 1995), pp. 40–1.
76. Darcee L. McLaren, 'On the edge of forever: understanding the *Star Trek* phenomenon as myth', in J. E. Porter and D. L. McLaren (eds), *Star Trek and Sacred Ground: Explorations of Star Trek, Religion and American Culture* (Albany, NY: State University of New York Press, 1999), p. 231.
77. Matt Hills, 'To boldly go where others have gone before …? Star Trek and (academic) narratives', *Scope*, November 2000. Available at: www.nottingham.ac.uk/film/journal/bookrev/star-trek.htm (accessed 2 November 2000, no longer online 22 September 2016).

78. Djoymi Baker, 'From the Doctor to Captain Kirk: actors and their mythic heroes', in J. Perlich and D. Whitt (eds), *Millennial Mythmaking: Essays on the Power of Science Fiction and Fantasy Literature, Films and Games* (Jefferson, NC: McFarland, 2010), pp. 129–46.
79. For a comparison of the myths of *Star Trek* and *Star Wars*, see Lincoln Geraghty, 'Creating and comparing myth in twentieth-century science fiction: Star Trek and Star Wars', *Literature/Film Quarterly*, 33/3 (2005), pp. 191–200. For reasons of scope this book remains focused on *Star Trek*; however, it would nonetheless be fruitful to examine how other long-lasting franchises may similarly market their mythic status.
80. John Fiske, *Television Culture* (London and New York: Methuen, 1987), p. 130.
81. Henry Jenkins, 'Star Trek rerun, reread and rewritten: fan writing as textual poaching', in C. Penley, E. Lyons, L. Spigel and J. Bergstrom (eds), *Close Encounters: Film, Feminism, and Science Fiction* (Minneapolis, MN: University of Minnesota Press, 1991). Henry Jenkins, *Textual Poachers: Television Fans and Participatory Culture* (New York: Routledge, 1992). John Tulloch and Henry Jenkins, *Science Fiction Audiences: Watching Doctor Who and Star Trek* (London and New York: Routledge, 1995).
82. Jenkins, *Textual Poachers*, pp. 23–4. Robert V. Kozinets, 'Inno-tribes: Star Trek as Wikimedia', in Bernard Cova, Robert V. Kozinets and Avi Shankar (eds), *Consumer Tribes* (Amsterdam: Butterworth-Heinemann, 2007), p. 202.
83. Johnston, 'The classic *Star Trek*', p. 68.
84. Tulloch and Jenkins, *Science Fiction Audiences*, p. 191. Michael A. Hemmingson, *Star Trek: A Post-Structural Critique of the Original Series* (San Bernardino, CA: Borgo Press, 2009), p. 13.
85. Henry Jenkins, *Convergence Culture: Where Old and New Media Collide* (New York: New York University Press, 2006), pp. 95–6.
86. Henry Jenkins, 'Transmedia Storytelling 101', *Confession of an Aca-Fan* (blog). Available at http://henryjenkins.org/2007/03/transmedia_storytelling_101.html (accessed 24 November 2015).
87. William Proctor, 'Beginning again: the reboot phenomenon in comic books, film and beyond' (PhD diss., University of Sunderland, 2015), p. 303. Mike Johnson and Tim Jones, *Star Trek: Countdown* (London: Titan, 2009).
88. Mike Johnson and David Messina, *Star Trek: Countdown to Darkness* (London: Titan, 2013).
89. Chris Gregory, *Star Trek: Parallel Narratives* (Houndsmills, Hampshire and London: Macmillan Press, 2000), pp. 38, 41. Marc Okuda and Denise Okuda, *Star Trek Chronology: The History of the Future* (New York: Pocket Books, 1996), p. vii.

90. Angela Ndalianis, 'Enter the Aleph: superhero worlds and hypertime realities', in A. Ndalianis (ed.), *The Contemporary Comic Book Superhero* (New York: Routledge, 2009), p. 282.
91. Proctor, 'Beginning again: the reboot phenomenon in comic books, film and beyond', pp. 303–305.
92. Chris Cooper, *Star Trek: Telepathy War*, 1/1, November 1997.
93. Collins, *Architectures of Excess*, pp. 45, 47. Jenkins, *Textual Poachers*, p. 27.
94. Collins, *Architectures of Excess*, pp. 40–1.
95. Fiske, *Television Culture*, p. 130.
96. Hills, 'To boldly go where others have gone before …?'. Robert Asa, 'Classic *Star Trek* and the death of God: a case study of "Who Mourns for Adonais?"' in J. E. Porter and D. L. McLaren (eds), *Star Trek and Sacred Ground: Explorations of Star Trek, Religion and American Culture* (Albany, NY: State University of New York Press, 1999). Wagner and Lundeen, *Deep Space and Sacred Time*.
97. Pearson and Messenger Davies, *Star Trek and American Television*, p. 10.
98. Michael Idato, 'Star Trek explores next frontier with new television and streaming series', *The Age*, 3 November 2015. Available at www.theage.com.au/entertainment/tv-and-radio/star-trek-explores-next-frontier-with-new-television-and-streaming-series-20151103-gkp629.html (accessed 23 November 2015).
99. Jim Collins, 'Batman: the movie, the narrative, the hyperconscious', in R. E. Pearson and W. Uricchio (eds), *The Many Lives of the Batman: Critical Approaches to a Superhero and His Media* (New York: Routledge and London: BFI, 1991), p. 179.
100. Ibid., pp. 179–80.
101. Robert A. Segal, *Myth and Ritual Theory: An Anthology* (Malden, MA and Oxford: Blackwell, 1998), p. 13.
102. Emma Stafford, *Herakles* (Hoboken, NY: Taylor and Francis, 2013), pp. 24, 52.
103. Daryl G. Frazetti, 'Star Trek and the Culture of Fandom', 26 April 2011. Available at www.startrek.com/article/star-trek-and-the-culture-of-fandom (accessed 21 June 2017).
104. See, for example: Dflorence in Dave Gonzales, 'Star Trek Beyond will ignore most of Into Darkness', *Geek*, 17 December 2015. Available at www.geek.com/news/star-trek-beyond-will-ignore-most-of-into-darkness-1642409/ (accessed 18 February 2016).
105. Quoted in Henry Barnes, 'Simon Pegg joins criticism of Star Trek Beyond trailer', *Guardian*, 18 December 2015. Available at www.theguardian.com/film/2015/dec/18/simon-pegg-critical-of-star-trek-beyond-trailer-justin-lin (accessed 18 February 2016).

Chapter 1: Myth and Early US TV

1. As Kovacs notes, the title is taken from Percy Bysshe Shelley's poem 'Adonais'. George Kovacs, 'Moral and mortal in Star Trek: The Original Series', in B. M. Rogers and B. E. Stevens, *Classical Traditions in Science Fiction* (New York: Oxford University Press, 2015), p. 204.
2. See, for example: Jeffrey Scott Lamp, 'Biblical interpretation in the *Star Trek* universe', in J. E. Porter and D. L. McLaren (eds), *Star Trek and Sacred Ground: Explorations of Star Trek, Religion, and American Culture* (Albany, NY: State University of New York Press, 1999). Anne MacKenzie Pearson, 'From thwarted gods to reclaimed mystery? An overview of the depiction of religion in *Star Trek*', in J. E. Porter and D. L. McLaren (eds), *Star Trek and Sacred Ground*. Jon Wagner and Jan Lundeen, *Deep Space and Sacred Time: Star Trek in the American Mythos* (Westport, CT: Praeger, 1998).
3. Matt Hills, 'To boldly go where others have gone before …? Star Trek and (academic) narratives', *Scope*, November 2000. Available at: www.nottingham.ac.uk/film/journal/bookrev/star-trek.htm (accessed 2 November 2000, no longer online 22 September 2016).
4. Solomon does mention some of the key television programmes, but only those based in 'ancient' settings and whose continuing premise is myth. Jon Solomon, *The Ancient World in the Cinema* (New Haven, CT: Yale University Press, 2001), pp. xviii–xix.
5. Secondary sources such as TV guides from the period have been relied upon where the programmes themselves or specific episodes could not be located.
6. Jonathan Gray, *Show Sold Separately: Promos, Spoilers, and Other Media Paratexts* (New York: New York University Press, 2010), p. 141.
7. The term 'away team' is used in this and subsequent series to denote the group of personnel selected for missions away from the spaceship.
8. As indeed the Greeks themselves thought. For example, historian Thucydides assumes the Trojan war is historical fact. Thucydides, *The Peloponnesian War*, trans. Richard Crawley, J. M. Dent (London and New York: E. P. Dutton, 2008), 6.2.1.
9. Lamp, 'Biblical interpretation in the *Star Trek* universe', pp. 194, 198. Kovacs, 'Moral and mortal in Star Trek', pp. 207–208.
10. Pearson, 'From thwarted gods to reclaimed mystery?' p. 20.
11. Robert Asa, 'Classic *Star Trek* and the death of God: a case study of "Who Mourns for Adonais?" ' in J. E. Porter and D. L. McLaren (eds), *Star Trek and Sacred Ground*, pp. 39, 44, 53, n. 3.
12. Ibid., p. 47.
13. Ibid., p. 45.
14. Hills, 'To boldly go where others have gone before …?'.

15. Asa, 'Classic *Star Trek* and the death of God'. Wagner and Lundeen, *Deep Space and Sacred Time*. Hills, 'To boldly go where others have gone before ...?'
16. Asa, 'Classic *Star Trek* and the death of God', p. 53, n. 5.
17. Ibid.
18. Wagner and Lundeen, *Deep Space and Sacred Time*, pp. 20, 237 n.1. Apollodorus, *The Library*, trans. James G. Frazer, Vol. 1 (Cambridge, MA: Harvard University Press, London: William Heinemann, 1921, 1967), 1.3.6.
19. Wagner and Lundeen, *Deep Space and Sacred Time*, p. 237, n.1.
20. Martin M. Winkler, *Cinema and Classical Texts: Apollo's New Light* (Cambridge: Cambridge University Press, 2009), p. 87.
21. Ibid.
22. Kovacs, 'Moral and mortal in Star Trek', p. 202.
23. Maria Wyke, *Projecting the Past: Ancient Rome, Cinema and History* (New York and London: Routledge, 1997), p. 13. Pierre Sorlin, *The Film in History: Restaging the Past* (Oxford: Basil Blackwell, 1980).
24. Jay David Bolter and Richard Grusin, *Remediation: Understanding New Media* (Cambridge, MA: MIT Press, 1999), p. 47.
25. Ibid., p. 44.
26. Rick Altman, *Film/Genre* (London: BFI, 1999), pp. 38, 62–3, 69–82.
27. Ibid., p. 38.
28. Ibid., pp. 78–9, 82.
29. Andrew Ford, 'Epic as genre', in I. Morris and B. Powell (eds), *A New Companion to Homer* (Leiden and New York: Brill, 1997), p. 399.
30. Vivian Sobchack, ' "Surge and splendor": a phenomenology of the Hollywood historical epic', in B. K. Grant (ed.), *Film Genre Reader II* (Austin, TX: University of Texas Press, 1995), p. 286.
31. Ibid., p. 286, emphasis in original.
32. George MacDonald Fraser, *The Hollywood History of the World* (London: Penguin, 1988), p. 7. See also Sobchack, 'Surge and splendor', p. 286.
33. Steve Neale, 'Epics and spectacles', *Genre and Hollywood* (London and New York: Routledge, 2000), p. 87.
34. Solomon, *The Ancient World in the Cinema*, p. 102.
35. Tino Balio, 'Introduction to Part I', in T. Balio (ed.), *Hollywood in the Age of Television* (Boston, MA: Unwin Hyman, 1990), p. 23. John Belton, *Widescreen Cinema* (Cambridge, MA: Harvard University Press, 1992), pp. 70, 73. Sobchack, 'Surge and splendor', p. 297. Solomon, *The Ancient World in the Cinema*, p. 13.
36. Belton, *Widescreen Cinema*, pp. 77, 191.
37. Sobchack, 'Surge and splendor', pp. 299, 300. Early miniseries included *Rich Man, Poor Man* (1976), *Roots* (1977), *Jesus of Nazareth* (1977), *The Winds of War* (1983) and *North and South* (1985). On these and the miniseries

generally, see: N. D. Batra, 'The mini-series: epic in the age of television', *The Hour of Television: Critical Approaches* (Metuchen, NJ: Scarecrow Press, 1987), p. 199. Sobchack, 'Surge and splendor', p. 299. Solomon, *The Ancient World in the Cinema*, p. 17.

38. Hank Werba, 'Italo TV "Odyssey" hits a Homer', *Variety*, 22 May 1968, no pagination. Reprinted in H. H. Prouty (ed.), *Variety Television Reviews, Vol. 9, 1966-1969* (New York: Garland, 1989-91).
39. W. Stephen Bush, 'Homer's Odyssey. Three Reels. (Milano Films.)', *The Moving Picture World*, 11/11, 16 March 1912, p. 941.
40. Ibid.
41. Epes Winthrop Sargent, 'Advertising for exhibitors', *The Moving Picture World*, 11/8, 24 February 1912, p. 666.
42. Ibid., p. 763.
43. Trau., 'With its third season under the aegis of the Ford Foundation ...', *Variety*, 6 April 1955, no pagination. Reprinted in H. H. Prouty (ed.), *Variety Television Reviews, Vol. 5, 1954-1956* (New York: Garland, 1989-91).
44. Trau., 'With its third season under the aegis of the Ford Foundation ...'
45. Werba, 'Italo TV "Odyssey" hits a Homer'.
46. Horo., 'Leonard Bernstein and the N.Y. Philharmonic', *Variety*, 1 March 1961, no pagination. Reprinted in H. H. Prouty (ed.), *Variety Television Reviews, Vol. 7, 1960-1962* (New York: Garland, 1989-91).
47. Guy., 'Oedipus', *Variety*, 9 November 1960, no pagination. Reprinted in H. H. Prouty (ed.), *Variety Television Reviews, Vol. 7, 1960-1962*.
48. Continued as *Jane Wyman Presents The Fireside Theatre* (1955-8).
49. Lynn Spigel, 'Installing the television set: popular discourses on television and domestic space, 1948-1955', in L. Spigel and D. Mann (eds), *Private Screenings: Television and the Female Consumer* (Minneapolis, MN: University of Minnesota Press, 1992), pp. 12, 13-15. Lynn Spigel, *Make Room for TV: Television and the Family Ideal in Postwar America* (Chicago, IL: University of Chicago Press, 1992), p. 138.
50. Ibid., pp. 16-24.
51. Les., 'Search for Ulysses', *Variety*, 19 January 1966, no pagination. Reprinted in H. H. Prouty (ed.), *Variety Television Reviews, Vol. 9, 1966-1969*.
52. Ibid.
53. Ibid.
54. The format was borrowed from the successful radio programme that also featured Cronkite, originally broadcast in 1947 as *CBS is There* and continuing in 1948-50 as *You Are There*. George W. Woolery, *Children's Television: The First Thirty-Five Years, 1946-1981, Part II: Live, Film and Tape Series* (Metuchen, NJ: The Scarecrow Press, 1985), p. 567. See also Maria Wyke, 'Film style and Fascism: *Julius Caesar*', *Film Studies*, 4, Summer (2004), p. 69.

55. Also known as *Hercules and the Princess of Troy*. Solomon, *The Ancient World in the Cinema*, pp. 17, 123.
56. Pit., 'Hercules', *Variety*, 15 September 1965, no pagination. Reprinted in H. H. Prouty (ed.), *Variety Television Reviews, Vol. 8, 1963-1965* (New York: Garland, 1989-91).
57. Pit., 'Hercules'.
58. George W. Woolery, *Children's Television: The First Thirty-Five Years, 1946-1981, Part I: Animated Cartoon Series* (Metuchen, NJ: The Scarecrow Press, 1983), p. 183.
59. George W. Woolery, *Children's Television Part II*, p. 342.
60. Ibid., pp. 342-3.
61. Ibid., pp. 557-8.
62. Stuart Fischer, *Kids' TV: The First 25 Years* (New York: Facts on File Publications, 1983), p. 22.
63. *Variety*, 'You Are There', 21 April 1954, no pagination. Reprinted in H. H. Prouty (ed.), *Variety Television Reviews, Vol. 5, 1954-1956*.
64. Fischer, *Kids' TV*, p. 4.
65. Ibid., p. 4.
66. On the high/low culture distinction, see Lynn Spigel, *Welcome to the Dreamhouse: Popular Media and Postwar Suburbs* (Durham, NC: Duke University Press, 2001), pp. 265-309.
67. Woolery, *Children's Television Part II*, pp. 586-8. Spigel, *Welcome to the Dreamhouse*, pp. 191-5.
68. Spigel, *Welcome to the Dreamhouse*, pp. 192-3, 195.
69. Ibid., p. 195. See also Evalyn Grumbine, 'Reaching juvenile markets', *Psychology of Juvenile Appeal* (New York: McGraw-Hill, 1938). Reprinted in H. Jenkins (ed.), *The Children's Culture Reader* (New York: New York University Press, 1998), p. 461. Dorothy Walter Baruch, 'Radio rackets, movie murders and killer cartoons', *New Ways to Discipline: You and Your Child Today* (New York: McGraw-Hill 1949). Reprinted in H. Jenkins (ed.), *The Children's Culture Reader*, pp. 493, 494. *Variety* warned against children watching the *Space Patrol* television programme, calling it 'disturbing'. Jose., 'Space Patrol', *Variety*, 8 September 1954, no pagination; reprinted in H. H. Prouty (ed.), *Variety Television Reviews, Vol. 5, 1954-1956*.
70. Richard Reynolds, *Super Heroes - A Modern Mythology* (London: B.T. Batsford, 1992), p. 53.
71. Jose., 'Mr. I. Magination', *Variety*, 6 September 1950. Reprinted in H. H. Prouty (ed.), *Variety Television Reviews, Vol. 3, 1923-1950* (New York: Garland, 1989-91). Stal., 'Mr. I. Magination', *Variety*, 27 April 1949. Reprinted in H. H. Prouty (ed.), *Variety Television Reviews, Vol. 3, 1923-1950*. Fredric Wertham, *Seduction of the Innocent* (London: Museum Press, 1954), p. 369.

72. Woolery, *Children's Television Part I*, p. 170. Woolery, *Children's Television Part II*, pp. 17–18.
73. Ibid., p. 18.
74. Mark Siegel, 'Science fiction and fantasy TV', in B. G. Rose (ed.), *TV Genres* (Westport, CT: Greenwood Press, 1985), p. 92.
75. Spigel, *Welcome to the Dreamhouse*, p. 200.
76. Woolery, *Children's Television Part II*, p. 566.
77. Ibid., p. 396.
78. Fischer, *Kids' TV*, p. xiii.
79. Jeffrey Sconce, 'Science fiction programs', in H. Newcomb (ed.), *Encyclopedia of Television*, 2nd edn (New York and London: Fitzroy Dearborn, 2004), pp. 2026–7. See also Gerald Duchovnay, 'From big screen to small box: adapting science fiction film for television', in J. P. Telotte (ed.), *The Essential Science Fiction Television Reader* (Lexington, KY: University Press of Kentucky, 2008), pp. 69–70.
80. David Weinstein, 'Captain Video: television's first fantastic voyager', *Journal of Popular Film and Television*, 30/3, Fall 2002, p. 150.
81. Gilb., 'Space Patrol', *Variety*, 13 June 1951, no pagination. Reprinted in H. H. Prouty (ed.), *Variety Television Reviews, Vol. 4, 1951–1953* (New York: Garland, 1989–91).
82. Helm., 'Space Patrol', *Variety*, 7 September 1954, no pagination. Reprinted in H. H. Prouty (ed.), *Daily Variety Television Reviews, Vol. 1, 1946–1956* (New York: Garland, 1989–991). See also Kap., 'Space Patrol', *Variety*, 18 January 1954. Reprinted in H. H. Prouty (ed.), *Daily Variety Television Reviews, Vol. 1, 1946–1956*. *Variety* also suggested that *Buck Rogers* might attract an adult following in part due to its cinema serial forerunner. Stal., 'Buck Rogers', *Variety*, 19 April 1950. Reprinted in H. H. Prouty (ed.), *Variety Television Reviews, Vol. 3, 1923–1950*.
83. *Variety* also suggested that *Tom Corbett*, although a children's show, 'may pick up a few adult viewers through its fanciful science fiction theme and setting'. Chan., 'Tom Corbett, Space Cadet', *Variety*, 4 October 1950. Reprinted in H. H. Prouty (ed.), *Variety Television Reviews, Vol. 3, 1923–1950*.
84. Spigel, *Welcome to the Dreamhouse*, p. 197.
85. Rod Serling, 'Reviews: Science Fiction Theater', *TV Guide*, 11 June 1955, p. 18.
86. See for example Daku., 'The Man from 1997 (*Conflict*)', *Variety*, 29 November 1956. Reprinted in H. H. Prouty (ed.), *Daily Variety Television Reviews, Vol. 1, 1946–1956*.
87. Siegel, 'Science fiction and fantasy TV', pp. 93–4.
88. *Hercules Against the Moon Men* (1964) was a notable exception.
89. *Captain Video and His Video Rangers* is often listed as the first science fiction programme on television, and while this is true of the broadcast era proper, a

science fiction short was nonetheless broadcast in early tests. Fischer, *Kids' TV*, p. 13. Erik Barnouw, *Tube of Plenty: The Evolution of American Television*, 2nd edn (New York: Oxford University Press, 1990), p. 61.

90. Joe Sarno, 'Captain Video, Daily Episodes (1949–1955)', *Comic Kingdom* (n.d.). Available at http://home.earthlink.net/~joesarno/tvscifi/captainvdaily.htm (accessed 6 January 2005, no longer online 23 September 2016).
91. Ibid.
92. Woolery, *Children's Television Part II*, p. 109.
93. Ibid., p. 110. Wertham, *Seduction of the Innocent*, p. 369.
94. Art., 'Captain Video', *Variety*, 13 July 1955, no pagination. Reprinted in H. H. Prouty (ed.), *Variety Television Reviews, Vol. 5, 1954–1956*. During his testimony, he was 'continually addressed by investigators as "Captain".' Woolery, *Children's Television Part II*, p. 110.
95. In 1951 *Variety* had criticised *Captain Video* for its lack of educational material. *Variety*, 'DuMont's Captain Video', 25 April 1951. Reprinted in H. H. Prouty (ed.), *Variety Television Reviews, Vol. 4, 1951–1953* (New York: Garland, 1989–91).
96. To a much lesser extent, this naming strategy can also be found in adult genres, such as the 1955 'The Argonauts' episode of *Playhouse of Stars*, which depicted not Jason's adventures but rather an ordinary worker who dreams of sailing away. Helm., 'The Argonauts (*Playhouse of Stars*)', *Variety*, 1 June 1955. Reprinted in H. H. Prouty (ed.), *Daily Variety Television Reviews, Vol. 1, 1946–1956*.
97. *Flash Gordon* had also been branded as 'most objectionable' by the National Association for Better Radio and Television, and the earlier film serials had similarly attracted criticism. Woolery, *Children's Television*, p. 174.
98. Aired 26 September 1953. *TV Guide*, 'Tom Corbett, Space Cadet', 15 September 1953, p. A-10.
99. Trau., 'Star Trek', *Variety*, 14 September 1966, no pagination. Reprinted in H. H. Prouty (ed.), *Variety Television Reviews, Vol. 9, 1966–1969* (New York: Garland, 1989–91). On the scheduling, see Allan Asherman, *The Star Trek Compendium* (New York: Pocket Books, 1989, 1993), p. 31.
100. Trau., 'Star Trek'.
101. Mor., 'The Time Tunnel', *Variety*, 14 September 1966. Reprinted in H. H. Prouty (ed.), *Variety Television Reviews, Vol. 9, 1966–1969*. Cleveland Amory, 'The Time Tunnel', *TV Guide*, 29 October 1966, p. 25. In 'Revenge of the Gods' (1966), time travellers Doug Phillips and Tony Newman find themselves in the midst of the Trojan war, although like in *You Are There*, the role of the gods has been omitted. Myth is presented as history.
102. Cleveland Amory, 'The Invaders', *TV Guide*, 18 February 1967, p. 12.
103. Mor., 'Star Trek', *Variety*, 25 September 1968, no pagination. Reprinted in H. H. Prouty (ed.), *Variety Television Reviews, Vol. 9, 1966–1969*. This

very move to late Friday night cut the programme's young adult audience. Asherman, *The Star Trek Compendium*, p. 103.
104. Asa, 'Classic *Star Trek* and the death of God', pp. 53–4, n. 7. Wagner and Lundeen, *Deep Space and Sacred Time*, p. 20. Asherman, *The Star Trek Compendium*, p. 73.
105. Wagner and Lundeen, *Deep Space and Sacred Time*, p. 20.
106. Woolery, *Children's Television Part II*, pp. 110, 634.
107. *Tom Corbett, Space Cadet*, 'The Mercurian Invasion' (1950, VHS cover).
108. *TV Guide*, ' "Ride" The New *Apollo* Moonship!' 18 February (1967), p. A41. The impact of the Space Race on science fiction will be explored more fully in Chapter Three.
109. Susan J. Drucker and Robert S. Cathcart, 'The Hero as a communication phenomenon', in S. J. Drucker and R. S. Cathcart (eds), *American Heroes in a Media Age* (Creskill, NJ: Hampton Press, 1994), p. 2, emphasis in original.
110. Lance Strate, 'Heroes: a communication perspective', in S. J. Drucker and R. S. Cathcart (eds), *American Heroes in a Media Age*, p. 15.
111. Quoted in Emily Kennard 'What's in a Name?', *NASA* (2009). Available at www.nasa.gov/centers/glenn/about/history/silverstein_feature.html (accessed 22 September 2016).
112. Derek Elley, *The Epic Film: Myth and History* (London: Routledge, 1984), p. 165.
113. Ibid.
114. Roy Kinnard, *Science Fiction Serials* (Jefferson, NC, and London: McFarland, 1998), p. 36. Woolery, *Children's Television Part I*, p. 331.
115. *TV Guide*, 'Straight from the Drawing Board: More Comic Strip Characters Head Toward Television', 13 November 1954, p. 16.
116. Wertham, *Seduction of the Innocent*, p. 359.
117. Leslie Raddatz, 'Product of Two Worlds: Leonard Nimoy, as the hybrid Mr. Spock, has made it big in outer space', *TV Guide*, 4 March 1967, p. 24.
118. Les., 'Land of the Giants', *Variety*, 25 September 1968, no pagination. Reprinted in H. H. Prouty (ed.), *Variety Television Reviews, Vol. 9, 1966–1969*. See, for example: Lynn Spigel and Henry Jenkins, 'Same bat channel, different bat times: mass culture and popular memory', in R. E. Pearson and
119. W. Uricchio (eds), *The Many Lives of the Batman: Critical Approaches to a Superhero and his Media* (New York: Routledge & London: BFI, 1991), p. 129.
120. Wertham, *Seduction of the Innocent*, p. 381.
121. Reynolds, *Super Heroes*, p. 53.
122. By contrast, *Wonder Woman* (1941–) had drawn on the Greek myths of the Amazons, but was not originally herself a Greek hero.

123. Stan Lee and Jack Kirby, 'Thor the Mighty and The Stone Men from Saturn', *Journey into Mystery*, 1/83 (1962). Reprinted in S. Lee and J. Kirby, *Essential Thor*, Vol. 1 (New York: Marvel Comics, 2001).
124. Reynolds, *Super Heroes*, p. 53.
125. Reynolds, *Super Heroes*, p. 58. Stan Lee and Jack Kirby, 'The Coming of the Avengers!', *The Avengers*, 1/1 (1963). Reprinted in S. Lee, J. Kirby and D. Heck, *Essential Avengers*, Vol. 1 (New York: Marvel Comics, 2001).
126. Jason Mittell, *Genre and Television: From Cop Shows to Cartoons in American Culture* (New York: Routledge, 2004), p. 65.
127. Mor., 'Marvel Super-Heroes', *Variety*, 26 October 1966, no pagination. Reprinted in H. H. Prouty (ed.), *Variety Television Reviews, Vol. 9, 1966–1969*.
128. Susan Sontag explains that 'camp' embraces 'artifice and exaggeration' and rejects 'ordinary aesthetic judgment'. Susan Sontag, 'Notes on "Camp"', *Against Interpretation and Other Essays* (London: Eyre & Spottiswoode, 1967), pp. 275, 286.
129. On *Batman*, Pop art and camp, see Spigel and Jenkins, 'Same bat channel'. *Batman* also borrowed from myth. See episodes 'Ring Around the Riddler' (1967), 'The Wail of the Siren' (1967) and 'Minerva, Mayhem and Millionaires' (1968).
130. *TV Guide*, 'From the Underground', 4 March 1967, p. A2.
131. While Thor made frequent references to his godly identity, he was 'rarely used as a pretext for expounding Norse mythology'. Reynolds, *Super Heroes*, p. 60. The Norse Thor revealed in *The Poetic Edda* (ninth to twelfth centuries ce) is a much more formidable figure, prone to fits of violent vengeance.
132. Superhero based very loosely on Egyptian mythology. George W. Woolery, *Children's Television, Part I*, p. 47.
133. Reynolds, *Super Heroes*, p. 53.
134. Ibid. Similarly, a review of the 1953 television debut of Superman cites the opening as taking place 'on a mythical planet', the origins of Superman's 'super qualities'. Daku., 'Superman on Earth (*Superman*)', *Variety*, 11 February (1953). Reprinted in H. H. Prouty (ed.), *Daily Variety Television Reviews, Vol. 1, 1946–1956* (New York: Garland, 1989–91).
135. Reynolds, *Super Heroes*, pp. 9–10, 61.
136. *TV Guide*, 'Time Tunnel', 3 September 1966, p. A81. *TV Guide*, 'Star Trek', 8 September 1966, p. A72.

Chapter 2: The New Mythology

1. See the Introduction for an overview of these changes in the Greek understanding of myth.

2. Lowell Edmunds, 'Myth in Homer', in I. Morris and B. Powell (eds), *A New Companion to Homer* (Leiden and New York: Brill, 1997), pp. 415–18, 420.
3. Ibid., p. 420. See also Gregory Nagy, *Greek Mythology and Poetics* (Ithaca, NY, and London: Cornell University Press, 1990), pp. 8–9.
4. Richard Lattimore (trans.), *The Iliad of Homer* (London: University of Chicago Press, 1951), 1.352. Jan Bremmer (ed.), *Interpretations of Greek Mythology* (London: Croom Helm, 1987), p. 3.
5. Bremmer, *Interpretations of Greek Mythology*, pp. 3, 5.
6. Ibid., p. 3.
7. Ibid., p. 4. T. P. Van Baaren, 'The flexibility of myth', in A. Dundes (ed.), *Sacred Narrative: Readings in the Theory of Myth* (Berkeley, CA: University of California Press, 1984), p. 221. Bremmer, *Interpretations of Greek Mythology*, p. 4.
8. John M. Foley, 'Oral tradition and its implications', in I. Morris and B. Powell (eds), *A New Companion to Homer* (Leiden and New York: Brill, 1997), pp. 165–8. Robert Parker, 'Myths of early Athens', in J. Bremmer (ed.), *Interpretations of Greek Mythology*, p. 188.
9. In the Greek context, from the mid-seventh century BCE scenes from myths began to appear on vases. Ken Dowden, *The Uses of Greek Mythology* (London and New York: Routledge, 1992), p. 12.
10. Parker, 'Myths of early Athens', p. 188.
11. Ibid., pp. 188–9.
12. See also Bremmer, *Interpretations of Greek Mythology*, pp. 5–6.
13. Dowden, *The Uses of Greek Mythology*, p. 8. Ken Dowden, 'Approaching women through myth: Vital tool or self-delusion?' in R. Hawley and B. Levick (eds), *Women in Antiquity: New Assessments* (London and New York: Routledge, 1995), p. 47.
14. Ken Dowden, 'Homer's sense of text', *Journal of Hellenic Studies* cxvi (1996), p. 51.
15. Richard Lattimore, trans., *The Odyssey of Homer* (New York: Harper Perennial, 1965, 1975), 12.70. Howard W. Clarke, *Homer's Readers: A Historical Introduction to the Iliad and the Odyssey* (Newark, DE: University of Delaware Press, 1981), p. 192.
16. Dowden, 'Homer's sense of text', p. 52.
17. Ibid. p. 60. Malcolm Willcock, 'Neoanalysis', in I. Morris and B. Powell (eds), *A New Companion to Homer*, p. 174.
18. Dowden, 'Homer's sense of text', p. 52. Laura M. Slatkin, *The Power of Thetis: Allusion and Interpretation in the* Iliad (Berkeley, CA: University of California Press, 1991), p. 4.
19. Edmunds, 'Myth in Homer', p. 420.
20. For the complex use of allusion in Homer, see especially Slatkin, *The Power of Thetis*.

21. See Wolfgang Kullmann, 'Oral poetry theory and neoanalysis in Homeric research', *Homerische Motive* (Stuttgart: Franz Steiner Verlag, 1992), pp. 141–2, 144, 146.
22. Foley, 'Oral tradition and its implications', pp. 167–8.
23. John M. Foley, *Immanent Art: From Structure to Meaning in Traditional Oral Epic* (Bloomington and Indianapolis, IN: Indiana University Press, 1991), pp. 6–7.
24. This is despite the fact that both writers adopt quite different theoretical stances (oral formulism and neoanalysis, respectively).
25. Edmunds, 'Myth in Homer', p. 420. Foley, *Immanent Art*, p. 7.
26. John M. Foley, *The Singer of Tales in Performance* (Bloomington and Indianapolis, IN: Indiana University Press, 1995), p. xii.
27. Parker, 'Myths of early Athens', pp. 188–9.
28. Vivian Sobchack, ' "Surge and splendor": a phenomenology of the Hollywood historical epic', in B. K. Grant (ed.), *Film Genre Reader II* (Austin, TX: University of Texas Press, 1995), p. 286. The cinematic epic and television epic have their own particular history beyond the scope of the present endeavour. See, for example: Derek Elley, *The Epic Film: Myth and History* (London: Routledge, 1984). Gary A. Smith, *Epic Films: Casts, Credits and Commentary on over 250 Historical Spectacle Movies* (Jefferson, NC: McFarland and Co., 1991). Constantine Santas, Jim Wilson, Maria Colavito and Djoymi Baker, *The Encyclopedia of Epic Films* (Lanham, MD: Rowman & Littlefield, 2014).
29. Pierre Sorlin, *The Film in History: Restaging the Past* (Oxford: Basil Blackwell, 1980), p. 20.
30. Ibid., pp. 20–1.
31. Sobchack, 'Surge and Splendor', p. 286. Wyke, *Projecting the Past*, p. 13.
32. Foley's metonymy within a generic field created by the word myth in this respect can be seen to resemble iconographic approaches to cinema genres. See, for example: Christine Gledhill, 'History of genre criticism', in P. Cook (ed.), *The Cinema Book* (London: BFI, 1996), p. 60. Edward Buscombe, 'The idea of genre in the American cinema', in B. K. Grant (ed.), *Film Genre Reader II* (Austin, TX: University of Texas Press, 1995).
33. As noted in Chapter 1, this iconography also draws from the *mise-en-scène* of the 'peplum' epic, whose popularity was only just beginning to wane. See, for example: Elley, *The Epic Film*, p. 21. Sobchack, 'Surge and splendor', p. 297.
34. Asa, 'Classic *Star Trek* and the death of God', p. 36. See, for example: Apollodorus, *The Library*, trans. James G. Frazer, Vol. 1 (Cambridge, MA: Harvard University Press, London: William Heinemann, 1921, 1967), 3.12.5.
35. We might consider this a post-modern combination of time periods. See Jean Baudrillard, 'Hysterisis of the millennium', *The Illusion of the End*, trans.

Chris Turner (Cambridge: Polity Press, 1994), p. 118. Jim Collins, *Uncommon Cultures: Popular Culture and Post-Modernism* (New York: Routledge, 1989), p. 132.
36. Collins, *Uncommon Cultures*, p. 61.
37. Homer, *Odyssey*, 12.70.
38. On lost world stories and Atlantis, see, for example: John Clute and Peter Nicholls, *The Encyclopedia of Science Fiction* (London: Orbit, 1993, 1999), p. 735.
39. Matthew Richardson, *The Halstead Treasury of Ancient Science Fiction* (Rushcutters Bay, NSW: Halstead Classics, 2001), p. 10.
40. Clute and Nicholls, *The Encyclopedia of Science Fiction*, p. 67.
41. Bremmer, *Interpretations of Greek Mythology*, p. 3.
42. Indeed, *The Epic of Gilgamesh* (third millennium BCE) seems to form the narrative basis of the episode itself, in its story of two strangers who are at first enemies and then friends, and whose battle with a monster results in the death of the hero's new friend.
43. The *Enterprise* computer and Data characterise the Tamarian stories as 'mythohistorical'. Later in the episode, Picard refers simply to their 'mythology'.
44. Claude Lévi-Strauss, *The Raw and the Cooked: Introduction to a Science of Mythology*, trans. John and Doreen Weightman (London: Jonathan Cape, 1969). Sheila Johnston, 'Film narrative and the structuralist controversy', in P. Cook (ed.), *The Cinema Book* (London: BFI, 1985), p. 233.
45. Edmunds, 'Myth in Homer', pp. 415–18, 420.
46. For a contrary reading, see: Paul A. Cantour, 'From Shakespeare to Wittgenstein: "Darmok" and cultural literacy', in J. T. Eberl and Kevin S. Decker (ed.), *Star Trek and Philosophy: The Wrath of Kant* (Chicago and La Salle, IL: Open Court, 2008), p. 17.
47. Mikhail Bakhtin, 'Discourse in the novel', in M. Holquist (ed.), *The Dialogic Imagination: Four Essays*, trans. Caryl Emerson and Michael Holquist (Austin, TX, and London: University of Texas Press, 1981), p. 315.
48. Ibid., p. 284.
49. Ibid., pp. 326, 332. On dialogic debates between characters in *Star Trek* about war and terrorism (but not mythic discourses), see also Roberta Pearson and Máire Messenger Davies, *Star Trek and American Television* (Berkeley, CA: University of California Press, 2014), pp. 176–84.
50. Ibid., p. 293. See also Julia Kristeva, *Desire in Language: A Semiotic Approach to Literature and Art*, trans. T. Gora, A. Jardine and L. S. Roudiez, ed. L. S. Roudiez (New York: Columbia University Press, 1980), p. 65.
51. Bakhtin, 'Discourse in the novel', p. 282.
52. Ibid., p. 403.
53. Ibid., p. 369.
54. Ibid., p. 370.

55. Ibid., p. 361. Robert Stam, *Subversive Pleasures: Bakhtin, Cultural Criticism, and Film* (Baltimore, MD and London: Johns Hopkins University Press, 1989), p. 50.
56. Jon Wagner and Jan Lundeen, *Deep Space and Sacred Time: Star Trek in the American Mythos* (Westport, CT: Praeger, 1998), pp. 11–12. See also Susan L. Schwartz, 'Enterprise engaged: mythic enactment and ritual performance', in R. S. Kraemer, W. Cassidy and S. Schwartz, *Religions of Star Trek* (Boulder, CO: Westview Press, 2001), pp. 141, 147–52.
57. Wagner and Lundeen, *Deep Space and Sacred Time*, p. 11.
58. Stam, *Subversive Pleasures*, p. 188.
59. Bremmer, *Interpretations of Greek Mythology*, p. 3.
60. Lillian Eileen Doherty, *Siren Songs: Gender, Audiences, and Narrators in the Odyssey* (Ann Arbor, MI: University of Michigan Press, 1998), pp. 163, 169, n. 21, 186, 189.
61. Bakhtin, 'Discourse in the novel', p. 420.
62. Collins, *Uncommon Cultures*, pp. 59, 61.
63. Bakhtin, 'Discourse in the novel', pp. 326, 315. Stam, *Subversive Pleasures*, p. 60.
64. Bakhtin, 'Discourse in the novel', p. 349.
65. See Horace Newcomb and Paul M. Hirsch, 'Television as cultural forum', in H. Newcomb (ed.), *Television: The Critical View* (Oxford: Oxford University Press, 1987). See also Stam, *Subversive Pleasures*, p. 257, n. 3. John Fiske, *Television Culture* (London and New York: Methuen, 1987), pp. 89–90.
66. A similar interplay is evident in the use of (diegetic) Klingon myths, in *TNG* and *Voyager* and particularly in *DS9*.
67. Edmunds, 'Myth in Homer', pp. 415–18, 420.
68. Bakhtin, 'Discourse in the novel', p. 360.
69. Denny Atkin, 'The science of *Star Trek*', *Omni*, 17/8, Fall (1995), p. 51.
70. 'Emissary, Parts I and II' (1993). Chroniton weapons reappear in the series in 'The Reckoning' (1998) and 'Tears of the Prophets' (1998).
71. *Star Trek* continually mobilises complex temporal dynamics, the effects of which will be explored in subsequent chapters.
72. Terry J. Erdmann with Paula M. Block, *Star Trek: Deep Space Nine Companion* (New York: Pocket Books, 2000), p. 593. On semi-divine heroes, see: Lord Raglan, 'The hero of tradition', in A. Dundes (ed.), *The Study of Folklore* (Englewood Cliffs, NJ: Prentice-Hall, 1965), p. 151.
73. This had been intended as an apotheosis, but was made deliberately ambiguous so that Sisko could promise to return to his pregnant wife. Erdmann and Block, *Star Trek: Deep Space Nine Companion*, pp. 709–10.
74. Clute and Nicholls, *The Encyclopedia of Science Fiction*, p. 849.
75. Parker, 'Myths of early Athens', pp. 188–9.
76. Ibid.

77. Umberto Eco, *Faith in Fakes*, trans. William Weaver (London: Secker and Warburg, 1986), p. 200.
78. Ibid., p. 202.
79. Ibid., p. 201.
80. Ibid., pp. 209-10.
81. Ibid. Despite this, Daniel Leonard Bernardi argues that 'the "ricketiness" and subsequent cult status of [...] the Trek mega-text more generally seems not unlike Eco's *Casablanca*'. Daniel Leonard Bernardi, *Star Trek and History: Race-Ing Toward a White Future* (New Brunswick, NJ: Rutgers University Press, 1998), p. 191, n. 7.
82. Jim Collins, 'Batman: the movie, the narrative, the hyperconscious', in R. E. Pearson and W. Uricchio (eds), *The Many Lives of the Batman: Critical Approaches to a Superhero and His Media* (New York: Routledge and London: BFI, 1991), p. 170.
83. Ibid., pp. 170-1, emphasis in original. This is similar to Dowden's argument regarding Greek mythology as an intertext. Dowden, *The Uses of Greek Mythology*, p. 8.
84. Collins, 'Batman', pp. 170-1.
85. Tony Bennett, and Janet Woollacott, *Bond and Beyond: The Political Career of a Popular Hero* (New York: Methuen, 1987), pp. 42-3, 53.
86. Ibid.
87. Collins, 'Batman', p. 167.
88. Ibid.
89. Ibid., pp. 179-80.
90. Collins, *Uncommon Cultures*, p. 98. Similarly, Laurence Coupe argues that with post-modern texts, 'we must not speak of "myth"' in the singular but rather "myths"'. Laurence Coupe, *Myth* (London and New York: Routledge, 1997), p. 84.
91. Will Wright, *Six-Guns and Society* (Berkeley, CA: University of California Press, 1975), p. 187. Collins, *Uncommon Cultures*, p. 97. Jim Collins, *Architectures of Excess: Cultural Life in the Information Age* (New York: Routledge, 1995), pp. 130-1.
92. For example, he uses myth to mean a false belief. Collins, *Uncommon Cultures*, pp. 18, 127, 95.
93. Collins, 'Batman', pp. 179-80.
94. Dowden, *The Uses of Greek Mythology*, p. 8.
95. Ibid.
96. Bremmer, *Interpretations of Greek Mythology*, p. 3.
97. Foley, *Immanent Art*, pp. 6-7. Foley, 'Oral tradition and its implications', pp. 167-8.
98. Collins, *Architectures of Excess*, pp. 155-6.

99. On ratings, see: Allan Asherman, *The Star Trek Compendium* (New York: Pocket Books, 1989, 1993), p. 68.
100. Other episodes of *TOS* also draw upon the ancient Greco-Roman world as a means of creating narrative conflict. In 'Bread and Circuses' (1968), the crew of the *Enterprise* discover a civilisation based on the Roman Empire, while 'Plato's Stepchildren' (1968) examines an alien race that has attempted to recreate Plato's *Republic*. For a discussion, see George Kovacs, 'Moral and mortal in Star Trek: The Original Series', in B. M. Rogers and B. E. Stevens, *Classical Traditions in Science Fiction* (New York: Oxford University Press, 2015).
101. Asherman, *The Star Trek Compendium*, p. 106.
102. *TOS*, 'Catspaw' (1967).
103. *TOS*, 'Wolf in the Fold' (1967).
104. *TOS*, 'A Piece of the Action' (1968).
105. *TOS*, 'Spectre of the Gun' (1968).
106. *TOS*, 'The Conscience of the King' (1966) and 'Elaan of Troyius'.
107. *TOS*, 'The Cloudminders' (1969).
108. *TOS*, 'City on the Edge of Forever' (1967).
109. *TOS*, 'Assignment: Earth' (1968) and 'Tomorrow is Yesterday' (1967).
110. *TOS*, 'Patterns of Force' (1968).
111. *TOS*, 'The Paradise Syndrome' (1968).
112. Quoted in William Blake Tyrell, '*Star Trek* as myth and television as mythmaker', *Journal of Popular Culture* 10/4 (1977), pp. 711–19. Reprinted in M. W. Kapell (ed.), *Star Trek as Myth: Essays on Symbol and Archetype at the Final Frontier* (Jefferson, NC: McFarland, 2010), p. 19.
113. Indeed, Collins argues that contemporary texts have 'polylogic rather than dialogic relationships with multiple "already saids"'. Collins, *Uncommon Cultures*, p. 134. However, Bakhtin's dialogism can itself incorporate many voices from the heteroglossia, so we can interpret late twentieth-century texts as being *particularly* dialogic.
114. Greek mythology is referenced in the Season 4 *Enterprise* episode 'Daedalus' (2005), linking the inventor of the transporter with the Greek mythic inventor Daedalus. Apollodorus, *The Library*, 1.13.
115. *DS9*, 'The Way of the Warrior' (1995).
116. *TNG*, 'Qpid' (1991).
117. *Voyager*, 'Heroes and Demons' (1996).
118. *DS9*, 'Bar Association' (1996), 'Accession' (1996).
119. *Voyager*, 'The Cloud' (1995).
120. *Voyager*, 'Bliss' (1998).
121. Porthos, Captain Archer's dog on *Enterprise*, is named after one of the musketeers from the novel by Alexandre Dumas, as revealed in 'A Night in Sick Bay' (2002).

122. *TNG*, 'Lonely Among Us' (1987), 'Elementary, Dear Data' (1988).
123. Ilsa J. Bick, 'Boys in space: *Star Trek*, latency, and the neverending story', in T. Harrison, S. Projansky, K. A. Ono and E. R. Helford (eds), *Enterprise Zones: Critical Positions on Star Trek* (Boulder, CO: Westview Press, 1996), p. 206. On *Star Trek*'s many literary references, see also Larry Kreitzer, 'The cultural veneer of *Star Trek*', *Journal of Popular Culture*, 30/2, Fall (1996), pp. 1–28.
124. Bick, 'Boys in space', pp. 206–207. As noted in Chapter 1, comic books have used similar strategies. Richard Reynolds, *Super Heroes – A Modern Mythology* (London: B.T. Batsford, 1992), p. 53.
125. Bick, 'Boys in space', p. 207.
126. *The Animated Series* revisited the Tribbles in 'More Tribbles, More Troubles' (1973), one of the earliest examples of *Star Trek* referencing its own earlier episodes. 'More Tribbles, More Troubles' does not, however, revisit its past in the literal sense embodied in 'Trials and Tribble-ations'.
127. Cult aspects of *Star Trek*'s fan following are explored in Chapter 4.
128. Kim Campbell, 'Star Trek crew still "Troubled with Tribbles," 30 years later', *The Christian Science Monitor*, 7 November 1996. Available at http://www.csmonitor.com/1996/1107/110796.feat.whathapp.1.html (accessed 21 June 2017).
129. Collins, 'Batman', p. 180.
130. 'Klingon Discrepancy Theories: Where Did the Ridges Go?' StarTrek.com, 22 July 2003. Available at http://startrek.com/startrek/view/series/ENT/feature/1614.html (accessed 26 January 2008, no longer online 22 September 2016).
131. Ina Rae Hark, *Star Trek* (London: BFI & New York: Palgrave Macmillan, 2008), p. 143.
132. For technical and background information, see 'Trials and Tribble-ations: Uniting Two Legends' (2003) and 'Trials and Tribble-ations: An Historic Endeavor' (2003), *DS9*, Season 5, disc 7, Special Features, Paramount 2004.
133. As Richard Reynolds notes, the longer a fictional character or world lasts, 'the more continuity [to which] there is to cohere'. Reynolds, *Super Heroes*, p. 38.
134. Bick, 'Boys in space', pp. 204, 207.
135. Bakhtin, 'Discourse in the novel', p. 421.
136. Collins, *Architectures of Excess*, p. 135.
137. Ibid., p. 137.
138. ' "Saga" is an Icelandic term and was originally applied to supposedly true histories of families/clans or of kins.' Dowden, *The Uses of Greek Mythology*, p. 6. Worf's use of the term suggests that the continuing characters of the *Star Trek* franchise similarly function as a futuristic, heroic family.

139. In this sense, Worf's nostalgia cannot be conceptualised in terms of Collins' 'new sincerity', works that try to recapture older, simpler story models. Collins, *Architectures of Excess*, pp. 125–56.
140. *Voyager* 4.12, containing 'Living Witness' (1998) and 'Demon' (1998).
141. Stephen Edward Poe, *A Vision of the Future: Star Trek Voyager* (New York: Pocket Books, 1998), pp. 346, 351–2.
142. Hark, *Star Trek*, p. 136.
143. Caillan, 'UPN "Enterprise" Promos Feature New Footage', *TrekToday*, 2 August 2010. Available at www.trektoday.com/news/020801_01.shtml (accessed 26 January 2008).
144. Homer, *Odyssey*, 9–12. Although 'Favorite Son' is told in the present tense, Harry's recitation of the Sirens story at the end of the episode seems to occur in the context of telling his adventure to fellow crew members Tom Paris and Neelix. Many other *Voyager* episodes use the flashback method of storytelling.
145. See also Spagna, who compares *Voyager* with the *Odyssey* but argues for a closer alignment with Virgil's *Aeneid*. Amy Spagna, '*Voyager* and ancient epic', *Now Voyager: The Official Newsletter of the Kate Mulgrew Appreciation Society*, 4/1 (1997), pp. 35–7. Available at www.littlereview.com/kmas/nowvoy19.txt (accessed 27 November 2015).
146. Poe, *A Vision of the Future*, p. 352.
147. Ibid.
148. Dowden, *The Uses of Greek Mythology*, p. 8.
149. Bakhtin argues, 'The historical life of classic works is in fact the uninterrupted process of their social and ideological re-accentuation'. Bakhtin, 'Discourse in the novel', p. 421.
150. Homer, *Odyssey*, 12.39–54, 12.165–200. In one of many inversions, Odysseus binds himself to protect himself against the Sirens, whereas the victims of the Taresians are bound by them during the marriage ceremony. Binding becomes a method of capture rather than evasion, and Harry only just avoids being bound himself.
151. Jennifer Neils, 'Les femmes fatales: Skylla and the Sirens in Greek art', in B. Cohen (ed.), *The Distaff Side: Representing the Female in Homer's Odyssey* (New York: Oxford University Press, 1995), p. 175.
152. Homer, *Odyssey*, 12.184–191. Pietro Pucci, 'The songs of the Sirens', in S. L. Schein (ed.), *Reading the Odyssey: Selected Interpretive Essays* (Princeton, NJ: Princeton University Press, 1996), p. 196.
153. In this sense, the heroic and narrative role played by Odysseus is here split between Harry and Captain Janeway, who leads the remaining crew.
154. Homer, *Odyssey*, 12.69–70.
155. Charles Segal, '*Kleos* and its ironies in the Odyssey', in S. L. Schein (ed.), *Reading the Odyssey: Selected Interpretive Essays*, p. 215.

156. For example, Odysseus chooses to be remembered as a hero among mortals, rather than staying with Kalypso for a good, but ultimately unheroic, life. Homer, *Odyssey*, 5.219-24. Seth L. Schein, 'Female representations and interpreting the Odyssey', in B. Cohen (ed.), *The Distaff Side: Representing the Female in Homer's Odyssey*, p. 20.
157. Segal, '*Kleos* and its ironies in the Odyssey', p. 214.
158. Homer, *Odyssey*, 12.166-170. Segal, '*Kleos* and its ironies in the Odyssey', p. 214.
159. Homer, *Odyssey*, 12.40-46.
160. Ibid., 12.45-6, 12.188.
161. After Harry is already marooned on Taresia, *Voyager* is warned by hostile aliens that 'no one who "comes home" to Taresia every leaves again'. *Voyager* is unable to communicate this warning to Harry.
162. Karin Blair, 'Sex and *Star Trek*', *Science-Fiction Studies*, 10/31 (1983), p. 292.
163. See, for example: A. J. Graham, 'The Odyssey, history, and women', in B. Cohen (ed.), *The Distaff Side: Representing the Female in Homer's Odyssey*, p. 13.
164. Lillian Eileen Doherty, 'Sirens, muses and female narrators in the *Odyssey*', in B. Cohen (ed.), *The Distaff Side: Representing the Female in Homer's Odyssey*, p. 84. Schein, 'Female representations and interpreting the Odyssey', p. 21.
165. In Greek vase painting there is a stronger connection between the Sirens and sexuality. John Pollard, 'The Boston Siren Aryballos', *American Journal of Archaeology*, 53 (1949), pp. 357-9.
166. See, for example: Blair, 'Sex and *Star Trek*', pp. 292-7. Anne Cranny-Francis, 'Sexuality and sex-role stereotyping in *Star Trek*', *Science Fiction Studies*, 12/ 37 (1985), pp. 274-84.
167. *TNG*, 'When the Bough Breaks' (1988), in which a sterile alien race steals children from the *Enterprise*. Picard warns them 'that human parents are quite willing to die for their children'. This is mirrored in 'Favorite Son', when a Taresian woman tells Harry that 'any father should be willing to sacrifice himself for the sake of his children'. The other *TNG* episode referred to by the sleeve is 'Up the Long Ladder' (1989), in which a society that reproduces by cloning attempts to steal new DNA from *Enterprise* crew members.
168. While the videotape sleeve for 'Favorite Son' links the episode with its *Star Trek* past, other episodes, such as *Voyager*'s 'Heroes and Demons' (1995), use the sleeve to provide information on the appropriated text. In this episode, the medieval epic *Beowulf* forms the broad basis for the story, and the sleeve provides historical information on that text.
169. Dowden, *The Uses of Greek Mythology*, p. 8. Collins, 'Batman', pp. 167, 170-1, 179-80.
170. Irad Malkin, *The Returns of Odysseus: Colonization and Ethnicity* (Berkeley, CA: University of California Press, 1998), p. 3.

171. Diana Buitron-Oliver and Beth Cohen, 'Between Skylla and Penelope: female characters of the Odyssey in Archaic and Classical Greek art', in B. Cohen (ed.), *The Distaff Side: Representing the Female in Homer's Odyssey*, pp. 31–3.

Chapter 3: *Star Trek* Title Sequences and Cosmology as Myth

1. Carl Sagan, *Cosmos* (New York: Ballantine Books, 1980), p. 159.
2. Karl S. Guthke, *The Last Frontier: Imagining Other Worlds, from the Copernican Revolution to Modern Science Fiction*, trans. Helen Atkins (Ithaca, NY, and London: Cornell University Press, 1990), p. 32.
3. Ibid., p. 33.
4. Astronomy, meaning the arrangement of the stars, is similarly closely related, and even up until the seventeenth century was not always clearly distinguished from astrology, the study of the influence of the heavenly bodies on human fate. This said, astronomy and astrology tend not to be used to categorise ancient myths about the universe.
5. Hesiod, 'Theogony', *The Homeric Hymns and Homerica*, trans. Hugh G. Evelyn-White (Cambridge, MA: Harvard University Press & London: William Heinemann Ltd, 1914), ll. 115–39.
6. Lauri Honko, 'The problem of defining myth', in A. Dundes (ed.), *Sacred Narrative: Readings in the Theory of Myth* (Berkeley, CA: University of California Press, 1984), p. 47.
7. On this communal notion of myth, see, for example: Gregory Nagy, *Greek Mythology and Poetics* (Ithaca, NY and London: Cornell University Press, 1990), p. 8.
8. Alexander Heidel, *The Babylonian Genesis: The Story of Creation*, 2nd edn (Chicago, IL and London: University of Chicago Press, 1951), pp. 72–3.
9. Sagan, *Cosmos*, pp. xv–xvi.
10. Jacob A. Arlow, 'Scientific cosmogony, mythology, and immortality', *Psychoanalytic Quarterly*, 51 (1982), p. 177.
11. Ibid., p. 181.
12. Sagan, *Cosmos*, p. 12.
13. Stephen Hawking, 'The Origin of the Universe' (2005). Available at www.hawking.org.uk/the-origin-of-the-universe.html (accessed 11 February 2016). Douglas Heaven, 'What came before the Big Bang? And other questions physics can't answer ... yet', *New Scientist*, 227/3037 (2015), pp. 30–1.
14. Arlow, 'Scientific cosmogony', pp. 180, 187.
15. Earl R. MacCormac argues that science becomes myth when it is believed as fact instead of hypothesis, and when proof is accepted as absolute rather than

partial and subject to revision. Earl R. MacCormac, *Metaphor and Myth in Science and Religion* (Durham, NC: Duke University Press, 1976). See also Stanley J. Grenz, 'Why do theologians need to be scientists?', *Zygon*, 35/2, June 2000, p. 351, emphasis in the original.
16. William R. Stoeger, 'Astronomy's integrating impact on culture: a Ladrierean hypothesis', *Leonardo*, 29/2 (1996), p. 153.
17. Ibid.
18. Ibid.
19. Charles R. Garoian and John D. Mathews, 'A common impulse in art and science', *Leonardo*, 29/3 (1996), p. 194.
20. Ibid., p. 195.
21. Guy J. Consolmagno, 'Astronomy, science fiction and popular culture: 1277 to 2001 (and beyond)', *Leonardo*, 29/2 (1996), p. 127.
22. Kathleen Freeman, *The Pre-Socratic Philosophers* (Oxford: Basil Blackwell, 1953), p. 41. Stephen L. Harris and Gloria Platzner, *Classical Mythology: Images and Insights*, 3rd edn (Mountain View, CA: Mayfield Publishing, 2001), p. 35.
23. See, for example: 'Scipio's Dream' in Cicero's *On The Republic* (51 BCE), or *True History* by Lucian of Somosata (160 ce). Consolmagno, 'Astronomy, science fiction and popular culture', pp. 127–8. Edward W. Ploman, *Space, Earth and Communication* (Westport, CT: Quorum Books, 1984), p. 1.
24. Robert S. Westman, 'Proof, poetics and patronage: Copernicus's preface to *De revolutionibus*', in D. C. Lindberg and R. S. Westman (eds), *Reappraisals of the Scientific Revolution* (Cambridge and New York: Cambridge University Press, 1990), p. 170. Brian Easlea, *Witch Hunting, Magic and the New Philosophy: An Introduction to Debates of the Scientific Revolution 1450–1750* (Brighton: Harvester Press & Atlantic Highlands, NJ: Humanities Press, 1980), pp. 58–68.
25. Westman, 'Proof, poetics and patronage', p. 170, emphasis in original.
26. Johannes Kepler, *Kepler's Dream*, trans. Patricia Frueh Kirkwood (Berkeley and Los Angeles, CA: University of California Press, 1965), pp. 102–58. See also John Lear, 'Introduction and interpretation', in Johannes Kepler, *Kepler's Dream*, trans. P. F. Kirkwood (Berkeley and Los Angeles, CA: University of California Press, 1965), p. 3.
27. Kepler, *Kepler's Dream*, p. 114.
28. Ibid., p. 114, n. 96.
29. Ibid., pp. 165–6. See also Guthke, *The Last Frontier*, p. 99.
30. Kepler, *Kepler's Dream*, pp. 97–102.
31. Lear, 'Introduction and interpretation', pp. 17–18, 21–38. For more on beliefs of witchcraft in the sixteenth and seventeenth centuries, see Easlea, *Witch Hunting*, pp. 1–44.

32. I. Bernard Cohen, *Album of Science: From Leonardo to Lavoisier 1450-1800* (New York: Scribner, 1980), p. xii. Easlea, *Witch Hunting*.
33. Cohen, *Album of Science*, p. 25.
34. For further examples of science/science fiction works of the era, see: Peter Remnant and Jonathan Bennett, 'Notes', in G. W. Leibniz, *New Essays on Human Understanding*, trans. and eds Peter Remnant and Jonathan Bennett (Cambridge: Cambridge University Press, 1996), p. lxxix. Guthke, *The Last Frontier*. Angela Ndalianis, *Neo-Baroque Aesthetics and Contemporary Entertainment* (Cambridge, MA: The MIT Press, 2004), pp. 235, 237.
35. Bruno was burnt at the stake for such views. Hazel Muir, 'Does the universe go on forever?' *New Scientist*, 180/2416, October 11 (2003), p. 7.
36. Sagan, *Cosmos*, p. 119.
37. Guthke, *The Last Frontier*, p. 44. Sagan, *Cosmos*, p. 121.
38. Cohen, *Album of Science*, p. 3.
39. Ibid., p. 274.
40. Ibid., p. 29.
41. Ibid.
42. Miles Harvey, *The Island of Lost Maps: A True Story of Cartographic Crime* (New York: Random House, 2000), pp. 17-43.
43. William B. Ashworth, Jr., 'Allegorical astronomy', *The Sciences*, 25/5 (1985), p. 34.
44. Ibid.
45. Ibid.
46. Ibid.
47. Ibid., p. 36. See also Erwin Panofsky, 'More on Galileo and the arts', *Isis*, 47/148, June 1956, p. 185. Mario Biagioli, 'Galileo the emblem maker', *Isis*, 81 (1990), p. 230.
48. Cohen, *Album of Science*, p. 45. Kitty Ferguson, *Tycho and Kepler: The Strange Partnership that Revolutionised Astronomy* (London: Review, 2002), p. 142.
49. Cohen, *Album of Science*, p. 45.
50. Horst Bredekamp, 'Gazing hands and blind spots: Galileo as draftsman', *Science in Context*, 13/3-4 (2000), pp. 423-4, 445. Erwin Panofsky, 'Galileo as a critic of the arts', *Isis*, 47/148, March (1956), pp. 3-4. Cohen, *Album of Science*, p. 12.
51. See, for example: Remnant and Bennett, 'Notes', p. lxxix.
52. As Guthke writes, science fiction has a 'role of interpreting for the nonscientist the implications of the present state of scientific knowledge'. Guthke, *The Last Frontier*, p. 23.
53. Rima D. Apple and Michael W. Apple, 'Screening science', *Isis*, 84 (1993), pp. 751-2.
54. Constance Penley, *NASA/TREK: Popular Science and Sex in America* (London: Verso, 1997), pp. 9-10.

55. David Pringle, 'What is this thing called space opera?' in Gary Westfahl (ed.), *Space and Beyond: The Frontier Theme in Science Fiction* (Westport, CT: Greenwood Press, 2000), p. 41. See also Jack Williamson, 'On the final frontier', in G. Westfahl (ed.), *Space and Beyond: The Frontier Theme in Science Fiction*, p. 51.
56. Penley, *NASA/TREK*.
57. Gene Roddenberry, 'A Tribute to Gene Roddenberry', *Star Trek: The Next Generation*, DVD, Season 5, Disc 7, 1988.
58. Quoted in Penley, *NASA/TREK*, p. 19. TOS' *Enterprise* model had been housed at the museum since 1974. Rick Worland, 'From the new frontier to the final frontier: *Star Trek* from Kennedy to Gorbachev', *Film & History*, 24/1–2 (1994), p. 27.
59. Stephen Hawking, 'Foreword', in L. M. Krauss, *The Physics of Star Trek* (London: Flamingo, 1995), p. xi.
60. The holodeck is a holographic role-playing domain on the *Enterprise*.
61. Consolmagno, 'Astronomy, science fiction and popular culture', p. 130.
62. James R. Hansen, *Spaceflight Revolution: NASA Langley Research Center from Sputnik to Apollo* (Washington, DC: The NASA History Series, National Aeronautics and Space Administration, 1995). Available at http://history.nasa.gov/SP-4308/sp4308.htm (accessed 26 August 2006). NASA, 'Vanguard rocket explodes on launch pad', Image VAN-9, 6 December 1957. Available at http://nasaimages.lunaimaging.com/luna/servlet/detail/nasaNAS~5~5~24178~127619:Vanguard-rocket-explodes-on-launch- (accessed 23 September 2016).
63. Ploman, *Space, Earth and Communication*, pp. 4–5. Jet Propulsion Laboratory, 'Mission to Earth – Explorer 1' (n.d.). Available at http://www.jpl.nasa.gov/missions/explorer-1/ (accessed 22 September 2016).
64. John F. Kennedy, 'Special Message to the Congress on Urgent National Needs', John F. Kennedy Library and Museum, 25 May 1961. Available at www.jfklibrary.org/Research/Research-Aids/JFK-Speeches/United-States-Congress-Special-Message_19610525.aspx (accessed 22 September 2016).
65. John F. Kennedy, 'Rice University', 12 September 1962. Available at www.jfklibrary.org/Asset-Viewer/MkATdOcdU06X5uNHbmqm1Q.aspx (accessed 22 September 2016). Kennedy had also used frontier imagery in his nomination speech of 15 July 1960. Peter Müller, 'Star Trek: The American Dream Continued? The Crisis of the American Dream in the 1960s and its Reflection in a Contemporary TV Series' (1994). Available at www.pmueller.de/downloads. html (accessed 22 September 2016). John F. Kennedy, 'Address of Senator John F. Kennedy Accepting the Democratic Party Nomination for the Presidency of the United States', John F. Kennedy Library and Museum, 15 July 1960. Available at https://www.jfklibrary.org/Research/Research-Aids/JFK-Speeches/Democratic-Party-Nomination_19600715.aspx (accessed 22 September 2016).

66. Cleveland Amory, 'Review: Star Trek', *TV Guide*, 25 November 1967, p. 1. On *Star Trek*'s Cold War politics, see Mark P. Lagon, ' "We Owe It to Them to Interfere": *Star Trek* and US statecraft in the 1960s and the 1990s', *Extrapolation*, 34/3 (1993), p. 259. Reid-Jeffery, 'Star Trek: the last frontier in modern American myth', pp. 35, 41. Worland, 'Captain Kirk Cold Warrior', pp. 112, 114–15.
67. Müller, 'Star Trek: The American Dream Continued?' 3.2.1.
68. Ivan D. Ertel and Roland W. Newkirk, with Courtney G. Brooks, *The Apollo Spacecraft: A Chronology*, NASA SP-4009, Volume IV (Washington, DC: The NASA Historical Series, Scientific and Technical Information Office, National Aeronautics and Space Administration, 1978), Part 1 E. Available at www.hq.nasa.gov/office/pao/History/SP-4009/cover.htm (accessed 6 October 2003).
69. *TV Guide*, 'Star Trek', pp. A72–A73.
70. *The Time Tunnel* (1966–7) also debuted that year, another cross-generational sci-fi programme. For further discussion, see Chapter One. *The Jetsons* (1962–3) and *My Favorite Martian* (1963–6) were science fiction sit-coms with cross-generational appeal. Similarly, *Lost in Space* (1965–8) drew on comedy but could be regarded as the first specifically spacefaring programme with cross-generational pitch.
71. Amory, 'Review: Star Trek', p. 1.
72. Ibid.
73. Isaac Asimov, 'What are a few galaxies among friends?' *TV Guide*, 26 November 1966, p. 9, emphasis in original.
74. Leslie Raddatz, 'Product of two worlds: Leonard Nimoy, as the hybrid Mr. Spock, has made it big in outer space', *TV Guide*, 4 March 1967', p. 25. Leslie Raddatz, ' "Star Trek" wins the Ricky Schwartz', *TV Guide*, 18 November 1967, p. 28.
75. Ibid. On the JPL, see: Edward C. Ezell and Linda N. Ezell, *On Mars: Exploration of the Red Planet, 1958–1978* (Washington, DC: National Aeronautics and Space Administration, The NASA History Series, SP-4212, Scientific and Technical Information Branch, 1984). Available at www.history.nasa.gov/SP-4212/on-mars.html (accessed 8 December 2004).
76. Quoted in Raddatz, ' "Star Trek" wins the Ricky Schwartz', p. 28.
77. Isaac Asimov, 'Mr. Spock is dreamy', *TV Guide*, 29 April 1967, p. 11.
78. Kennedy, 'Special Message to the Congress on Urgent National Needs'.
79. Kennedy, 'Rice University'. In his address, Kennedy also compares the old Western frontier and the new frontier of space. Similarly, *Star Trek* was conceptualised by creator Gene Roddenberry as a '*Wagon Train* to the stars'. Roddenberry, quoted in William Blake Tyrell, '*Star Trek* as myth and television as mythmaker', *Journal of Popular Culture* 10/4 (1977), pp. 711–19. Reprinted in M. W. Kapell (ed.), *Star Trek as Myth: Essays on Symbol and Archetype at the Final Frontier* (Jefferson,

NC: McFarland, 2010), p. 19. The early US space missions have frequently been interpreted in terms of an extended Western frontier. See, for example: Wilbur R. Jacobs, *The Historical World of Frederick Jackson Turner: with Selections from his Correspondence* (New Haven, CT and London: Yale University Press, 1968), p. 163. Ralph Brauer with Donna Brauer, *The Horse, The Gun and the Piece of Property: Changing Images of the TV Western* (Bowling Green, OH: Bowling Green University Popular Press, 1975), p. 103. Lynn Spigel, 'From domestic space to outer space: the 1960s fantastic family sit-com', in Constance Penley et al (eds), *Close Encounters: Film, Feminism and Science Fiction* (Minneapolis, MN: University of Minnesota Press, 1991). Similarly, as noted in the book's Introduction, scholars have frequently linked *Star Trek* with the American West. For a discussion of earlier drafts of Kirk's voice-over, see Lincoln Geraghty, 'Eight days that changed American television: Kirk's opening narration', in L. Geraghty (ed.), *The Influence of Star Trek on Television, Film and Culture* (Jefferson, NC: McFarland, 2008), p. 13.
80. Barthes, *Image Music Text*, pp. 38–40. See also Ellen Seiter, 'Semiotics, structuralism, and television', in R. C. Allen (ed.), *Channels of Discourse Reassembled: Television and Contemporary Criticism*, 2nd edn (London: Routledge, 1993), p. 44.
81. Seiter, 'Semiotics, structuralism, and television', p. 56. See also John Ellis, *Visible Fictions: Cinema: Television: Video* (London: Routledge, 1982, 1992), p. 129.
82. Quoted in Pamela Haskin, 'Saul, can you make me a title?' *Film Quarterly*, 50/1, Fall (1996), pp. 12–13. See also Pat Kirkham, 'The jeweller's eye', *Sight and Sound*, 7/4 (1997), p. 18.
83. As Hartley argues, 'these boundary sequences are structured not to take us *through*, but to take us *in*'. John Hartley, 'Out of bounds: the myth of marginality', in Len Masterman (ed.), *Television Mythologies: Stars, Shows and Signs* (London and New York: Comedia Publishing Group and MK Media Press, 1984), p. 122. See also Jim Supanick, 'Saul Bass', *Film Comment*, 33/2, March–April 1997, pp. 72–7. John Fiske and John Hartley, *Reading Television* (London: Methuen, 1978), pp. 165–8. Stacey Abbott, ' "I want to do bad things with you": The television horror title sequence', in L. Geraghty (ed.), *Popular Media Cultures: Fans, Audiences and Paratexts* (New York: Palgrave Macmillan, 2015), pp. 112–13.
84. See Abbott, 'I want to do bad things with you', p. 112.
85. Cathy Schwichtenberg, '*The Love Boat*: the packaging and selling of love, heterosexual romance, and family', in H. Newcomb (ed.), *Television: The Critical View*, 4th edn (New York: Oxford University Press, 1987), p. 130.
86. Ellis, *Visible Fictions*, pp. 119–20. See also Hartley, 'Out of Bounds', p. 122. For a discussion of these issues in relation to film, see Supanick, 'Saul Bass'.
87. Rick Altman, 'Television Sound', in Newcomb, H. (ed.), *Television: The Critical View*, p. 574. Ellis, *Visible Fictions*, p. 130.

88. Quoted in Abbott, 'I want to do bad things with you', p. 111.
89. Simon Frith, *Music for Pleasure: Essays in the Sociology of Pop* (Cambridge: Polity Press, 1988), p. 134.
90. Jeff Bond, *The Music of Star Trek* (Los Angeles, CA: Lone Eagle, 1999), p. 13.
91. Ibid., pp. 13-14. Jessica L. Getman, 'A series on the edge: social tensions in *Star Trek*'s title cue', *Journal of the Society for American Music*, 9/3, August 2015, p. 301.
92. Bond, *The Music of Star Trek*, p. 13.
93. Quoted in ibid., p. 64.
94. Quoted in ibid., p. 66.
95. Ibid.
96. Ibid., p. 14.
97. Neil Lerner, 'Hearing the boldly goings', in K. J. Donnelly and P. Hayward (eds), *Music in Science Fiction Television: Tuned to the Future* (Hoboken, NJ: Taylor and Francis, 2012), p. 133.
98. Getman, 'A series on the edge', p. 306.
99. In Season 1, the written credits featured the series title, along with 'William Shatner' and 'Leonard Nimoy as Mr. Spock'. For Season 2, 'De Forest Kelley as Dr. McCoy' was added. The only other visual changes were the removal of a shift in the camera's direction through the stars from Season 1. In Season 3, the final season, the lettering changed from yellow to blue and Gene Roddenberry as creator was noted alongside the title.
100. The sight of Earth photographed from space facilitated this conceptual shift. In 1948, astronomer Fred Hoyle argued 'once a photograph of earth, taken from outside is available – once the sheer isolation of earth becomes plain, a new idea as powerful as any in history will be let loose'. Quoted in Ploman, *Space, Earth and Communication*, p. 7. Guthke argues that the Apollo 8 pictures of Earth from space marked a shift in 'human consciousness', by allowing millions of TV viewers to see 'with their own eyes images that confirmed […] that Earth was merely one of the planets'. Guthke, *The Last Frontier*, pp. 4–5. NASA, 'Apollo 8 Earthrise', 25 June 2013. Available at www.nasa.gov/multimedia/imagegallery/image_feature_1249.html (accessed 22 September 2016). NASA, 'Earth from Apollo 8', Image AS8-16-2606, 12 January 1968. Available at: www.history.nasa.gov/ap08fj/photos/16-a/hr/as08-16-2606hr.jpg (accessed 22 September 2016).
101. 'Turnabout Intruder', *Star Trek*, Herb Wallerstein, broadcast 3 June 1969.
102. Spigel, 'From domestic space to outer space', p. 212.
103. Quoted in ibid., p. 229. See also S. N. Johnson-Roehr, 'These are mine', 14 August 2012. Available at http://astronomy.snjr.net/blog/?p=677 (accessed 28 June 2017).
104. Ploman, *Space, Earth and Communication*, p. 14.

105. Lerner, 'Hearing the boldly goings', pp. 134–5.
106. It was in 1986 that plans for *The Next Generation* began in earnest. Larry Nemecek, *The Star Trek The Next Generation Companion* (New York: Pocket Books, 1995), p. 2.
107. I have chosen not to examine the title sequences of the various *Star Trek* feature films in this chapter for reasons of scope. The posters of the feature films are examined in the book's conclusion.
108. Penley, *NASA/TREK*, pp. 32–3.
109. Ibid., p. 41.
110. This relationship calls to mind 'the old analogy of the *palimpsest*: on the same parchment, one text can become superimposed upon another, which it does not quite conceal but allows to show through'. Gérard Genette, *Palimpsests: Literature in the Second Degree*, trans. Channa Newman and Claude Doubinsky (Lincoln, NE, and London: University of Nebraska Press, 1997), pp. 398–9. However, with *TNG* we have a case of direct *quotation* of voice-over, music and format. See ibid., p. 2.
111. Nemecek, *The Star Trek The Next Generation Companion*, p. 5.
112. Clyde Wilcox, 'To boldly return where others have gone before: cultural change and the old and new *Star Treks*', *Extrapolation*, 33/1 (1992), p. 90.
113. See, for example: Wilcox, 'To boldly return where others have gone before', pp. 88–100. Rhonda V. Wilcox, 'Shifting roles and synthetic women in *Star Trek: The Next Generation*', *Studies in Popular Culture*, 13/2 (1991), pp. 53–65. Marleen S. Barr, ' "All Good Things...": the end of *Star Trek: The Next Generation*, the end of Camelot – the end of the tale about woman as handmaid to patriarchy as Superman', in Taylor Harrison et al. (eds), *Enterprise Zones: Critical Positions on Star Trek* (Boulder, CO: Westview Press, 1996). Lynne Joyrich, 'Feminist Enterprise: *Star Trek: The Next Generation* and the occupations of femininity', *Cinema Journal*, 35/2 (1996), pp. 61–84. Sarah Projansky, 'When the body speaks: Deanna Troi's tenuous authority and the rationalization of Federation superiority in *Star Trek: The Next Generation* rape narratives', in T. Harrison et al. (eds), *Enterprise Zones: Critical Positions on Star Trek*. Penley, *NASA/TREK*, p. 90. Robin Roberts, *Sexual Generations*: Star Trek: The Next Generation *and Gender* (Urbana, IL: University of Illinois Press, 1999).
114. Jay Chattaway, 'The Making of a Legend', Mission Logs Year One, *TNG*, DVD, Season 1, Disc 7.
115. Bond, *The Music of Star Trek*, p. 88.
116. Irwin, 'Boots and starships', p. 23.
117. Consolmagno similarly notes of *Star Trek*: 'Planets had become places where people we knew had adventures.' Consolmagno, 'Astronomy, science fiction and popular culture', p. 130.

118. At the same time, the tune at least partially reflects the fashion for bolder science fiction soundtracks, ushered in by John Williams' music for *Star Wars* (George Lucas) in 1977. Indeed, Goldsmith 'was reportedly asked to write a '*Star Wars*-type' title theme for *Star Trek: The Motion Picture*'. Bond, *The Music of Star Trek*, p. 87.
119. Bond, *The Music of Star Trek*, p. 168.
120. Text changes reflected changes in cast, but were also stylistic, identifying only actors' names and not their characters for the 'Encounter' episode, but listing both thereafter. In Season 5 a shadow effect was added to the lettering of the show's title.
121. Michael Jindra, 'Star Trek fandom as a religious phenomenon', *Sociology of Religion*, 55/1 (1994), p. 41.
122. The centrality of Earth is also suggested by the fact that the *Star Trek* 'universe [...] is excessively endowed with Earth-like planets'. Athena Andreadis, 'The Enterprise finds twin Earths everywhere it goes, but future colonizers of distant planets won't be so lucky', *Astronomy*, January (1999), p. 64. *Astronomy*, 'Interview With An Alien: Although Tim Russ plays an alien on *Star Trek Voyager*, his interest in astronomy is no act', 28/9, September 2000, p. 44.
123. In this sense, we might recall the theories of Lévi-Strauss, who argued that myths symbolically resolve cultural contractions. Lévi-Strauss, 'The structural study of myth', pp. 189–90.
124. Nemecek, *The Star Trek The Next Generation Companion*, p. 12.
125. See Brooks Landon, *The Aesthetics of Ambivalence* (Westport, CT, and London: Greenwood Press, 1992), pp. 89–90.
126. The text of *TNG*'s title appears as the camera slowly moves forward through space. The lettering is blue, in keeping with the final season of *TOS*, another visual cue that in this case suggests continuity between the two programmes.
127. Nemecek, *The Star Trek The Next Generation Companion*, p. 99.
128. Sarah Kozloff, 'Narrative theory and television', in R. C. Allen (ed.), *Channels of Discourse, Reassembled: Television and Contemporary Criticism*, 2nd edn (London: Routledge, 1992), p. 91. Ellis, *Visible Fictions*, pp. 120, 123.
129. Although the event takes place within *TNG* timeline, the footage itself is new for *DS9*.
130. Raul D. Tovares, 'Teaser', in H. Newcomb (ed.), *Museum of Broadcast Communication Encyclopedia of Television*, vol. 3 (Chicago, IL, and London: Fitzroy Dearborn Publishers, 1997), p. 1629.
131. Nemecek, *The Star Trek The Next Generation Companion*, p. 139.
132. Zimmerman quoted in Erdmann and Block, *Star Trek: Deep Space Nine Companion*, pp. 5–6.
133. Lawrence M. Krauss, *The Physics of Star Trek* (London: Flamingo, 1995), pp. 37–41. A. Swarup, 'How to spot a wormhole in space', *New Scientist*, 31 January

2008. Available at www.newscientist.com/article/mg19726414.600-how-to-spot-a-wormhole-in-space.html (accessed 27 February 2012).
134. Kathy E. Ferguson, 'This species which is not one: identity practices in *Star Trek: Deep Space Nine*', *Strategies*, 15/2 (2002), p. 183.
135. Ibid., p. 182.
136. Executive Producer Michael Pillar describes the Bajorans as being in a 'sort of a Palestinian- or Israeli- or American Indian [...] situation of a disenfranchised people dominated for years'. Quoted in David Bischoff, 'Behind the scenes of *Star Trek: Deep Space Nine*', *Omni*, 15/5, February–March (1993).
137. Erdmann and Block, *Star Trek: Deep Space Nine Companion*, p. 4.
138. Rick Berman, quoted in ibid., p. 4. In a different interview, Berman says, 'Deep Space Nine [sic] has more edge to it'. Quoted in ibid. Production Designer Herman Zimmerman argues that the show 'promises to be a darker, grittier, more visceral adventure than has gone before'. Herman Zimmerman, 'Architect of illusion: designing *Deep Space Nine*', *Omni*, 15/5, February–March(1993), p. 44.
139. Peter Linford, 'Deeds of power: respect for religion in *Star Trek: Deep Space Nine*', in J. E. Porter and D. L. McLaren (eds), *Star Trek and Sacred Ground: Explorations of Star Trek, Religion, and American Culture* (Albany, NY: State University of New York Press, 1999), p. 85.
140. Anne MacKenzie Pearson, 'From thwarted gods to reclaimed mystery? An overview of the depiction of religion in *Star Trek*', in J. E. Porter and D. L. McLaren (eds), *Star Trek and Sacred Ground*, p. 29. Gregory Peterson, 'Religion and science in *Star Trek: The Next Generation*: God, Q, and evolutionary eschatology on the final frontier', in J. E. Porter and D. L. McLaren (eds), *Star Trek and Sacred Ground*, pp. 61–2.
141. Bond, *The Music of Star Trek*, p. 173.
142. Michèle Barrett and Duncan Barrett, *Star Trek: The Human Frontier* (New York: Routledge 2001), p. 37. See also ibid., p. 48.
143. See, for example: Linford, 'Deeds of power', p. 85.
144. Consolmagno, 'Astronomy, science fiction and popular culture', p. 131.
145. See Linford, 'Deeds of power', pp. 86–95.
146. Erdmann and Block, *Star Trek: Deep Space Nine Companion*, p. 593.
147. Barrett and Barrett, *Star Trek: The Human Frontier*, p. 37.
148. Landon, *The Aesthetics of Ambivalence*, pp. 89–90.
149. Erdmann and Block, *Star Trek: Deep Space Nine Companion*, p. 257.
150. See Roger Hagedorn, 'Doubtless to be continued: a brief history of serial narrative', in R. C. Allen (ed.), *To Be Continued ... Soap Operas Around the World* (New York: Routledge, 1995), p. 39.
151. Denny Atkin, 'The science of *Star Trek*', *Omni*, 17/8, Fall (1995), p. 52.

152. 'The name Maquis was used by members of the French underground in World War II.' Marc Okuda and Denise Okuda with Debbie Mirek, *The Star Trek Encyclopedia: A Reference Guide to the Future* (New York: Pocket Books, 1999), p. 287. Writer Jeri Taylor also compares it with the 'Israeli–West Bank situation', and Stephen Edward Poe compares it with the American Civil War. Stephen Edward Poe, *A Vision of the Future: Star Trek Voyager* (New York: Pocket Books, 1998), pp. 200, 202.
153. Erdmann and Block, *Star Trek: Deep Space Nine Companion*, p. 134.
154. Ibid.
155. Ibid.
156. The terms Native American and American Indian are much contested, with some preferring Indigenous or First Americans, First Peoples or First Nation, but the last two may potentially cause confusion in the context of this episode, given that it is a colony on another planet. Amanda Blackhorse, 'Blackhorse: do you prefer "Native American" or "American Indian"? 6 prominent voices respond', *Indian Country Today Media Network*, 21 May 2015. Available at www.indiancountrytodaymedianetwork.com/2015/05/21/blackhorse-do-you-prefer-native-american-or-american-indian-6-prominent-voices-respond (accessed 18 February 2016).
157. Nemecek, *The Star Trek The Next Generation Companion*, p. 290.
158. Rick Berman, quoted in Poe, *A Vision of the Future*, p. 192.
159. Quoted in Bond, *The Music of Star Trek*, p. 98. The title music won an Emmy Award. Ibid., p. 173.
160. Ibid., p. 175.
161. See Chapter 2 for more detail.
162. Although the cast listings changed, the visuals of the titles for *Voyager* remained constant through seven seasons.
163. David Lyon, *The Sailing Navy List: All the Ships of the Royal Navy Built, Purchased and Captured 1688–1860* (London: Conway Maritime Press, 1993), p. 192.
164. Chris Paterson, 'Space program and television', in H. Newcomb (ed.), *Museum of Broadcast Communication Encyclopedia of Television*, vol. 3 (Chicago, IL, and London: Fitzroy Dearborn Publishers, 1997), p. 1538. Allan Asherman, *The Star Trek Compendium* (New York: Pocket Books, 1989, 1993), p. 151.
165. Asherman, *The Star Trek Compendium*, p. 151.
166. *NASA*, 'President Bush Offers New Vision for NASA', 14 January 2004. Available at www.nasa.gov/missions/solarsystem/bush_vision.html (accessed 26 August 2006).
167. *NASA*, 'Star Trek Honors NASA with Voyager Award', 23 February (2004). Available at www.nasa.gov/vision/earth/everydaylife/star_trek.html (accessed 26 August 2006).

168. A. Nevills, 'Final Frontier Astronauts Land on Star Trek', NASA's Johnson Space Center, 13 May 2005. Available at www.nasa.gov/vision/space/features/Astros_on_StarTrek.html (accessed 26 August 2006).
169. Sharon Sharp, 'Nostalgia for the future: retrofuturism in *Enterprise*', *Science Fiction Film and Television*, 4/1, Spring (2011), p. 29.
170. Cohen, *Album of Science*, pp. 3, 274.
171. Frith, *Music for Pleasure*, p. 129. Patricia Aufderheide, 'The look of the sound', in T. Gitlin (ed.), *Watching Television* (New York: Pantheon, 1986), p. 116.
172. Frith, *Music for Pleasure*, p. 130, emphasis in original.
173. Ibid.
174. While I am using the lyrics here as a focus of analysis, I am also mindful that those lyrics gain meaning in musical context, an issue that I will address below. See Johan Fornäs, 'The words of music', *Popular Music and Society*, 26/1, February (2003), pp. 42, 48. For reasons of copyright, I am unable to reproduce the full lyrics here, but they are readily available online.
175. Geraghty, 'Eight days that changed American television', p. 18. Lincoln Geraghty, 'Truly American Enterprise: *Star Trek*'s post-9/11 politics', in D. M. Hassler and C. Wilcox (eds), *New Boundaries of Political Science Fiction* (Columbia, SC: University of South Carolina Press, 2008), p. 164.
176. Andrew Goodwin, *Dancing in the Distraction Factory: Music Television and Popular Culture* (Minneapolis, MN: University of Minnesota Press, 1992), p. 72.
177. Ibid., p. 75.
178. Ibid., p. 76. In the case of music videos, Will Straw argues that the performer exists as a blurred 'performer/character' identity'. Will Straw, 'Popular music and postmodernism in the 1980s', in S. Frith, A. Goodwin and L. Grossberg (eds), *Sound and Vision: The Music Video Reader* (London: Routledge, 1993), p. 16. Frith argues that music videos prioritise the 'singer-as-star' rather than the singer as character/protagonist of the lyrics. Frith, *Music for Pleasure*, pp. 21, 217.
179. Jane Garcia, 'Trekking boldly back to the beginning', *The Age, Green Guide*, 21 February (2002), p. 14.
180. Roman Jakobson, *Selected Writings, Volume II: Word and Language* (The Hague: Mouton, 1971), p. 132.
181. Ibid., emphasis in original.
182. Ibid., pp. 701–702.
183. Ibid., p. 132.
184. Schwichtenberg, 'The Love Boat', p. 131. See also Ellis, *Visible Fictions*, p. 139.
185. By contrast, the soundtrack for *Enterprise* includes a performance music video featuring Watson.
186. Cochrane is played by James Cromwell (uncredited), who played the same character in *Star Trek: First Contact*, creating continuity between the film and the series.

187. Executive Producer Rick Berman has also tended to use 'man' in interviews rather than 'one'. See, for example: Joal Ryan, ' "Star Trek": where no franchise has gone before', *Variety*, 387/2, 27 May 2002, p. S1.
188. The title footage accompanying this part of the song shows a hot air balloon, Charles Lindbergh's *Spirit of St Louis*, and the space shuttle *Enterprise*, providing little context for the unnamed obstructive parties. Fan James R. Kratzer has also argued for reading the song as a reference to the Vulcans. James R. Kratzer, 'Different Strokes for Different Folks', 13 December 2002. Available at www.amazon.com/exec/obidos/tg/detail/-/B0000658PQ/ref=cm_cr_dp_2_1/002-0132310-7164857?v=glance&s=music&vi=customer-reviews (accessed 26 September 2003).
189. Guthke, *The Last Frontier*, p. 18.
190. Andreadis, 'The Enterprise finds twin Earths', p. 64.
191. Indeed, Hark argues that the negative portrayal of the Vulcans was one of the reasons for the programme's poor reception. Hark, *Star Trek*, pp. 143–6.
192. A Music Fan from Lafayette, 'Another effective McCarthy score', 16 May 2002. Available at www.amazon.com/exec/obidos/tg/d…r-reviews&show=-submittime&start-at=21 (accessed 26 September 2003, no longer online 22 September 2016).
193. The *Enterprise* version is shorter and is performed by British singer Russell Watson, because the rights for the Rod Stewart version were too expensive. Garcia, 'Trekking boldly back to the beginning', p. 14.
194. Ibid.
195. Charles Murray and Mike Marqusee, 'To boldly go back', *The Age*, *The Culture*, 12 February (2002), p. 1. Some fans sent in petitions to have the song removed. Garcia, 'Trekking boldly back to the beginning', p. 14.
196. Lerner, 'Hearing the boldly goings', p. 144.
197. Frith, *Music for Pleasure*, p. 91.
198. Ibid., p. 154, emphasis in original. My thanks to Diana Sandars for this connection. See Diana Sandars, 'The Hollywood Musical from 1980 to 2000', (PhD diss., the University of Melbourne, 2006).
199. Fornäs, 'The words of music'.
200. Frith, *Music for Pleasure*, p. 120.
201. Ibid., p. 133.
202. Murray and Marqusee, 'To boldly go back', p. 1. Some fans have noted the musical similarities between the *Enterprise* soundtrack and former series, either to praise its continuity or criticise its lack of originality. Reginald D. Garrard, 'A new "sound" for a new take on the Star Trek saga!', 26 May 2002. Available at www.amazon.com/exec/obidos/tg/detail/-/B0000658PQ/ref=cm_rev_next/102-9724734-3849729?v=glance&s=music&vi=customer-reviews&show=-submittime&start-at=21 (accessed 16 October 2003).

A Music Fan from Miami, 'More bland filler music', 19 May 2002. Available at www.amazon.com/exec/obidos/tg/d...r-reviews&show=-submittime&start-at=21 (accessed 26 September 2003, no longer online 22 September 2016). See also Gao-kutari, 'Not really the Final Frontier', 23 July 2002. Available at www.amazon.com/exec/obidos/tg/detail/-/B0000658PQ/ref=cm_rev_next/102-9724734-3849729?v=glance&s=music&vi=customer-reviews&show=-submittime&start-at=11 (accessed 16 October 2003).
203. As Ryan notes, 'In the old beginning there was Captain James T. Kirk, of the 23rd century. And in the new beginning, there is Captain Jonathan Archer, of the 22nd century.' Ryan, ' "Star Trek": where no franchise has gone before', p. S1.
204. Frith, *Music for Pleasure*, p. 167.
205. Before and during the pilot episode 'Broken Bow' on UPN, *Buffy*'s Sarah Michelle Gellar and Scott Bakula gave post-September 11 appeals for blood and financial support for the American Red Cross. One fan also noted that the *Enterprise* soundtrack was recorded on September 10 and 11, 2001, connecting the terrorist attack with the hope suggested by *Star Trek* as a whole and the *Enterprise* soundtrack in particular. Adam D. Pave, 'Inspiring', 6 June 2002. Available at www.amazon.com/exec/obidos/tg/det...c_1/002-0132310-7164857?v=glance&s=music (accessed 26 September 2003, no longer online 22 September 2016).
206. Richard P. Martin, *The Language of Heroes: Speech and Performance in the* Iliad (Ithaca, NY and London: Cornell University Press, 1989), p. xiv.
207. Starfleet Library, 'Dispatch: Enterprise NX-01 Salutes Enterprise CVN 65', 16 November 2001. Available at www.starfleetlibrary.com/enterprise/welcome_home_uss_enterprise.htm (accessed 16 September 2003, no longer online 22 September 2016).
208. Murray and Marqusee, 'To boldly go back', p. 3.
209. Mark O. Piggot, 'Enterprise Sailors "Beam Up" to TV's "Enterprise"', 28 March 2003. Available at www.navy.mil/Submit/display.asp?story_id=6403> (accessed 22 September 2016).
210. Barrett and Barrett note the naval connections throughout the franchise. In particular, they note, 'the NCC prefixing the various *Enterprise* ships, stands for "Naval Construction Contract"'. Barrett and Barrett, *Star Trek: The Human Frontier*, pp. 9–51, 12. More generally, David Pringle has argued for connections between ship-focused space operas and ship-based seas stories. Pringle, 'What is this thing called space opera?', p. 37. Consolmagno has noted that many spacefaring science fiction stories have military associations. Consolmagno, 'Astronomy, science fiction and popular culture', p. 131.
211. Quoted in Raddatz, ' "Star Trek" wins the Ricky Schwartz', p. 28.
212. 'Broken Bow', James L. Conway 2001.

213. Whether such a 'double address' constitutes a break depends on the context, with Goodwin arguing that it is 'a conventions of pop performance' for music video singers to present themselves both as musicians and fictional characters. Goodwin, *Dancing in the Distraction Factory*, p. 76.
214. Jane Feuer, 'Narrative form in American network television', in C. MacCabe (ed.), *High Theory/Low Culture: Analysing Television and Film* (Manchester: Manchester University Press, 1986), pp. 104–105, emphasis in original.
215. Murray and Marqusee, 'To boldly go back', p. 3.
216. Worland, 'From the new frontier to the final frontier', p. 25.
217. On this episode and Vietnam politics, see: Worland, 'Captain Kirk Cold Warrior', p. 113. Kapell, *Exploring the Next Frontier*, pp. 159–63.
218. Steffen Hantke, '*Star Trek*'s mirror universe episodes and US military culture through the eyes of the other', *Science Fiction Studies*, 41/3 (2014), p. 571.
219. Charlie Jane Anders, 'Simon Pegg's Star Trek Reboot Theory: Is this the "Mirror" Crew?' *i09*, 9 May 2013. Available at http://io9.com/simon-peggs-star-trek-reboot-theory-is-this-the-mirro-499064330 (accessed 26 November 2015).
220. See also Sharon Sharp's analysis of the Season 4 episodes 'Storm Front: Part I' (2004) and 'Storm Front: Part II' (2004), in which the crew travel back in time to fight the Nazis in WWII, and therefore take part in a conflict and time period in which 'enemies and heroes were more clearly defined in the popular imagination'. Sharp, 'Nostalgia for the future', pp. 25–40.
221. Pearson and Messenger Davies, *Star Trek and American Television*, p. 147.
222. Reviving an idea first suggested by Aristarchus of Samos (c.310–230 BCE). Thomas S. Kuhn, *The Copernican Revolution: Planetary Astronomy in the Development of Western Thought* (Cambridge, MA: Harvard University Press, 1957, 1985), p. 42.
223. William Blake Tyrell, '*Star Trek*'s myth of science', *Journal of American Culture*, 2/1, Spring (1979), p. 293. Grenz, 'Why do theologians need to be scientists?', p. 345

Chapter 4: Fans, Bards and Rituals

1. *Star Trek: The Experience* won the award for best attraction at the 1998 Thea (Themed Entertainment Association) Awards.
2. Sean Alfano, 'CBS, Viacom Formally Split: Now Traded Separately on Wall Street, Shares of Two Companies Rise', 3 January 2006. Available at www.cbsnews.com/stories/2006/01/03/business/main1176111.shtml?tag=mncol (accessed 1 June 2010).

3. Ken Dowden, *The Uses of Greek Mythology* (London and New York: Routledge, 1992), pp. 27–8. Jaan Puhvel, *Comparative Mythology* (Baltimore, MD: The Johns Hopkins University Press, 1987), p. 15.
4. Puhvel, *Comparative Mythology*, p. 15. See also: Robert A. Segal, *Myth and Ritual Theory: An Anthology* (Malden, MA, and Oxford: Blackwell, 1998), p. 1.
5. Sir James G. Frazer, *The Golden Bough: A Study in Magic and Religion* (London: Macmillan, 1915). Dowden, *The Uses of Greek Mythology*, p. 27.
6. Puhvel, *Comparative Mythology*, pp. 15–16. The ritual approach also paved the way for the heroic biography approach, which examined heroic figures in terms of ritual formula applied over a lifetime.
7. Dowden, *The Uses of Greek Mythology*, p. 34, emphasis mine.
8. Ibid.
9. Lucia Nixon, 'The cults of Demeter and Kore', in R. Hawley and B. Levick (eds), *Women in Antiquity: New Assessments* (London & New York: Routledge, 1995), pp. 75–96.
10. Anonymous, 'The Homeric Hymn to Demeter', trans. Helene P. Foley, in H. P. Foley, *The Homeric 'Hymn to Demeter': Translation, Commentary, and Interpretive Essays* (Princeton, NJ: Princeton University Press, 2013), ll 459–582.
11. Nixon, 'The cults of Demeter and Kore', p. 75.
12. Ibid., pp. 85–6.
13. Ibid., p. 86.
14. Ibid., p. 91.
15. Ibid., pp. 91–2.
16. Ibid., p. 92.
17. Applied to the work of former and present scholars of the Instituto di Studi storico-religiosi at the University of Rome.
18. Dowden, *The Uses of Greek Mythology*, pp. 35–6.
19. Ibid., p. 35.
20. Segal, *Myth and Ritual Theory*, pp. 8–9.
21. Ibid., p. 10. See also Dowden, *The Uses of Greek Mythology*, p. 7.
22. Sally F. Moore and Barbara G. Myerhoff, *Secular Ritual* (Amsterdam: Van Gorcum, 1977).
23. Segal, *Myth and Ritual Theory*, p. 13.
24. Victor Turner, 'Variations on a theme of liminality', in S. F. Moore and B. G. Meyerhoff (eds), *Secular Ritual* (Amsterdam: Van Gorcum 1977), pp. 42–3, emphasis in original.
25. Horace Newcomb and Paul M. Hirsch, 'Television as cultural forum', in H. Newcomb (ed.), *Television: The Critical View* (Oxford: Oxford University Press, 1987), p. 468. Jennifer E. Porter, 'To boldly go: *Star Trek* convention

attendance as pilgrimage', in J. E. Porter and D. L. McLaren (eds), *Star Trek and Sacred Ground: Explorations of Star Trek, Religion, and American Culture* (Albany, NY: State University of New York Press, 1999), pp. 246–67.
26. Jim Kitses, *Horizons West: Anthony Mann, Budd Boetticher, Sam Peckinpah – Studies of Authorship within the Western* (London: BFI, 1969), p. 20. However, Kitses believed that myths should, by definition, contain gods, and that the Western could not, therefore, be a myth in any convention sense. As I have discussed throughout this book, this narrow conception of myth is not in keeping with the word's origins and subsequent development.
27. John G. Cawelti, *The Six-Gun Mystique* (Bowling Green, OH: Bowling Green University Press, 1971), p. 32. See also p. 73.
28. Thomas Schatz, 'The structural influence: new directions in film genre study', in B. K. Grant (ed.), *Film Genre Reader* (Austin, TX: University of Texas Press, 1986), p. 95.
29. J. P. Telotte, 'Beyond all reason: the nature of the cult', in J. P. Telotte (ed.) *The Cult Film Experience: Beyond All Reason* (Austin, TX: University of Texas Press, 1991), p. 13. See also Bruce Kawin, 'After midnight', in J. P. Telotte (ed.), *The Cult Film Experience: Beyond All Reason*, p. 23.
30. Chris Gregory, *Star Trek: Parallel Narratives* (Houndsmills, Hampshire and London: Macmillan Press, 2000), p. 108.
31. Henry Jenkins, *Textual Poachers: Television Fans and Participatory Culture* (New York: Routledge, 1992), p. 12. Because I am specifically interested in the connection between fandom, myth and ritual, I will not be revisiting scholarly work on other areas of fandom such as fan art, fiction and conventions. For other influential early work in this field, see in particular Camille Bacon-Smith, *Enterprising Women: Television Fandom and the Creation of Popular Myth* (Philadelphia, PA: University of Pennsylvania Press, 1992). Lisa Lewis, *The Adoring Audience: Fan Culture and Popular Media* (London: Routledge, 1992). Joe Sanders (ed.), *Science Fiction Fandom* (Westport, CT: Greenwood Press, 1994). John Tulloch and Henry Jenkins, *Science Fiction Audiences: Watching Doctor Who and Star Trek* (London and New York: Routledge, 1995). Constance Penley, *NASA/TREK: Popular Science and Sex in America* (London: Verso, 1997).
32. Jenkins, *Textual Poachers*, p. 12.
33. Ibid., p. 13.
34. Gregory, *Star Trek: Parallel Narratives*, p. 108.
35. James A. Herrick, *Scientific Mythologies: How Science and Science Fiction Forge New Religious Beliefs* (Downers Grove, IL: InterVarsity Press, 2008).
36. Michael Jindra, 'Star Trek fandom as a religious phenomenon', *Sociology of Religion*, 55/1 (1994), p. 30.
37. Ibid., p. 32.

38. Ibid., p. 46.
39. Ibid., p. 50.
40. Ibid., p. 47.
41. For an analysis of rituals performed within the *Star Trek* diegesis itself, see Susan L. Schwartz, 'Enterprise engaged: mythic enactment and ritual performance', in R. S. Kraemer, W. Cassidy and S. Schwartz, *Religions of Star Trek* (Boulder, CO: Westview Press, 2001).
42. Segal, *Myth and Ritual Theory*, p. 7.
43. Clyde Kluckholn, 'Myths and rituals: a general theory', in R. A. Segal (ed.), *Myth and Ritual Theory: An Anthology* (Malden, MA and Oxford: Blackwell, 1998), p. 322.
44. Segal, *Myth and Ritual Theory*, pp. 12–13.
45. Walter Burkert, 'Homo Necans', in R. A. Segal (ed.), *Myth and Ritual Theory: An Anthology*, p. 346.
46. Thus, Chris Gregory notes, 'The experience of watching [TV...] becomes "ritualised" as part of a pattern of lifestyle.' Gregory, *Star Trek: Parallel Narratives*, p. 105.
47. John Fiske and John Hartley, *Reading Television* (London: Methuen, 1978), p. 85.
48. John Hartley and Tom O'Regan, 'Quoting not science but sideboards', in J. Hartley, *Tele-ology: Studies in Television* (London & New York: Routledge, 1992), p. 206.
49. Ibid.
50. John Hartley, *Tele-ology: Studies in Television*, p. 112.
51. Ellis, *Visible Fictions*, p. 113.
52. See for example ibid., pp. 128, 161–2.
53. Djoymi Baker, 'Terms of excess: binge-viewing as epic-viewing in the streaming era', in M. Wiatrowski and C. Barker (eds), *The Age of Netflix: Critical Essays on Streaming Media, Digital Delivery and Instant Access* (Jefferson, NC: McFarland, 2017).
54. Fiske and Hartley, *Reading Television*, pp. 85–7.
55. Ibid., p. 88.
56. Ibid., p. 86, emphasis in original.
57. Ibid.
58. Ibid., p. 85.
59. Ibid., p. 86.
60. Ibid.
61. Ibid., pp. 124–5.
62. Ibid., pp. 86–7.
63. Ibid., p. 87.
64. Ibid., p. 89.

65. Roland Barthes, *Mythologies*, trans. Annette Lavers (London: Vintage, 1957, 1993), p. 157.
66. Fiske and Hartley, *Reading Television*, pp. 114, 145, 174.
67. Ibid., p. 85, emphasis in original.
68. Ibid.
69. Proinsias Mac Cana, *The Learned Tales of Medieval Ireland* (Dublin: Dublin Institute for Advanced Studies, 1980), pp. 16, 27, 31.
70. See, for example: Jan de Vries, *Heroic Legend and Heroic Song*, trans. B. J. Timmer (New York: Arno Press, 1978), pp. 164–70.
71. Mac Cana, *The Learned Tales of Medieval Ireland*, pp. 6–7.
72. Ibid., pp. 16, 27.
73. Ibid., pp. 3, 27.
74. Ibid., pp. 3–4, 13, 24.
75. Ibid., pp. 6, 13.
76. Ibid., pp. 18, 31.
77. Ibid., pp. 13.
78. Janet H. Murray, *Hamlet on the Holodeck: The Future of Narrative in Cyberspace* (New York: The Free Press, 1997), pp. 185–213.
79. Ibid., p. 188.
80. Ibid., p. 194.
81. Ibid., p. 195.
82. Ibid., p. 196.
83. Ibid., p. 204.
84. Mac Cana, *The Learned Tales of Medieval Ireland*, p. 15.
85. Murray, *Hamlet on the Holodeck*, p. 200.
86. Ibid., p. 203.
87. Ibid., p. 208.
88. Myths are inherently multi-authored. For example, Homer drew upon numerous pre-existing stories as building blocks to his own works. Laura M. Slatkin, *The Power of Thetis: Allusion and Interpretation in the* Iliad (Berkeley, CA: University of California Press, 1991), p. xv.
89. Ellis, *Visible Fictions*, pp. 128, 161–2.
90. Segal, *Myth and Ritual Theory*, p. 13.
91. Porter, 'To boldly go: *Star Trek* convention attendance as pilgrimage', p. 245.
92. Ibid., p. 246.
93. Alan Morinis, 'Introduction', in A. Morinis (ed.), *Sacred Journeys: The Anthropology of Pilgrimage* (Westport, CT: Greenwood, 1992), pp. 4, 19.
94. Victor Turner, *The Ritual Process: Structure and Anti-Structure* (Chicago, IL: Aldine, 1974), p. 166.
95. Ibid., pp. 166–7.
96. Ibid., p. 273.

97. Ibid., p. 251.
98. David D. Gilmore, 'Carnival, ritual, and the anthropologists', *Carnival and Culture: Sex, Symbol, and Status in Spain* (New Haven, CT and London: Yale University Press, 1998), p. 35. Turner, 'Variations on a theme of liminality', pp. 43–4.
99. Turner, *The Ritual Process*, p. 169.
100. Turner, 'Variations on a theme of liminality', pp. 41–3. Victor Turner, 'Social dramas and stories about them', *Critical Inquiry*, Autumn (1980), p. 159.
101. Victor Turner, *Dramas, Fields and Metaphors: Symbolic Action in Human Society* (Ithaca, NY: Cornell University Press, 1974), pp. 260. Turner, 'Variations on a theme of liminality', pp. 34–5, 43. See also Porter, 'To boldly go: *Star Trek* convention attendance as pilgrimage', pp. 246–7. Erik Cohen, 'Pilgrimage and tourism: convergence and divergence', in A. Morinis (ed.), *Sacred Journeys: The Anthropology of Pilgrimage* (Westport, CT: Greenwood, 1992), p. 56.
102. Cohen, 'Pilgrimage and tourism', pp. 52–3.
103. Turner, 'Social dramas and stories about them', pp. 156, 159.
104. Porter, 'To boldly go: *Star Trek* convention attendance as pilgrimage', pp. 246–7.
105. Ibid.
106. Michael Jindra notes, 'In recent years the number of Star Trek [sic] places of "pilgrimage" and commemorative exhibitions has been increasing' (1994: 39). Jindra, 'Star Trek fandom as a religious phenomenon', p. 39. One fan told Jindra of her tour of the *Star Trek* set, 'we pilgrimage out there; it's our Mecca'. Quoted in ibid., p. 40.
107. Morinis, 'Introduction', pp. 8–9.
108. Ibid., p. 8.
109. Christopher Anderson, *Hollywood TV: The Studio System in the Fifties* (Austin, TX: University of Texas Press, 1994), pp. 150–1. Douglas Gomery, 'Disney's business history: a reinterpretation', in E. Smoodin (ed.), *Disney Discourse: Producing the Magic Kingdom* (New York: Routledge, 1994), p. 76.
110. Thomas Hine, *Populuxe* (New York: Alfred A. Knopf, 1986), p. 151.
111. Scott Bukatman, 'There's always a Tomorrowland: Disney and the hypercinematic experience', *October* 57, Summer (1991), p. 61. Angela Ndalianis, 'Theme parks, neo-baroque experiences, and entertainment cities', *Eyeline*, 41, Summer (1999/2000), p. 12. Beth Dunlop, *Building a Dream: The Art of Disney Architecture* (New York: Harry N. Abrams, 1996), pp. 13, 29. Jay David Bolter and Richard Grusin, *Remediation: Understanding New Media* (Cambridge, MA: MIT Press, 1999), p. 170.
112. Quoted in Anderson, *Hollywood TV*, p. 141.
113. Quoted in Dunlop, *Building a Dream*, p. 37.

114. See also: Michael Sorkin, 'Introduction: variations on a theme park' and 'See you in Disneyland', in M. Sorkin (ed.), *Variations on a Theme Park: The New American City and the End of Public Space* (New York: Hill & Wang, 1992), pp. xiii, 208, 232. Jim Collins, *Architectures of Excess: Cultural Life in the Information Age* (New York: Routledge, 1995), pp. 38–9. Matt Hills, *Fan Cultures* (London: Routledge, 2002), p. 152.
115. Quoted in Anderson, *Hollywood TV*, p. 134.
116. Ibid., p. 153.
117. Justin Wyatt, *High Concept: Movies and Marketing in Hollywood* (Austin, TX: University of Texas Press, 1994), p. 70. Paramount in particular became known for the close interaction between production, distribution and marketing, and Viacom (now operating as CBS Corp.) used its subsidiary companies to produce related merchandise, such as the *Star Trek* novels produced by Pocket Books. Ibid., pp. 87–8, 133.
118. T. L. Stanley, 'Paramount Parks get $10M in ads, Viacom synergy', *Brandweek*, 36/14, 3 April 1995, pp. 1–2.
119. Judith Rubin, 'Are you experienced?' *TCI*, 32/4, April 1998, p. 35. The attraction had been intended for inclusion in existing Paramount theme parks, but was scaled down to the single Vegas attraction for reasons of cost. Greg Dudsic, 'Hotels win big on high-tech attractions', *Variety*, 10 August 1998, pp. 32–3.
120. The new themed casinos in this era included Excalibur (1990), Treasure Island (1993), Luxor (1993) and MGM Grand (1993).
121. Russell W. Belk, 'Three coins in a Caesar's Palace fountain: interpreting Las Vegas', *Advances in Consumer Research*, 25 (1998), p. 7. Yvette Cardazo and Bill Hirsh, 'Take a Look at Las Vegas', *Daily Herald*, Chicago (n.d.). Available at www.dailyherald.com/oldtravel/leadstory/dhhtm/leadstory41.htm (accessed 13 August 2004, no longer online 22 September 2016). Julian Coman, 'Sin City opts for flesh rather than families after big losses', *The Age*, 16 December 2002, p. 11. Tim Frost, 'Just an illusion', *Home Entertainment*, April 1994, p. 34. Las Vegas was compared with Disney as early as 1963. Theming also has a long Vegas history. Images of the earlier frontier West marked the first phase with El Rancho Vegas (1941) and Hotel Last Frontier (1942), and Last Frontier Village (1947). This was ten years before Disneyland's Frontierland, so perhaps Disneyland should have been called a grotesque Las Vegas. After a lull in the 1950s, the theming trend was revived by Caesars Palace (1966). Alan Hess, *Viva Las Vegas: After-Hours Architecture* (San Francisco, CA: Chronicle Books, 1993), pp. 10, 17, 26–33, 84, 88, 89.
122. Henry Jenkins, 'Transmedia 202: Further Reflections', *Confession of an Aca-Fan* (blog), (2011). Available at http://henryjenkins.org/2011/08/defining_transmedia_further_re.html (accessed 2 February 2016).
123. On ' "entering" the cult text', see Hills, *Fan Cultures*, p. 151.

124. Rubin, 'Are you experienced?', p. 37.
125. Steve Friess, 'Vegas Steels for Borg Invasion', *Wired News*, 5 March 2004. Available at http://archive.wired.com/gaming/gamingreviews/news/2004/03/62538?currentPage=all (accessed 22 September 2016). Scott Migaldi, 'Great Fun while in Las Vegas!' 8 April 2004. Available at www.imdb.com/title/tt0356069/ (accessed 14 August 2004).
126. Oskar Garcia, ' "Trek" fans, want Picard's chair? It's for sale', Associated Press, 9 April 2010. Available at www.democraticunderground.com/discuss/duboard.php?az=view_all&address=105x9327273 (accessed 23 June 2017).
127. The Las Vegas Hilton's Vice President of Sales, Michael Gasta, noted: 'Because we're off the strip, we need to install an attraction to draw the leisure guests to our hotel.' Quoted in Martha I. Finney, 'High-stakes relationships', *Association Management*, March, 49/3 (1997). Hess notes that in the 1960s, the distances between hotels was a means of keeping customers within the one complex. Hess, *Viva Las Vegas*, pp. 74–5. By the 1990s, this was no longer the case, with Michael J. Dear arguing that theming is a way to keep guests inside. Michael J. Dear, 'A tale of two cities. 2. Las Vegas', *The Postmodern Urban Condition* (Malden, MA: Blackwell Publishers, 2000), p. 204.
128. This movement proved to be too successful, with Hilton fined by the Nevada Gaming Commission for allowing underage visitors to line up for the attraction in the casino area. Dave Berns, 'Hilton fined for Trek incident', *Las Vegas Review-Journal*, 22 May 1998. Available at www.reviewjournal.com/lvrj_home/1998/May-22-Fri-1998/business/7544970.html (accessed 3 January 2003, no longer online 22 September 2916).
129. Russell Belk, 'May the farce be with you: on Las Vegas and consumer infantalization', *Consumption, Markets and Culture*, 4/2 (2000), p. 103.
130. For example, Excalibur draws on Arthurian legend, Luxor on ancient Egypt, and MGM Grand on MGM's movie history.
131. Mark Gottdiener, *The Theming of America: Dreams, Visions and Commercial Spaces* (Boulder, CO: Westview Press, 1997), p. 107.
132. Viacom ran advertisements for the attraction at the beginning of various *Star Trek* videos released at this time, including *Voyager* volume 4.11, containing 'The Omega Directive' (1998) and 'Unforgettable' (1998).
133. *Star Trek: The Experience* (n.d.). Available at www.startrekexp.com (accessed 7 January 2008, no longer online 23 September 2016). Anthony Esparza, the Senior Vice President of Design and Entertainment for Paramount Parks, similarly says, 'What others do in 2-D, we do in 3-D.' Quoted in Dudsic, 'Hotels win big'.
134. Belton, *Widescreen Cinema*, p. 79.
135. Anderson, *Hollywood TV*, p. 153.

136. Cohen, 'Pilgrimage and tourism', pp. 58–9.
137. Turner, *Dramas, Fields and Metaphors*, p. 169.
138. 'Don't go on a ride. Go on a mission', *What's On Las Vegas*, 15–28 May 2001, p. 61.
139. Although Karpovich notes, that with few European visitors, the possibility of being the ancestor to a French Starfleet captain would seem remote to most. Angela I. Karpovich, 'Locating the "*Star Trek* experience"', in L. Geraghty (ed.), *The Influence of Star Trek on Television, Film and Culture* (Jefferson, NC: McFarland, 2008), p. 207.
140. 'BORG Invasion 4D Opens', *The Arizona Newsroom*, 10 February 2004. Available at www.azreporter.com/idirectory/lasvegas/news/borginvasion.html (accessed 14 August 2004, no longer online 22 September 2016).
141. *Star Trek: The Experience* (n.d.).
142. While all fan fiction is a reworking of the text to suit personal tastes, 'Mary Sue' stories create characters based on the fan authors themselves. Jenkins, *Textual Poachers*, pp. 171, 173. Bacon-Smith, *Enterprising Women*, pp. 94–114. The Mary Sue Society (2002). Available at www.web.archive.org/web/20040624085452/http://www.subreality.com/marysue/explain.htm (accessed 16 February 2021).
143. J. Coyle, '"Veronica Mars" Kickstarter legacy is cloudy', *Huffington Post*, 13 March 2014. Available at www.huffingtonpost.com/2014/03/13/veronica-mars-kickstarter_n_4958016.html (accessed 10 February 2016, no longer online 22 September 2016). Bertha Chin, Bethan Jones, Myles McNutt and Luke Pebler, 'Veronica Mars Kickstarter and crowd funding', *Transformative Works & Cultures*, 15 (2014), p. 5.
144. 'Win a Walk-On Role in Star Trek Beyond', StarTrek.com, 14 July 2015. Available at www.startrek.com/article/win-a-walk-on-role-in-star-trek-beyond (accessed 30 November 2015).
145. Similarly, Kurt Lancaster has noted that numerous theme park attractions allow visitors to act out scenes from particular films or television programmes, 'thus becoming the heroes that, perhaps, they never were or wish to become'. Kurt Lancaster, 'When spectators become performers: contemporary performance-entertainments meet the needs of an "unsettled" audience', *Journal of Popular Culture*, 30/4, Spring (1997), p. 79.
146. Markku Eskelinen, 'The gaming situation', *Game Studies*, 1/1, July 2001. Available at www.gamestudies.org/0101/eskelinen/ (accessed 8 December 2004). Here I am concerned primarily with the marketing strategies of games rather than the games per se.
147. Roman Jakobson, *Selected Writings, Volume II: Word and Language* (The Hague: Mouton, 1971), pp. 130–4.
148. Ibid., pp. 701–702.
149. Schwichtenberg, '*The Love Boat*', p. 131. See also: Ellis, *Visible Fictions*, p. 139.

150. Turner, *Dramas, Fields and Metaphors*, pp. 273, 251.
151. Turner, 'Variations on a theme of liminality', pp. 41–3. Turner, 'Social dramas and stories about them', pp. 156, 159.
152. Turner, 'Variations on a theme of liminality', p. 45.
153. Porter, 'To boldly go: *Star Trek* convention attendance as pilgrimage', pp. 248–52.
154. Turner, 'Variations on a theme of liminality', pp. 38, 40. Turner, *Dramas, Fields and Metaphors*, p. 243.
155. Turner, 'Variations on a theme of liminality', p. 41.
156. Porter 'To boldly go: *Star Trek* convention attendance as pilgrimage', p. 249. See also: Jindra, 'Star Trek fandom as a religious phenomenon', p. 47.
157. Robin Roberts, 'Performing science fiction: Television, theater, and gender in Star Trek: The Experience', *Extrapolation*, 42/4, Winter (2001), pp. 340–56.
158. The voice-overs and filmed appearances of *Star Trek: Next Generation* characters remain the same, however, and noticeably male, as Roberts points out. Roberts, 'Performing science fiction'. However, the 'Borg Invasion 4D' ride added in 2004 features crew members from *Voyager*, in which the participant is rescued from the Borg by Admiral Kathryn Janeway. Migaldi, 'Great Fun While in Las Vegas!' The Borg threat is also feminised, through the Borg Queen.
159. Turner, *Dramas, Fields and Metaphors*, p. 243.
160. Porter, 'To boldly go: *Star Trek* convention attendance as pilgrimage', pp. 249–52.
161. Marc Okrand, *The Klingon Dictionary* (New York: Pocket Books, 1992). Marc Okrand, *Klingon for the Galactic Traveller* (New York: Pocket Books, 1997). Marc Okrand and Michael Dorn, *Star Trek: Conversational Klingon* (S & S Audio 1992). *Klingon Language Institute* (n.d.). Available at www.kli.org (accessed 8 January 2003).
162. Turner, *Dramas, Fields and Metaphors*, p. 263.
163. Morinis, 'Introduction', p. 18.
164. Ibid.
165. Bukatman, 'There's always a Tomorrowland', pp. 59–60. See also: Alan Bryman, *Disney and His Worlds* (London and New York: Routledge, 1995), p. 136.
166. Rubin, 'Are you experienced?' p. 35.
167. Quoted in ibid.
168. T. L. Stanley, 'How long can the ride continue?' *Brandweek*, 11 September 1995, pp. 34–6.
169. Jeff Mason, 'The disappearing bum: a look at time travels in Star Trek', in W. Irwin and G. B. Love (eds), *The Best of the Best of Trek II* (New York: ROC, 1992), p. 357.

170. Ibid., p. 359. That said, *Star Trek* has inspired a number of real-life technologies, such as mobile phones, spray-on drugs, and research into teleportation. Mary-Anne Toy, 'Melbourne team finds key to spray-on drugs', *The Age*, 27 August 1999, pp. 1–2. Nathan Cochrane, 'Back to the future: Scotty, you'll flip over our antique mobile phone', *The Age*, 3 March 1998, p. E4. NASA named a US space shuttle *Enterprise* in 1976 after requests from *Star Trek* fans. Jim Dumoulin, 'Enterprise (OV-101)', Kennedy Space Center (1994). Available at www.science.ksc.nasa.gov/shuttle/resources/orbiters/enterprise.html (accessed 18 December 2016).
171. Mason, 'The disappearing bum', pp. 355–7.
172. On the complex use of history in *Star Trek*, see Lincoln Geraghty, ' "Carved from the rock experiences of our daily lives": Reality and Star Trek's multiple histories', *European Journal of American Culture*, 21/3 (2002), pp. 160–76.
173. The war culminates in the double episode 'Storm Front' (2004), at the end of which Temporal Cold War agent Daniels assures Archer that the correct timeline has been restored.
174. Proctor, 'Beginning again: the reboot phenomenon in comic books, film and beyond', pp. 287–8.
175. See, for example: Ina Rae Hark, 'Franchise fatigue? The marginalization of the television series after *The Next Generation*', in L. Geraghty (ed.), *The Influence of Star Trek on Television, Film and Culture* (Jefferson, NC: McFarland, 2007), pp. 54–5.
176. Jack Teiwes, 'Crisis of Infinite Intertexts! Continuity as Adaptation in the Superman Multimedia Franchise' (PhD diss., University of Melbourne, 2015), p. 123. Proctor, 'Beginning again: the reboot phenomenon in comic books, film and beyond', p. 313. See also Shane Denson, 'Marvel Comics' Frankenstein: a case study in the media of serial figures', *Amerikastudien*, 56/ 4 (2011), pp. 531–53. William Proctor, 'Beginning again: the reboot phenomenon in comic books and film', *Scan: Journal of Media Arts and Culture*, 9, 1 (2012). Available at www.scan.net.au/scn/journal/vol9number1/William-Proctor.html (accessed 24 November 2015). William Proctor, 'Ctl-Alt-Delete: retcon, relaunch, or reboot?' *Sequart*, 8 February (2013). Available at www.sequart.org/magazine/18508/ctl-alt-delete-retcon-relaunch-or-reboot (accessed 6 September 2013). For use of 'reboot' in the popular press, see for example: D. McNary, ' "Star Trek: Beyond" gets new release date', *Variety*, 17 September 2015. Available at www.variety.com/2015/film/news/star-trek-beyond-gets-new-release-date-1201596328/ (accessed 27 November 2015, no longer online 18 December 2016).
177. Proctor, 'Beginning again: the reboot phenomenon in comic books, film and beyond', p. 291. Michael A. Hemmingson, *Star Trek: A Post-Structural Critique of the Original Series* (San Bernardino, CA: Borgo Press, 2009), p. 114.

178. 'Future's End, Part 1' (1996).
179. Rowan Hooper, 'Multiverse me: should I care about my other selves?' *New Scientist*, 223/2988, 27 September 2014. Available at www.newscientist.com/article/mg22329880-400-multiverse-me-should-i-care-about-my-other-selves/ (accessed 26 November 2015).
180. Proctor, 'Beginning again: the reboot phenomenon in comic books, film and beyond', p. 312.
181. Hark, 'Franchise fatigue?' p. 55.
182. Quoted in Mark Julian, 'J. J. Abrams discusses the altered timeline of his Star Trek movies', *Comic Book Movie*, 8 June 2011. Available at www.comicbook-movie.com/scifi_movies/star_trek/jj-abrams-discusses-the-altered-timeline-of-his-star-trek-a51999 (accessed 1 September 2015).
183. Marc Okuda and Denise Okuda, *Star Trek Chronology: The History of the Future* (New York: Pocket Books, 1996), pp. viii, 21–2.
184. Djoymi Baker, ' "Every old trick is new again": myth in quotations and the *Star Trek* Franchise', *Popular Culture Review*, 12/1, February (2001), pp. 67–77. Reprinted in M. W. Kapell (ed.), *Star Trek as Myth: Essays on Symbol and Archetype at the Final Frontier* (Jefferson, NC: McFarland, 2010).
185. Books such as Krauss' *The Physics of Star Trek* explore the potential to turn *Star Trek*'s fictional technology into real technology.
186. Quoted in Roberts, 'Performing science fiction', p. 344.
187. Ibid., p. 347.
188. Turner, *Dramas, Fields and Metaphors*, pp. 273, 251. Turner, 'Variations on a theme of liminality', pp. 41–3.
189. Author's own transcription.
190. Jenkins, 'Transmedia 202'.
191. Morinis, 'Introduction', p. 6.
192. See Hemmingson for a discussion of fan consumerism in general as creating a class system and commodity fetishism. Hemmingson, *Star Trek: A Post-Structural Critique*, p. 40. See also Lincoln Geraghty on merchandising at the San Diego Comic-Con, which is nonetheless different to *The Experience* in being held at the San Diego Convention Center, 'an empty and blank space'. Lincoln Geraghty, *Cult Collectors* (Florence: Taylor and Francis, 2014), pp. 96, 99, 112–18. By contrast, *The Experience* environs were fully themed as a faux space station.
193. See, for example: *DS9* 'Rules of Acquisition', *Star Trek: Deep Space Nine* (1993), and Ira Steven Behr, *The Ferengi Rules of Acquisition* (New York: Pocket Books, 1995).
194. Indeed, Alan Bryman argues that this blurring of shopping with other, themed activities can be seen as part of a larger process of 'Disneyization', and that Las Vegas' 'casinos, hotels, restaurants, shopping, and theme parks' are

a prime example. Bryman, *Disney and His Worlds*, p. 36. The mix of restaurant, shop and rides can also be compared with what John Hannigan terms 'shoppertainment' and 'eatertainment', creating synergies between different forms of consumption. John Hannigan, *Fantasy City: Pleasure and Profit in the Postmodern Metropolis* (New York: Routledge, 1998), pp. 87, 89–90, 93.

195. Hills, *Fan Cultures*, pp. 30, 153. See also Jenkins, *Textual Poachers*, p. 280. Kurt Lancaster, *Interacting with Babylon 5: Fan Performance in a Media Universe* (Austin, TX: University of Texas Press, 2001), p. 156.
196. Turner, *Dramas, Fields and Metaphors*, p. 273.
197. See, for example: Roger C. Aden, *Popular Stories and Promised Lands: Fan Cultures and Symbolic Pilgrimages* (Tuscoloosa, AL and London: University of Alabama Press, 1999), p. 248.
198. Belk, 'May the farce be with you', p. 101.
199. Ibid. See, for example: Arnold Van Gennep, *The Rites of Passage*, trans. M. B. Visedom and G. L. Caffee (Chicago, IL: University of Chicago Press, 1960). Turner, *The Ritual Process*. Mikhail Bakhtin, *Rabelais and his World*, trans. Helene Iswolsky (Cambridge, MA: MIT Press, 1968).
200. Belk, 'May the farce be with you', p. 116.
201. Ibid.
202. See, for example, Henry Jenkins' analysis of the 1987 William Shatner skit that appeared on *Saturday Night Live*. Jenkins, *Textual Poachers*, p. 10.
203. Turner, 'Variations on a theme of liminality', p. 37.
204. Ibid., emphasis in original.
205. Ibid., pp. 37, 47.
206. Ibid., p. 47. Indeed, Morinis notes that there are many different types of pilgrimage. Morinis, 'Introduction', pp. 10–14. *The Experience* was tailored towards group participation on the 'Klingon Encounter' ride, but also in its recreation of Quark's bar, defined in *DS9* as a social hub that would lose its textual affinity if only patronised by a few individual visitors.
207. For example, Alexander Moore has argued that Walt Disney World operates as a pilgrimage site, a space away from the everyday with its own associated rituals. Alexander Moore, 'Walt Disney World: bonded ritual space and the playful pilgrimage center', *Anthropological Quarterly*, 35, October 1980, pp. 207–18.
208. Bryman, *Disney and His Worlds*, p. 98.
209. Cohen, 'Pilgrimage and tourism', pp. 58–9. Turner, *Dramas, Fields and Metaphors*, p. 169.
210. Cohen, 'Pilgrimage and tourism', p. 59.
211. Quoted in Dudsic, 'Hotels win big on high-tech attractions'.
212. Hess, *Viva Las Vegas*, pp. 118–19.
213. Ibid., p. 119.
214. Bryman, *Disney and His Worlds*, p. 98.

215. Morinis, 'Introduction', p. 4.
216. Porter, 'To boldly go: *Star Trek* convention attendance as pilgrimage', p. 253. Similarly, Lancaster argues that interactive, performative engagements with *Babylon 5* allow fans to 'see or experience *Babylon 5* from different perspectives'. Lancaster, *Interacting with Babylon 5*, p. 162.
217. Porter, 'To boldly go: *Star Trek* convention attendance as pilgrimage', p. 269 n.9.
218. Morinis, 'Introduction', p. 4.
219. A dual online and in-person fan convention was held at *The Experience* on 2–4 August 2002. *Vir-Con* (2002). Available at www.vir-con.net (accessed 1 August 2002, no longer online 24 June 2017). The online version allowed participants to choose an avatar from different race, gender and rank possibilities, although higher ranks required a more costly ticket. Mark Baard, 'Trekkies Go Boldly, Virtually', *Wired News*, 24 July 2002. Available at www.wired.com/news/culture/0,1284,53876,00.html (accessed 14 August 2004, no longer online 22 September 2016).
220. Djoymi Baker, 'Contested spaces: the internet ate my TV, the TV company ate my internet site', *The Refractory: A Journal of Entertainment Media*, 1, October 2002. Available at https://refractory-journal.com/contested-spaces-the-internet-ate-my-tv-the-tv-company-ate-my-internet-site-djoymi-baker/ (accessed 16 February 2021).
221. This customer feedback was solicited through the official website. *Star Trek: The Experience* (n.d.). Available at www.StarTrekExp.com (accessed 7 January 2008, no longer online 23 September 2016).
222. Like the 'Klingon Encounter', advertising for the new ride personalised its address, this time directly from the Borg: 'We are coming for you.' Ibid. The ride similarly picked out the guest as special, in potentially having a genetic immunity to Borg technology. See Friess, 'Vegas Steels for Borg Invasion'. Migaldi, 'Great Fun While in Las Vegas!'
223. Coman, 'Sin City opts for flesh', p. 11. Eugene Martin Christiansen, 'Gaming and entertainment: an imperfect union?', *Cornell Hotel & Restaurant Administration Quarterly*, April, 36/2 (1995), pp. 79–93. Elaine Underwood, 'Casino gambling's new deal', *Brandweek*, 36/15, 10 April 1995, pp. 21–5.
224. Coman, 'Sin City', p. 11.
225. Ferdinand Tan, quoted in ibid.
226. Quoted in Dunlop, *Building a Dream*, p. 18.
227. Christopher Grove, 'Rollercoasters or high rollers?' *Variety*, 368/1, 11 August 1997, pp. 38–9. Underwood, 'Casino gambling's new deal'.
228. Art Daudelin, 'In Vegas, Resistance is Futile: Trekkers Flock to Borg Invasion 4D', (2004). Available at www.radioworld.com/article/In-Vegas-Resistance-is-Futile/184774 (accessed 22 September 2016). Berns calls *The Experience*

venture 'an ill-fated effort to lure younger customers'. Dave Berns, 'A new direction: new owner promises to make major changes in transformation of Las Vegas Hilton's image', *Hotel & Motel Management*, 215/14, 14 August 1998, p. 28. Mike Weatherford, 'Vegas shows can be unique', reviewjournal. com, 8 February 2004. Available at www.reviewjournal.com/lvrj_home/2004/Feb-08-Sun-2004/living/23149767.html (accessed 14 August 2004, no longer online 23 September 2016).

229. For example: Big Hairy Kev, ' "Star Trek: The Experience" is about to close', 25 March 2006. Available at www.bighairykev.proboards.com/search/results?captcha_id=captcha_search&what_at_least_one=%27Star +Trek%3A+The+Experience%27+is+about+to+close&who_only_made_by=0&display_as=0&fc-token=79157d3c62e7850b7.29426177%7Cr%3Dap-southeast-1%7Cmetaiconclr%3D%2523c0c1c2%7Cmeta%3D1%7Cguitextcolor%3D%2523fc5526%7Cmetabgclr%3D%2523FFFFFF%7Cmeta%3D3%7Cpk%3DC0F5B1D6-CFF5-1D52-0F76-87F4E9F50EC0%7Cinjs%3Dhttps%3A%2F%2Fcdn.funcaptcha.com%2Ffc%2Fassets%2Fgraphics%2Fproboards%2Fproboards-fix.js%7Cat%3D100%7Crid%3D36%7Csurl%3Dhttps%3A%2F%2Ffuncaptcha.com (accessed 10 September 2016).

230. *ipetitions*, 'Save Star Trek: The Experience', (2008). Available at www.ipetitions.com/petition/savestartrekexp/ (accessed 18 September 2008).

231. See Karpovich for an analysis and personal experience of the *Star Trek Adventure*. Karpovich, 'Locating the *"Star Trek* Experience"', p. 216.

232. Roberts, 'Performing science fiction'.

233. The attraction opened in London on 18 December 2002. It featured a number of different experiences, including a *Voyager* shuttle craft ride simulator, a trivia game, props from the feature film *Star Trek: Nemesis* (2002) and the television series *Enterprise*, behind the scenes footage, the three-storey set of Quark's Bar from *DS9*, the *TOS* bridge set, the bridge and warp core sets of 1701-D *Enterprise*, food outlets, the *Enterprise* Federation Mess Hall and the Space Dock Lounge, merchandise at the Starfleet Exchange store, and photo and video superimposition into *TOS* and *TNG*. For the Spanish attraction, see StarTrek.com 'Exhibition Premieres in Spain' (2010). Available at www.startrek.com/article/exhibition-premieres-in-spain (accessed 1 September 2013).

234. 'Starfleet Academy Experience to open on NYC's Intrepid', *StarTrek.com*, 28 April 2016. Available at www.startrek.com/article/starfleet-academy-experience-to-open-july-9-on-nycs-intrepid#sthash.TU0Zmaph.dpuf (accessed 2 June 2017).

235. *Roadside America*, 'Future Birthplace of James T. Kirk', (n.d.). Available at www.roadsideamerica.com/attract/IARIV.html (accessed 29 January 2001) and www.roadsideamerica.com/story/2081 (accessed 23 June 2017). The town

of Vulcan in Alberta, Canada, also has a *Star Trek* festival. 'Vulcan Tourism and Trek Station', (n.d.), *Vulcan Tourism*. Available at www.vulcantourism.com (accessed 23 September 2016). Similarly, Matt Hills notes that Las Vegas tourist guides advertise Kirk's place of death from *Star Trek: Generations* (1994). Hills, *Fan Cultures*, p. 201, n. 29.

236. *Trekfest* (2015). Available at www.trekfest.com (accessed 18 December 2016).
237. Janet Murray and Henry Jenkins, 'Before the holodeck: translating *Star Trek* into digital media', in G. M. Smith (ed.), *On a Silver Platter: CD-ROMS and the Promises of a New Technology* (New York and London: New York University Press, 1999), p. 54.
238. Collins, 'Batman', p. 167.
239. Such as Vir-con. See also Baard, 'Trekkies go boldly, virtually'.
240. John, 'The impact of the internet on a television-based society', *Technology in Society* 22 (2000), p. 284.
241. James A. Knapp, 'Essayistic messages: internet newsgroups as an electronic public sphere', in D. Porter (ed.), *Internet Culture* (New York: Routledge, 1997), p. 183. Linda Carroli, 'Virtual encounters: community or collaborations on the internet?' *Leonardo*, 30/5 (1997), p. 359.
242. Knapp, 'Essayistic messages', pp. 182, 192–4. For a contrary view, see Carroli, 'Virtual encounters', p. 362.
243. Richard Wise, *Multimedia: A Critical Introduction* (London & New York: Routledge, 2000), pp. 184–95.
244. Ibid., pp. 193, 198.
245. See, for example: Bacon-Smith, *Enterprising Women*. Jenkins, *Textual Poachers*. Lewis, *The Adoring Audience*. Sanders, *Science Fiction Fandom*. Tulloch and Jenkins, *Science Fiction Audiences*. Penley, *NASA/TREK*.
246. Murray and Jenkins, 'Before the holodeck', p. 39.
247. Ibid., p. 55. Steve Silberman, 'Fox Slams Bootleg *Millennium* Sites', *Hotwired* Special (1996). Available at http://hotwired.lycos.com/special/millennium/ (accessed 1 April 2001, no longer online 23 September 2016).
248. David Wertheimer, 'Dear Star Trek fan ...' Paramount (1997). Available at www.paramount.com/openletter/ (accessed 19 July 2000, no longer online 23 September 2016).
249. Amanda Lang, 'Viacom Cracks Down on Trek Web Sites', *Financial Post*, 10 January 1997. Available at www.canoe.ca/JamStarTrek/jan10_treksites .html (accessed 1 April 2001, no longer online 22 September 2016).
250. Similarly, the official *Xena: The Warrior Princess* website excluded fans interested in exploring the programme's lesbian subtext. Kirsten Pullen, 'I -love-Xena.com: creating online fan communities', in D. Gauntlett (ed.), *Web.Studies: Rewiring Media Studies for the Digital Age* (London: Arnold, 2000), p. 59.

251. Similarly, when 20th Century Fox threatened *Buffy* fan sites with legal action, one *Buffy* fan argued that Fox's stance was 'akin to a vampire feeding off my blood'. Simoun, quoted in Lynn Burke, 'Fox wants *Buffy* fan sites slain', *Wired*, 1 March 2000. Available at http://archive.wired.com/techbiz/media/news/2000/03/34563 (accessed 22 September 2016). Brian Courtis, 'Buffy Battle', *The Age, Green Guide*, 30 December 1996, p. 6.
252. Kevin Atkinson, 'Viacom as Borg Info Page' (2002). Available at www.kevina.org/protest/ (accessed 1 September 2013).
253. *TNG*, 'I, Borg' (1992).
254. Aeron Davies, *Promotional Cultures: The Rise and Spread of Advertising, Public Relations, Marketing and Branding* (Cambridge: Polity Press, 2013), p. 49. See also: Proctor, 'Beginning again: the reboot phenomenon in comic books, film and beyond', pp. 49–50.
255. I agree with Sue Short, who argues that academic ideas of nerdy Trekkers and heroic Trekkers are 'equally simplistic'. Sue Short, '*Star Trek*: the franchise! – poachers, pirates, and Paramount', in L. Geraghty (ed.), *The Influence of Star Trek on Television, Film and Culture* (Jefferson, NC: McFarland, 2008), p. 184. What I am arguing here is that fans have knowingly constructed themselves as heroic characters within fictional *Star Trek* storytelling.
256. Jason Ellis, 'Big Brother is watching you!' *Wired*, December 1996. Available at http://members.aol.com/mprofile/edit9701.htm (accessed 1 April 2001, no longer online 22 September 2016).
257. Robert V. Kozinets, 'Inno-tribes: *Star Trek* as Wikimedia', in Bernard Cova, Robert V. Kozinets and Avi Shankar (eds), *Consumer Tribes* (Amsterdam: Butterworth-Heinemann, 2007), p. 207.
258. Henry Jenkins, 'Afterword: the future of fandom', in J. Gray, C. Sandvoss and C. L. Harrington (eds), *Fandom: Identities and Communities in a Media World* (New York and London: New York University Press, 2007), pp. 358, 361–2.
259. Joshua Green and Henry Jenkins, 'The moral economy of Web 2.0', in J. Holt and A. Perren (eds), *Media Industries: History, Theory, and Method* (Oxford: Wiley-Blackwell, 2009).
260. Ibid. Henry Jenkins, 'Why Participatory Culture is Not Web 2.0: Some Basic Distinctions', *Confession of an Aca-Fan* (blog). Available at http://henryjen-kins.org/2010/05/why_participatory_culture_is_n.html (accessed 9 February 2016).
261. Derek Johnson, 'Fan-tagonism: factions, institutions, and constitutive hegemonies of fandom', in J. Gray, C. Sandvoss and C. L. Harrington (eds), *Fandom: Identities and Communities in a Media World*, p. 295.
262. Green and Jenkins, 'The moral economy of Web 2.0', p. 222.

263. Thomas Vinciguerra, 'A "Trek" script is grounded in cyberspace', *New York Times*, 28 March 2012. Available at www.nytimes.com/2012/03/29/arts/television/cbs-blocks-use-of-unused-star-trek-script-by-spinrad.html?_r=3&partner=rss&emc=rss& (accessed 1 September 2013).
264. 'CBS's "Rules of Engagement" for Star Trek Fan Films', *The Trek BBS* (2012). Available at www.trekbbs.com/showthread.php?t=187825 (accessed 1 September 2013).
265. Quoted in Vinciguerra, 'A "Trek" script is grounded in cyberspace'.
266. Mircea Eliade, *Rites and Symbols of Initiation*, trans. Willard R. Trask (New York: Harper & Row, 1958, 1994), p. 55.

Conclude ... Then Reboot

1. Djoymi Baker, 'From the Doctor to Captain Kirk: actors and their mythic heroes', in J. Perlich and D. Whitt (eds), *Millennial Mythmaking: Essays on the Power of Science Fiction and Fantasy Literature, Films and Games* (Jefferson, NC: McFarland, 2010), pp. 129–46.
2. Alex Zalben, '10 Totally Spoilery "Star Trek Into Darkness" Easter Eggs', *MTV*, 15 June 2013. Available at http://geek-news.mtv.com/2013/05/16/10-star-trek-into-darkness-easter-eggs/ (accessed 1 September 2013).
3. Box Office Mojo, 'Franchises: Star Trek', (n.d.). Available at www.boxoffic-emojo.com/franchises/chart/?id=startrek.htm (accessed 11 September 2016).
4. Ben Child, 'Into Darkness voted worst Star Trek film by trekkies', *Guardian*, 15 August 2013. Available at www.theguardian.com/film/2013/aug/14/star-trek-into-darkness-voted-worst (accessed 11 September 2016).
5. H. A. Shapiro, 'Old and new heroes: narrative, composition, and subject in Attic Black-Figure', *Classical Antiquity*, 9/1 (1990), p. 148.
6. Abraham Kawa, 'Skewed villainy: the problematic image of the eastern antagonist (or, Dr. No was a monkey)', *The International Journal of the Image*, 4 (2014), p. 53. Ian Crouch, 'Star Trek's best enemy gets reheated', *New Yorker*, 20 May 2013. Available at www.newyorker.com/culture/culture-desk/star-treks-best-enemy-gets-reheated (accessed 17 December 2016).
7. See, for example: Catherine Shoard, 'George Takei: making Sulu gay in new Star Trek is "really unfortunate"', *Guardian*, 8 July 2016. Available at www.the-guardian.com/film/2016/jul/08/star-trek-beyond-george-takei-sulu-really-unfortunate (accessed 12 July 2016).
8. Henry Barnes, 'Simon Pegg joins criticism of Star Trek Beyond trailer', *Guardian*, 18 December 2015. Available at www.theguardian.com/film/2015/dec/18/simon-pegg-critical-of-star-trek-beyond-trailer-justin-lin (accessed 18 February 2016).

9. Luke Holland, 'New Star Trek show in the Netflix era?' *Guardian*, 4 November 2015. Available at www.theguardian.com/culture/2015/nov/03/star-trek-can-prosper-netflix-and-chill-era (accessed 12 July 2016).
10. Jonathan Gray, *Show Sold Separately: Promos, Spoilers, and Other Media Paratexts* (New York: New York University Press, 2010), p. 51.
11. Robert Parker, 'Myths of early Athens', in J. Bremmer (ed.), *Interpretations of Greek Mythology* (London: Croom Helm, 1987), pp. 188–9.
12. John Fiske, *Television Culture* (London and New York: Methuen, 1987), p. 130.
13. 'Captain Kirk tweets space station', *New Scientist*, 2899, 12 January 2013, pp. 4–5

Afterword

1. Michael G. Robinson, 'These are the Voyages? The Post-Jubilee *Trek* Legacy on the *Discovery*, the *Orville*, and the *Callister*', in S. Mittermeier and M. Spychala (eds), *Fighting for the Future: Essays on Star Trek: Discovery* (Liverpool: Liverpool University Press, 2020), p. 85.
2. Sarah Iles Johnston, 'The Greek Mythic Story World', *Arethusa*, 38/3 (2015), p. 309. Eva Miller, 'Retelling Gilgamesh in Star Trek: The Next Generation', in A. Garcia-Ventura and L. Verderame (eds), *Receptions of the Ancient Near East in Popular Culture and Beyond* (Atlanta GA: Lockwood Press, 2020), p. 144. Djoymi Baker, 'Hercules: Transmedia Superhero Mythology', in N. Diak (ed.), *The New Peplum: Essays on Sword and Sandal Films and Television Programs Since the 1990s* (Jefferson NC: McFarland, 2018), pp. 44-62.
3. Robinson, 'These are the Voyages?', pp. 86-87.
4. Clayton Davis, 'Celebrating William Shatner: Top 10 "Star Trek" Movies and TV Shows of the Franchise', *Variety*, 22 March 2021. Available at https://variety.com/lists/best-star-trek-movies-tv-shows-ranked/ (accessed 15 April 2021).
5. Akiva Goldsman quoted in James Hibberd, '"Star Trek" showrunner discusses "Strange New Worlds" Plan, Evolving Q for "Picard"', *The Hollywood Reporter*, 12 April 2021. Available at https://www.hollywoodreporter.com/heat-vision/star-trek-producer-reveals-strange-new-worlds-plan-evolving-q-for-picard (accessed 13 April 2021).
6. Alex Kurtzman quoted in Anthony Pascale, 'Alex Kurtzman says "Section 31" series writers building a "very surprising" Star Trek show', *TrekMovie*, 26 August 2020. Available at https://trekmovie.com/2020/08/26/alex-kurtman-says-writing-team-building-a-very-surprising-section-31-star-trek-series/ (accessed 15 April 2021).
7. Joy Press, 'The Star Trek TV Universe is CBS All Access' Secret Weapon. Will It Keep Expanding Infinitely?', *Vanity Fair*, 29 November 2019. Available at

https://www.vanityfair.com/hollywood/2019/11/the-star-trek-tv-universe-is-cbs-all-access-secret-weapon-can-it-keep-expanding-infinitely (accessed 19 April 2021). Hibberd, '"Star Trek" showrunner'.
8. StarTrek.com, 'INTERVIEW: Discovery Showrunner Aaron Harberts', 14 September 2017. Available at https://intl.startrek.com/article/interview-discovery-showrunner-aaron-harberts (accessed 19 April 2021). See also Liz Shannon Miller, '"Star Trek: Discovery" Star on How Character-Focused "Short Treks" Add to the Epic Mythology of the Franchise', *IndieWire*, 4 October 2018. Available at https://www.indiewire.com/2018/10/star-trek-discovery-mary-wiseman-on-short-treks-tilly-interview-1202009417/ (accessed 19 April 2021).
9. Michael Chabon, 'Notes on the Myth of Ganmadan (The end of the world)', *Medium*, 1 April 2021. Available at https://michaelchabon.medium.com/notes-on-the-myth-of-ganmadan-the-end-of-the-world-e2b1595cdb46 (accessed 21 April 2021). The twin planets Romulus and Remus are named after the mythical twin founders of Rome who were raised by a she-wolf.
10. Scott Collura, 'Star Trek: "Calypso" writer Michael Chabon on Trek time jumps, adapting The Odyssey, rethinking Picard and more', *IGN*, 10 November 2018. Available at https://www.ign.com/articles/2018/11/09/star-trek-calypso-writer-michael-chabon-on-trek-time-jumps-adapting-the-odyssey-rethinking-picard-and-more (accessed 21 April 2021). Ruth Richards, 'Calypso: The Posthuman female *in Star Trek Discovery*', unpublished paper presented to *Popular Culture Association of Australia and New Zealand* conference, July 2019, RMIT University, Australia.
11. The Indigenous American character Chakotay in *Voyager* was not authentically cast but was nonetheless used to fashion a fictional myth of the Sky Spirits in 'Tattoo' (1995), albeit in rather broad and problematic terms. Christian Jimenez, 'Disturbing Parallel: The shifting politics of racial inclusion and exclusion in *Star Trek: Voyager*', in R. L. Lively (ed.), *Exploring Star Trek: Voyager Critical Essays* (Jefferson NC: McFarland, 2020), pp. 198, 202-203.
12. Eva Miller, 'Retelling Gilgamesh in *Star Trek: The Next Generation*', p. 155. Indeed, upon reflection I would suggest this imbalance is also evident in my own reading of 'Darmok' in *To Boldly Go*.
13. Michael Wessels, *Bushman Letters: Interpreting /Xam narrative* (Johannesburg: Witz University Press, 2010), p. 242.
14. Wessels, *Bushman Letters*, pp. 241-262.
15. StarTrek.com, 'Warp Five with Brandon Schultz', 13 December 2019. Available at https://intl.startrek.com/news/warp-five-with-brandon-schultz (accessed 20 April 2021). Ryan Britt, '*Star Trek* returns to animation for a short that was almost in the *Discovery* finale', *SyFyWire*, 14 December 2019. Available at https://www.syfy.com/syfywire/star-trek-returns-to-animation-for-a-short-that-was-almost-in-the-discovery-finale (accessed 20 April 2021).

16. Kwasu David Tembo, '"Far from gay cities and the ways of men": Exploring wandering and homecoming in *The Odyssey* and *Star Trek: Voyager*', in R. L. Lively (ed.), *Exploring Star Trek: Voyager Critical Essays* (Jefferson NC: McFarland, 2020), pp. 15-31.
17. Leora Hadas, 'J. J. Abrams, "Star Trek", and promotional authorship', *Cinema Journal*, 56/2 (2017), pp. 46-66.
18. M. Keith Booker, *Star Trek: A Cultural History* (Lanham: Rowman & Littlefield, 2018), p. 136.

Bibliography

Abbott, Stacey, "'I want to do bad things with you': The television horror title sequence', in L. Geraghty (ed.), *Popular Media Cultures: Fans, Audiences and Paratexts* (New York: Palgrave Macmillan, 2015).

Aden, Roger C., *Popular Stories and Promised Lands: Fan Cultures and Symbolic Pilgrimages* (Tuscoloosa, AL, and London: University of Alabama Press, 1999).

Alfano, Sean, 'CBS, Viacom Formally Split: Now Traded Separately on Wall Street, Shares of Two Companies Rise', 3 January 2006. Available at www.cbsnews.com/stories/2006/01/03/business/main1176111.shtml?tag=mncol (accessed 1 June 2010).

Altman, Rick, 'Television Sound', in H. Newcomb (ed.), *Television: The Critical View*, 4th edn (New York: Oxford University Press, 1987).

Altman, Rick, *Film/Genre* (London: BFI, 1999).

Amory, Cleveland, 'The Time Tunnel', *TV Guide*, 29 October 1966, p.25.

Amory, Cleveland, 'The Invaders', *TV Guide*, 18 February 1967, p. 12.

Amory, Cleveland, 'Review: Star Trek', *TV Guide*, 25 November 1967, p. 1.

A Music Fan from Lafayette, 'Another effective McCarthy score', 16 May 2002. Available at www.amazon.com/exec/obidos/tg/d...r-reviews&show=-submittime&start-at=21 (accessed 26 September 2003, no longer online 22 September 2016).

A Music Fan from Miami, 'More bland filler music', 19 May 2002. Available at www.amazon.com/exec/obidos/tg/d...r-reviews&show=-submittime&start-at=21 (accessed 26 September 2003, no longer online 22 September 2016).

Anders, Charlie Jane, 'Simon Pegg's Star Trek Reboot Theory: Is this the 'Mirror' Crew?' *i09*, 9 May 2013. Available at http://io9.com/simon-peggs-star-trek-reboot-theory-is-this-the-mirro-499064330 (accessed 26 November 2015).

Anderson, Christopher, *Hollywood TV: The Studio System in the Fifties* (Austin, TX: University of Texas Press, 1994).

Andreadis, Athena, 'The Enterprise finds twin Earths everywhere it goes, but future colonizers of distant planets won't be so lucky', *Astronomy*, Jan (1999), p. 64.

Anonymous, 'The Homeric Hymn to Demeter', trans. Helene P. Foley, in H. P. Foley, *The Homeric 'Hymn to Demeter': Translation, Commentary, and Interpretive Essays* (Princeton, NJ: Princeton University Press, 2013).

Apollodorus, *The Library*, trans. James G. Frazer, Vol. 1 (Cambridge, MA: Harvard University Press, London: William Heinemann, 1921, 1967). Available at www

Bibliography

.perseus.tufts.edu/cgi-bin/ptext?lookup=Apollod.+1.1.1 (accessed 22 September 2016).

Apple, Rima D. and Apple, Michael W., 'Screening science', *Isis*, 84 (1993), pp. 750–4.

The Arizona Newsroom, 'BORG Invasion 4D Opens', 10 February 2004. Available at www.azreporter.com/idirectory/lasvegas/news/borginvasion.html (accessed 14 August 2004, no longer online 22 September 2016).

Arlow, Jacob A., 'Scientific cosmogony, mythology, and immortality', *Psychoanalytic Quarterly*, 51 (1982), pp. 177–195.

Art. [*sic*], 'Captain Video', *Variety*, 13 July 1955, no pagination. Reprinted in H. H. Prouty (ed.), *Variety Television Reviews, Vol. 5, 1954–1956* (New York: Garland, 1989-91).

Asa, Robert, 'Classic *Star Trek* and the death of God: a case study of "Who Mourns for Adonais?"', in J. E. Porter and D. L. McLaren (eds), *Star Trek and Sacred Ground: Explorations of Star Trek, Religion and American Culture* (Albany, NY: State University of New York Press, 1999).

Asherman, Allan, *The Star Trek Compendium* (New York: Pocket Books, 1989, 1993).

Ashworth, William B., Jr., 'Allegorical astronomy', *The Sciences*, 25/5 (1985), pp. 34–7.

Asimov, Isaac, 'What are a few galaxies among friends?' *TV Guide*, 26 November 1966, pp. 6–9.

Asimov, Isaac, 'Mr. Spock is Dreamy', *TV Guide*, 29 April 1967), pp. 9–11.

Astronomy, 'Interview With An Alien: Although Tim Russ plays an alien on *Star Trek Voyager*, his interest in astronomy is no act,' 28/9, September (2000), p. 44.

Atkin, Denny, 'The science of *Star Trek*', *Omni*, 17/8, Fall (1995), p. 46.

Atkinson, Kevin, 'Viacom as Borg Info Page', (2002). Available at www.kevina.org/protest/ (accessed 1 September 2013).

Aufderheide, Patricia, 'The look of the sound', in T. Gitlin (ed.), *Watching Television* (New York: Pantheon, 1986).

Baard, Mark, 'Trekkies go boldly, virtually', *Wired News*, 24 July 2002. Available at www.wired.com/news/culture/0,1284,53876,00.html (accessed 14 August 2004, no longer online 22 September 2016).

Bacon-Smith, Camille, *Enterprising Women: Television Fandom and the Creation of Popular Myth* (Philadelphia, PA: University of Pennsylvania Press, 1992).

Baker, Djoymi, "'Every old trick is new again': myth in quotations and the Star Trek franchise', *Popular Culture Review* 12/1 (2001), pp. 67–77. Reprinted in M. W. Kapell (ed.), *Star Trek as Myth: Essays on Symbol and Archetype at the Final Frontier* (Jefferson, NC: McFarland, 2010).

Baker, Djoymi, 'Contested Spaces: The internet ate my TV, the TV company ate my internet site', *The Refractory: A Journal of Entertainment Media*, 1, October (2002). Available at https://refractory-journal.com/contested-spaces-the-internet-ate-my-tv-the-tv-company-ate-my-internet-site-djoymi-baker/ (accessed 16 February 2021).

Bibliography

Baker, Djoymi, 'Are we there yet? Star Trek and the future history of space exploration', in *Resistance is Futile*, exhibition catalogue (Southbank, VCA Margaret Lawrence Gallery, 2006). Reprinted in K. Daw and V. McInnes (eds), *Bureau* (Melbourne: VCA Margaret Lawrence Gallery, University of Melbourne, 2008).

Baker, Djoymi, "'The illusion of magnitude': adapting the epic from film to television", *Senses of Cinema*, 41 (2006). Available at www.sensesofcinema.com/2006/film-history-conference-papers/adapting-epic-film-tv/ (accessed 6 September 2013).

Baker, Djoymi, 'From the Doctor to Captain Kirk: actors and their mythic heroes,' in J. Perlich and D. Whitt (eds), *Millennial Mythmaking: Essays on the Power of Science Fiction and Fantasy Literature, Films and Games* (Jefferson, NC: McFarland, 2010).

Baker, Djoymi, 'Terms of excess: binge-viewing as epic-viewing in the streaming era', in M. Wiatrowski and C. Barker (eds), *The Age of Netflix: Critical Essays on Streaming Media, Digital Delivery and Instant Access* (Jefferson, NC: McFarland, 2017).

Baker, Djoymi, 'Hercules: Transmedia superhero mythology', in N. Diak (ed.), *The New Peplum: Essays on Sword and Sandal Films and Television Programs Since the 1990s* (Jefferson NC: McFarland, 2018).

Bakhtin, Mikhail, 'Discourse in the novel', in M. Holquist (ed.), *The Dialogic Imagination: Four Essays*, trans. Caryl Emerson and Michael Holquist (Austin, TX, and London: University of Texas Press, 1981).

Bakhtin, Mikhail, *Rabelais and his World*, trans. Helene Iswolsky (Cambridge, MA: MIT Press, 1968).

Balio, Tino, 'Introduction to Part I', in T. Balio (ed.), *Hollywood in the Age of Television* (Boston, MA: Unwin Hyman, 1990).

Barnes, Henry, 'Simon Pegg joins criticism of Star Trek Beyond trailer', *The Guardian*, 18 December 2015. Available at www.theguardian.com/film/2015/dec/18/simon-pegg-critical-of-star-trek-beyond-trailer-justin-lin (accessed 18 February 2016).

Barnouw, Erik, *Tube of Plenty: The Evolution of American Television*, 2nd edn (New York: Oxford University Press, 1990).

Barr, Marleen S., "'All good things ...': the end of *Star Trek: The Next Generation*, the end of Camelot – the end of the tale about woman as handmaid to patriarchy as Superman', in Taylor Harrison et al (eds), *Enterprise Zones: Critical Positions on Star Trek* (Boulder, CO: Westview Press, 1996).

Barrett, Michèle and Duncan Barrett, *Star Trek: The Human Frontier* (New York: Routledge 2001).

Barthes, Roland, *Mythologies*, trans. Annette Lavers (London: Vintage, 1957, 1993).

Barthes, Roland, *Image Music Text*, trans. Stephen Heath (London: Fontana Press, 1977).

Bibliography

Barthes, Roland, 'Theory of the text', in R. Young (ed.), *Unifying the Text: A Post-Structuralist Reader* (London and New York: Routledge, 1981).

Baruch, Dorothy Walter, 'Radio rackets, movie murders and killer cartoons', *New Ways to Discipline: You and Your Child Today* (New York: McGraw-Hill, 1949). Reprinted in H. Jenkins (ed.), *The Children's Culture Reader* (New York: New York University Press, 1998).

Bascom, William, "The forms of folklore: prose narratives', *Journal of American Folklore* 78 (1965), pp. 3–20. Reprinted in A. Dundes (ed.), *Sacred Narrative: Readings in the Theory of Myth* (Berkeley, CA: University of California Press, 1984).

Batra, N. D., 'The mini-series: epic in the age of television', in *The Hour of Television: Critical Approaches* (Metuchen, NJ: Scarecrow Press, 1987).

Baudrillard, Jean, 'Hysterisis of the millennium', *The Illusion of the End*, trans. Chris Turner (Cambridge: Polity Press, 1994).

Behr, Ira Steven, *The Ferengi Rules of Acquisition* (New York: Pocket Books, 1995).

Belk, Russell W., 'Three coins in a Caesar's Palace fountain: interpreting Las Vegas', in *Advances in Consumer Research*, 25 (1998), pp. 7–9.

Belk, Russell W., 'May the farce be with you: on Las Vegas and consumer infantalization', *Consumption, Markets and Culture*, 4/2 (2000), pp. 102–24.

Bellows, Henry Adams, trans., *The Poetic Edda* (Princeton, NJ: Princeton University Press & New York: American Scandinavian Foundation, 1936). Available at www.sacred-texts.com/neu/poe/index.htm (accessed 13 August 2004).

Belton, John, *Widescreen Cinema* (Cambridge, MA: Harvard University Press, 1992).

Bennett, Tony and Woollacott, Janet, *Bond and Beyond: The Political Career of a Popular Hero* (New York: Methuen, 1987).

Bernardi, Daniel Leonard, *Star Trek and History: Race-ing Toward a White Future* (New Brunswick, NJ: Rutgers University Press, 1998).

Berns, Dave, 'Hilton fined for Trek incident', in *Las Vegas Review-Journal*, 22 May 1998. Available at www.reviewjournal.com/lvrj_home/1998/May-22-Fri-1998/business/7544970.html (accessed 3 January 2003, no longer online 22 September 2016).

Berns, Dave, 'A new direction: new owner promises to make major changes in transformation of Las Vegas Hilton's image', in *Hotel & Motel Management*, 215/14, 14 August 1998, p. 28.

Biagioli, Mario, 'Galileo the Emblem Maker', *Isis*, 81 (1990), pp. 230–58.

Bick, Ilsa J., 'Boys in space: *Star Trek*, latency, and the neverending story', in T. Harrison, S. Projansky, K. A. Ono and E. R. Helford (eds), *Enterprise Zones: Critical Positions on Star Trek* (Boulder, CO: Westview Press, 1996).

Big Hairy Kev, "Star Trek: The Experience' is about to close', 25 March 2006. Available at www.bighairykev.proboards.com/search/results?captcha_id=captcha_search

Bibliography

&what_at_least_one=%27Star+Trek%3A+The+Experience%27+is+about+to+close&who_only_made_by=0&display_as=0&fc-token=79157d3c62e7850b7.29426177%7Cr%3Dap-southeast-1%7Cmetaiconclr%3D%2523c0c1c2%7Cmeta%3D1%7Cguitextcolor%3D%2523fc5526%7Cmetabgclr%3D%2523FFFFFF%7Cmeta%3D3%7Cpk%3DC0F5B1D6-CFF5-1D52-0F76-87F4E9F50EC0%7Cinjs%3Dhttps%3A%2F%2Fcdn.funcaptcha.com%2Ffc%2Fassets%2Fgraphics%2Fproboards%2Fproboards-fix.js%7Cat%3D100%7Crid%3D36%7Csurl%3Dhttps%3A%2F%2Ffuncaptcha.com (accessed 10 September 2016).

Bischoff, David, 'Behind the scenes of Star Trek: Deep Space Nine', *Omni*, 15/5, Feb–March (1993), pp. 34–41.

Blackhorse, Amanda, 'Blackhorse: do you prefer 'Native American' or 'American Indian'? 6 prominent voices respond', *Indian Country Today Media Network*, 21 May 2015. Available at www.indiancountrytodaymedianetwork.com/2015/05/21/blackhorse-do-you-prefer-native-american-or-american-indian-6-prominent-voices-respond (accessed 18 February 2016).

Blair, Karin, 'The garden in the machine: the why of *Star Trek*', *Journal of Popular Culture*, 13/2, Fall (1979), pp. 310–20.

Blair, Karin, 'Sex and *Star Trek*', *Science-Fiction Studies*, 10/31 (1983), pp. 292–7.

Bolter, Jay David and Grusin, Richard, *Remediation: Understanding New Media* (Cambridge, MA: MIT Press, 1999).

Bond, Jeff, *The Music of Star Trek* (Los Angeles, CA: Lone Eagle, 1999).

Booker, M. Keith, *Star Trek: A Cultural History* (Lanham: Rowman & Littlefield, 2018).

Box Office Mojo, 'Franchises: *Star Trek*', (n.d.). Available at www.boxofficemojo.com/franchises/chart/?id=startrek.htm (accessed 11 September 2016).

Brauer, Ralph with Brauer, Donna, *The Horse, The Gun and the Piece of Property: Changing Images of the TV Western* (Bowling Green, OH: Bowling Green University Popular Press, 1975).

Bremmer, Jan (ed.), *Interpretations of Greek Mythology* (London: Croom Helm, 1987).

Bredekamp, Horst, 'Gazing hands and blind spots: Galileo as draftsman', *Science in Context*, 13/3–4 (2000), pp. 423–62.

Britt, Ryan, '*Star Trek* returns to animation for a short that was almost in the *Discovery* finale', *SyFyWire*, 14 December 2019. Available at https://www.syfy.com/syfywire/star-trek-returns-to-animation-for-a-short-that-was-almost-in-the-discovery-finale (accessed 20 April 2021).

Brockway, Robert W., *Myth: From the Ice Age to Mickey Mouse* (Albany, NY: State University of New York Press, 1993).

Brode, Douglas, 'Introduction', in D. Brode and S. T. Brode (eds), *The Star Trek Universe: Franchising the Final Frontier* (Lanham, MD: Rowman & Littlefield, 2015).

Bibliography

Brooks, Tim and Marsh, Earle F. (eds), *The Complete Directory of Prime Time Network and Cable TV Shows 1946–Present*, 7th edn (New York: Ballantine Books, 1999).

Bryman, Alan, *Disney and His Worlds* (London and New York: Routledge, 1995).

Bryman, Alan, 'The Disneyization of Society', *Sociological Review*, 47/1, February (1999).

Buitron-Oliver, Diana and Cohen, Beth, 'Between Skylla and Penelope: female characters of the Odyssey in Archaic and Classical Greek art', in B. Cohen (ed.), *The Distaff Side: Representing the Female in Homer's Odyssey* (New York: Oxford University Press, 1995).

Bukatman, Scott, "There's always a Tomorrowland: Disney and the hypercinematic experience", October 57, Summer (1991), pp. 55–78.

Burke, Lynn, 'Fox Wants *Buffy* fan sites slain', *Wired*, 1 March 2000. Available at http://archive.wired.com/techbiz/media/news/2000/03/34563 (accessed 22 September 2016).

Burkert, Walter, *Structure and History in Greek Mythology and Ritual* (Berkeley, CA: University of California Press, 1979).

Burkert, Walter, 'Homo Necans', in R. A. Segal (ed.), *Myth and Ritual Theory: An Anthology* (Malden, MA, and Oxford: Blackwell, 1998).

Buscombe, Edward, "The idea of genre in the American cinema', in B. K. Grant (ed.), *Film Genre Reader II* (Austin, TX: University of Texas Press, 1995).

Bush, W. Stephen, 'Homer's Odyssey. Three Reels. (Milano Films.)', pp. 941–2.

Caillan, 'UPN 'Enterprise' Promos Feature New Footage', *Trek Today*, 2 August 2010. Available at www.trektoday.com/news/020801_01.shtml (accessed 26 January 2008).

Caldwell, Richard S., *The Origins of the Gods: A Psychoanalytic Study of Greek Theogonic Myth* (New York and Oxford: Oxford University Press, 1989).

Campbell, Kim, 'Star Trek crew still 'Troubled with Tribbles,' 30 years later', *The Christian Science Monitor*, 7 November 1996. Available at http://www.csmonitor .com/1996/1107/110796.feat.whathapp.1.html (accessed 21 June 2017).

Cantour, Paul A., 'From Shakespeare to Wittgenstein: 'Darmok' and cultural literacy', in J. T. Eberl and Kevin S. Decker (ed.), *Star Trek and Philosophy: The Wrath of Kant* (Chicago & La Salle, IL: Open Court, 2008)

Cardazo, Yvette and Hirsch, Bill, 'Take a Look at Las Vegas', *Daily Herald*, Chicago (n.d.). Available at www.dailyherald.com/oldtravel/leadstory/dhhtm /leadstory41.htm (accessed 13 August 2004, no longer online 22 September 2016).

Carroll, Larry, 'J. J. Abrams Responds to "Star Trek" Fans' Theories', *MTV*, 20 May 2009. Available at http://www.mtv.com/news/1611878/jj-abrams-responds-to -star-trek-fans-theories/ (accessed 22 September 2016).

Bibliography

Carroli, Linda, 'Virtual encounters: community or collaborations on the internet?' *Leonardo*, 30/5 (1997), pp. 359–63.

Cawelti, John G., *The Six Gun Mystique* (Bowling Green, OH: Bowling Green University Press, 1971).

Chabon, Michael, 'Notes on the Myth of Ganmadan (The end of the world)', *Medium*, 1 April 2021. Available at https://michaelchabon.medium.com/notes-on-the-myth-of-ganmadan-the-end-of-the-world-e2b1595cdb46 (accessed 21 April 2021).

Chan. [*sic*], 'Tom Corbett, Space Cadet', *Variety*, 4 October 1950. Reprinted in H. H. Prouty (ed.), *Variety Television Reviews, Vol. 3, 1923–1950* (New York: Garland, 1989–91).

Chesebro, James W., 'Communication, values, and popular television series – a four year assessment', in H. Newcomb (ed.), *Television: The Critical View* (New York: Oxford University Press, 1987).

Child, Ben, 'Into Darkness voted worst Star Trek film by trekkies', *The Guardian*, 15 August 2013. Available at www.theguardian.com/film/2013/aug/14/star-trek-into-darkness-voted-worst (accessed 11 September 2016).

Chin, Bertha, Bethan Jones, Myles McNutt, and Luke Pebler 'Veronica Mars Kickstarter and crowd funding', *Transformative Works & Cultures*, 15 (2014).

Christiansen, Eugene Martin and Brinkerhoff-Jacobs, Julie, 'Gaming and entertainment: an imperfect union?' *Cornell Hotel & Restaurant Administration Quarterly*, April, 36/2 (1995), pp. 79–93.

Clarke, Howard W., *Homer's Readers: A Historical Introduction to the Iliad and the Odyssey* (Newark, DE: University of Delaware Press, 1981).

Claus, Peter J., 'A structuralist appreciation of "Star Trek"', in J. B. Cole (ed.), *Anthropology for the Eighties* (New York: The Free Press, 1982).

Clute, John and Nicholls, Peter, *The Encyclopedia of Science Fiction* (London: Orbit, 1993, 1999).

Cochrane, Nathan, 'Back to the future: Scotty, you'll flip over our antique mobile phone', *The Age*, 3 March 1998, p. E4.

Cohen, Erik, 'Pilgrimage and tourism: convergence and divergence', in A. Morinis (ed.), *Sacred Journeys: The Anthropology of Pilgrimage* (Westport, CT: Greenwood, 1992).

Cohen, I. Bernard, *Album of Science: From Leonardo to Lavoisier 1450–1800* (New York: Scribner, 1980).

Collins, Jim, *Uncommon Cultures: Popular Culture and Post-Modernism* (New York: Routledge, 1989).

Collins, Jim, 'Batman: the movie, the narrative, the hyperconscious', in R. E. Pearson and W. Uricchio (eds), *The Many Lives of the Batman: Critical Approaches to a Superhero and His Media* (New York, NY: Routledge & London: BFI, 1991).

Bibliography

Collins, Jim, *Architectures of Excess: Cultural Life in the Information Age* (New York: Routledge, 1995).

Collura, Scott, 'Star Trek: 'Calypso' writer Michael Chabon on Trek time jumps, adapting The Odyssey, rethinking Picard and more', *IGN*, 10 November 2018. Available at https://www.ign.com/articles/2018/11/09/star-trek-calypso-writer-michael-chabon-on-trek-time-jumps-adapting-the-odyssey-rethinking-picard-and-more (accessed 21 April 2021).

Coman, Julian, 'Sin City opts for flesh rather than families after big losses', *The Age*, 16 December 2002, p. 11.

Cooper, Chris, *Star Trek: Telepathy War*, 1/1, November (1997).

Consolmagno, Guy J., 'Astronomy, science fiction and popular culture: 1277 to 2001 (and beyond)', *Leonardo*, 29/2 (1996), pp. 127–32.

Coupe, Laurence, *Myth* (London and New York: Routledge, 1997).

Courtis, Brian, 'Buffy Battle', *The Age*, Green Guide, 30 December 1996), p. 6.

Coyle, J., "Veronica Mars' Kickstarter legacy is cloudy', *Huffington Post*, 13 March 2014. Available at www.huffingtonpost.com/2014/03/13/veronica-mars-kickstarter_n_4958016.html (accessed 10 February 2016, no longer online 22 September 2016).

Cranny-Francis, Anne, 'Sexuality and sex-role stereotyping in Star Trek', *Science Fiction Studies*, 12/37 (1985), pp. 274–84.

Crouch, Ian, 'Star Trek's best enemy gets reheated', *New Yorker*, 20 May 2013. Available at www.newyorker.com/culture/culture-desk/star-treks-best-enemy-gets-reheated (accessed 17 December 2016).

Daku. [sic], 'Superman on Earth (*Superman*)', *Variety*, 11 February 1953. Reprinted in H. H. Prouty (ed.), *Daily Variety Television Reviews, Vol. 1, 1946–1956* (New York: Garland, 1989–91).

Daku. [sic], 'The Man from 1997 (*Conflict*)', *Variety*, 29 November 1956. Reprinted in H. H. Prouty (ed.), *Daily Variety Television Reviews, Vol. 1, 1946–1956* (New York: Garland, 1989–91).

Daudelin, Art, 'In Vegas, Resistance is Futile: Trekkers Flock to Borg Invasion 4D', (2004). Available at www.radioworld.com/article/In-Vegas-Resistance-is-Futile/184774 (accessed 22 September 2016).

Davies, Aeron, *Promotional Cultures: The Rise and Spread of Advertising, Public Relations, Marketing and Branding* (Cambridge: Polity Press, 2013).

Davis, Clayton, 'Celebrating William Shatner: Top 10 'Star Trek' movies and TV shows of the Franchise', *Variety*, 22 March 2021. Available at https://variety.com/lists/best-star-trek-movies-tv-shows-ranked/ (accessed 15 April 2021).

Dear, Michael J., 'A tale of two cities. 2. Las Vegas', *The Postmodern Urban Condition* (Malden, MA: Blackwell Publishers, 2000).

Denson, Shane, 'Marvel Comics' Frankenstein: a case study in the media of serial figures', *Amerikastudien*, 56/4 (2011), pp. 531–53.

Bibliography

Detienne, Marcel, *The Creation of Mythology*, trans. Margaret Cook (Chicago, IL: University of Chicago Press, 1986).

De Vries, Jan, *Heroic Legend and Heroic Song*, trans. B. J. Timmer (New York: Arno Press, 1978).

Doherty, Lillian Eileen, 'Sirens, muses and female narrators in the *Odyssey*', in B. Cohen (ed.), *The Distaff Side: Representing the Female in Homer's Odyssey* (New York: Oxford University Press, 1995).

Doherty, Lillian Eileen, *Siren Songs: Gender, Audiences, and Narrators in the Odyssey* (Ann Arbor, MI: University of Michigan Press, 1998).

Dowden, Ken, *The Uses of Greek Mythology* (London and New York: Routledge, 1992).

Dowden, Ken, 'Approaching women through myth: Vital tool or self-delusion?' in R. Hawley and B. Levick (eds), *Women in Antiquity: New Assessments* (London and New York: Routledge, 1995).

Dowden, Ken, 'Homer's sense of text', *Journal of Hellenic Studies* cxvi (1996), pp. 47–61.

Drucker, Susan J., and Cathcart, Robert S., 'The Hero as a communication phenomenon', in S. J. Drucker and R. S. Cathcart (eds), *American Heroes in a Media Age* (Creskill, NJ: Hampton Press, 1994).

Duchovnay, Gerald, 'From big screen to small box: adapting science fiction film for television', in J. P. Telotte (ed.), *The Essential Science Fiction Television Reader* (Lexington, KY: University Press of Kentucky, 2008).

Dudsic, Greg, 'Hotels win big on high-tech attractions', *Variety*, 10 August 1998, pp. 32–3.

Dumoulin, Jim, 'Enterprise (OV-101)', Kennedy Space Center (1994). Available at www.science.ksc.nasa.gov/shuttle/resources/orbiters/enterprise.html (accessed 18 December 2016).

Dundes, Alan (ed.), *Sacred Narrative: Readings in the Theory of Myth* (Berkeley, CA: University of California Press, 1984).

Dunlop, Beth, *Building a Dream: The Art of Disney Architecture* (New York: Harry N. Abrams, 1996).

Easlea, Brian, *Witch Hunting, Magic and the New Philosophy: An Introduction to Debates of the Scientific Revolution 1450–1750* (Brighton: Harvester Press & Atlantic Highlands, NJ: Humanities Press, 1980).

Eckert, Charles W., 'The English cine-structuralists', *Film Comment* 9/3 (1973), pp. 46–51.

Eckert, Charles W., 'Shall we deport Lévi-Strauss?' *Film Quarterly*, 27/3, Spring (1974), pp. 63–5.

Eco, Umberto, *Faith in Fakes*, trans. William Weaver (London: Secker & Warburg, 1983).

Edmunds, Lowell, 'Myth in Homer', in I. Morris and B. Powell (eds), *A New Companion to Homer* (Leiden and New York: Brill, 1997).

Bibliography

Eliade, Mircea, *Rites and Symbols of Initiation*, trans. Willard R. Trask (New York: Harper & Row, 1958, 1994).
Elley, Derek, *The Epic Film: Myth and History* (London: Routledge, 1984).
Ellington, Jane E. and Critelli, Joseph W., 'Analysis of a modern myth: The Star Trek series', *Extrapolation* 24/3 (1983), pp. 241–50.
Ellis, John, *Visible Fictions: Cinema: Television: Video* (London: Routledge, 1982, 1992).
Ellis, Jason, 'Big Brother is watching you!' *Wired*, December 1996. Available at http://members.aol.com/mprofile/edit9701.htm (accessed 1 April 2001, no longer online 22 September 2016).
Erdmann, Terry J. with Block, Paula M., *Star Trek: Deep Space Nine Companion* (New York: Pocket Books, 2000).
Ertel, Ivan D., and Newkirk, Roland W., with Brooks, Courtney G., *The Apollo Spacecraft: A Chronology*, NASA SP-4009, Volume IV (Washington, DC: The NASA Historical Series, Scientific and Technical Information Office, National Aeronautics and Space Administration, 1978), Part 1 E. Available at www.hq.nasa.gov/office/pao/History/SP-4009/cover.htm (accessed 6 October 2003).
Eskelinen, Markku, 'The gaming situation', *Game Studies*, 1/1, July (2001). Available at www.gamestudies.org/0101/eskelinen/ (accessed 8 December 2004).
Ezell, Edward C. and Ezell, Linda N., *On Mars: Exploration of the Red Planet, 1958–1978* (Washington, DC: National Aeronautics and Space Administration, The NASA History Series, SP-4212, Scientific and Technical Information Branch, 1984). Available at www.history.nasa.gov/SP-4212/on-mars.html (accessed 8 December 2004).
Ferguson, Kathy E., 'This species which is not one: identity practices in *Star Trek: Deep Space Nine*', *Strategies*, 15/2 (2002), pp. 181–95.
Ferguson, Kitty, *Tycho and Kepler: The Strange Partnership that Revolutionised Astronomy* (London: Review, 2002).
Feuer, Jane, 'Narrative form in American network television', in C. MacCabe (ed.), *High Theory/Low Culture: Analysing Television and Film* (Manchester: Manchester University Press, 1986).
Finney, Martha I., 'High-stakes relationships', Association Management, March, 49/3 (1997), pp. 64–9.
Fischer, Stuart, *Kids' TV: The First 25 Years* (New York: Facts on File Publications, 1983).
Fiske, John, *Television Culture* (London and New York: Methuen, 1987).
Fiske, John and Hartley, John, *Reading Television* (London: Methuen, 1978).
Foley, John M., *Immanent Art: From Structure to Meaning in Traditional Oral Epic* (Bloomington and Indianapolis, IN: Indiana University Press, 1991).
Foley, John M., *The Singer of Tales in Performance* (Bloomington and Indianapolis, IN: Indiana University Press, 1995).

Bibliography

Foley, John M., 'Oral tradition and its implications', in I. Morris and B. Powell (eds), *A New Companion to Homer* (Leiden and New York: Brill, 1997).

Ford, Andrew, 'Epic as genre', in I. Morris and B. Powell (eds), *A New Companion to Homer* (Leiden and New York: Brill, 1997).

Fornäs, Johan, 'The words of music', *Popular Music and Society*, 26/1, February (2003), pp. 37–51.

Fraser, George MacDonald, *The Hollywood History of the World* (London: Penguin, 1988).

Frazer, *The Golden Bough: A Study in Magic and Religion* (London: Macmillan, 1915).

Frazetti, Daryl G., 'Star Trek and the Culture of Fandom', 26 April 2011. Available at http://www.startrek.com/article/star-trek-and-the-culture-of-fandom (accessed 21 June 2017).

Freeman, Kathleen, *Ancilla to the Pre-Socratic Philosophers* (Oxford: Basil Blackwell, 1948).

Freeman, Kathleen, *The Pre-Socratic Philosophers* (Oxford: Basil Blackwell, 1953).

Friess, Steve, 'Vegas Steels for Borg Invasion', *WiredNews*, 5 March 2004. Available at http://archive.wired.com/gaming/gamingreviews/news/2004/03/62538?currentPage=all (accessed 22 September 2016).

Freud, Sigmund, *The Standard Edition of the Complete Psychological Works of Sigmund Freud*, trans. James Strachey (London: Hogarth, 1955).

Frith, Simon, *Music for Pleasure: Essays in the Sociology of Pop* (Cambridge: Polity Press, 1988).

Frost, Tim, 'Just an illusion', *Home Entertainment*, April (1994), pp. 34–8.

Gao-kutari, 'Not really the Final Frontier', 23 July 2002. Available at www.amazon.com/exec/obidos/tg/detail/-/B0000658PQ/ref=cm_rev_next/102-9724734-3849729?v=glance&s=music&vi=customer-reviews&show=-submittime&start-at=11 (accessed 16 October 2003).

Garcia, Jane, 'Trekking boldly back to the beginning', *The Age*, Green Guide, 21 February 2002, p. 14.

Garcia, Oskar, "'Trek' fans, want Picard's chair? It's for sale", Associated Press, 9 April 2010. Available at www.democraticunderground.com/discuss/duboard.php?az=view_all&address=105x9327273 (accessed 23 June 2017).

Garoian, Charles R. and Mathews, John D., 'A common impulse in art and science', *Leonardo*, 29/3 (1996), pp. 193–6.

Garrard, Reginald D., 'A new 'sound' for a new take on the Star Trek saga!' 26 May 2002. Available at www.amazon.com/exec/obidos/tg/detail/-/B0000658PQ/ref=cm_rev_next/102-9724734-3849729?v=glance&s=music&vi=customer-reviews&show=-submittime&start-at=21 (accessed 16 October 2003).

Genette, Gérard, *Palimpsests: Literature in the Second Degree*, trans. Channa Newman and Claude Doubinsky (Lincoln, NE, and London: University of Nebraska Press, 1997).

Bibliography

Geraghty, Lincoln, '"Carved from the rock experiences of our daily lives": Reality and Star Trek's multiple histories', *European Journal of American Culture*, 21/3 (2002), pp. 160–76.

Geraghty, Lincoln, 'Creating and comparing myth in twentieth-century science fiction: Star Trek and Star Wars', *Literature/Film Quarterly*, 33/3 (2005), pp. 191–200.

Geraghty, Lincoln, *Living with Star Trek: American Culture and the Star Trek Universe* (London: I.B.Tauris, 2007).

Geraghty, Lincoln, 'Eight days that changed American television: Kirk's opening narration', in L. Geraghty (ed.), *The Influence of Star Trek on Television, Film and Culture* (Jefferson, NC: McFarland, 2008).

Geraghty, Lincoln, 'Truly American Enterprise: Star Trek's post-9/11 politics', in D. M. Hassler and C. Wilcox (eds), *New Boundaries of Political Science Fiction* (Columbia, SC: University of South Carolina Press, 2008).

Geraghty, Lincoln, *Cult Collectors* (Florence: Taylor and Francis, 2014).

Geraghty, Lincoln, 'Introduction: fans and paratexts', in L. Geraghty (ed.), *Popular Media Cultures: Fans, Audiences and Paratexts* (New York: Palgrave Macmillan, 2015).

Getman, Jessica L., 'A series on the edge: social tensions in *Star Trek*'s title cue', *Journal of the Society for American Music*, 9/3, August (2015), pp. 293–320.

Gilb. [sic], 'Space Patrol', *Variety*, 13 June 1951, no pagination. Reprinted in H. H. Prouty (ed.), *Variety Television Reviews, Vol. 4, 1951–1953* (New York: Garland, 1989–91).

Gill, Christopher, 'Plato on falsehood – not fiction', in C. Gill and T. P. Wiseman (eds), *Lies and Fiction in the Ancient World* (Exeter: University of Exeter Press, 1993).

Gilmore, David D., 'Carnival, ritual, and the anthropologists', *Carnival and Culture: Sex, Symbol, and Status in Spain* (New Haven, CT & London: Yale University Press, 1998).

Gledhill, Christine, 'History of genre criticism', in P. Cook (ed.), *The Cinema Book* (London: BFI, 1996).

Glenn, Justin, 'Psychoanalytic writings on Classical mythology and religion: 1909–1960', *The Classical World*, December/January (1976–77), pp. 225–47.

Gomery, Douglas, 'Disney's business history: a reinterpretation', in E. Smoodin (ed.), *Disney Discourse: Producing the Magic Kingdom* (New York: Routledge, 1994).

Gonzales, Dave, 'Star Trek Beyond will ignore most of Into Darkness', *Geek*, 17 December 2015. Available at www.geek.com/news/star-trek-beyond-will-ignore-most-of-into-darkness-1642409/ (accessed 18 February 2016).

Goodwin, Andrew, *Dancing in the Distraction Factory: Music Television and Popular Culture* (Minneapolis, MN: University of Minnesota Press, 1992).

Bibliography

Gottdiener, Mark, *The Theming of America: Dreams, Visions and Commercial Spaces* (Boulder, CO: Westview Press, 1997).

Gould, Eric, *Mythical Intentions in Modern Literature* (Princeton, NJ: Princeton University Press, 1981).

Graham, A. J., 'The Odyssey, history, and women', in B. Cohen (ed.), *The Distaff Side: Representing the Female in Homer's Odyssey* (New York: Oxford University Press, 1995).

Gray, Jonathan, *Show Sold Separately: Promos, Spoilers, and Other Media Paratexts* (New York: New York University Press, 2010).

Green, Joshua and Jenkins, Henry, 'The moral economy of Web 2.0', in J. Holt & A. Perren (eds), *Media Industries: History, Theory, and Method* (Oxford: Wiley-Blackwell, 2009).

Gregory, Chris, *Star Trek: Parallel Narratives* (Houndsmills, Hampshire and London: Macmillan Press, 2000).

Grenz, Stanley J., 'Why do theologians need to be scientists?', *Zygon*, 35/2, June (2000), pp. 331–356.

Griffin, J., 'Speech in the *Iliad*', *The Classical Review*, New Series XLI/I (1991), pp. 1–5.

Grove, Christopher, 'Rollercoasters or high rollers?' *Variety*, 368/1, 11 August 1997, pp. 38–9.

Grumbine, E. Evalyn, 'Reaching juvenile markets', *Psychology of Juvenile Appeal* (New York: McGraw-Hill, 1938). Reprinted in H. Jenkins (ed.), *The Children's Culture Reader* (New York: New York University Press, 1998).

Guthke, Karl S., *The Last Frontier: Imagining Other Worlds, from the Copernican Revolution to Modern Science Fiction*, trans. Helen Atkins (Ithaca, NY, and London: Cornell University Press, 1990).

Guy. [sic], 'Oedipus', *Variety*, 9 November 1960, no pagination. Reprinted in H. H. Prouty (ed.), *Variety Television Reviews, Vol. 7, 1960–1962* (New York, NY: Garland, 1989–91)..

Hadas, Leora, 'J. J. Abrams, 'Star Trek', and promotional authorship', *Cinema Journal*, 56/2 (2017), pp. 46–66.

Hagedorn, Roger, 'Doubtless to be continued: a brief history of serial narrative', in R. C. Allen (ed.), *To Be Continued ... Soap Operas Around the World* (New York: Routledge, 1995).

Hannigan, John, *Fantasy City: Pleasure and Profit in the Postmodern Metropolis* (New York: Routledge, 1998).

Hansen, James R., *Spaceflight Revolution: NASA Langley Research Center from Sputnik to Apollo* (Washington, DC: The NASA History Series, National Aeronautics and Space Administration, 1995). Available at http://history.nasa.gov/SP-4308/sp4308.htm (accessed 26 August 2006).

Hantke, Steffen, '*Star Trek*'s mirror universe episodes and US military culture through the eyes of the other', *Science Fiction Studies*, 41/3 (2014), pp. 562–78.

Bibliography

Hark, Ina Rae, 'Franchise fatigue? The marginalization of the television series after *The Next Generation*', in L. Geraghty (ed.), *The Influence of Star Trek on Television, Film and Culture* (Jefferson, NC: McFarland, 2007).

Hark, Ina Rae, *Star Trek* (London: BFI & New York: Palgrave Macmillan, 2008).

Harris, Stephen L. and Platzner, Gloria, *Classical Mythology: Images and Insights*, 3rd edn (Mountain View, CA: Mayfield Publishing, 2001).

Hartley, John and O'Regan, Tom, 'Quoting not science but sideboards', in J. Hartley, *Tele-ology: Studies in Television* (London and New York: Routledge, 1992).

Hartley, John, 'Out of bounds: the myth of marginality', in Len Masterman (ed.), *Television Mythologies: Stars, Shows and Signs* (London and New York: Comedia Publishing Group & MK Media Press, 1984).

Hartley, John, *Tele-ology: Studies in Television* (London and New York: Routledge, 1992).

Harvey, Miles, *The Island of Lost Maps: A True Story of Cartographic Crime* (New York: Random House, 2000).

Haskin, Pamela, 'Saul, can you make me a title?' *Film Quarterly*, 50/1, Fall (1996), pp. 10–17.

Havick, John, 'The impact of the internet on a television-based society', *Technology in Society* 22 (2000), pp. 273–87.

Hawking, Stephen, 'Foreword', in L. M. Krauss, *The Physics of Star Trek* (London: Flamingo, 1995).

Hawking, Stephen, 'The Origin of the Universe' (2005). Available at www.hawking.org.uk/the-origin-of-the-universe.html (accessed 11 February 2016).

Heaven, Douglas, 'What came before the Big Bang? And other questions physics can't answer … yet', *New Scientist*, 227/3037 (2015), pp. 30–1.

Heidel, Alexander, *The Babylonian Genesis: The Story of Creation*, 2nd edn (Chicago, IL, and London: University of Chicago Press, 1951).

Helm. [*sic*], 'Space Patrol', *Variety*, 7 September 1954, no pagination. Reprinted in H. H. Prouty (ed.), *Daily Variety Television Reviews, Vol. 1, 1946–1956*, (New York: Garland, 1989–91).

Helm. [*sic*], 'The Argonauts (*Playhouse of Stars*)', *Variety*, 1 June 1955. Reprinted in H. H. Prouty (ed.), *Daily Variety Television Reviews, Vol. 1, 1946–1956* (New York: Garland, 1989–91).

Hemmingson, Michael A., *Star Trek: A Post-Structural Critique of the Original Series* (San Bernardino, CA: Borgo Press, 2009).

Henderson, Brian, 'Critique of cine-structuralism, part 1', *Film Quarterly*, 26/5 Autumn (1973), pp. 25–34.

Henderson, Brian, 'Critique of cine-structuralism, part 2', *Film Quarterly*, 27/2, Winter (1973/4), pp. 37–46.

Herodotus, *The Histories*, trans. A. D. Godley (Cambridge, MA: Harvard University Press, 1920).

Bibliography

Herrick, James A., *Scientific Mythologies: How Science and Science Fiction Forge New Religious Beliefs* (Downers Grove, IL: InterVarsity Press, 2008).

Hesiod, *The Homeric Hymns and Homerica*, trans. Hugh G. Evelyn-White (Cambridge, MA: Harvard University Press & London: William Heinemann Ltd, 1914). Available at www.perseus.tufts.edu/cgi-bin/ptext?lookup=Hes.+Th.+5 (accessed 29 June 2002).

Hess, Alan, *Viva Las Vegas: After-Hours Architecture* (San Francisco, CA: Chronicle Books, 1993).

Hibberd, James, '"Star Trek" showrunner discusses "Strange New Worlds" Plan, Evolving Q for "Picard"', *The Hollywood Reporter*, 12 April 2021. Available at https://www.hollywoodreporter.com/heat-vision/star-trek-producer-reveals-strange-new-worlds-plan-evolving-q-for-picard (accessed 13 April 2021).

Hills, Matt, 'To boldly go where others have gone before …? Star Trek and (academic) narratives', *Scope*, November (2000). Available at: www.nottingham.ac.uk/film/journal/bookrev/star-trek.htm (accessed 2 November 2000, no longer online 22 September 2016).

Hills, Matt, *Fan Cultures* (London: Routledge, 2002).

Hine, Thomas, *Populuxe* (New York: Alfred A. Knopf, 1986).

Holland, Luke, 'New Star Trek show in the Netflix era?' *The Guardian*, 4 November 2015. Available at www.theguardian.com/culture/2015/nov/03/star-trek-can-prosper-netflix-and-chill-era (accessed 12 July 2016).

Honko, Lauri, 'The problem of defining myth', in A. Dundes (ed.), *Sacred Narrative: Readings in the Theory of Myth* (Berkeley, CA: University of California Press, 1984).

Hooper, Rowan, 'Multiverse me: should I care about my other selves?' *New Scientist*, 223/2988, 27 September 2014. Available at www.newscientist.com/article/mg22329880-400-multiverse-me-should-i-care-about-my-other-selves/ (accessed 26 November 2015).

Horo. [sic], 'Leonard Bernstein and the N.Y. Philharmonic', *Variety*, 1 March 1961, no pagination. Reprinted in H. H. Prouty (ed.), *Variety Television Reviews, Vol. 7, 1960–1962* (New York: Garland, 1989–91).

Iaccino, James F., *Jungian Reflections Within the Cinema: A Psychological Analysis of Sci-Fi and Fantasy Archetypes* (Westport, CT: Praeger, 1998).

Idato, Michael, 'Star Trek explores next frontier with new television and streaming series', *The Age*, 3 November 2015. Available at www.theage.com.au/entertainment/tv-and-radio/star-trek-explores-next-frontier-with-new-television-and-streaming-series-20151103-gkp629.html (accessed 23 November 2015).

Ipetitions, 'Save Star Trek: The Experience', (2008). Available at www.ipetitions.com/petition/savestartrekexp/ (accessed 18 September 2008).

Irwin, Walter, 'Boots and starships,' in W. Irwin and G. B. Love (eds), *The Best of the Best of Trek II* (New York: ROC, 1992).

Bibliography

Jacobs, Wilbur R., *The Historical World of Frederick Jackson Turner: with Selections from his Correspondence* (New Haven, CT, and London: Yale University Press, 1968).

Jakobson, Roman, *Selected Writings, Volume II: Word and Language* (The Hague: Mouton, 1971).

Jenkins, Henry, 'Star Trek rerun, reread and rewritten: fan writing as textual poaching', in C. Penley, E. Lyons, L. Spigel and J. Bergstrom (eds), *Close Encounters: Film, Feminism, and Science Fiction* (Minneapolis, MN: University of Minnesota Press, 1991).

Jenkins, Henry, *Textual Poachers: Television Fans and Participatory Culture* (New York: Routledge, 1992).

Jenkins, Henry, *Convergence Culture: Where Old and New Media Collide* (New York: New York University Press, 2006).

Jenkins, Henry, 'Afterword: the future of fandom', in J. Gray, C. Sandvoss and C. L. Harrington (eds), *Fandom: Identities and Communities in a Media World* (New York and London: New York University Press, 2007)

Jenkins, Henry, 'Transmedia Storytelling 101', *Confession of an Aca-Fan* (blog). Available at http://henryjenkins.org/2007/03/transmedia_storytelling_101.html (accessed 24 November 2015).

Jenkins, Henry, 'Why Participatory Culture is Not Web 2.0: Some Basic Distinctions', *Confession of an Aca-Fan* (blog). Available at http://henryjenkins.org/2010/05/why_participatory_culture_is_n.html (accessed 9 February 2016).

Jenkins, Henry, 'Transmedia 202: Further Reflections', *Confession of an Aca-Fan* (blog), (2011). Available at http://henryjenkins.org/2011/08/defining_transmedia_further_re.html (accessed 2 February 2016).

Jet Propulsion Laboratory, 'Mission to Earth – Explorer 1', (n.d.). Available at http://www.jpl.nasa.gov/missions/explorer-1/ (accessed 22 September 2016).

Jimenez, Christian, 'Disturbing Parallel: The shifting politics of racial inclusion and exclusion in Star Trek: Voyager', in R. L. Lively (ed.), *Exploring Star Trek: Voyager Critical Essays* (Jefferson, NC: McFarland, 2020).

Jindra, Michael, 'Star Trek fandom as a religious phenomenon', *Sociology of Religion*, 55/1 (1994), pp. 27–51.

Johnson, Derek, 'Fan-tagonism: factions, institutions, and constitutive hegemonies of fandom', in J. Gray, C. Sandvoss and C. L. Harrington (eds), *Fandom: Identities and Communities in a Media World* (New York and London: New York University Press, 2007).

Johnson, Mike and Jones, Tim, *Star Trek: Countdown* (London: Titan, 2009).

Johnson, Mike and Messina, David, *Star Trek: Countdown to Darkness* (London: Titan, 2013).

Johnson-Roehr, S. N., 'These are mine', 14 August 2012. Available at http://astronomy.snjr.net/blog/?p=677 (accessed 28 June 2017).

Bibliography

Johnston, Linda, 'The classic *Star Trek*', in W. Irwin and G. B. Love (eds), *The Best of the Best of Trek II* (New York: ROC, 1992).

Johnston, Sarah Iles, 'The Greek Mythic Story World', *Arethusa*, 38/3 (2015), pp. 283–311.

Johnston, Sheila, 'Film narrative and the structuralist controversy', in P. Cook (ed.), *The Cinema Book* (London: BFI, 1985).

Jose. [sic], 'Mr. I. Magination', *Variety*, 6 September 1950. Reprinted in H. H. Prouty (ed.), *Variety Television Reviews, Vol. 3, 1923–1950* (New York: Garland, 1989–91).

Jose. [sic], 'Space Patrol', *Variety*, 8 September 1954, no pagination; reprinted in H. H. Prouty (ed.), *Variety Television Reviews, Vol. 5, 1954–1956* (New York: Garland, 1989–91).

Joyrich, Lynne, 'Feminist Enterprise: *Star Trek: The Next Generation* and the occupations of femininity', *Cinema Journal*, 35/2 (1996), pp. 61–84.

Julian, Mark, 'J. J. Abrams Discusses the Altered Timeline of His Star Trek Movies', *Comic Book Movie*, 8 June 2011. Available at www.comicbookmovie.com/scifi_movies/star_trek/jj-abrams-discusses-the-altered-timeline-of-his-star-trek-a51999 (accessed 1 September 2015).

Jung, Carl G., *Flying Saucers: A Modern Myth of Things Seen in the Skies*, trans. R. F. C. Hull (Princeton, NJ: Princeton University Press, 1978).

Jung, Carl G., *Jung: Selected Writings*, A. Storr (ed.), (Bungay, Suffolk: Fontana, 1983).

Kap. [sic], 'Space Patrol', *Variety*, 18 January 1954. Reprinted in H. H. Prouty (ed.), *Daily Variety Television Reviews, Vol. 1, 1946–1956* (New York: Garland, 1989–91).

Kapell, Matthew Wilhelm (ed.), *Star Trek as Myth: Essays on Symbol and Archetype at the Final Frontier* (Jefferson, NC: McFarland, 2010).

Kapell, Matthew Wilhelm (ed.), *Exploring the Next Frontier: Vietnam, NASA, Star Trek and Utopia in 1960s and 70s American Myth and History* (New York: Routledge, 2016).

Karpovich, Angela I., 'Locating the "*Star Trek* Experience"', in L. Geraghty (ed.), *The Influence of Star Trek on Television, Film and Culture* (Jefferson, NC: McFarland, 2008).

Kawa, Abraham, 'Skewed villainy: the problematic image of the eastern antagonist (or, Dr. No was a monkey)', *The International Journal of the Image*, 4 (2014), pp. 51–6.

Kawin, Bruce, 'After midnight', in J. P. Telotte (ed.), *The Cult Film Experience: Beyond All Reason* (Austin, TX: University of Texas Press, 1991).

Kennard, Emily, 'What's in a name?' *NASA* (2009). Available at www.nasa.gov/centers/glenn/about/history/silverstein_feature.html (accessed 22 September 2016).

Bibliography

Kennedy, John F., 'Address of Senator John F. Kennedy Accepting the Democratic Party Nomination for the Presidency of the United States', John F. Kennedy Library and Museum, 15 July 1960. Available at https://www.jfklibrary.org/Research/Research-Aids/JFK-Speeches/Democratic-Party-Nomination_19600715.aspx (accessed 22 September 2016).

Kennedy, John F., 'Special Message to the Congress on Urgent National Needs', John F. Kennedy Library and Museum, 25 May 1961. Available at www.jfklibrary.org/Research/Research-Aids/JFK-Speeches/United-States-Congress-Special-Message_19610525.aspx (accessed 22 September 2016).

Kennedy, John F., 'Rice University', 12 September 1962. Available at www.jfklibrary.org/Asset-Viewer/MkATdOcdU06X5uNHbmqm1Q.aspx (accessed 22 September 2016).

Kepler, Johannes, *Kepler's Dream*, trans. Patricia Frueh Kirkwood (Berkeley & Los Angeles, CA: University of California Press, 1965).

Kinnard, Roy, *Science Fiction Serials* (Jefferson, NC, and London: McFarland, 1998).

Kirk, G. S., 'On defining myths', *Phronesis: A Journal for Ancient Philosophy*, 1 (1973), pp. 61–9. Reprinted in A. Dundes (ed.), *Sacred Narrative: Readings in the Theory of Myth* (Berkeley, CA: University of California Press, 1984).

Kirk, G. S., *The Nature of Greek Myths* (Harmondsworth, Middlesex: Penguin, 1974).

Kirkham, Pat, 'The jeweller's eye', *Sight and Sound*, 7/4 (1997), pp. 18–9.

Kitses, Jim, *Horizons West: Anthony Mann, Budd Boetticher, Sam Peckinpah – Studies of Authorship within the Western* (London: BFI, 1969).

Klecker, Cornelia, 'The other kind of film frames: a research report on paratexts in film', *Word & Image* 31 (2015), pp. 402–13

Klingon Language Institute (n.d.). Available at www.kli.org (accessed 8 January 2003).

Kluckhohn, Clyde, "Myths and rituals: a general theory', in R. A. Segal (ed.), *Myth and Ritual Theory: An Anthology* (Malden, MA & Oxford: Blackwell, 1998).

Knapp, James A., 'Essayistic messages: internet newsgroups as an electronic public sphere', in D. Porter (ed.), *Internet Culture* (New York: Routledge, 1997).

Kovacs, George, 'Moral and mortal in Star Trek: The Original Series', in B. M. Rogers and B. E. Stevens, *Classical Traditions in Science Fiction* (New York: Oxford University Press, 2015).

Kozinets, Robert V., 'Inno-tribes: *Star Trek* as Wikimedia', in Bernard Cova, Robert V. Kozinets and Avi Shankar (eds), *Consumer Tribes* (Amsterdam: Butterworth-Heinemann, 2007).

Kozloff, Sarah, 'Narrative theory and television', in R. C. Allen (ed.), *Channels of Discourse, Reassembled: Television and Contemporary Criticism*, 2nd edn (London: Routledge, 1992).

Bibliography

Kratzer, James R., 'Different Strokes for Different Folks', 13 December 2002. Available at www.amazon.com/exec/obidos/tg/detail/-/B0000658PQ/ref=cm_cr_dp_2_1/002-0132310-7164857?v=glance&s=music&vi=customer-reviews (accessed 26 September 2003).

Krauss, Lawrence M., *The Physics of Star Trek* (London: Flamingo, 1995).

Kreitzer, Larry, 'The cultural veneer of *Star Trek*', *Journal of Popular Culture*, 30/2, Fall (1996), pp. 1–28.

Kristeva, Julia, *Desire in Language: A Semiotic Approach to Literature and Art*, trans. T. Gora, A. Jardine, and L. S. Roudiez, (ed.) L. S. Roudiez (New York: Columbia University Press, 1980).

Kuhn, Thomas S., *The Copernican Revolution: Planetary Astronomy in the Development of Western Thought* (Cambridge, MA: Harvard University Press, 1957, 1985).

Kullmann, Wolfgang, 'Oral poetry theory and neoanalysis in Homeric research', *Homerische Motive* (Stuttgart: Franz Steiner Verlag, 1992).

Lagon, Mark P., '"We Owe It to Them to Interfere": *Star Trek* and US statecraft in the 1960s and the 1990s', *Extrapolation*, 34/3 (1993), pp. 251–64.

Lamp, Jeffrey Scott, 'Biblical interpretation in the *Star Trek* universe', in J. E. Porter and D. L. McLaren (eds), *Star Trek and Sacred Ground* (Albany, NY: State University of New York Press, 1999).

Lancaster, Kurt, 'When spectators become performers: contemporary performance-entertainments meet the needs of an 'unsettled' audience', *Journal of Popular Culture*, 30/4, Spring (1997), pp. 75–88.

Lancaster, Kurt, *Interacting with Babylon 5: Fan Performance in a Media Universe* (Austin, TX: University of Texas Press, 2001).

Landon, Brooks, *The Aesthetics of Ambivalence* (Westport, CT, and London: Greenwood Press, 1992).

Lang, Amanda, 'Viacom Cracks Down on Trek Web Sites', *Financial Post*, 10 January 1997. Available at www.canoe.ca/JamStarTrek/jan10_treksites.html (accessed 1 April 2001, no longer online 22 September 2016).

Lattimore, Richard (trans.), *The Iliad of Homer* (London: University of Chicago Press, 1951).

Lattimore, Richard (trans.), *The Odyssey of Homer* (New York: Harper Perennial, 1965, 1975).

Lear, John, 'Introduction and interpretation', in Johannes Kepler, *Kepler's Dream*, trans. P. F. Kirkwood (Berkeley & Los Angeles, CA: University of California Press, 1965)

Lee, Stan and Kirby, Jack, 'Thor the Mighty and the Stone Men from Saturn', *Journey into Mystery*, 1/83 (1962). Reprinted in S. Lee and J. Kirby, *Essential Thor*, Vol. 1 (New York: Marvel Comics, 2001).

Bibliography

Lee, Stan and Kirby, Jack, 'The Coming of the Avengers!' *The Avengers*, 1/1 (1963). Reprinted in S. Lee, J. Kirby and D. Heck, *Essential Avengers*, Vol. 1 (New York: Marvel Comics, 2001).

Lerner, Neil, 'Hearing the boldly goings', in K. J. Donnelly and P. Hayward (eds), *Music in Science Fiction Television: Tuned to the Future* (Hoboken, NJ: Taylor and Francis, 2012).

Les. [*sic*], 'Search for Ulysses', *Variety*, 19 January 1966, no pagination. Reprinted in H. H. Prouty (ed.), *Variety Television Reviews, Vol. 9, 1966–1969* (New York: Garland, 1989–91).

Les. [*sic*], 'Land of the Giants', *Variety*, 25 September 1968, no pagination. Reprinted in H. H. Prouty (ed.), *Variety Television Reviews, Vol. 9, 1966–1969* (New York: Garland, 1989–91).

Lévi-Strauss, Claude, *The Raw and the Cooked: Introduction to a Science of Mythology*, trans. John and Doreen Weightman (London: Jonathan Cape, 1969).

Lévi-Strauss, Claude, 'The structural study of myth', in R. and F. De George (eds), *The Structuralists from Marx to Levi-Strauss* (New York: Doubleday, Anchor, 1972).

Lewis, Lisa, *The Adoring Audience: Fan Culture and Popular Media* (London: Routledge, 1992).

Lincoln, Bruce, *Theorizing Myth: Narrative, Ideology, Scholarship* (Chicago, IL, and London: University of Chicago Press, 1999).

Linford, Peter, 'Deeds of power: respect for religion in *Star Trek: Deep Space Nine*', in J. E. Porter and D. L. McLaren (eds), *Star Trek and Sacred Ground: Explorations of Star Trek, Religion, and American Culture* (Albany, NY: State University of New York Press, 1999).

Lyon, David, *The Sailing Navy List: All the Ships of the Royal Navy Built, Purchased and Captured 1688–1860* (London: Conway Maritime Press, 1993), p. 192.

Mac Cana, Proinsias, *The Learned Tales of Medieval Ireland* (Dublin: Dublin Institute for Advanced Studies, 1980).

MacCormac, Earl R., *Metaphor and Myth in Science and Religion* (Durham, NC: Duke University Press, 1976).

Malkin, Irad, *The Returns of Odysseus: Colonization and Ethnicity* (Berkeley, CA: University of California Press, 1998).

Martin, Richard P., *The Language of Heroes: Speech and Performance in the* Iliad (Ithaca, NY, and London: Cornell University Press, 1989).

The Mary Sue Society (2002). Available at www.web.archive.org/web/20040624085452/http://www.subreality.com/marysue/explain.htm (accessed 16 February 2021).

Mason, Jeff, 'The disappearing bum: a look at time travels in Star Trek', in W. Irwin and G. B. Love (eds), *The Best of the Best of Trek II* (New York: ROC, 1992).

Bibliography

McLaren, Darcee L., 'On the edge of forever: understanding the *Star Trek* phenomenon as myth', in J. E. Porter and D. L. McLaren (eds), *Star Trek and Sacred Ground: Explorations of Star Trek, Religion and American Culture* (Albany, NY: State University of New York Press, 1999).

McNary, D., "Star Trek: Beyond' gets new release date', *Variety*, 17 September 2015. Available at www.variety.com/2015/film/news/star-trek-beyond-gets-new-release-date-1201596328/ (accessed 27 November 2015, no longer online 18 December 2016).

Migaldi, Scott, 'Great Fun While in Las Vegas!', 8 April 2004. Available at www.imdb.com/title/tt0356069/ (accessed 14 August 2004).

Miller, Eva, 'Retelling Gilgamesh in *Star Trek: The Next Generation*', in A. Garcia-Ventura and Lorenzo Verderame (eds), *Receptions of the Ancient Near East in Popular Culture and Beyond* (Atlanta, GA: Lockwood Press, 2020).

Miller, Liz Shannon, "Star Trek: Discovery' Star on How Character-Focused 'Short Treks' Add to the Epic Mythology of the Franchise', *IndieWire*, 4 October 2018. Available at https://www.indiewire.com/2018/10/star-trek-discovery-mary-wiseman-on-short-treks-tilly-interview-1202009417/ (accessed 19 April 2021).

Mittell, Jason, *Genre and Television: From Cop Shows to Cartoons in American Culture* (New York: Routledge, 2004).

Moore, Alexander, 'Walt Disney World: bonded ritual space and the playful pilgrimage center', *Anthropological Quarterly*, 35, October (1980), pp. 207–18.

Moore, Sally F. and Myerhoff, Barbara G., *Secular Ritual* (Amsterdam: Van Gorcum, 1977).

Mor. [sic], 'The Time Tunnel', *Variety*, 14 September 1966, no pagination. Reprinted in H. H. Prouty (ed.), *Variety Television Reviews, Vol. 9*, 1966–1969 (New York: Garland, 1989–91).

Mor. [sic], 'Marvel Super-Heroes', *Variety*, 26 October 1966, no pagination. Reprinted in H. H. Prouty (ed.), *Variety Television Reviews, Vol. 9, 1966–1969* (New York: Garland, 1989–91).

Mor. [sic], 'Star Trek', *Variety*, 25 September 1968, no pagination. Reprinted in H. H. Prouty (ed.), *Variety Television Reviews, Vol. 9, 1966–1969* (New York: Garland, 1989–91).

Morgan, Kathryn A., 'Designer history: Plato's Atlantis story and fourth-century ideology', *Journal of Hellenic Studies* 118 (1998), pp. 101–18.

Morinis, Alan, 'Introduction', in A. Morinis (ed.), *Sacred Journeys: The Anthropology of Pilgrimage* (Westport, CT: Greenwood, 1992).

Muir, Hazel, 'Does the universe go on forever?' *New Scientist*, 180/2416, October 11 2003, pp. 6–7.

Müller, Peter, 'Star Trek: The American Dream Continued? The Crisis of the American Dream in the 1960s and its Reflection in a Contemporary TV Series'

Bibliography

(1994). Available at www.pmueller.de/downloads.html (accessed 22 September 2016).

Murray, Charles and Marqusee, Mike, 'To boldly go back', *The Age, The Culture*, 12 February 2002, p. 1.

Murray, Janet H., *Hamlet on the Holodeck: The Future of Narrative in Cyberspace* (New York: The Free Press, 1997).

Murray, Janet and Jenkins, Henry, 'Before the holodeck: translating *Star Trek* into digital media', in G. M. Smith (ed.), *On a Silver Platter: CD-ROMS and the Promises of a New Technology* (New York & London: New York University Press, 1999).

Myers, Steve, 'Psychological vs. visionary sources of myth in film', *International Journal of Jungian Studies*, 4/2 (2012), pp. 150–61.

Nagy, Gregory, *Greek Mythology and Poetics* (Ithaca, NY, and London: Cornell University Press, 1990).

NASA, 'Vanguard rocket explodes on launch pad', Image VAN-9, 6 December 1957. Available at http://nasaimages.lunaimaging.com/luna/servlet/detail/nasaNAS ~5~5~24178~127619:Vanguard-rocket-explodes-on-launch- (accessed 23 September 2016).

NASA, 'Earth from Apollo 8', Image AS8-16-2606, 12 January 1968. Available at: www.history.nasa.gov/ap08fj/photos/16-a/hr/as08-16-2606hr.jpg (accessed 22 September 2016).

NASA, 'President Bush Offers New Vision for NASA', 14 January 2004. Available at www.nasa.gov/missions/solarsystem/bush_vision.html (accessed 26 August 2006).

NASA, 'Star Trek Honors NASA With Voyager Award', 23 February 2004. Available at www.nasa.gov/vision/earth/everydaylife/star_trek.html (accessed 26 August 2006).

NASA, 'Apollo 8 Earthrise', 25 June 2013. Available at www.nasa.gov/multimedia/ imagegallery/image_feature_1249.html (accessed 22 September 2016).

Ndalianis, Angela, 'Theme parks, neo-baroque experiences, and entertainment cities', *Eyeline*, 41, Summer (1999/2000), pp. 12–15.

Ndalianis, Angela, *Neo-Baroque Aesthetics and Contemporary Entertainment* (Cambridge, MA: The MIT Press, 2004).

Ndalianis, Angela, 'Enter the Aleph: superhero worlds and hypertime realities', in A. Ndalianis (ed.), *The Contemporary Comic Book Superhero* (New York: Routledge, 2009).

Neale, Steve, 'Epics and spectacles', *Genre and Hollywood* (London and New York: Routledge, 2000).

Neils, Jennifer, 'Les femmes fatales: Skylla and the Sirens in Greek art', in B. Cohen (ed.), *The Distaff Side: Representing the Female in Homer's Odyssey* (New York: Oxford University Press, 1995).

Bibliography

Nemecek, Larry, *The Star Trek The Next Generation Companion* (New York: Pocket Books, 1995).

Nevills, A., 'Final Frontier Astronauts Land on Star Trek', NASA's Johnson Space Center, 13 May 2005. Available at www.nasa.gov/vision/space/features/Astros_on_StarTrek.html (accessed 26 August 2006).

Newcomb, Horace and Hirsch, Paul M., 'Television as cultural forum', in H. Newcomb (ed.), *Television: The Critical View* (Oxford: Oxford University Press, 1987).

New Scientist, 'Captain Kirk tweets space station', 2899, 12 January 2013, pp. 4–5.

Nixon, Lucia, 'The cults of Demeter and Kore', in R. Hawley and B. Levick (eds), *Women in Antiquity: New Assessments* (London and New York: Routledge, 1995).

Nowell Smith, Geoffrey, 'I was a Star*Struck Structuralist', *Screen*, 14/3, Autumn (1973), pp. 92–9.

Okrand, Marc, *The Klingon Dictionary* (New York: Pocket Books, 1992).

Okrand, Marc, *Klingon for the Galactic Traveller* (New York: Pocket Books, 1997).

Okrand, Marc and Dorn, Michael, *Star Trek: Conversational Klingon* (S & S Audio, 1992).

Okuda, Marc and Okuda, Denise, *Star Trek Chronology: The History of the Future* (New York: Pocket Books, 1996).

Okuda, Marc and Okuda, Denise with Mirek, Debbie, *The Star Trek Encyclopedia: A Reference Guide to the Future* (New York: Pocket Books, 1999).

Pascale, Anthony, 'Alex Kurtzman says 'Section 31' series writers building a 'very surprising' Star Trek show', *TrekMovie*, 26 August 2020. Available at https://trekmovie.com/2020/08/26/alex-kurtman-says-writing-team-building-a-very-surprising-section-31-star-trek-series/ (accessed 15 April 2021).

Panofsky, Erwin, 'Galileo as a critic of the arts', *Isis*, 47/148, March (1956), pp. 3–15.

Panofsky, Erwin, 'More on Galileo and the arts', *Isis*, 47/148, June (1956), pp. 182–5.

Parker, Robert, 'Myths of early Athens', in J. Bremmer (ed.), *Interpretations of Greek Mythology* (London: Croom Helm, 1987).

Paterson, Chris, 'Space program and television', in H. Newcomb (ed.), *Museum of Broadcast Communication Encyclopedia of Television*, vol. 3 (Chicago, IL, and London: Fitzroy Dearborn Publishers, 1997).

Pave, Adam D., 'Inspiring', 6 June 2002. Available at www.amazon.com/exec/obidos/tg/det…c_1/002-0132310-7164857?v=glance&s=music (accessed 26 September 2003, no longer online 22 September 2016).

Pearson, Anne MacKenzie, 'From thwarted gods to reclaimed mystery? An overview of the depiction of religion in Star Trek', in J. E. Porter and D. L. McLaren (eds), *Star Trek and Sacred Ground: Explorations of Star Trek, Religion, and American Culture* (Albany, NY: State University of New York Press, 1999).

Bibliography

Pearson, Roberta and Messenger Davies, Máire, *Star Trek and American Television* (Berkeley, CA: University of California Press, 2014).

Penley, Constance, *NASA/TREK: Popular Science and Sex in America* (London: Verso, 1997).

Peradotto, John, *Man in the Middle Voice: Name and Narration in The Odyssey* (Princeton, NJ: Princeton University Press, 1990).

Peterson, Gregory 'Religion and science in *Star Trek: The Next Generation*: God, Q, and evolutionary eschatology on the final frontier', in J. E. Porter and D. L. McLaren (eds), *Star Trek and Sacred Ground: Explorations of Star Trek, Religion, and American* Culture (Albany, NY: State University of New York Press, 1999).

Piggott, Mark O. 'Enterprise Sailors "Beam Up" to TV's "Enterprise"', 28 March 2003. Available at www.navy.mil/Submit/display.asp?story_id=6403> (accessed 22 September 2016).

Pindar, Odes, trans. Diane Svarlien, revised by T. K. Hubbard (1990). Available at www.perseus.tufts.edu/cgi-bin/ptext?doc=Perseus%3Atext%3A1999.01.0162 (accessed 8 December 2004).

Pit. [sic], 'Hercules', *Variety*, 15 September 1965, no pagination. Reprinted in H. H. Prouty (ed.), *Variety Television Reviews, Vol. 8, 1963–1965* (New York: Garland, 1989–91).

Ploman, Edward W., *Space, Earth and Communication* (Westport, CT: Quorum Books, 1984).

Plato, *The Republic*, trans. Desmond Lee, 2nd edn (London: Penguin Books, 2003),

Plato, 'Extract from *Timaeus*', and '*Critias*', in M. Richardson (ed.), *The Halstead Treasury of Ancient Science Fiction* (Rushcutters Bay, NSW: Halstead Classics, 2001).

Poe, Stephen Edward, *A Vision of the Future: Star Trek Voyager* (New York: Pocket Books, 1998).

Pollard, John, 'The Boston Siren Aryballos', *American Journal of Archaeology*, 53 (1949), pp. 357–9.

Porter, Jennifer E., 'To boldly go: *Star Trek* convention attendance as pilgrimage', in J. E. Porter and D. L. McLaren (eds), *Star Trek and Sacred Ground: Explorations of Star Trek, Religion, and American Culture* (Albany, NY: State University of New York Press, 1999).

Press, Joy, 'The Star Trek TV Universe is CBS All Access' Secret Weapon. Will it keep expanding infinitely?', *Vanity Fair*, 29 November 2019. Available at https://www.vanityfair.com/hollywood/2019/11/the-star-trek-tv-universe-is-cbs-all-access-secret-weapon-can-it-keep-expanding-infinitely (accessed 19 April 2021).

Pringle, David, 'What is this thing called space opera?' in Gary Westfahl (ed.), *Space and Beyond: The Frontier Theme in Science Fiction* (Westport, CT: Greenwood Press, 2000).

Bibliography

Proctor, William, 'Beginning again: the reboot phenomenon in comic books and film', *Scan: Journal of Media Arts and Culture*, 9, 1 (2012). Available at www.scan.net.au/scn/journal/vol9number1/William-Proctor.html (accessed 24 November 2015).

Proctor, William, 'Ctl-Alt-Delete: retcon, relaunch, or reboot?' *Sequart*, 8 February 2013. Available at www.sequart.org/magazine/18508/ctl-alt-delete-retcon-relaunch-or-reboot (accessed 6 September 2013).

Proctor, William, 'Beginning again: the reboot phenomenon in comic books, film and beyond' (PhD diss., University of Sunderland, 2015).

Projansky, Sarah, 'When the body speaks: Deanna Troi's tenuous authority and the rationalization of Federation superiority in *Star Trek: The Next Generation* rape narratives', in T. Harrison et al (eds), *Enterprise Zones: Critical Positions on Star Trek* (Boulder, CO: Westview Press, 1996).

Propp, Vladmir, *Morphology of the Folktale* (Austin, TX, and London: University of Texas Press, 1968).

Pucci, Pietro, 'The songs of the Sirens', in S. L. Schein (ed.), *Reading the Odyssey: Selected Interpretive Essays* (Princeton, NJ: Princeton University Press, 1996).

Puhvel, Jaan, *Comparative Mythology* (Baltimore, MD: The Johns Hopkins University Press, 1987).

Pullen, Kirsten, 'I-love-Xena.com: creating online fan communities', in D. Gauntlett (ed.), *Web.Studies: Rewiring Media Studies for the Digital Age* (London: Arnold, 2000).

Raddatz, Leslie, 'Product of Two Worlds: Leonard Nimoy, as the hybrid Mr. Spock, has made it big in outer space', *TV Guide*, 4 March 1967, pp. 23–6.

Raddatz, Leslie, '"Star Trek" wins the Ricky Schwartz', *TV Guide*, 18 November 1967, pp. 25–8.

Raglan, Lord, 'The hero of tradition', in A. Dundes (ed.), *The Study of Folklore* (Englewood Cliffs, NJ: Prentice-Hall, 1965).

Reid-Jeffery, Donna, 'Star Trek: the last frontier in modern American myth', *Folklore and Mythology Studies*, 6, Spring (1982), pp. 34–41.

Remnant, Peter and Bennett, Jonathan, 'Notes', in G. W. Leibniz, *New Essays on Human Understanding*, trans. and eds Peter Remnant and Jonathan Bennett (Cambridge: Cambridge University Press, 1996).

Reynolds, Richard, *Super Heroes – A Modern Mythology* (London: B. T. Batsford, 1992).

Richards, Ruth, 'Calypso: The Posthuman female in Star Trek Discovery', unpublished paper presented to *Popular Culture Association of Australia and New Zealand* conference, July 2019, RMIT University, Australia.

Richardson, Matthew (ed.), *The Halstead Treasury of Ancient Science Fiction* (Rushcutters Bay, NSW: Halstead Classics, 2001).

Bibliography

Roadside America, 'Future Birthplace of James T. Kirk', (n.d.). Available at www.roadsideamerica.com/attract/IARIV.html (accessed 29 January 2001) and www.roadsideamerica.com/story/2081 (accessed 23 June 2017).

Roberts, Robin, 'Performing science fiction: Television, theater, and gender in Star Trek: The Experience', *Extrapolation*, 42/4, Winter (2001), pp. 340–56.

Roberts, Robin, *Sexual Generations:* Star Trek: The Next Generation *and Gender* (Urbana, IL: University of Illinois Press, 1999).

Robinson, Michael G., 'These are the Voyages? The Post-Jubilee *Trek* Legacy on the *Discovery*, the *Orville*, and the *Callister*', in S. Mittermeier and M. Spychala (eds), *Fighting for the Future: Essays on Star Trek: Discovery* (Liverpool: Liverpool University Press, 2020).

Rogerson, J. W., 'Slippery words: myth', in A. Dundes (ed.), *Sacred Narrative: Readings in the Theory of Myth* (Berkeley, CA: University of California Press, 1984).

Rose, Peter, 'Teaching Greek myth and contemporary myths', in M. M. Winkler (ed.), *Classics and Cinema* (Lewisburg, PA: Bucknell University Press, 1991).

Rubin, Judith, 'Are you experienced?' *TCI*, 32/4, April (1998), pp. 34–8, 56–8.

Ryan, Joal, '"Star Trek": where no franchise has gone before', *Variety*, 387/2, 27 May 2002, p. S1.

Sagan, Carl, *Cosmos* (New York: Ballantine Books, 1980).

Sandars, Diana, 'The Hollywood Musical from 1980 to 2000', (PhD diss., University of Melbourne, 2006).

Sandars, N. K. (trans.), *The Epic of Gilgamesh* (London: Penguin, 1960, 1972).

Sanders, Joe (ed.), *Science Fiction Fandom* (Westport, CT: Greenwood Press, 1994).

Santas, Constantine, Jim Wilson, Maria Colavito and Djoymi Baker, *The Encyclopedia of Epic Films* (Lanham, MD: Rowman & Littlefield, 2014).

Sargent, Epes Winthrop, 'Advertising for exhibitors', *The Moving Picture World*, 11/8, 24 February 1912, pp. 666, 763.

Sarno, Joe, 'Captain Video, Daily Episodes (1949–1955)', *Comic Kingdom* (n.d.). Available at http://home.earthlink.net/~joesarno/tvscifi/captainvdaily.htm (accessed 6 January 2005, no longer online 23 September 2016).

Schatz, Thomas, 'The structural influence: new directions in film genre study', in B. K. Grant (ed.), *Film Genre Reader* (Austin, TX: University of Texas Press, 1986).

Schein, Seth L., 'Female representations and interpreting the Odyssey', in B. Cohen (ed.), *The Distaff Side: Representing the Female in Homer's Odyssey* (New York: Oxford University Press, 1995).

Schiller, Dan, 'O what a tangled web we weave', *Index on Censorship*, 26/3, May–June (1997), pp. 68–76.

Schwartz, Susan L., 'Enterprise engaged: mythic enactment and ritual performance', in R. S. Kraemer, W. Cassidy and S. Schwartz, *Religions of Star Trek* (Boulder, CO: Westview Press, 2001).

Bibliography

Schwichtenberg, Cathy, '*The Love Boat*: the packaging and selling of love, heterosexual romance, and family', in H. Newcomb (ed.), *Television: The Critical View*, 4th edn (New York: Oxford University Press, 1987).

Sconce, Jeffrey, 'Science fiction programs', in H. Newcomb (ed.), *Encyclopedia of Television*, 2nd edn (New York, NY, and London: Fitzroy Dearborn, 2004).

Segal, Charles, 'Greek myth as a semiotic and structural system and the problem of tragedy', *Interpreting Greek Tragedy: Myth, Poetry, Text* (Ithaca, NY: Cornell University Press, 1986).

Segal, Charles, '*Kleos* and its ironies in the Odyssey', in S. L. Schein (ed.), *Reading the Odyssey: Selected Interpretive Essays* (Princeton, NJ: Princeton University Press, 1996).

Segal, Robert A. (ed.), *Myth and Ritual Theory: An Anthology* (Malden, MA & Oxford: Blackwell, 1998).

Seiter, Ellen, 'Semiotics, structuralism, and television', in R. C. Allen (ed.), *Channels of Discourse Reassembled: Television and Contemporary Criticism*, 2nd edn (London: Routledge, 1993).

Serling, Rod, 'Reviews: Science Fiction Theater', *TV Guide*, 11 June 1955, p. 18.

Shapiro, H. A., 'Old and new heroes: narrative, composition, and subject in Attic Black-Figure', *Classical Antiquity*, 9/1 (1990), pp. 114–48.

Sharp, Sharon, 'Nostalgia for the future: retrofuturism in *Enterprise*', *Science Fiction Film and Television*, 4/1, Spring (2011), pp. 25–40.

Shoard, Catherine, 'George Takei: making Sulu gay in new Star Trek is "really unfortunate"', *The Guardian*, 8 July 2016. Available at www.theguardian.com /film/2016/jul/08/star-trek-beyond-george-takei-sulu-really-unfortunate (accessed 12 July 2016).

Short, Sue, '*Star Trek*: the franchise! – poachers, pirates, and Paramount', in L. Geraghty (ed.), *The Influence of Star Trek on Television, Film and Culture* (Jefferson, NC: McFarland, 2008).

Siegel, Mark, 'Science fiction and fantasy TV', in B. G. Rose (ed.), *TV Genres* (Westport, CT: Greenwood Press, 1985).

Silberman, Steve, 'Fox Slams Bootleg *Millennium* Sites', *Hotwired* Special (1996). Available at http://hotwired.lycos.com/special/millennium/ (accessed 1 April 2001, no longer online 23 September 2016).

Silberman, Steve, 'Paramount Locks Phasers on *Trek* Fan Sites', *Wired*, 18 December 1996. Available at http://archive.wired.com/culture/lifestyle/news/1996/12 /1076 (accessed 23 September 2016).

Slatkin, Laura M., *The Power of Thetis: Allusion and Interpretation in the* Iliad (Berkeley, CA: University of California Press, 1991).

Smith, Gary A., *Epic Films: Casts, Credits and Commentary on over 250 Historical Spectacle Movies* (Jefferson, NC: McFarland and Co., 1991).

Bibliography

Sobchack, Vivian, "Surge and splendor': a phenomenology of the Hollywood historical epic', in B. K. Grant (ed.), *Film Genre Reader II* (Austin, TX: University of Texas Press, 1995).

Solomon, Jon, *The Ancient World in the Cinema* (New Haven, CT: Yale University Press, 2001).

Sontag, Susan, 'Notes on "Camp"', *Against Interpretation and Other Essays* (London: Eyre & Spottiswoode, 1967).

Sorkin, Michael, 'Introduction: variations on a theme park' and 'See you in Disneyland', in M. Sorkin (ed.), *Variations on a Theme Park: The New American City and the End of Public Space* (New York: Hill & Wang, 1992).

Sorlin, Pierre, *The Film in History: Restaging the Past* (Oxford: Basil Blackwell, 1980).

Spagna, Amy, '*Voyager* and ancient epic', *Now Voyager: The Official Newsletter of the Kate Mulgrew Appreciation Society*, 4/1 (1997), pp. 35–7. Available at www.littlereview.com/kmas/nowvoy19.txt (accessed 27 November 2015).

Spigel, Lynn, 'From domestic space to outer space: the 1960s fantastic family sitcom', in Constance Penley et al (eds), *Close Encounters: Film, Feminism and Science Fiction* (Minneapolis, MN: University of Minnesota Press, 1991).

Spigel, Lynn, 'Installing the television set: popular discourses on television and domestic space, 1948–1955', in L. Spigel and D. Mann (eds), *Private Screenings: Television and the Female Consumer* (Minneapolis, MN: University of Minnesota Press, 1992).

Spigel, Lynn, *Make Room for TV: Television and the Family Ideal in Postwar America* (Chicago, IL: University of Chicago Press, 1992).

Spigel, Lynn, *Welcome to the Dreamhouse: Popular Media and Postwar Suburbs* (Durham, NC: Duke University Press, 2001).

Spigel, Lynn and Jenkins, Henry, 'Same bat channel, different bat times: mass culture and popular memory', in R. E. Pearson and W. Uricchio (eds), *The Many Lives of the Batman: Critical Approaches to a Superhero and his Media* (New York: Routledge & London: BFI, 1991).

Stafford, Emma, *Herakles* (Hoboken: Taylor and Francis, 2013).

Stal. [*sic*], 'Mr. I. Magination', *Variety*, 27 April 1949. Reprinted in H. H. Prouty (ed.), *Variety Television Reviews, Vol. 3, 1923–1950* (New York: Garland, 1989–91).

Stal. [*sic*], 'Buck Rogers', *Variety*, 19 April 1950. Reprinted in H. H. Prouty (ed.), *Variety Television Reviews, Vol. 3, 1923–1950* (New York: Garland, 1989–91).

Stam, Robert, *Subversive Pleasures: Bakhtin, Cultural Criticism, and Film* (Baltimore, MD, and London: Johns Hopkins University Press, 1989).

Stanley, T. L., 'Paramount Parks get $10M in ads, Viacom synergy', *Brandweek*, 36/14 3 April 1995, pp. 1–2.

Stanley, T. L., 'How long can the ride continue?' *Brandweek*, 11 September 1995, pp. 34–6.

Bibliography

Starfleet Library, 'Dispatch: Enterprise NX-01 Salutes Enterprise CVN 65', 16 November 2001. Available at www.starfleetlibrary.com/enterprise/welcome_home_uss_enterprise.htm (accessed 16 September 2003, no longer online 22 September 2016).

StarTrek.com, 'Klingon Discrepancy Theories: Where Did the Ridges Go?' 22 July 2003. Available at http://startrek.com/startrek/view/series/ENT/feature/1614.html (accessed 26 January 2008, no longer online 22 September 2016).

StarTrek.com, 'Borg Invasion 4D', 3 February 2004. Available at www.startrek.com/startrek/view/news/article/4393.html (accessed 14 August 2004, no longer online 22 September 2016).

StarTrek.com, 'Exhibition Premieres in Spain' (2010). Available at www.startrek.com/article/exhibition-premieres-in-spain (accessed 1 September 2013).

StarTrek.com, 'Win a Walk-On Role in Star Trek Beyond', 14 July 2015. Available at www.startrek.com/article/win-a-walk-on-role-in-star-trek-beyond (accessed 30 November 2015).

StarTrek.com, 'Starfleet Academy Experience to open on NYC's Intrepid', 28 April 2016. Available at www.startrek.com/article/starfleet-academy-experience-to-open-july-9-on-nycs-intrepid#sthash.TU0Zmaph.dpuf (accessed 2 June 2017).

StarTrek.com, 'Warp Five with Brandon Schultz', 13 December 2019. Available at https://intl.startrek.com/news/warp-five-with-brandon-schultz (accessed 20 April 2021).

StarTrek.com, 'INTERVIEW: Discovery Showrunner Aaron Harberts', 14 September 2017. Available at https://intl.startrek.com/article/interview-discovery-showrunner-aaron-harberts (accessed 19 April 2021).

Star Trek: The Adventure (n.d.). Available at www.startrektheadventure.co.uk/ (accessed 8 January 2003, no longer online 23 September 2016).

Star Trek: The Experience (n.d.). Available at www.startrekexp.com (accessed 7 January 2008, no longer online 23 September 2016).

Stoeger, William R., 'Astronomy's integrating impact on culture: a Ladrierean hypothesis', *Leonardo*, 29/2 (1996), pp. 151–4.

Strate, Lance, 'Heroes: a communication perspective', in S. J. Drucker and R. S. Cathcart (eds), *American Heroes in a Media Age* (Creskill, NJ: Hampton Press, 1994).

Straw, Will, 'Popular music and postmodernism in the 1980s', in S. Frith, A. Goodwin and L. Grossberg (eds), *Sound and Vision: The Music Video Reader* (London: Routledge, 1993).

Supanick, Jim, 'Saul Bass', *Film Comment*, 33/2, March–April (1997), pp. 72–7.

Swarup, A., 'How to spot a wormhole in space', *New Scientist*, 31 January 2008. Available at www.newscientist.com/article/mg19726414.600-how-to-spot-a-wormhole-in-space.html (accessed 27 February 2012).

Bibliography

Teiwes, Jack, 'Crisis of Infinite Intertexts! Continuity as Adaptation in the Superman Multimedia Franchise' (PhD diss., University of Melbourne, 2015).

Telotte, J. P., 'Beyond all reason: the nature of the cult', in J. P. Telotte (ed.) *The Cult Film Experience: Beyond All Reason* (Austin, TX: University of Texas Press, 1991).

Tembo, Kwasu David, "Far from gay cities and the ways of men': Exploring wandering and homecoming in *The Odyssey* and *Star Trek: Voyager*', in R. L. Lively (ed.), *Exploring Star Trek: Voyager Critical Essays* (Jefferson, NC: McFarland, 2020).

Terrace, Vincent (ed.), *The Complete Encyclopedia of Television Programs 1947-1979*, 2nd edn., Vols 1 & 2 (South Brunswick, NJ, and New York: A. S. Barnes & Company & London: Thomas Yoseloff Ltd, 1976, 1979).

Thucydides, *The Peloponnesian War*, trans. Richard Crawley, J. M. Dent (London & New York: E. P. Dutton, 2008).

Tovares, Raul D., 'Teaser', in H. Newcomb (ed.), *Museum of Broadcast Communication Encyclopedia of Television*, Vol. 3 (Chicago, IL, and London: Fitzroy Dearborn Publishers, 1997).

Toy, Mary-Anne, 'Melbourne team finds key to spray-on drugs', *The Age*, 27 August 1999, pp. 1-2.

Trau. [sic], 'With its third season under the aegis of the Ford Foundation ...' *Variety*, 6 April 1955, no pagination. Reprinted in H. H. Prouty (ed.), *Variety Television Reviews, Vol. 5, 1954-1956* (New York: Garland, 1989-91).

Trau. [sic], 'Star Trek', *Variety*, 14 September 1966, no pagination. Reprinted in H. H. Prouty (ed.), *Variety Television Reviews, Vol. 9, 1966-1969* (New York: Garland, 1989-91).

The Trek BBS, 'CBS's "Rules of Engagement" for Star Trek Fan Films' (2012). Available at www.trekbbs.com/showthread.php?t=187825 (accessed 1 September 2013).

Trekfest (2015). Available at www.trekfest.com/ (accessed 18 December 2016).

Tudor, Andrew, 'Genre: theory and mispractice in film criticism', *Screen*, 11/6, Nov-Dec (1970), pp. 33-43.

Tulloch, John and Jenkins, Henry, *Science Fiction Audiences: Watching Doctor Who and Star Trek* (London and New York: Routledge, 1995).

Turner, Victor, *The Ritual Process: Structure and Anti-Structure* (Chicago, IL: Aldine, 1974).

Turner, Victor, *Dramas, Fields and Metaphors: Symbolic Action in Human Society* (Ithaca, NY: Cornell University Press, 1974).

Turner, Victor, 'Variations on a theme of liminality', in S. F. Moore and B. G. Meyerhoff (eds), *Secular Ritual* (Amsterdam: Van Gorcum 1977).

Turner, Victor, 'Social dramas and stories about them', *Critical Inquiry*, Autumn (1980), pp. 141-68.

TV Guide, 'Tom, Corbett, Space Cadet', 15 September 1953, p. A-10.

Bibliography

TV Guide, 'Straight from the drawing board: more comic strip characters head toward television', 13 November 1954, pp. 16-17.
TV Guide, 'Star Trek', 8 September 1966, pp. A72-A73.
TV Guide, 'Time Tunnel', 3 September 1966, p. A81.
TV Guide, 'From The Underground', March 4 1967, pp. A2-A4.
TV Guide, "Ride' The New *Apollo* Moonship!' 18 February 1967, pp. A41-A44.
Tyrell, William Blake, 'Greek myth and *Star Trek*', *The Classical Bulletin*, 53, January (1977), pp. 36-9.
Tyrell, William Blake, '*Star Trek* as myth and television as mythmaker', *Journal of Popular Culture* 10/4 (1977), pp. 711-19. Reprinted in M. W. Kapell (ed.), *Star Trek as Myth: Essays on Symbol and Archetype at the Final Frontier* (Jefferson, NC: McFarland, 2010).
Tyrell, William Blake, '*Star Trek*'s myth of science', *Journal of American Culture*, 2/1, Spring (1979), pp. 288-96.
Underwood, Elaine, 'Casino gambling's new deal', *Brandweek*, 36/15 10 April 1995, pp. 21-5.
Van Baaren, T. P., 'The flexibility of myth,' in A. Dundes (ed.), *Sacred Narrative: Readings in the Theory of Myth* (Berkeley, CA: University of California Press, 1984).
Van der Horst, Pieter, 'M. Winiarczk, Euhemeros von Messene. Leben, Werk und Nachwirkung', Bryn Mawr Classical Review (2002). Available at http://bmcr.brynmawr.edu/2002/2002-07-21.html (accessed 10 September 2016).
Van Gennep, Arnold, *The Rites of Passage*, trans. M. B. Visedom and G. L. Caffee (Chicago, IL: University of Chicago Press, 1960).
Variety, 'DuMont's Captain Video', 25 April 1951. Reprinted in H. H. Prouty (ed.), *Variety Television Reviews, Vol. 4, 1951-1953* (New York: Garland, 1989-91).
Variety, 'You Are There', 21 April 1954, no pagination. Reprinted in H. H. Prouty (ed.), *Variety Television Reviews, Vol. 5, 1954-1956* (New York: Garland, 1989-91).
Vinciguerra, Thomas, 'A 'Trek' script is grounded in cyberspace', *New York Times*, 28 March 2012. Available at www.nytimes.com/2012/03/29/arts/television/cbs-blocks-use-of-unused-star-trek-script-by-spinrad.html?_r=3&partner=rss&emc=rss& (accessed 1 September 2013).
Vir-Con (2002). Available at www.vir-con.net (accessed 1 August 2002, no longer online 24 June 2017).
Vogler, Christopher, *The Writer's Journey: Mythic Structure for Storytellers and Screenwriters* (Studio City, CA: M. Wiese, 1998).
Vulcan Tourism, 'Vulcan Tourism and Trek Station,' (n.d.). Available at www.vulcantourism.com (accessed 23 September 2016).
Wagner, Jon and Jan Lundeen, *Deep Space and Sacred Time: Star Trek in the American Mythos* (Westport Connecticut: Praeger, 1998).

Bibliography

Weatherford, Mike, 'Vegas shows can be unique', *reviewjournal.com*, 8 February 2004. Available at www.reviewjournal.com/lvrj_home/2004/Feb-08-Sun-2004/living/23149767.html (accessed 14 August 2004, no longer online 23 September 2016).

Weinstein, David, 'Captain Video: Television's First Fantastic Voyager,' *Journal of Popular Film and Television*, 30/3, Fall (2002), pp. 148–157.

Werba, Hank, 'Italo TV 'Odyssey' hits a Homer', *Variety*, 22 May 1968, no pagination. Reprinted in H. H. Prouty (ed.), *Variety Television Reviews, Vol. 9, 1966–1969* (New York: Garland, 1989–91).

Wertham, Fredric, *Seduction of the Innocent* (London: Museum Press, 1954).

Wertheimer, David, 'Dear Star Trek fan…' Paramount (1997). Available at www.paramount.com/openletter/ (accessed 19 July 2000, no longer online 23 September 2016).

Wessels, Michael, *Bushman Letters: Interpreting /Xam narrative* (Johannesburg: Witz University Press, 2010).

Westman, Robert S., 'Proof, poetics and patronage: Copernicus's preface to *De revolutionibus*', in D. C. Lindberg and R. S. Westman (eds), *Reappraisals of the Scientific Revolution* (Cambridge and New York: Cambridge University Press, 1990).

What's On Las Vegas, 'Don't go on a ride. Go on a mission', 15–28 May 2001, p. 61.

Wilcox, Clyde, 'To boldly return where others have gone before: cultural change and the old and new *Star Treks*', *Extrapolation*, 33/1 (1992), pp. 88–100.

Wilcox, Rhonda V., 'Shifting roles and synthetic women in *Star Trek: The Next Generation*', *Studies in Popular Culture*, 13/2 (1991), pp. 53–65.

Willcock, Malcolm, 'Neoanalysis', in I. Morris and B. Powell (eds), *A New Companion to Homer* (Leiden and New York: Brill, 1997).

Williamson, Jack, 'On the final frontier', in G. Westfahl (ed.), *Space and Beyond: The Frontier Theme in Science Fiction* (Westport, CT: Greenwood Press, 2000).

Wilson, Carl and Wilson, Garrath T., 'Future Technology in the 'Star Trek' Reboots: Complex Future(s)', *Pop Matters*, 13 October 2016. Available at www.popmatters.com/feature/future-technology-in-the-star-trek-reboots-complex-futures/ (accessed 17 December 2016).

Winkler, Martin M., *Cinema and Classical Texts: Apollo's New Light* (Cambridge: Cambridge University Press, 2009).

Wise, Richard, *Multimedia: A Critical Introduction* (London and New York: Routledge, 2000).

Wollen, Peter, *Signs and Meaning in the Cinema* (London: Thames and Hudson & BFI, 1969).

Woods, Louis A. and Harmon, Gary L., 'Jung and *Star Trek: The Coincidentia Oppositorium* and images of the shadow', *Journal of Popular Culture*, 28/2 (1994), pp. 169–84.

Bibliography

Woolery, George W., *Children's Television: The First Thirty-Five Years, 1946–1981, Part I: Animated Cartoon Series* (Metuchen, NJ: The Scarecrow Press, 1983).

Woolery, George W., *Children's Television: The First Thirty-Five Years, 1946–1981, Part II: Live, Film and Tape Series* (Metuchen, NJ: The Scarecrow Press, 1985).

Worland, Rick, 'Captain Kirk Cold Warrior', *The Journal of Popular Film and Television*, 16/3, Fall (1988), pp. 109–17.

Worland, Rick, 'From the new frontier to the final frontier: *Star Trek* from Kennedy to Gorbachev', *Film & History*, 24/1–2 (1994), pp. 19–35.

Wright, M. R., Wright, 'Myth, Science and Reason in the *Timaeus*,' *Reason and Necessity: Essays on Plato's Timaeus* (London: Duckworth, 2000).

Wright, Will, *Six-Guns and Society* (Berkeley, CA: University of California Press, 1975).

Wyatt, Justin, *High Concept: Movies and Marketing in Hollywood* (Austin, TX: University of Texas Press, 1994).

Wyke, Maria, *Projecting the Past: Ancient Rome, Cinema and History* (New York and London: Routledge, 1997).

Wyke, Maria, 'Film style and Fascism: *Julius Caesar*', *Film Studies*, 4, Summer (2004), pp. 58–74.

Xenophanes of Colophon, *Fragments*, trans. J. H. Lesher (Toronto: University of Toronto Press, 1992).

Zalben, Alex, '10 Totally Spoilery "Star Trek Into Darkness" Easter Eggs', *MTV*, 15 June 2013. Available at http://geek-news.mtv.com/2013/05/16/10-star-trek-into-darkness-easter-eggs/ (accessed 1 September 2013).

Zimmerman, Herman, 'Architect of illusion: designing Deep Space Nine', *Omni*, 15/5, Feb–March (1993), pp. 42–7.

Index

Page numbers in italics refer to figures

9/11, 135
'11.59' (television episode, STV, 1999), 168, *169*

Abrams, J.J., 3, 5, 171, 191
Adventures of Danny Dee, The (television programme, 1954-5), 37, 42
advertising, 5, 19, 21, 31, 34, 48, 86, 94, 96, 110, 114, 117, 126, 153, 156, 159, 160-1, 162-3, 165, 172, 183, 193, 194, 247n.132, 253n.222, 254-1n.235
  see also marketing; paratexts; posters; trailers
Agamemnon (Greek hero), 25, 43, 48
Aldrin, Buzz, 195
animation, 16, 18, 38-9, *39*, 44, 46, 51-3, *53*, 54, 92, 113, 223n.126
Apollo (Greek god), 9, 18, 23, 25, 26, 27, 37, *38*, 46, 47, 48-9, 53, 64-5, 75, 79
Apollo Program, NASA, 48, 49, 108, 113
Aquaman (television programme, 1967-9), 49, 54
Archer, Jonathan (character), 130, 131-3, *132*, 134-5, *135*, 136-7, 138, 190
Argonautica, 46, 48, 61, 66, 89, 90, 92, 214n.96
Aristotle, 30
Armstrong, Neil, 195
Asimov, Isaac, 109

'Assignment, The' (television episode, *DS9*, 1996), 73-6
astronomy, 97, 99, 102, 103, 106, 119, 121
  see also cosmology
Atlantis, 10, 65-7
audiences, 5, 16, 17, 40-1, 44, 45, 47, 50-1, 59, 60-2, 63, 64, 71, 78, 81-2, 85, 89, 92, 94, 106, 108, 110-11, 115-18, 120-2, 128-9, 132-3, 142, 147-8, 149-50, 152, 158, 161, 163, 173-4, 187, 189, 190-1, 232n.100
authenticity, 9, 58, 60, 175, 176, 190, 194
authorship, 20, 26, 35, 58, 79, 142, 152, 153, 161, 184, 185, 186, 194

Babylon 5 (television programme, 1993, 1994-8), 120, 253n.216
Bacon, Francis, 101-2
Bajorans (fictional species), 72-3, 75, 118, 119, 120-2
Bakhtin, Mikhail, 57, 68-9, 71-2, 74, 85
Bakula, Scott, 125, 130, 133, 134-5, *135*, 136-7, 138
bards, 20, 142, 148-53, 165, 175, 181, 182, 184, 185, 186
Barthes, Roland, 10, 12-13, 110, 149, 150
Bashir, Julian (character), 82, 117, 119
Bass, Saul, 110
Batman (character), 49, 52, 77-8

294

Index

Batman (television programme, 1966–8), 49, 52
Battlestar Galactica (television programme, 2004–9), 15
Beany and Cecil (television programme, 1963), 37
Beastie Boys, 1, 2–3, 4–5, 7, 21
Beowulf, 80, 125, 225n.168
'Best of Both Worlds, Part 1, The' (television episode, *TNG*, 1990), 115
'Best of Both Worlds, Part II, The' (television episode, *TNG*, 1990), 118
Birdman (television programme, 1967–8), 54
Bond, James (character), 15, 77
Borg (fictional species), 90, 117, 118, 159, 161, 169, 179–80, 184–5
'Borg Invasion 4D' (ride, 2004–2008), 159, 161, 179–80, 249n.158
'Broken Bow' (television episode, *STE*, 2001), 130–133, *132*, 239n.205
'Brother' (television episode, *STD*, 2019), 199
Bruno, Giordano, 101
Buck Rogers (television programme, 1950–1), 213n.82
Buffy: The Vampire Slayer (television programme, 1997–2003), 15
Burnham, Michael (character), *192*
Bush, George W., 126, 137

'Calypso' (television episode, *STST*, 2018), 199
camp, 29, 49, 52, 53–4, 55
Campbell, Joseph, 7
canon, 16–17, 55, 162, 170–1, 181
Captain Video and his Video Rangers (television programme, 1949–55), 37, 39, 42, 44–6, 48, 49, 55, 56, 117
Cardassians (fictional species), 119, 123, 138

'Caretaker' (television episode, *STV*, 1995), 123
carnivals, 155, 176
Casablanca (film, 1942), 76
CBS, 19, 42, 142, 154, 180, 186, 187, 188, 192, 193
Celestial Temple, 120–1, 123, 138
Challenger, space shuttle, 113
Chakotay (character), 124, 259n.11
Chekov, Pavel (character), 16
children's television, 18, 23, 28, 31, 35, 38–45, 47, 48, 50–1, 54–5, 58, 106, 108–9
Circe, 46, 89, 91
'Civilization' (television episode, *STE*, 2001), 134, 136
Cochrane, Zefram (character), 130
Cold War, 20, 48
  see also Temporal Cold War
colonialism, 119, 123, 131–2
comic books, 16–17, 39, 41, 48, 49, 50–52, 223n.124
communitas *see* rites of passage
computer games, 21, 151, 162–3, 188
Computer Generated Imagery (CGI), 116, 122
  see also special effects
computer storytelling, 151–3, 184–5
Conflict (television programme, 1956–7), 45
conglomerates, 141, 142, 145, 147, 156, 157, 160, 175, 181, 183, 185
Copernican revolution, 100, 103, 105, 112, 115, 120–1, 124–5, 127, 131
Copernicus, Nicholas, 96, 100–1, 103, 139
  see also Copernican revolution
copyright, 20, 41, 142, 179, 183–7
cosmology, 19–20, 96, 97–9, 100–128, 139–40, 193
  see also astronomy

Index

costumes, 37, *38*, 52, 53, *53*, 64, 92, *93*, 127, 145, 165, 166, 173, 174
Courage, Alexander, 111, 113
Critias, 10, 66
Cronkite, Walter, 35, *36*, 40
cult, 76, 81, 94, 143–8, 189, 193
Cumberbatch, Benedict, 190
Cyclops, 32, 42, 47

'Darmok' (television episode, *TNG*, 1991), 67–69
Data (character), 68–71, *71*, *171*, 106
Dax, 81, 82
Defiant, 122
De Lancie, John, 173
Demeter (Greek goddess), 143–4
'Demon' (television episode, *STV*, 1998), 89–90, 224n.140
'Descent' (television episode, *TNG*, 1993), 106, 184
dialogism, 57, 68–72, 74
Disney, Walt, 156–7
Disneyland, 154, 156–60, 166–7, 178
Disneyland (television programme, 1954–8), 156–7
'Divergence' (television episode, *STE*, 2005), 83
Doctor Who (television programme, 1963–89, 1996, 2005–), 15
Dorn, Michael, 85, 122
DVDs, 84, 86, 92, 93, 182, 190

Eco, Umberto, 76–7, 80
Einstein, Albert, 100, 106, 119
'Elaan of Troyius' (television episode, *TOS*, 1968), 79
'Emissary' (television episode, *DS9*, 1993), 117–18, 119, 121
'Encounter at Farpoint' (television episode, *TNG*, 1988), 114
'Ensign Ro' (television episode, *TNG*, 1991), 123–4
Enterprise see *Star Trek: Enterprise* (*STE*) (television programme, 2001–5)

Enterprise, space shuttle, 126, 136, 238n.188, 250n.170
Enterprise, Starship, 84, 85, 92, 106, 108, 109, 110, 112, 115, 116, 117, 120, 126, 128, 134, 136, 137, 158, 168, 191
Enterprise, USS, aircraft carrier, 134–8
Enterprize, HMS, 125, 128, 136, 138
epic, 11, 19, 24, 25, 29–38, 40, 43, 45, 49, 54, 63, 80, 89–91, 94, 96, 120, 125, 133, 142, 151, 172, 190, 193, 194, 219n.42, 225n.168
epithet formulas, 61–2
etymology, 8, 13, 62, 150
Euhemerus of Messene, 10

fan conventions, 145, 153–5, 163–5, 173, 178–9, 182, 186, 190
fan websites, 182–6, 187
'Favorite Son' (television episode, *STV*, 1997), 87–94, *93*
Ferengi (fictional species), 174–5
Finder, The (television programme, 1954–5), 37, 42
'Flashback' (television episode, *STV*, 1996), 81–2
Flash Gordon (television programme, 1954–5), 37, 46, 49, 50, 55, 110
Flash Gordon Conquers the Universe (cinema serial, 1940), 123
folk tales, 11, 143, 151–2
Forrest Gump (film, 1994), 84
franchise, 1, 3–6, 12–13, 15–16, 18–21, 50, 56, 57–8, 63, 65, 72, 77–8, 80–2, 94, 105, 120, 121, 124, 137, 139–40, 141, 145, 153–4, 159, 166–8, 172, 180, 185–6, 191–3, 194
frontier myth, 6, 109, 111–12, 115, 119, 124, 125, 127, 132, 137, 140

Gagarin, Yuri, 107, 129
Galileo, 101, 103
gambling, 73, 159, 160, 176, 177

Index

Gemini Program, NASA, 113
gender, 91–2, 112, 114, 134, 143–4, 164, 253n.219
genre, 11, 12, 17, 19, 24, 28–31, 33, 39, 44, 47, 53, 54–5, 58, 71, 78–80, 144, 145, 161, 194, 214n.96, 218n.32
 see also epic; science fiction; superheroes; sword-and-sandal; Western genre
Georgiou, Philippa (character), 198
'Girl Who Made the Stars, The' (television episode, *STST*, 2019), 199
Golden Bough, The, 143
Goldsmith, Jerry, 114, 124
Greek mythology, 7, 8–11, 15, 18, 23, 25–6, 37, 38, 47, 50, 53, 55, 59–61, 64–6, 75, 78–80, 87–92, 100, 143–4, 215n.122, 221n.83, 222n.114

Hadfield, Chris, 195
Hawking, Stephen, 106
Heracles (Greek hero), 21
Hercules (film, 1958), 36
Hercules (Greek and Roman hero), 21, 38–40, 42, 46, 52–3, 74, 101
Hercules (television programme, 1965), 36–7
Hercules: The Legendary Journeys (television programme, 1995–9), 43
Herodotus, 9
Hesiod, 8, 98
'Home' (television episode, *STE*, 2004), 137
Homer, 7–10, 13, 32–6, 43, 46, 59, 61, 66, 68, 74, 87–8, 91–2, 135, 151, 193
Homeric Hymn to Demeter, 143–4
Homeric Hymn to Hermes, 64
Homer's Odyssey (film, 1911), 32
Honeymooners, The (television programme, 1955–6), 45

Huygens, Christiaan, 101

iconography, 17, 52, 53, 55, 58, 64, 92, 121, 125, 191, 218n.32, 218n.33
ideology, 10, 11, 13, 69, 73, 96, 114, 121, 134–9, 140, 149, 150, 182–3, 224n.149
Iliad, 8, 33, 43, 46, 61
'In a Mirror Darkly' (television episode, *STE*, 2005), 137–9, *138*
Indigenous Americans, 79, 102, 124
infantilisation, 45, 176–7
intertextuality, 13–14, 17, 24, 57, 60–5, 72, 76–8, 80, 82, 89, 92, 94, 133, 144, 168, 181, 188, 221n.83
Invaders, The (television programme, 1967–8), 47

Janeway, Kathryn (character), 86–8, 91, 159, *169*, 170, 249n.158
Jason (Greek hero), 46, 48, 61, 66, 89, 90, 214n.96
Jenkins, Henry, 16, 17, 146, 158, 174, 181, 183, 186–7, 252n.202
Jetsons, The (television programme, 1962–3), 230n.70
'Journey's End' (television episode, *TNG*, 1994), 124
Jung, Carl, 7
juvenile delinquency, 41, 46

Kelvin timeline, 3–4, 167, 189
Kennedy, John F., 107–8, 109, 111–13, 115, 137
Kepler, Johannes, 100–2, 106
Khan, also known as Khan Noonien Singh (character), 171, 189–90
Kim, Harry (character), 87–91, 93, *93*
Kira, Nerys (character), 119
Kirk, James T. (character), 2–3, *3*, 5, 21, 23, 25–6, *38*, 49, 65, 79–80, *81*, 83, 86, 92–3, 108–12, 114–15, 130, 137, 180–1, 187, 190–1, 195

Index

'Klingon Encounter' (ride, 1998–2008), 158–9, 161–6, 172
Klingons (fictional species), 82–4, 158, 165, 174, 191, 220n.66
Koenig, Walter, 16

La Forge, Geordi (character), 158
Land of the Giants (television programme, 1968–70), 50
Las Vegas, 20, 141–2, 154, 157–9, 163, 174, 176, 178–80, 186, 188, 190
legitimisation, 7, 12, 14, 15, 18, 21, 32–6, 40–1, 43, 46, 52, 54, 80, 83–4, 110, 113, 135
Lévi-Strauss, Claude, 11, 12, 68, 234n.123
liminality, 122, 136, 147, 154–5, 156, 160, 164–6, 172–3, 176–7, 179, 181, 183–6, 188
Lin, Justin, 21
linguistics, 129–34, 163
'Lorelei Signal, The' (television episode, *TAS*, 1973), 92–3
Lost in Space (television programme, 1965–8), 110, 230n.70
Love Boat, The (television programme, 1977–86), 129

'Maquis, The' (television episode, *DS9*, 1994), 123
marketing, 1, 4–6, 12, 14–16, 18–21, 58, 86, 96, 142, 150, 156, 160, 162, 168, 172, 190–3
  see also advertising; posters; trailers
Martin-Green, Sonequa, 199
Marvel Comics, 17, 50–2
Marvel Superheroes (television programme, 1966), 51–3, 53
Mary Sue, 161–2
'Masks' (television episode, *TNG*, 1994), 69–71, 71, 75–6
Mason, James, 34–5
masquerade, 164–5
McCarthy, Dennis, 120, 122, 133

McCoy, Leonard (character), 2, 49, 232n.99
memory, 17, 61, 64, 66, 73–4, 77–8, 81, 90–4, 132, 145, 153, 190–1
merchandising, 48, 55–6, 86, 156–8, 175, 254n.233
Mercury Program, NASA, 113
metonymy, 61–4, 68, 79, 88, 92
Metropolis (film, 1926), 79
Mighty Hercules, The (television programme, 1963), 38–9, *39*, 53–4
Mighty Thor, The (television programme, 1966), 49, 51–3, *53*
military, 111, 114, 134–6, 137–9, 182
'Mirror, Mirror' (television episode, *TOS*, 1967), 137, 170
mirror universe, 137–9, 170
Moby Dick, 80
Mount, Anson, 198
Mr. I. Magination (television programme, 1949–52), 37, 40, 42
Mulgrew, Kate, 88
music, 2, 34, 59, 111–14, 122, 124–6, 133–4, 139, 146, 172
  see also pop music; theme songs
music videos, 2, 4, 237n.178, 237n.185, 240n.213
My Favorite Martian (television programme, 1963–6), 230n.70

NASA, 49, 105–6, 108, 109, 113, 126–7, 137
National Air and Space Museum, 106
Navy, 125, 135–6, 137
Nemean Odes, 9
neoanalysis, 61, 218n.24
Newton, Isaac, 106
Nimoy, Leonard, 4, *4*, 109, 195
nostalgia, 44, 77, 81, 85, 124–5, 127, 131, 134, 167, 224n.139

O'Brien, Keiko (character), 73
O'Brien, Miles (character), 73–5, 82

Index

Odysseus (Greek hero), 25, 42, 46, 48, 61, 66, 87, 88–92, 94
   see also Ulysses (Greek and Roman hero)
Odyssey, 34, 46, 48, 59, 61, 66, 71, 87–92, 94, 125
Odyssey, The (television programme, 1968), 31–2, 34
Oedipus at Colonus, 34
Oedipus Rex, 34
Omnibus (television programme, 1952–61), 33–4, 37
One Step Beyond (television programme, 1959–61), 45
opening titles *see* title sequences
oral formulism, 61–2, 151, 218n.24
orality, 7, 8, 11, 59–61, 66, 68, 73–4, 78, 97–8, 147, 149, 150–2, 182, 194
Outer Limits, The (television programme, 1963–5), 117

Pah-wraiths (fictional species), 73, 75
'Parallels' (television episode, *TNG*, 1993), 170–1, *171*
Paramount, 86, 88, 126, 142, 154, 157–9, 160, 178, 183, 192, 201n.6, 246n.117
Paramount Parks, 154, 157–8, 178
Paramount Plus, 198
paratexts, 5–6, 24, 84, 86, 92–4, 110, 117, 135, 138–9, 142, 161–2, 172, 191
   see also advertising; marketing; posters; title sequences; trailers
'Past Prologue' (television episode, *DS9*, 1992), 119
Patch Adams (film, 1998), 133
Pegg, Simon, 21, 138, 191
Peloponnesian War, The, 9, 209n.8
Picard, Jean-Luc (character), 66, 67–70, 86, 114–15, 117, 158, 161–2, 166, 185, 190, 225n.167

Pike, Christopher (character), 198
pilgrimage, 20, 141, 153–8, 160, 162–3, 165–6, 175–9, 180–3, 188, 193
Pillars of Hercules, 101
Pindar, 9
Plato, 9–10, 66–7, 93, 222n.100
'Plato's Stepchildren' (television episode, *TOS*, 1968), 93, 222n.100
play, 48, 141, 146–7, 158, 160, 164–6, 172–7, 179, 181–5, 188, 229n.60
pop art, 52–3
pop music, 1–4, 7, 21, 129, 130, 133–4, 240n.213
posters, 5, 29, 190, 191
postmodernism, 221n.90
poststructuralism, 13–4
'Preemptive Strike' (television episode, *TNG*, 1994), 124
'Private Little War, A' (television episode, *TOS*, 1967), 137
Prophets (fictional species), 73–5, 120–2
Propp, Vladimir, 151–2
psychoanalysis, 7, 76, 155

Q (character), 173, 184
Quantum Leap (television programme, 1989–93), 125, 129, 133
quantum mechanics, 170–1
Quinto, Zachary, 4
'Q Who' (television episode, *TNG*, 1989), 184

race, 26, 82–3, 91, 93–4, 107–8, 121, 131, 164, 165, 189–91, 253n.219
rape, 47, 64, 233n.113
reboot, 2, 16–17, 20, 141, 154, 169–70, 180, 181, 189, 190, 191
recaps, 117, 122
Red Dwarf (television programme, 1988–), 63

Index

religion, 25–6, 27, 55, 65, 72–4, 97, 120–2, 142, 144–6, 155–6, 166, 175, 188
remediation, 29–30, 31, 34, 49, 50, 52
Republic, The, 9–10, 222n.100
retro-futures, 167, 181, 190
retrospective continuity, also known as retcon, 81, 83, 169, 191
reviews, 15, 23–5, 29–34, 36, 37, 44, 45, 47, 50, 52, 54–5, 58, 108, 193
Riker, Will (character), 65, 70, 158
rites of passage, 154–6, 163, 176–8, 185
ritual, 1, 14, 20, 21, 56, 70, 110, 141–8, 151, 153–6, 158–60, 162–6, 173–7, 181–2, 184–8, 193
Riverside, Iowa, 180–1
Rocky Jones, Space Ranger (television programme, 1953), 37, 46, 55
Robe, The (film, 1953), 34
Roddenberry, Gene, 3, 5, 16, 26, 55, 79, 105, 109, 111, 112, 136, 153, 230n.79, 232n.99
Romulans (fictional species), 198

Samson and Delilah (film, 1949), 31, 33
science fiction, 44–9, 87–8
Science Fiction Theater (television programme, 1955–7), 45
scientific revolution, 19–20, 97, 100, 127
    see also Copernican revolution
Scott, Montgomery, also known as 'Scotty' (character), 138
'Search, Part 1, The' (television episode, *DS9*, 1994), 122
Search for Ulysses (television programme, 1966), 34–5
Section 31 (television programme), 198, 258n.6
seriality, 17, 19, 21, 49, 50, 72, 85, 110, 117–18, 122–4, 147–8, 213n.82, 214n.97

Serling, Rod, 45
Seven of Nine (character), 169, 184
Shakespeare, William, 79, 80, 130
Shatner, William, 3, *38*, *81*, 109, 110, 137, 195, 232n.99, 252n.202
Shepard, Alan, 107, 128
'Shore Leave' (television episode, *TOS*, 1966), 108
Siddig, Alexander, 122
Sirens, 32, 87–94, 111, 216n.129
Sisko, Benjamin, 74, *81*, 118, 121–2
slave labour, 119
Small Fry Club (television programme, 1947–51), 40–1
Socrates, 9–10
Sophocles, 34
sound, 52, 111, 129, 133
    see also music
Space Ghost (television programme, 1966–8), 47
space opera, 105, 239n.210
Space Patrol (television programme, 1950–5), 37, 44–6, 49, 55, 108, 212n.69
Space Race, 20, 48, 107–9, 112–13, 124, 126, 127, 131
'Space Seed' (television episode, *TOS*, 1967), 171
space shuttle program, 113, 127
    see also *Challenger*, space shuttle; *Enterprise*, space shuttle
special effects, 9, 17, 32, 84, 115–16, 122, 123, 140
    see also Computer Generated Imagery (CGI)
spectatorship *see* audiences
Spock (character), 2, 4, *4*, 27, 80, 82, 86, 109, 191, 195, 232n.99
spin-offs, 2, 16, 19, 24, 50, 54, 94, 113, 156
Sputnik, 106–7
Starfleet, 65, 70, 72, 114, 122, 137, 172, 180
Starfleet Academy (comic book, 1996–8), 17

300

Index

Starfleet Academy Experience, The (exhibition, 2016), 180
Star Trek (film, 2009), 1–5, *3*, *4*, 20, 82, 141, 154, 167, 169–71, 181, 191
Star Trek: Bridge Commander (video game, 2001), 163
Star Trek: Countdown (comic book, 2009), 16
Star Trek: Countdown to Darkness (comic book, 2013), 16
Star Trek: Deep Space Nine (DS9) (television programme, 1993–9), 2, 15, 17, 58, 72–5, 80–7, *81*, 116–24, 127, 132, 138, 158, 165, 172, 173, 220n.66, 222n.115, 222n.118
Star Trek: Discovery (television programme, 2017–), 5, 18, 86, 191, *192*
Star Trek: Enterprise (STE) (television programme, 2001–5), 2, 15, 20, 58, 80, 83, 86, 96, 105, 116, 125–139, *132*, *138*, 168–70, 172, 190, 222n.121, 254n.233
Star Trek: First Contact (film, 1996), 126, 131, 237n.186
Star Trek: Generations (film, 1994), 190–1
Star Trek: Lower Decks (television programme, 2020–), 198
Star Trek: Nemesis (2002), 191, 254n.233
Star Trek: Picard (television programme, 2020–), 198
Star Trek: Prodigy (television programme), 198
Star Trek: Short Treks (STST) (television programme, 2018–), 198, 199
Star Trek: Strange New Worlds (television programme), 198
Star Trek: Telepathy War (comic book, 1997), 17
Star Trek: The Adventure (exhibition, 2002), 180
Star Trek: The Animated Series (TAS) (television programme, 1973), 16, 18, 39, 92, 113, 223n.126
Star Trek: The Exhibition (exhibition, 2010), 180
Star Trek: The Experience (theme park, 1998–2008), 153–68, 171–86
Star Trek: The Exploration (exhibition, 2010), 180
Star Trek: The Motion Picture (film, 1979), 190, 191, 234n.118
Star Trek: The Next Generation (TNG) (television programme, 1988–94), 2, 4, 15, 17, 65–70, *71*, 85, 87, 92, 96, 106, 113–20, 122–4, 127, 130, 131, 133, 158, 161, 169–71, *171*, 173, 184, 190, 204n.43, 220n.66, 222n.116, 223n.122, 225n.167, 254n.233, 256n.253
Star Trek: The Original Series (TOS) (television programme, 1966–9), 2–7, 16–20, 23–9, 33, 37–8, *38*, 44, 45, 47–50, 52–6, 63–5, 67, 75, 79–80, 81–6, 91–3, 105–16, 118, 120, 122, 124, 126–7, 130–1, 133–4, 136–7, 153, 167–72, 187, 190–1, 194, 195, 222n.102–11, 229n.58, 234n.126, 254n.233
Star Trek: Timelines (computer game, 2016), 170
Star Trek: Voyager (STV) (television programme, 1995–2001), 2, 15, 20, 58, 80, 81, 86–94, *93*, 96, 116, 123–7, 159, 168, *169*, 170, 172–3, 184, 220n.66, 222n.117, 222n.119, 222n.120, 224n.140, 234n.122, 247n.132, 249n.158, 254n.233
Star Trek II: The Wrath of Khan (film, 1982), 189–90
Star Trek IV: The Voyage Home (film, 1986), 113, 168

Index

Star Trek V: The Final Frontier (film, 1989), 16
Star Trek VI: The Undiscovered Country (film, 1991), 16
Star Trek Beyond (film, 2016), 162, 190, 191
Star Trek Into Darkness (film, 2013), 16, 138, 189, 190
Star Trek New Voyages: Phase II (online programme, 2004), 187
Star Wars (film, 1977), 15, 123, 234n.118
Stewart, Rod, 133
streaming services, 19, 92, 148, 182, 190
structuralism, 11, 14, 68, 145, 194, 234n.123
  see also poststructuralism
Sub-Mariner (television programme, 1966), 49, 54
Sulu, Hikaru (character), 82, 190, 195
superheroes, 38–9, 44, 49–55
Superman (character), 15, 54, 216n.134
sword-and-sandal, 36–7, 43
synergy, 156–8, 181

Takei, George, 82, 195
Tales of Tomorrow (television programme, 1951–3), 45
Taliban, 135
Taming of the Shrew, The, 79
'Tattoo' (television episode, *STV*, 1995), 259n.11
Taylor, Jeri, 123, 236n.152
teasers, 5, 86, 114, 117–18, 124, 130–1, 134, 191–2, *192*
technobabble, 74, 140
Temporal Cold War, 168–70
terrorism, 123, 135, 190, 219n.49
Theagenes of Rhêgium, 9
theme parks, 154, 156–9, 166, 177–8, 246n.119, 248n.145, 251n.194
theme songs, 38, 128–34

Theogony, 98
'These Are the Voyages ...' (television episode, *STE*, 2005), 190
Thor (Norse god), 51
Thor (superhero), 49, 51–3, *53*, 55
Three Musketeers, The, 80
Timaeus, 10, 66
Time Tunnel, The (television programme, 1966–7), 28, 45, 47, 55, 230n.70
title sequences, 5, 17, 20, 95–6, 105, 109–30, 131–34, 136–9, 140–1
Tom Corbett, Space Cadet (television programme, 1950–5), 37, 46, 48, 49, 56, 115
'Tomorrow is Yesterday' (television episode, *TOS*, 1967), 108, 222n.109
tourism, 155–6, 177, 180, 188, 255–6n.235
trailers, 2, 4–5, 7, 21, 128, 190–2, *192*
transmedia, 1, 16–18, 58, 141–2, 156, 158, 160, 172, 174, 181, 193
Trekkies (film, 1997), 173
'Trials and Tribble-ations' (television episode, *DS9*, 1996), 80–5, *81*, 86
'Trouble with Tribbles, The' (television episode, *TOS*, 1967), 80, 82–3, 187
Troy, (film, 2004), 9
Turner, Victor, 144, 154–6, 163–6, 177
Twilight Zone, The (television programme, 1959–64), 45

Uhura, Nyota (character), *81*, 93, 170
Ulysses (Greek and Roman hero), 34–5, 42
Ulysses 31 (television programme, 1981), 63
'Unamatrix Zero' (television episode, *STV*, 2000), 184
utopianism, 104, 124, 146

Index

Veronica Mars (film, 2014), 161
VHS, 83–4, 86, 92–3
Viacom, 141–2, 154, 157, 160, 162, 175–6, 179, 180–1, 183–8, 192–3, 246n.117, 247n.132
viewers *see* audiences
Vulcans (fictional species), 130–2, 254n.235

Wagon Train (television programme, 1957–1965), 79, 230n.79
Wang, Garrett, 93, *93*
Watson, Russell, 129, 130, 133, 134
'Way of the Warrior, The' (television episode, *DS9*, 1995), 85, 122, 222n.115
Web 2.0, 186–8
Wertham, Fredric, 50–1
Western genre, 11, 41, 79, 145, 230–7n.79
'What You Leave Behind' (television episode, *DS9*, 1999), 74, 121
'When the Bough Breaks' (television episode, *TNG*, 1988), 65–7, 72–3, 75, 204n.43, 225n.167
'Where My Heart Will Take Me' (song), 128–34

see also theme songs
Whistling Wizard, The (television programme, 1951–2), 37, 40
'Who Mourns for Adonais?' (television episode, *TOS*, 1967), 18, 23–8, 37–8, *38*, 47–9, 52, 55, 63–5, 67, 75, 79, 92
'Wink of an Eye' (television episode, *TOS*, 1968), 92
witchcraft, 101
Wonder Woman (character), 215n.122
Worf (character), 82–3, 85, 170
wormholes, 73, 119–24, 138
'Wounded, The' (television episode, *TNG*, 1991), 123

Xena: Warrior Princess (television programme, 1995–2001), 15, 43, 255n.250
Xenophanes of Colophon, 8–9
X-Files, The (television programme, 1993–2002, 2016), 120

Yeoh, Michelle, 198
You Are There (television programme, 1953–7), 35–7, *36*, 40, 42–3, 45, 49, 214n.101

www.ingramcontent.com/pod-product-compliance
Lightning Source LLC
Chambersburg PA
CBHW051804230426
43672CB00012B/2627